A DICTIONARY OF
OPERA
and
SONG THEMES

A DICTIONARY OF
OPERA
and
SONG THEMES

INCLUDING CANTATAS, ORATORIOS
LIEDER, AND ART SONGS

Originally Published as
A Dictionary of Vocal Themes

Compiled by

SAM MORGENSTERN
and
HAROLD BARLOW

Crown Publishers, Inc.

NEW YORK

Introduction

WITH THE completion of our *Dictionary of Musical Themes*, we started on a book which would do for vocal music what *Musical Themes* did for instrumental works. It took several years of research to compile this *Dictionary of Vocal Themes*, which includes the salient and rememberable themes from operas, cantatas, oratorios, *Lieder* and art songs, as well as many miscellaneous vocal pieces not belonging to any of the above categories.

Since, in addition to the notation of the themes, this book contains the words of the music quoted, we have indexed first lines as well as titles. The reader can thereby identify a piece through its composer, title, or first line, as well as its notation.

Man has sung from the beginning of his existence, and one lifetime would not suffice to extract the themes from only those melodies which he has noted down. We were, consequently, forced to limit ourselves in some fashion or other, and decided to confine the contents of this book for the most part to those works which have been recorded here and in Europe.

The problems confronting the compiler of such a volume as this are legion. Should he include folk music? To what degree should he include popular songs? What about those works, ultra-modern ones in particular, in which a clearly defined theme is hardly discernible? Should he use original or English translations?

Having no precedent, we tried to solve these questions in what seemed to us the most practical and satisfactory manner. Folk themes and their endless variants could easily fill a book the size of this one. We therefore chose those which have been edited and arranged by composers steeped in their own national folk idiom—Bartók, Kodaly, Vaughan Williams, Warlock, Weckerlin, to name a handful—and which through recordings have become an international heritage. If a popular tune has been recorded several times by concert artists of repute, achieving thereby a kind of classical status, we have tried to include it in our book.

Operas such as *Pélleas and Mélisande, Electra* and *Salome* we omitted. Here, every vocal line is thematic or not, as you choose, and quoting them would have meant literally copying the whole score. What the general reader might remember from *Salome*—the themes from the "Dance of the Seven Veils"—is included in our first book. Most of the leitmotifs in the later Wagnerian operas appear in the orchestra rather than in the vocal line. Since these are plentifully quoted in our *Dictionary of Musical Themes,* we have used opening phrases from scenes as they are recorded. Otherwise, we would have been obliged again to quote line for line.

In such early church works as, for instance, Palestrina's *Missa Brevis* and the *Marcellus Mass* there is a constant melodic flow, any part of which could be thematic. We have quoted the opening phrases from the various sections of these Masses and the ecclesiastical motives which form their bases.

Wherever possible, we have gone to original sources for our material. All the Bach and Handel quotations were culled from the *Gesellschaft* editions. To have quoted the entire vocal output of Bach and Handel we would have had to compile two separate volumes. Here, too, our yardstick was the recorded works plus whatever we felt might be of use to the amateur, layman and professional musician. If there are any gross omissions we hope our readers will call them to our attention so that they may be included in subsequent editions.

An examination of scores of recital programs as well as record catalogues governed our choice of the songs of Schubert, who wrote close to six hundred *Lieder*. We handled Brahms, Wolf, Strauss and other great *Lieder* composers in the same manner.

Though we chose the arias and concerted numbers from operas, we did include a certain number of recitatives which are as well known as the arias which follow them.

In a limited number of songs where we felt the accompaniment theme was as important as the vocal line, if not more so, we quoted both. Thus, the eighty repetitions of the same note in the solo part of Peter Cornelius' *Ein Ton* are supplemented by their accompanying motive in the piano part. The accompaniment to Debussy's *Spleen* and the violin obbligato to Braga's *Angel's Serenade* follow immediately on their vocal themes.

Some composers, who in their lifetime may have been very prolific, are here represented by perhaps one or two songs. Time and neglect have made these composers practically obsolete, and their scores for the most part unavailable. We have, therefore, chosen a few pieces representative of their style and still occasionally heard, on the chance that some reader might recall their themes.

A few of the songs quoted here may seem unimportant to the American student. The international distribution of our *Dictionary of Musical Themes* was the basis for the inclusion of these pieces, unknown here but of interest to musicians and laymen in other lands.

Wherever possible we used original texts, though in many cases only translations were available. Of these we chose the best we could find. Because of script difficulties and the possibility of error in phonetic spelling, we used only translations of Russian texts. Here, the choice of French,

German or English was governed by the quality of the text and its adherence to the musical line.

The variety of interval combination in vocal literature is perhaps not so great as in instrumental works (what is playable is not always singable), and the reader will find a greater similarity in vocal than in instrumental themes. We came across a good deal of unconscious as well as conscious plagiarism. Though *La Paloma* is Yradier's best-known, almost only known, song, we also included his *El Areglito* because of its quasi note-for-note similarity to the "Habañera" from *Carmen*. When this obvious fact was called to Bizet's attention he frankly admitted the plagiarism, saying that he could not have invented a better theme for his "Habañera" than Yradier's.

Our own *Marines' Hymn* is, consciously or not, almost a photograph of the "Couplets des deux hommes d'armes" from Offenbach's *Geneviève de Brabant*. Though rhythmically dissimilar, the "S'io S'io dir potessi" from Handel's *Ottone* parallels the first subject of Bach's *G minor fugue* in the first book of the *Well Tempered Clavichord* and is in the same key. This is without doubt unconscious plagiarism, if plagiarism it can be called.

Of interest to readers will be the many and varied settings of the same lyrics, especially those of Heine, Goethe and Verlaine.

For the most part, we have catalogued the themes alphabetically according to categories (cantatas, *Lieder*, operas, oratorios, songs, etc.). However, in the case of some composers, we have catalogued them according to opus numbers. Mozart themes are numbered in the order of their Köchel listings.

We have proofed and re-proofed this book, yet we can only identify ourselves with the Chinese author who always included an error or two so that the reader would be flattered by recognizing it. No matter how minutely such a book is proofed some errors are bound to creep in. We shall be grateful to our readers if they call our attention to any.

A book such as this cannot be created without the help of many kind friends. First and foremost, we wish to thank Mr. Philip Miller of the Music Reference Division of the New York Public Library whose advice and aid were invaluable and constant. Mr. Miller examined our entire card index, adding a great number of works which he felt indispensable to such a book. We also wish to thank Edward Bauer, Louis Kabasakalian and Elma Alexander of his staff.

Miss Gladys Chamberlain, Director of the Music Library Branch on 58th Street, and her co-workers, Miss Mary Lee Daniels and Miss Lilly Goldberg, gave us unreservedly of their time and advice and turned over to us all the resources of their splendid collection. Misses Mildred Lorres, Heather Moon, Melva Peterson, Florence O'Neill and Margaret Quinn were also very cooperative.

We want to thank Mr. Herbert Weinstock and Mr. Ben Meiselman for the use of their scores. Dr. Hans Heinsheimer of G. Schirmer, Inc., put his entire vocal department at our disposal and Mrs. Verona Clifford, Willard Lanzillo, William Kulkman and William Terranova were more than helpful in suggesting works and supplying us with practically everything we needed in the Schirmer catalogue.

We are especially grateful to the music publishers who gave us full cooperation and assistance. However, one publisher refused to let us show the themes from certain compositions published by him. The law on the matter is not clear at this writing, and therefore there are certain entries without notation. We trust the reader will understand that these regrettable omissions were unavoidable.

Lastly, we want to thank Mr. Robert Simon of Crown Publishers for his constant advice and encouragement.

Sam Morgenstern

New York, N. Y.
September, 1950

A DICTIONARY OF
OPERA
and
SONG THEMES

ABT, Franz (1819-1885)

Am Neckar, am Rhein, Op. 89
O wär' ich am Neckar, O wär' ich am Rhein

Gute Nacht, du mein herziges Kind
All' Abend bevor-ch zur Ru-he geh' blick' ich hin-aus in die Nacht

Über den Sternen ist Ruh, Op. 128, No. 1
Ü-ber den Ster-nen ist Ruh, über den Ster-nen ist Ruh

Wenn die Schwalben heimwärts ziehn (Agathe)
Wenn die Schwal-ben heim-wärts ziehn, wenn die Ro- sen nicht mehr blühn

ACQUA, Eva dell' (1856- ?)

Chanson provençale
Par les nuits sans ri- va-les, Les bel-les nuits d'é-té

Villanelle
Copyright 1923, G. Schirmer, Inc.
J'ai vu pas-ser l'hi-ron-del-le Dans le ciel pur du ma-tin:

ADAM, Adolphe Charles (1803-1856)

Cantique pour Noël (Christmas Song)
Minuit, Chré-tiens, c'est l'heure so-len-nel-le

Vallons de la Helvétie, from Le Chalet
Val-lons de l'Hel-vé-ti-e ob-jet de mon a-mour

Mes amis, écoutez l'histoire, from Le Postillon de Longjumeau Act I (opera)
Mes a-mis, é-cou-tez l'his-toi-re d'un jeune et ga-lant pos-til-lon

Si J'Etais Roi (opera) Act I
Dans le som-meil l'a-mour, je ga-ge vous fit voir

J'i-gno-re son nom, sa nais-san-ce, lors-qu'é-per-du

Un re-gard de ses yeux vien-drait fi-nir ma pei-ne

Zé-pho-ris est bon ca- ma-ra-de, mais c'est un pê-cheur fort mau-vais:

Act II (Nemea's Aria) (A)
Des sou-ve-rains du ri-va-ge d'A-si-e

(B)
Dis un seul mot sou-dain ta cour va de-ve-nir le doux se-jour

Vous m'ai-mez dites-vous Ah! vot-re ma-jes-té veut se jou-er i-ci

Ah! Vous dirai-je, Maman, from Le
   Toreador (opera)
Folk song used by many composers,
   including Mozart in his Piano
   Variations K.265

Ah! vous di-rais-je ma-man Ce qui cau-se mon tour-ment   A

ADAM de la Halle (1220-1287)

Le Jeu de Robin et Marion

Ro - bin___ m'ai - me, Ro - bin___ m'a;   C

Hé! ré-veil-le toi, Ro-bin Car on em-mè-ne Ma-rot,   D

ADAMS, A. Emmett

The Bells of St. Mary's

ADAMS, Stephen (1844-1913)

The Holy City (A)

Last night I lay a-sleep-ing, There came a dream so fair   H

(B)

Je - ru - sa - lem, Je - ru - sa - lem, Lift up your gates and sing   I

The Midshipmite

'Twas in fif-ty-five on a win-ter's night, Cheer-i-ly, my lads, yo ho!   J

Nancy Lee

Of all___ the wives as e'er you know___ Yeo ho___ lads, ho!   K

The Star of Bethlehem

It was the eve of Christ-mas, The snow lay deep and white,   L

A Warrior Bold

In days of old, when knights were bold, And ba-rons held their sway   M

L'AFFILARD, Michel (17th-18th Cent.)

Iris

I - ris, cet-te nuit en dor-mant,___ J'é-tais dans un ra-vis-se-ment ___ O

AHLE, Johann Georg (1650-1706)

Brünstiges Verlangen

Komm, Je - su, komm doch her zu mir, Komm her, mein Le-ben, mei-ne Zier   Q

AIBLINGER, Johann Kaspar (1779-1867)

Jubilate Deo

Ju-bi-la-te De - o, ju-bi-la-te De - o   S

AICHINGER, Gregor (1564-1628)

Factus est — Fa- ctus est re-pen-te de coe-lo so - - - - - - - - nus   B

Regina Coeli — Re-gi-na coe-li loe-ta - - - - - - re, loe-ta - - - re, al-le-lu-ja   C

Salve, Regina — Sal- ve, Re-gi-na, Ma-ter, - - mi-se-ri-cor-di-ae, Vi-ta,dul-ce-do,   D

Ubi est Abel — U-bi est A- bel fra - - - - - - - - ter tu- us   E

ALABIEV, Alexander Nikolaevich (1787-1851)

The Nightingale — Nach-ti-gall, O Nach-ti- gall, san-ges - rei-che - -   G

ALAIN, Albert (15th Century)

Le Paradis — Beau ciel, tu m'ap-pa-rais - - Comme un lieu clair et frais - -   I

ALBÉNIZ, Isaac Manuel Francisco (1860-1909)

Amor, Summa Injuria
Copyright by Salabert, Paris, N. Y. — Par - don-ne: Quand tu m'as ai-mé - - Je fus cou-pa-ble - -   K

Le Paradis Retrouvé
Copyright by Salabert, Paris, N. Y. — Dans un jar-din, je ne sais où, - - Sont mille oi-seaux chan-teurs - -   L

Quand je te vois souffrir
Copyright by Salabert, Paris, N. Y. — Quand je te vois souf-frir - J'ou-blie les verts jar-dins, - le bleu du ciel   M

Le Refuge
Copyright by Salabert, Paris, N. Y. — J'ai re-non-cé à ce mon-de vain: Pour moi la coupe est vi-de,   N

ALBERT, Eugen d' (1864-1932)

Möchte wohl gerne ein Schmetterling sein, Op. 27, No. 2
By permission Associated Music Publishers, Inc. — Sag-te ein gol-de-ner Schmet-ter-ling zu sei-ner sil-ber-nen Frau   P

Tiefland (opera) Prologue
By permission Associated Music Publishers, Inc. — Ich grüss' noch ein - - -mal mei-ne Ber - ge.   Q

Act 1 Traumerzählung — Zwei Va-ter-un-ser bet' ich vor dem Schlaf-en geh'n, das er-ste bet' ich   R

Wolfserzählung — Mein Le - ben wagt ich drum, - ja, ja, mein Le - ben!   S

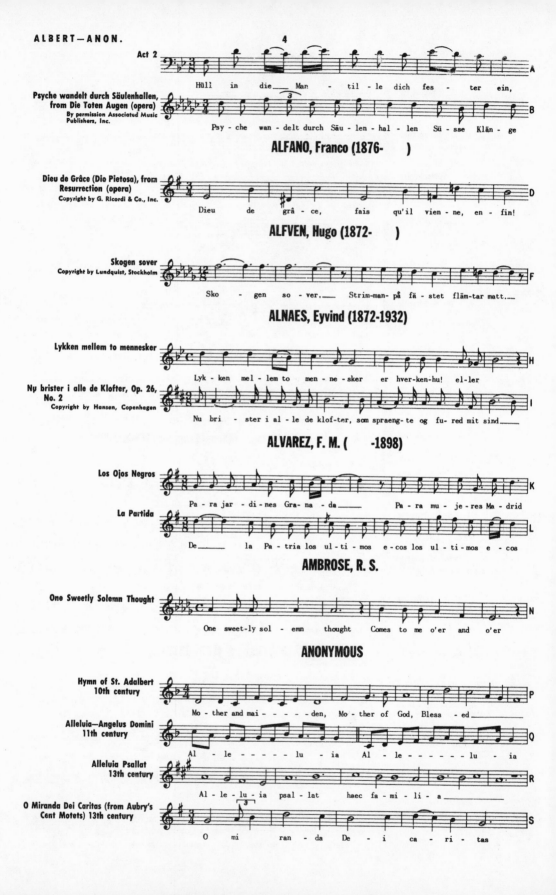

4

Act 2

Hüll in die Man - til - le dich fes - ter ein,

Psyche wandelt durch Säulenhallen, from Die Toten Augen (opera)
By permission Associated Music Publishers, Inc.

Psy - che wan - delt durch Säu - len-hal - len Sü - sse Klän - ge

ALFANO, Franco (1876-   )

Dieu de Grâce (Dio Pietosa), from Resurrection (opera)
Copyright by G. Ricordi & Co., Inc.

Dieu de grâ - ce, fais qu'il vien - ne, en - fin!

ALFVEN, Hugo (1872-   )

Skogen sover
Copyright by Lundquist, Stockholm

Sko - gen so - ver.___ Strim-man- på fä - stet fläm-tar matt.___

ALNAES, Eyvind (1872-1932)

Lykken mellem to mennesker

Lyk - ken mel - lem to men - ne - sker er hver-ken-hu! el - ler

Ny brister i alle de Klofter, Op. 26, No. 2
Copyright by Hansen, Copenhagen

Nu bri - ster i al - le de klof-ter, som spraeng-te og fu- red mit sind___

ALVAREZ, F. M. (-1898)

Los Ojos Negros

Pa - ra jar - di - nes Gra - na - da___ Pa - ra mu - je-res Ma - drid

La Partida

De___ la Pa - tria los ul - ti - mos e - cos los ul - ti - mos e - cos

AMBROSE, R. S.

One Sweetly Solemn Thought

One sweet-ly sol - emn thought Comes to me o'er and o'er

ANONYMOUS

Hymn of St. Adalbert
10th century

Mo - ther and mai - - - - - den, Mo - ther of God, Bless - ed___

Alleluia—Angelus Domini
11th century

Al - le - - - - - lu - ia Al - le - - - - - lu - ia

Alleluia Psallat
13th century

Al - le - lu - ia psal - lat haec fa - mi - li - a___

O Miranda Dei Caritas (from Aubry's Cent Motets) 13th century

O mi ran - da De - i ca - ri - tas

Puellare Gremium (End of 13th century—14th century?)
A
Pu - el - la - re gre - mi - um mun - do fu - dit

The Descent of the Holy Ghost (Spanish) 14th century
B
All bless-ings that our_ God hath giv'n, In to-ken of his_ dear son's love,

German Flagellants' Hymn Year of the Plague 1349
C
O Ma - ry Moth-er Vir-gin mild, For - get not Christ-en - dom_ thy child

Greensleeves
D
A - las! my love_ you do me wrong_ to cast me off_ dis-court-eous-ly

L'Amour de Moi 15th century
E
L'a - mour de moi s'y est en - clo____

Drink to me only with thine eyes
F
Drink to me on - ly with_ thine eyes_ And I_ will pledge with mine _

Have you seen but a whyte lillie grow
G
Have you seen but a whyte Lil - lie grow ____

Londonderry Air (Air from County Derry)
H
Would God I were the ten - der ap - ple blos - som

Oh! Dear! What Can the Matter Be?
I
Oh! dear! What can the mat - ter be? Dear! dear! What can the mat - ter be?

Ralph's Ramble to London
J
I am a poor in - no-cent clown,_ And late-ly I ram-bled to town _

The Slighted Swain
K
Chlo - e proves false,_ but still she is charm - ing

When Love is Kind
L
When love is kind,_ cheer - ful and free _

ARCADELT, Jacob (1514-1570)
(attributed to Arcadelt)

Ave Maria
N
A - ve Ma - ri - a! gra - ti - a ple - na

Il bianco e dolce cigno
O
Il bian - co e dol - ce cig - no Can - tan-do mo - re

ARCHANGELSKY, Alexander (1846-1924)

Hear My Prayer
Q
Hear my prayer, O God ____ O God, hear, O hear_ my _ prayer

ARDITI, Luigi (1822-1903)

Il Bacio (The Kiss)
S
Sul - le, Sul - le lab - bra, sul - le lab - bra se - po - tes - si

ARENSKY, Anton (1861-1906)

ARNE, Michael (1741-1786)

ARNE, Thomas A. (1710-1778)

AURIC, Georges (1899-   )

Le Gloxinia
By permission Associated Music Publishers, Inc.

Je vou-drais qu'à ma fe- nê- tre Fleurisse un ten-dre glo- xi- nia;

Printemps
By permission Durand & Cie, Paris; Elkan-Vogel Co., Inc., Phila., copyright owners

Quand ce beau prin-temps je voy, J'ap-per-çoy Ra- jeu-nir la terre

BACH, Carl Philipp Emanuel (1714-1788)
(See also BACH, Philipp Emanuel)

Die Himmel rühmen des ewigen Ehre

Die Him- mel rüh- men des E- wi- gen Eh- re

Jesus in Gethsemane

Schau' hin Dort in Geth-se- ma- ne klagt, trau-ert

Der Phoenix

Der Mann, der nach den Flit- ter- wo- chen aus Lie-be küsst

BACH, Johann Christian (1735-1782)

Non è ver, from Carattaco (opera)

Non è ver, che as-si- se in tro-no bel-le an-cor le col- pe so-no

BACH, Johann Michael (1648-1694)

Ich weiss dass mein Erlöser lebt

Ich weiss, dass mein Er- lo-ser lebt, ich weiss dass mein Er-lo-ser lebt

BACH, Johann Sebastian (1685-1750)

CANTATAS, Church, No. 4: Christ lag in Todesbanden (Easter Cantata) No. 1

Christ lag in To- des- ban- den

No. 3

Den Tod, Den Tod, Den Tod, Den Tod, Den Tod Nie- mand zwin- gen kunnt

No. 5

Hier ist das rech- te O- ster-lamm, das rech - - - te O-ster-lamm

No. 5: Wo soll ich fliehen hin No. 5

Ver- stum-me ver-stum-me, ver- stum- me, Höl - - - len- heer,

No. 6: Bleib' bei uns No. 1

Bleib' bei uns, bleib' bei uns, den es will A - - bend

No. 2

Hoch- ge- lob- ter Got- tes Sohn

No. 7: Christ unser Herr zum Jordan kam No. 6

Men- schen glaubt doch die- ser Gna- de

CANTATAS, Church, No. 8: Liebster Gott, wann werd' ich sterben?
No. 4

Doch wei - chet ihr tol - len ver-geb - - -li-chen sor - gen — A

No. 10: Mein Seel' erhebt den Herren No. 2

Herr, Herr, Herr, der du stark und mäch-tig bist, der du stark und mäch-tig bist — B

No. 3

Ge-wal - - - - - - - - - - - ti-ge, Ge-wal - - - - - ti-ge stösst Gott von — C

No. 6

Sein Sa - me muss-te sich so sehr wie Sand am Meer — D

No.12: Weinen, Klagen, Sorgen, Zagen No. 4

Kreuz und Kro-ne sind ver-bun-den, Kampf und Kleinod sind ver-eint. — E

No. 13: Meine Seufzer, meine Thränen No. 1

Mei - ne Seuf-zer, mei-ne Thrä-nen kön-nen nicht zu zäh - len sein — F

No. 2

Äch - zen und er - bärm - lich wei - nen, Äch - zen, — G

No. 17: Wer Dank opfert, der preiset mich No. 3

Herr, dei - ne Gü - te reicht, so weit der Him - mel ist, — H

No. 5

Welch Ü - ber-mass der Gü - te schenkst du mir! — I

No. 18: Gleich wie der Regen und Schnee von Himmel No. 4

Mein See - len-schatz ist Got-tes Wort, Mein See - len-schatz ist Got-tes Wort — J

No. 20: O Ewigkeit, du Donnerwort No. 3

E - - - -wig-keit du machst mir ban - - - - - - - - - ge — K

No. 6

O Mensch er - ret - te dei - ne See - le, ent - flie - - - - - - - he — L

Part II, No. 1

Wacht auf, wacht auf, wacht auf, wacht auf wacht auf, wacht auf, — M

No. 21: Ich hatte viel Bekümmerniss No. 2

Ich Ich, Ich, Ich hat-te viel Be-küm-mer-niss, Ich hat-te viel Be-küm-mer-niss — N

No. 3

Seuf-zer, Thrän-en, Kum- mer, Noth, Seuf-zer, Thrän-en, ängst-lich's — O

No. 5

Bä - che von ge - salz - nen Zäh - ren — P

Part II, No. 4

Er - freu - e dich See - le, er - freu - e dich, Her - ze — Q

No. 22: Jesus nahm zu sich die Zwölfe No. 2

Mein Je - su, zie - - - - - -he mich nach dir, — R

CANTATAS, Church, No. 69: Lobe den Herrn, meine Seele No. 5

A

Mein Er- lö- ser und Er- hal-ter, nimm mich stets in Hut und Wacht,_____

No. 70: Wachet, wachet, seid be- reit allezeit   Part I, No. 3

B

Wenn kommt der Tag aus dem_ wir zie- hen aus dem E- gyp-ten die- - - - ser Welt

Part I, No. 5

C

Lass' der_ Spöt- ter Zun- - - gen_ schmähen, es wird_doch, und_muss_ge- sche-hen

Part II, No. 1

D

Hebt eu- er._Haupt em- - - por und seid_ge-trost, ihr From- men,_____

Part II, No. 3

E

Se- - - - lig- - - - ster Er- qui- - - ckungs- tag

No. 71: Gott ist mein König   No. 4

F

Tag und Nacht,   Tag und Nacht ist dein, Tag und Nacht, Tag und Nacht,

No. 72: Alles nur nach Gottes Willen   No. 2 (Arioso)

G

Herr, so_ du_ willt,   so muss sich Al- les fü- - - gen!

H

Mit Al- lem, was ich hab' und bin Mit Al- lem was ich hab'_ und_ bin

No. 5

I

Mein Je- sus_will es, thun,   Er will dein Kreuz ver- sü- - ssen.

No. 73: Herr, wie du willt, so schick's mit mir   No. 4

J

Herr, so du willt,   Herr, so du willt, Herr, so du willt, Herr, so du willt,

No. 74: Wer mich liebet, der wird mein Wort halten   No. 4

K

Kommt!   Kommt!   ei - - - - - - - - - - - - - - - let!

No. 6

L

Nichts kann mich er- ret-ten von höl- li- schen Ket- - - - - - - - ten,

No. 75: Die Elenden sollen essen   No. 3

M

Mein   Je- - - sus_ soll- - - - - mein Al- les sein

No. 5

N

Ich neh- - - me mein Lei- - - - den mit Freu- den auf mich!

No. 76: Die Himmel erzählen die Ehre Gottes   Part I, No. 3

O

Hört, ihr Völ- ker,   Got-tes Stim- me, hört, ihr Völ-ker, Got-tes Stim- me

Part II, No. 3

P

Has- - - - - - - se nur, has- se mich recht, has- se nur, has-se mich recht,

Part II, No. 5

Q

Liebt,_ihr Chri- - - sten in_der That,   liebt_ihr Chri- - sten in_der That

No. 78: Jesu, der du meine Seele   No. 1

R

Je- su, der du mei- - - ne See- - - - - le,

No. 2

S

Wir ei- - - - - - - - - len mit schwa- chen, doch em- si-gen Schrit-ten

CANTATAS, Church, No. 90: Es reifet euch ein schreckliche Ende — No. 3

So löschet im Ei-fer der Rä-chen-de Rich-ter

No. 91: Gelobet seist du, Jesus Christ — No. 3

Gott, dem der Er-den-kreis zu klein, den we--der Welt noch Him--mel fas-sen,

No. 92: Ich hab' in Gottes Herz und Sinn — No. 6

Das Brau — — — — — — — — sen von den rauhen Win-den

No. 8

Mei--nem Hirten bleib' ich treu, mei--nem Hirten bleib' ich treu

No. 93: Wer nur den lieben Gott lässt walten — No. 3

Man hal-te nur ein we-nig stil-le, wenn sich die Kreu-zes-stun-de naht,

No. 94: Was frag' ich nach der Welt — No. 5

Die Welt kann ih-re Lust und| Freud',

No. 95: Christus, der ist mein Leben — No. 4

Ach, schlage doch bald, ach, schlage doch bald, schlage doch schlage doch

No. 97: In allen meinem Thaten — No. 4

Ich trau — — — — — e sei-ner Gna — — den,

No. 6

Leg' ich mich späte nie-der, er wa — — — che frühe wie-der,

No. 8

Ihm hab ich mich er-ge-ben zu ster-ben und zu le-ben so bald

No. 98: Was Gott tut, das ist wohlgetan — No. 1

Was Gott tut, das ist wohl-ge-than, es bleibt ge-recht sein Wil--le;

No. 3

Hört, ihr Au-gen, auf zu wei--nen,

No. 5

Mei-nen Je-sum lass'--ich nicht,

No. 99: Was Gott tut, das ist wohlgetan (second version) — No. 1

Was Gott thut, das ist wohl-ge-than es bleibt ge-recht sein Wil-le

No. 100: Was Gott tut, das ist wohlgetan (third version) — No. 4

Was Gott thut, das ist wohl-ge-than, was Gott thut, was Gott thut,

No. 5

Was Gott thut das ist wohl — — ge-than!

No. 101: Nimm von uns, Herr, du treuer Gott — No. 2

Han — — dle nicht nach dei — nen Rech-ten

No. 102: Herr, deine Augen sehen nach den Glauben — No. 3

Weh! der See-le, weh, der See-le,

No. 4

Ver-ach-test du den Reich--tum sei--ner Gna-de

CANTATAS, Church, No. 104: Du Hirte Israel, höre   No. 1

Du Hir - - - te I-srael du Hir - - - te I-srael.   A

No. 5

Be- glück-te Heer-de, Je- su Scha-fe,be- glück- te Heer- de Je-- su Scha- fe,   B

No. 105: Herr, gehe nich in's Gericht   No. 3

Wie zit- tern und wan- ken der Sün- der Ge- dan- ken,   C

No. 5

Kann ich nur Je- sum__ mir zum Freun-de ma- chen,   D

No. 106: Gottes Zeit ist die aller-beste Zeit   No. 1

Got- tes Zeit, Got- tes Zeit ist die al- ler-be - - - -ste,   E

In ihm le- ben we - - - - - - - - - - - - ben   F

Es ist der al- te Bund: Mensch, du musst ster - - - ben,du musst   G

No. 2

In dei- ne__ Hän- de, In dei-ne__ Hän-de be- fehl'_ich__mei-nen Geist   H

Mit Fried und Freud ich fahr da- hin in Got-tes Wil - - len,   I

No. 3

Glo- rie, Lob, Ehr' - - - - - und Herr - - - lich-keit   J

No. 110: Unser Mund, sei voll Lachens   No. 4

Ach Herr! was ist ein Men-schen-kind, dass du sein Heil so schmerzlich su-chest?   K

No. 6

Wacht auf,wacht auf!__ wacht auf, wacht auf!__ wacht auf, ihr A- dern   L

No. 112: Der Herr ist mein ge-treuer Hirt   No. 2

Zum rei- nen Was- ser er__ mich weist, das mich er- quick- en   M

No. 114: Ach, lieben Christen, seid getrost   No. 5

Du machst, O Tod,__ mir__ nun nicht fer- ner__ ban- ge   N

No. 115: Mache dich, mein Geist, bereit   No. 2

Ach,schläfri- ge See-le,_wie? Wie? Ach,'schläfri-ge See-le,wie? ru-hest du   O

No. 117: Sei Lob und Ehr' dem höchsten Gut   No. 7

Ich will dich all mein Le- ben lang, O Gott, von nun an eh - - -ren,   P

No. 120: Gott, man lobet dich in der Stille   No. 1

Gott,man lo - - - - - - - - - - - - - - bet dich in der Stil- le   Q

No. 4

Heil__ und Se- gen Heil__ und_Se - - -gen soll und muss zu al-ler Zeit,   R

No. 121: Christum wir sollen loben schon   No. 3

Jo- han - - - - nis freu- - - -den- vol- les Sprin - - - gen,   S

CANTATAS, Church, No. 122: Das neugebor'ne Kindelein No. 2

O Men-schen, die ihr täglich sündigt, die ihr täglich sündigt,   A

No. 127: Herr Jesu Christ, whar'r Mensch und Gott No. 3

Die See-le ruht in Je-su Hän-den,   B

No. 128: Auf Christi Himmelfahrt allein No. 3

Auf, auf, mit hel-lem Schall, mit hel-lem Schall   C

No. 129: Gelobet sei der Herr, mein Gott No. 4

Ge-lo-bet sei der Herr, mein Gott, der e-wig le-bet   D

Finale

Dem wir das Hei-lig itzt mit Freu-den las-sen klin-gen,   E

No. 133: Ich freue mich in dir No. 2

Ge-trost, ge-trost, ge-trost! es fasst ein heil'-ger Leib   F

No. 3

Wie lieb-lich klingt es in den Oh-ren!   G

No. 134: Ein Herz, das seinen Jesum lebend weiss No. 2

Auf, auf, auf, auf, Gläu-bi-ge   Auf, Gläu-bi-ge, sin-get die lieb-li-chen Lie-der   H

No. 135: Ach Herr, mich armen Sünder No. 3

Trö-ste mir, Je-su mein Ge-mü-the   I

No. 5

Weicht all' ihr Ü-bel-thä-ter, weicht!   J

No. 140: Wachet auf, ruft uns die Stimme No. 1

Wa-chet auf! ruft uns die Stim-me   K

No. 3

Wann kommst du, mein Heil Ich kom-me, dein Theil wann kommst du, ich kom-me.   L

No. 5

Zi-on hört die Wäch-ter sin-gen, das Herz tut ihr vor Freu-den sprin-gen,   M

No. 7

Mein Freund ist mein! Und ich bin dein! Die Lie-be soll nichts   N

No. 142: Uns ist ein Kind geboren No. 2

Uns ist ein Kind ge-bo-ren, ein Sohn' ist uns ge-bo-ren,   O

No. 3

Dein Ge-burtstag ist er-schie-nen, so er-for-dert mei-ne Pflicht.   P

No. 144: Nimm was dein ist, und gehe hin No. 2

Mur-re nicht, lie-ber Christ, Mur-re nicht, lie-ber Christ.   Q

No. 145: So du mit deinem Munde No. 5

Mer-ke, mein Her-ze, be-stän-dig nur dies,   R

No. 146: Wir müssen durch viel Trübsal No. 5

Ich sä-e mei-ne Zäh-ren mit ban-gem Her-zen,   S

CANTATAS, Church,

No. 147: Herz und Mund und Tat
und Leben No. 10 (Jesu, joy of
man's desiring)

No. 148: Bringet dem Herrn Ehre
seines Namens No. 4

No. 149: Man singet mit Freuden
vom Sieg No. 4

No. 151: Süsser Trost, mein Jesus
kömmt No. 1

No. 3

No. 152: Tritt auf die Glaubens-
bahn No. 4

No. 153: Schau', lieber Gott, wie
meine Feind! No. 6

No. 154: Mein liebster Jesus ist
verloren No. 1

No. 3

No. 155: Mein Gott, wie lang
No. 4

No. 156: Ich stehe mit einem
Fuss im Grabe No. 4

No. 159: Sehet, wir geh'n hinauf
gen Jerusalem No. 4

No. 160: Ich weiss dass mein
Erloser lebt No. 1

No. 161: Komm, du süsse Todes-
stunde No. 3

No. 167: Ihr Menschen rühmet
Gottes Liebe No. 1

No. 170: Vergnügte Ruh, beliebte
Seelenlust No. 1

No. 172: Erschallet, ihr Lieder
No. 3

No. 4

No. 175: Er rufet seinen Schafen
mit Namen No. 2

Je- sus blei- bet mei- ne Freu- de Mei- nes Her- zens Trost und Saft

Mund und Her- - - ze steht dir of- fen,

Got- tes En- gel wei- chen nie, sie sind bie mir al-ler- En-den,

Sü - - - - - - sser Trost, mein Je- sus, mein Je- sus kommt,

In Je- su De- muth kann ich Trost, in sei- ner Ar- muth

Stein, der ü- - ber al- - - - le Schätze, hilf,

Stürmt nur, stürmt, ihr Trüb- - - - - - sals- wet- ter.

Mein lieb- ster Je- - - - sus ist ver- lo- ren, O Wort, das mir

Je- su, lass dich fin- den, lass doch mei- ne Sün- den kei- ne di- cke Wol-ken sein,

Wirf, mein Her- ze, wirf dich noch in des Höch- sten Lie- bes- ar- me,

Herr, was du willst soll mir ge- fal- len, Herr, was du willst

Es ist voll- bracht, es ist voll- bracht, das Leid ist al- le;

Ich weiss, dass mein Er- lö- ser lebt Ich weiss dass mein Er- lö- ser lebt.

Mein Ver- lan- gen, mein Ver- lan- gen ist, dem Hei- land zu um- fan- gen

Ihr Men- schen, rüh- met Got- tes Lie- - - - be,

Ver- gnüg- - - - te Ruh', be- lieb- te See- len- lust,

Hei- lig- ste Drei- ei- nig- keit, gro- sser Gott, gro- sser Gott

O See- len- Pa- ra- dies, O See- len- Pa- - - - ra- dies,

Komm lei- te mich, es seh- net sich mein Geist auf grü- ne Wei- de,

BACH

CANTATAS, Secular, No. 194:
Höchsterwünschtes Freudenfest
No. 3

Was des Höch- sten Glanz___ er- füllt,wird in___ kei- ne Nacht_ver-hüllt, **A**

No. 201: Der Streit zwischen
Phoebus und Pan
No. 3

Pa- tron, Pa- tron, Pa- tron,das macht der Wind, Wind, Wind,das macht der Wind! **B**

No. 5

Mit_Ver-lan-gen, mit_Ver-lan-gen drück'_ich_deine zar - - - ten Wan-gen, **C**

No. 202: Weichet nur
No. 1

Wei - - - - chet___ nur, be-trüb- - - te___ Schat- ten___ **D**

No. 2

Phö- bus eilt___ **E**

No. 3

Wenn die___Frühlingslüf- te strei-chen und durch bun-te__ Fel- der wehn, **F**

No. 4

Sich ü- ben_ im lie- ben, im Scher-zen_ sich her-zen **G**

No. 5 Gavotte

See- - - het___ in Zu- frie- den- - - - heit **H**

No. 205: Der Zufriedengestellte
Aeolus
No. 3

Zweig'_____ und Aes- te, Zweig'_____ und Ae- - -ste, **I**

No. 3

Wie will ich lus-tig la - - - - - - - - - - - - chen___ **J**

No. 7

Kön- nen nicht die ro-then Wan-gen, wo-mit mei- ne_ Früch-te_ pran-gen, **K**

No. 206: Schleicht, spielende
Wellen (Birthday Cantata for
August III) No. 9

Hört_doch! der sanf-ten Flö-ten Chor___ er- freut- - die Brust,er-götzt_das Ohr, **L**

No. 208: Was mir behagt is nur
die munt're Jagd (Birthday Cantata) No. 9 (Sheep may safely
graze)

Scha- fe_ kön- nen si- cher_wei- den,_ wo ein_gu- ter Hir- te_wacht, **M**

No. 211: Schweigt stille, plau-
dert nicht (Coffee Cantata)
No. 2

Hat man nicht mit sei- nen Kin-dern hun-dert tau-send_ Hu- de- lei! **N**

No. 4

Ei! wie schmeckt der Cof-fee sü- sse,_ lieb-li-cher als tau-send Küs-se,_ **O**

No. 6

Mäd-chen, die von har-ten Sin- nen, die___ von_ har- ten Sin- nen, **P**

No. 8

Heu- te_ noch Heu- te_ noch, lie- ber_ Va- ter,thut es_ doch **Q**

No. 10

Die Ka- tze lässt das Mau- - - sen nicht, die Jung-- fern_blei-ben **R**

No. 212: Mer hahn en neue Oberkeet (Peasant Cantata)
No. 2

Mer___ hahn en neu- e_ O- ber-keet an un-sern Kam- mer- herrn. **S**

CANTATAS, Secular, No. 212: No. 4
Mer hahn en neue Oberkeet (Peasant Cantata)

Ach es schmeckt doch gar zu gut, gar zu gut, wenn ein Paar recht freund-lich tut;

No. 6

Ach Herr Schösser, geht nicht gar zu schlimm mit uns ar-men Bau-ers-leu-ten, üm,

No. 8

Un- ser treff-- lich- er lie- ber Kam-- mer-herr

No. 10

Das ist ga-lant, es spricht niemand von den ca-du-cken Scho-cken

No. 12

Fünf- zig Tha- ler baares Geld trock'-ner Wei se zu ver-schmau-sen,

No. 14

Klein-zschocher mü-sse so zart und sü-sse wie lau-ter Man-del-ker-ne sein

No. 16

Es neh- me zehn-tau-send Du-ca-ten der Kam-mer-herr al-le Tag' ein,

No. 18

Gieb, Schö- ne, viel Söh-ne von art'-ger Ge- stalt,

No. 20

Dein Wach- stum sei fe-ste und la-che vor Lust

No. 22

Und dass ihr's al- le wisst, es ist nun-mehr die Frist zu trin- ken,

No. 24

Wir gehn nun wo der Tu-del-sack, der Tu-del-Tu-del-Tu-del- Tu-del-

CHORALES: Ein feste Burg

Ein fe-ste Burg ist un-ser Gott, ein' gu-te Wehr und Waf-- fen

In dulci jubilo

In dul- ci ju- bi- lo sin- get und seid froh,

Lobet den Herrn

Lo- bet den Her- ren, lo-bet den Her- ren, denn er ist sehr freund-lich,

Die Sonn' hat sich mit ihrem Glanz

Die Sonn' hat sich mit ih- rem Glanz ge- wen- det, und, was sie soll

Vater unser in Himmelreich

Va- ter un- ser im Him- mel-reich, der du uns al- le heissest gleich

Wer den lieben Gott lässt walten

Wer nur den lie-ben Gott lässt wal-- ten, und hof-fet auf ihn al-- le-zeit

Magnificat in D 1. Chorus

Ma- - - - - - - -gni-fi-cat, ma-gni-fi-cat, ma-gni-fi-cat,

II. Aria

Et ex- ul- ta-- vit spi- ri- tus me- us

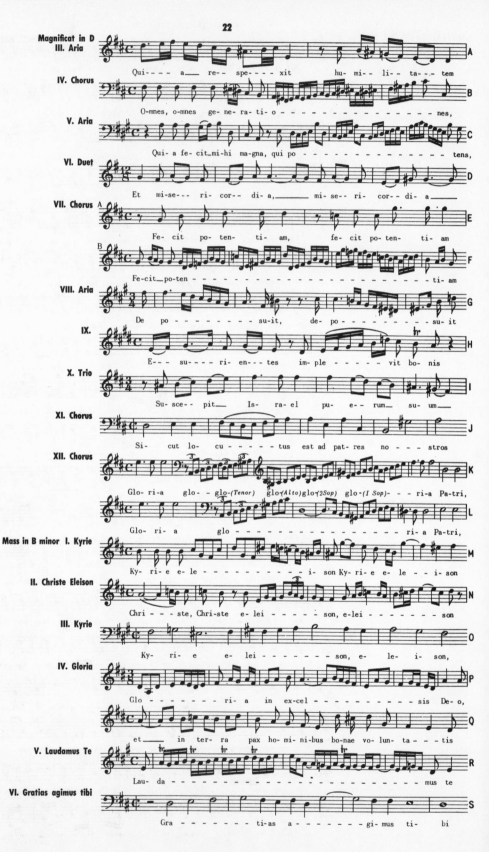

Christmas Oratorio

No. 4 — Be-rei-te dich,Zi-on,mit zärt-li-chen Trie-ben,den Schönsten,den Liebsten — A

No. 8 — Gro-sser Herr und star-ker Kö-nig, Lieb-ster Hei-land, o wie we-nig — B

No. 15 — Fro---he Hir---ten, eilt, ach ei-let, — C

No. 19 — Schla------fe,mein Lieb------ster,ge-nie---sse der Ruh, — D

No. 31 — Schlie-sse,mein Her---ze, dies se---li-ge Wun---der — E

No. 39 — Flösst, mein Hei-land, flösst, dein Na-men. flösst, mein Hei-land, — F

No. 41 — Ich will nur dir zu Eh-ren le------------ben, — G

No. 47 — Er-leucht' auch mei---ne fin----stre Sin---nen, — H

No. 57 — Nur ein Wink von sei-nen Hän-den sturzt ohnmächt'ger Menschen Macht — I

No. 62 — Nun mögt ihr stol--zen Fein--de schre--cken — J

Easter Oratorio

No. 3 — Kommt, ei-------let und lau---------fet, — K

No. 5 — See-le dei-ne Spe-ce-rei-----en sol-len nicht mehr Myrrhen sein — L

No. 7 — Sanf-te soll mein To-des-kum---mer nur ein Schlum-----mer, — M

No. 9 — Sa-get, sa-------------get, mir ge--schwin-de, — N

St. John Passion

Part I No. 1 A — Herr, Herr, Herr, un-ser Herr-----------scher — O

No. 1 B — Herr, un-ser Herr-----------scher,un-ser Herr-scher — P

No. 4 — O gro-sse Lieb', O Lieb' ohn al-le Maa---sse, — Q

No. 5 — Dein Will' ge-scheh',Herr Gott zu-gleich,auf Er-den wie im Him-mel-reich; — R

No. 6 — Von den Stri---cken mei-ner Sun---den mich zu ent-bin-den — S

St. John Passion

Part I No. 7
Ich fol--ge dir gleich-falls mit freu-di-gen Schrit-ten

No. 8
Wer hat dich so ge-schla-gen, mein Heil, und dich mit Pla- gen

No. 10
Ach, mein Sinn, ach, mein Sinn, wo willst du end-lich hin,

No. 11
Pet-rus, der nicht denkt zu-rück, sei-nen Gott ver-nei- net

Part II No. 12
Chri-stus, der uns se-lig macht, Kein Bös's hat be- gan-gen,

No. 13
Wä- re die-ser nicht ein Ü-bel-thä--ter, nicht ein Übel-thä-ter,

No. 18
Er-wä---ge, er-wä---ge er-wä-----ge, er-wä---- ge,

No. 19
Sei ge- grü-sset, lie-ber Ju- den- kö-nig, lie-ber Ju-den-kö-nig

No. 21
Wir ha-ben ein Ge- setz, und nach dem Ge-setz soll er ster------ ben

No. 26
Eilt, eilt, eilt, eilt, ihr an-ge- focht'-nen See-len,

No. 28
In mei-nes Her-zens Grun-de, dein Nam' und Kreuz al- lein

No. 31
Es ist voll--bracht, Es ist voll----bracht,

No. 34
Zer-flie---sse, mein Her-ze, in Flu-then der Zäh--ren,

No. 36
Ruht wohl, ruht wohl, ihr hei-li-gen Ge- bei--- ne

No. 37
Ach Herr, lass dein lieb' En-ge-lein am letz-ten End' die See-le mein

St. Matthew Passion
Part I No. 1
Kommt ihr Töch-ter, helft mir kla-----gen, helft mir kla-gen

Chorale Theme
O Lamm Got-tes un-schul-dig am Stamm des Kreu-zes

(Chorale) No. 3
Herz-lieb-ster Je---su, was hast du ver-bro---- chen

No. 10
Buss und Reu, Bus und Reu, knirscht das Sun-den--herz ent-zwei,

St. Matthew Passion
Part I No. 12

Blu- te nur, blu- te nur blu- te nur, du lie- bes Herz,   A

No. 16

Ich bin's, ich soll- te bü- ssen an Hän- den und an Fü- ssen   B

No. 17

Trin- ket al - - - le da- raus das ist mein Blut des neu- en Tes- ta- ments,   C

No. 19

Ich will dir mein Her- - - ze schen- ken, sen- - - ke_ dich, sen- - ke_ dich,   D

(Chorale) No. 21

Er- ken- ne mich, mein Hü- ter, mein Hir- te nimm_ mich an   E

No. 26

Ich will bei_ mei- nem Je- - - - - - - - su wa- chen   F

No. 29

Ger- ne will_ ich_ mich be- que- men, Kreuz und Be- cher an- zu- neh- men   G

(Chorale) No. 31

Was_ mein Gott will, das g'sceh' all- zeit, sein Will' der ist der_ be- ste   H

No. 33 A

So ist mein Je- sus nun ge- fan- - - - - - - - - - - - - - - gen,   I

No. 33 B

Sind Blitze, sind Don- ner in Wol- ken_ ver- - schwun- den,   J

No. 35

O Mensch, be- wein_ dein_ Sün- - - de_ gross_   K

Part II No. 36

Ach - - - - - - - - - - nun_ ist mein_ Je- sus_ hin,_ ach   L

(Chorale) No. 38

Mir hat die Welt - - - trüg- lich ge- richt't mit Lü- gen und mit fal- schem G'dicht,   M

No. 41

Ge- duld, Ge- duld! Ge- duld,_ Ge- duld!   N

(Chorale) No. 46

Wer hat dich so_ ge- schla- gen, mein Heil und dich mit_ Pla- gen   O

No. 48

Er bar- - - - - me_ dich,_ er- bar- - me dich, mein Gott,   P

(Chorale) No. 49

Bin ich gleich von dir ge- wi- chen, stell' ich mich doch_ wie- der ein   Q

No. 51

Gebt mir mei- - nen Je- - - sum wie- der, Gebt mir, gebt_ mir mei- nen Je- sum wie- der   R

(Chorale) No. 55

Wie wun- der- bar- lich ist doch die- se Stra- fe! der gu- te Hir- te lei- det   S

BACH
St. Matthew Passion
Part II No. 58

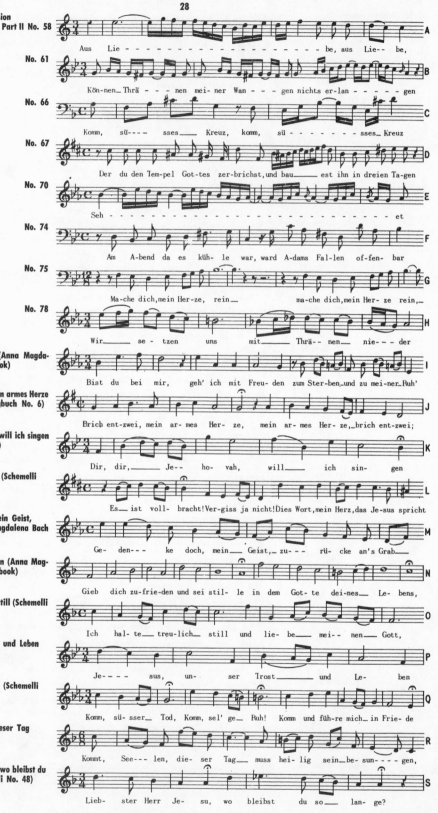

Aus Lie - - - - - - - - - - - - - - - be, aus Lie- be,

No. 61

Kön-nen Thrä - - - nen mei-ner Wan - - gen nichts er-lan - - - - gen

No. 66

Komm, sü- - - - sses Kreuz, komm, sü - - - - - sses Kreuz

No. 67

Der du den Tem-pel Got-tes zer-bricht,und bau - - est ihn in drei-en Ta-gen

No. 70

Seh - - - - - - - - - - - - - - - - - - - et

No. 74

Am A-bend da es küh - le war, ward A-dams Fal-len of-fen-bar

No. 75

Ma-che dich,mein Her-ze, rein — ma-che dich,mein Her- ze rein,—

No. 78

Wir— se-tzen uns mit— Thrä- - nen nie- - - der

SONGS

Bist du bei mir (Anna Magda-lena Bach Notebook)

Bist du bei mir, geh' ich mit Freu-den zum Ster-ben und zu mei-ner Ruh'

Brich entzwei, mein armes Herze (Schemelli Gesangbuch No. 6)

Brich ent-zwei, mein ar-mes Her- ze, mein ar-mes Her- ze,—brich ent-zwei;

Dir, dir, Jehovah, will ich singen (Schemelli No. 14)

Dir, dir,— Je-- ho-vah, will— ich sin- gen

Es ist vollbracht (Schemelli No. 20)

Es— ist voll- bracht!Ver-giss ja nicht!Dies Wort,mein Herz,das Je-sus spricht

Gedenke doch, mein Geist, zurücke (Anna Magdalena Bach Notebook)

Ge- den--- ke doch, mein Geist,— zu--- rü- cke an's Grab

Gieb dich zufrieden (Anna Mag-dalena Bach Notebook)

Gieb dich zu-frie-den und sei stil- le in dem Got-te dei-nes— Le- bens,

Ich halte treulich still (Schemelli No. 30)

Ich hal-te— treu-lich— still und lie- be— mei-- nen— Gott,

Jesus, unser Trost und Leben (Schemelli No. 39)

Je- - - - sus, un- ser Trost— und Le- ben

Komm, süsser Tod (Schemelli No. 42)

Komm, sü- sser Tod, Komm, sel' ge— Ruh! Komm und füh-re mich— in Frie- de

Kommt, Seelen, dieser Tag (Schemelli No. 43)

Kommt, See--- len, die-ser Tag— muss hei- lig sein—be-sun- - - gen,

Liebster Herr Jesu, wo bleibst du so lange (Schemelli No. 48)

Lieb- ster Herr Je- su, wo bleibst du so lan- ge?

SONGS

Mein Jesu, was für Seelenweh
(Schemelli No. 51)

Mein__ Je-su, was für See-len-weh be-fällt dich in Get-se-ma--ne

O Jesulein süss, o Jesulein mild
(Schemelli No. 58)

O Je-su-lein süss, O Je-su-lein mild, dein's Va-ters Will'n hast du er-füllt

Qui Tollis, from Mass in A major

Qui tollis pec-ca-ta, qui tol-lis pec-ca-ta, pec-ca-ta mun-di

So oft ich meine Tabakspfeife
(Anna Magdalena Bach Note-book)

So oft ich mei---ne Ta--baks-pfei--fe mit gu-tem Kna--ster an-ge-füllt,

Willst du dein Herz mir schenken
(Aria di Giovanni) (Anna Magda-lena Bach Notebook)

Willst du dein Herz mir schen-ken, so fang' es__ heim-lich an,

BACH, Philipp Emanuel   (see also Bach, Carl Philipp Emanuel)

Bitten

Gott, dei---ne Gü---te reicht__ so__ weit

Lied

Ich__ ging un-ter Er-len am küh-li-gen Bach

Passionslied

Er-for--sche mich, er-fahr__ mein__ Herz,

BACH, Wilhelm Friedemann (1710-1784)

Kein Hälmlein wächst auf Erden

Kein Hälm-lein wächst auf Er-den, der Him-mel__ hat's be-taut

BACHELET, Alfred Georges (1864-1943)

Chère Nuit

Chè----re nuit__ aux clar-tés__ se-rei----nes,

BACKER-GRONDAHL, Agathe (1847-1907)

Mot Kveld, Op. 42, No. 7

Al-le de dugg--vaa-te blom-ster har sennt, So-len det siss-te God-nat

BALAKIREV, Mily Alexeivich (1837-1910)

Oh come to me!
Copyright 1911, G. Schirmer, Inc.

Oh come to me when breez-es stir the si-lent trees with lan-guid sigh-ing

BALFE, Michael William (1808-1870)

Bohemian Girl (opera)

In the gyp-sy's life you read__ the life that all would like to lead__

Bohemian Girl (opera)

I dreamt that I dwelt_ in mar-ble halls, with vas-sals and serfs at my side,_ — A

The heart bow'd down by weight of woe, to weak-est hopes_ will_ cling — B

Then You'll Remember Me

When o-ther lips and o-ther_ hearts their tales of love shall tell — C

Trav'llers All of Ev'ry Station, from The Siege of La Rochelle (opera)

Trav'l-lers all of ev'-ry sta-tion, Trav'l-lers all of ev'ry sta-tion draw long — D

Come into the Garden, Maud

Come in-to the gar-den, Maud, For the black bat, Night has flown; — E

Excelsior

The shades of night were fall-ing fast As thro' an Al-pine vil-lage passed_ — F

Killarney

By Kil-lar-ney's_ lakes and fells, Em'-rald isles and_ wind-ing bays — G

BANTOCK, Sir Granville (1868-)

A Feast of Lanterns
By permission of Galaxy Music Corporation, N. Y., Copyright by Elkin & Co., Ltd.

In spring for sheer de-light I set the lan-terns swing-ing through the trees — I

The Parting
(Words by Ross)
Copyright by G. Ricordi & Co., Inc.

Oh he cam' whist-lin' up the glen,_ And, smi-lin' I gaed doon to meet him; — J

BARBER, Samuel (1910-)

The Daisies, Op. 2, No. 1
Copyright 1936, G. Schirmer, Inc.

In the scent-ed bud of the morn-ing O, when the wind-y grass — L

I hear an army, Op. 10, No. 3
Copyright 1939, G. Schirmer, Inc.

I hear an_ ar-my charg-ing up-on the land — M

A Nun Takes the Veil, Op. 13, No. 1
Copyright 1941, G. Schirmer, Inc.

I have de-sired to go where springs not fail — N

Sleep now, Op. 10, No. 2
Copyright 1939, G. Schirmer, Inc.

Sleep now, O sleep now O you un-qui-et heart! — O

Sure on this shining night, Op. 13, No. 3
Copyright 1941, G. Schirmer, Inc.

Sure on this shin-ing night of star-made shad-ows round, — P

With rue my heart is laden, Op. 2, No. 2
Copyright 1936, G. Schirmer, Inc.

With rue my heart is lad-en for gol-den friends I had — Q

BARLOW, S. M. L. (1892-)

The Cherry
Copyright by G. Ricordi & Co., Inc.

Jo-seph was an old man, an_ old man_ was he; — S

BARNABY, Sir Joseph (1838-1892)

Sweet and low

Sweet and low, sweet and low, wind of the wes- tern sea____

BARTLET, John (17th cent.)

Of all the birds that I do know

Of all the birds that I do know, Phil- ip my spar- row hath no peer

BARTLETT, James Carroll (1850-1929)

A Dream
Copyright by Oliver Ditson Co.
Used by permission.

Last night I was dream- ing of thee, love, was dream- ing,

BARTÓK, Béla (1881-1945)

Hungarian Folksong Settings
A gyulai kert alatt
By permission Boosey & Hawkes, Inc.,
copyright owners

A gyu- la- i kert a-latt, kert a- latt Bar-na le-gény roz-ma-rin- got a- rat

Által mennék én a Tiszán

Ál-tal-men-nék én a Ti-szán la- di-kon, la- di-kon, de la- di-kon,

Aszszonyok, Aszszonyok

Asz- szo-nyok, asz- szo- nyok, had' le- gyek tár- sa- tok,

Elindultam szép hazámbul

El- in-dul-tam szép ha- zám- bul, Hi- res kis ma-gyar- or- szág- bul.

Feketeföd
one theme

Fe- ke- te föd,____ fe- hér az én zseb- ken - - - -döm

El- ha- gyott a leg- ked- ve- sebb sze- re- töm

Ha kimegyek arr' a magas tetőre

Ha-ki- me-gyek arr' a ma-gas te- tő- re Ta-lá-lok én sze-re-tő-re ket-tő-re.

Istenem, Istenem
one theme

Is- te-nem, Is- te- nem á-raszd meg a vi- zet Had' vi-gyen el en- gem

a pám- ka- pu já- ra;____

Nem meszsze van ide kis Margitta

Nem mesz- sze van i- de kis Mar- git-ta, Hor-to-bágy-nak vi-ze kö-rül foly-ja.

Töltek a nagy erdö útját

Töl-tik a nagy er-dő út- - - - ját, Vi-szik a szé- kely ka-to- - - - nát

Vévig mentem a tárkányi sej, haj

Vé- vig men- tem a tár- ká- nyi sej, haj, nagy uc- cán;

32

BATESON, Thomas (1570-1630)

Cupid in a bed of roses

Cu-pid in a bed of Ro- ses in a bed of Ro- ses

Have I found her

Have I found her? have I found her O rich find- ing

BAX, Arnold (1883-   )

A Christmas Carol
By permission J. & W. Chester, Ltd., London, copyright owners

There is no rose of such vir- tue As__ is the rose_____ that bore

Cradle Song

I heard a Piper Piping
By permission Oxford Univ. Press, London, copyright owners

I heard a pi-per pi- ping the blue__ hills a- mong_____

Mater ora filium (unacc. double choir)

The White Peace
By permission J. & W. Chester, Ltd., London, copyright owners

It lies not on the sun- lit hill__ Nor__ on the sun-lit plain:

BAYLY, Anselm (1719-1794)

Long, long ago

Tell me the tales that to me were so dear, Long, long a- go, Long, long a-go

BEACH, Mrs. H. H. A. (1867-1944)

Ah, Love, But a Day
Copyright by Arthur P. Schmidt Co., Boston
Used by permission.

Ah, Love but__ a day____ And the world has changed!__

The Year's at the Spring, Op. 44, No. 1
Copyright by Arthur P. Schmidt Co., Boston
Used by permission.

The year's__at the spring,__ And day's_at the morn;__ Morn-ing's_at sev-en,

BECKER, Reinhold (1842-1924)

Frühlingszeit

Wenn der Früh- ling auf die Ber-- ge steigt

BEETHOVEN, Ludwig van (1770-1827)

**Fidelio, Op. 72 (Opera)
Act I, No. 2**

O wär' ich schon mit dir__ vereint, und dürf- te mann__ dich nen-nen!

No. 3 (Quartet)

Mir ist so wun- der-bar, es engt das Herz mir ein;

BEETHOVEN
Missa Solemnis, Op. 123
III Credo

34

Con sub-stan-ti- a- lem pa-tri per quem om-ni-a fac-ta sunt,

Et in-car-na-tus est de spi-ri-tu sanc- to ex Ma-ri- a vir-gi-ne,

Et vi-tam ven-tu-ri sae - - - - cu- li, a - - - - men, a - - men,

IV Sanctus

Sanc- - -tus_ Do- mi-nus, Do-mi-nus De-us Sa- - - ba-oth,

Ple- ni sunt coe- li et ter-ra glo - - - - - - - - - - ri-a tu- a

O- sa- na, O-sa-na in ex-cel - - - - sis, O-sa-na, O- sa-na

V Benedictus

Be-ne-dic - - - -tus, qui_ ve- nit, qui ve-nit in no- mi-ne Do-mi-ni,

VI Agnus Dei

Ag - - -nus, ag-nus De-i qui tol-lis pec-ca-ta, pec-ca-ta,pec-ca-ta mun- di,

Do - - - - - - - - - - na no- bis pa - - - - - - - - - cem,

pa- cem, pa -cem,

Do - - - - na no- - - bis pa - - - - - - - - - - - - - - - - - - -cem

Mount of Olives, Op. 85 (oratorio)
I

Mei-ne See-le ist er- schüt-tert von den Qua-len, von den Qua-len,die_mir_

II

Preist,preist des Er-lö-sers_ Gü- te, preist,Men-schen,_ sei- ne Huld

III

O Heil euch, heil euch, ihr_____ Er- lö- sten!

III

So ru- he denn_ mit gan-zer Schwe-re, mit gan-zer Schwe-re auf mir;

VI

In mei-nen A- dern wüh- len ge-rech-ter Zorn und Wuth

(Chorus)

Auf, auf! er- grei-fet den Ver- rä-ther,wei-let hier nun län-ger_ nicht!

(Chorus)

Wel-ten sin-gen, Wel-ten sin-gen, Wel-ten sin-gen Dank und Eh-re

(Chorus)

Prei-set ihn, ihr En-gel-chö-re,_ laut im heil'- gen Ju-bel- ton,

SONGS:
Abendlied

Wenn die Son- ne nie-der- sin-ket, und der Tag zur Ruh' sich neigt

Adelaide, Op. 46

Ein-sam wan- delt dein Freund im Früh- lings- gar- ten, mild von lieb- lich- en

Ah! Perfido, Op. 65 (Aria)

Per pie- tà, non dir- miad- di- o, non dir - - - - miad- di- o,

Di- te voi, se in tan- to af-fan- no non__ son__ de- gna di- pie- tà?__

Andenken

Ich den- ke dein,__ wenn durch den Hain der Nach-ti-gallen Ak- kor - - de schallen

An die ferne Geliebte, Op. 98, No. 1

Auf dem Hü- gel sitz' ich, spä- hend in das blau-e Ne- bel- land

No. 2

Wo die Ber- - ge so blau aus dem ne- - bli-gen Grau schau- en her- ein,

No. 3

Leich- te Seg- ler in den Hö- hen, und du Bäch- lein klein und schmal

No. 4

Die- se Wol- ken in den Hö- hen, die-ser Vög-lein munt' rer Zug

No. 5

Es keh-ret der Mai- en, es blü-het die Au'.Die Lüf-te,sie we-hen so mil-de,so lau,

No. 6

Nimm sie__ hin denn, die- se Lie-der, die ich dir, Ge- lieb- te, sang,__

An die Geliebte

O dass ich dir vom stil-len Au- ge in sei-nem lie- be-vol-len Schein,

An die Hoffnung, Op. 32

Die du so gern in heil'gen Näch- ten fei-erst und sanft und weich

Aus Goethe's Faust, Op. 75, No. 3

Es war ein-mal ein Kö- nig, der hatt' ei-nen gros-sen Floh,

Clärchen's Song, from Egmont, Op. 84

Die Trom- mel ge- rüh- ret! Das Pfeif- chen ge- spielt!

Freudvoll und leidvoll

Freud- voll und leid- voll, ge- dan- ken-voll sein;

Das Geheimniss

Wo bluht das Blüm-chen, das nie ver-blüht? Wo strahlt das Stern- lein,

Gellert Lieder, Op. 48, No. 1 Bitten

Gott, dei- ne Gü- te reicht- so weit, so weit die Wol- ken ge- hen

No. 2 Die Liebe des Nächsten

So Je-mand spricht: Ich lie- be Gott!__ und hasst doch sei- ne Brü- der,

BEETHOVEN

36

SONGS: Gellert Lieder, Op. 48,
No. 3 Vom Tode

Mei- ne Le- bens-zeit ver-streicht, stünd-lich eil' ich zu dem Gra- be, A

No. 4 Die Ehre Gottes aus der
Natur

Die Him-mel rüh-men des E- wi-gen Eh- re, ihr Schall pflanzt seinen Na-men- fort B

No. 5 Gottes Macht und Vorse-
hung

Gott ist mein Lied! Er ist der Gott der Stär- ke C

No. 6 Busslied

An dir al-lein, an dir hab' ich ge- sün-digt und ü- bel oft vor dir ge-than_ D

Ich liebe dich

Ich lie- be dich, so wie du mich, am A- bend und am Mor- gen, E

In questa tomba oscura

In que- sta tom- ba o- scu- ra la- scia-mi ri- po- sar; F

Irish Songs (voice and pianoforte
trio)
The British Light Dragoons

'Twas a mar- e-chal of France, and he fain would hon- our gain, G

Morning a Cruel Turmoiler Is

Mor-ning a cru- el tur-moil-er is, ban-ish- ing ease and re-pose H

The Morning Air Plays on my
Face

The morn- ing air_ plays on_ my face_ and, through_the gray mist peer- ing I

O Harp of Erin

O harp_ of E- rin thou art now_ laid low, J

O might I but my Patrick love

O might I but my Pat-rick love! My moth- er scolds se- vere- ly K

Oh! Who, my dear Dermot

Oh! who, my dear_ Der- mot, has dared to de- ceive thee, L

Once More I Hail Thee

Once more I_ hail thee, thou_ gloom- y De- cem- ber M

On the Massacre of Glencoe

Oh! tell me, Har-per, where-fore_ flow_ thy way-ward notes of wail and woe N

The Pulse of an Irishman

The pulse of an I- rish-man ev- er beats quick-er,when war is the sto- ry O

The Return to Ulster

Once a- gain, but how_ chang'd, since my wan- d'rings be- gan P

Sad and Luckless Was the
Season

Sad and luck-less was the sea-son, when to court fair_ El- len flew, Q

The Soldier

Then, Sol- dier!come_fill_ high the wine for we reck not of_ to- mor- row R

The Soldier in a Foreign Land

The_ pip- er who sat_ on his low_ mos- sy seat S

SONGS:

Kennst du das Land (Mignon) Op. 75, No. 1

Kennst du das Land, wo die Ci-tro- nen blüh'n, im dunk-len Laub

Der Kuss Op. 128 (ariette)

Ich war bei Chlo- en ganz al- lein, und kus-sen wollt' ich sie

Mailied Op. 52, No. 4

Wie herr- lich_ leuch-tet_ mir_ die Na-tur,_ wie glänzt die Son- ne,

Marmotte Op. 52, No. 7

Ich kom-me schon durch man-ches Land, a-vec que la_ mar-mot-te,

Mit einem gemalten Band, Op. 83, No. 3

Klei- ne_ Blu- men,_ klei-ne Blät- ter streu-en mir mit leich-ter_ Hand_

Neue Liebe, neues Leben, Op. 75 No. 2

Herz,mein Herz, was soll das ge- ben? Was be- drän- get dich so sehr?

La Partenza (Der Abschied)

Ec-co quel fie- ro i-stan- - - te! Ni- ce, mia Ni- ce, ad- di- - o!

Resignation

Lisch aus, lisch aus,mein Licht!_ was dir ge-bricht,_ das ist nun fort,

Scotch Songs: (Op. 108 for voice and pianoforte trio) Sally in our Alley

Of all the girls_ that are so smart_there's none like pret- ty Sal-ly

Auld Lang Syne

Should auld ac-quaintance be for-got and ne-ver brought to mind?

Charlie is my darling

O Char- lie is my dar- ling, my dar- ling, my dar- ling

No. 2 Sunset

The sun up-on the Weird-law hill, in Ett-rick's vale is sink- ing sweet;

No. 3 Oh sweet were the hours

Oh! sweet were the hours, when in mirth's frol- ic throng_

No. 7 Bonny laddie, highland laddie

Where got ye that sil- ver moon, bon- ny lad- die,_ high-land lad- die,

No. 8 The lovely lass of Inverness

The love-ly lass of In- ver-ness,_nae_ joy nor plea-sure can she see;

No. 14 O, how can I be blithe and glad

O, how can I_ be_ blithe and glad, or how can I_ gang_ brisk and braw;

No. 16 Could this ild world have been contriv'd

Could this ill world_ have been con- triv'd to stand

No. 17 O Mary, at thy window be

O Ma- ry, at thy win-dow be, It is the wish'd, the tryst-ed hour,

No. 20 Faithfu' Johnie

When will you come a- gain, my_ faith-fu' Joh- nie,

SONGS:

Scotch Songs, Op. 108 (voice and pianoforte trio)
No. 24. Again my Lyre

A- gain, my Lyre, yet once a- gain, with tears I wake

Welsh Songs: The Cottage Maid

I en- vy not the splen-dour fine that glit-ters in Sir Wat- kyn's hall;

Der Wachtelschlag

Horch, wie schallt's dor-ten so lieb-lich her- vor! Fürch-te Gott!

Wonne der Wehmut, Op. 83, No. 1

Trocknet nicht, trocknet nicht Thrä-nen der e- wi-gen Lie- be!

Symphony No. 9, "Choral", Op. 125: Finale

Freu- de schö-ner Göt-ter- fun- ken, Toch- ter aus E- ly- si- um

Seid um- schlun-gen, Mil- li- o- nen! Die-sen Kuss der gan- zen Welt!

Freu- - - - - - - de, Toch- ter aus E- ly- si- um

BELLINI, Vincenzo (1801-1835)

Norma (Opera) Act 1

I- te sul col-le O Dru- i-de i- te a spiar ne' cie - - -

Dell' au- ra tua pro- fe- ti- ca, ter- ri- bil Dio l'in-for- ma.

Me- co all'al-tar di ve-ne-re e ra Adal- gi- sa in' Ro- ma

Ca - - - - - sta Di - - va ca-sta Di va- che i nar-gen - - - ti

Ah! bel- lo a me ri- tor- na del fi- do amor pri-mie - - - ro

No. 6 Duet

Ah! si fa co- re e ab- brac- cia mi

Act II

Mira o Nor- ma, a tuoi gi-noc- chi que-sti ca- ri tuoi pargo- let- ti

Si fi-ne all' o- re all' o- re e-stre- me com- pag-na tu- a

Ah! del Te- bro al gio- go in- de- gno frem- o io pu- re fremo

Guer- ra, guer- ra le Gal- li-che sel- ve quan-te han quer- ce

Deh! non vo-ler- li vit- ti- me del mio fa- ta- le er- ro - - re

I Puritani (opera)   **Act 1**

A   Ah! per sem- pre io ti per-de- - -i, fior— d'a-mo-re

B   A te,o ca- ra,— a-mor ta-lo-ra,— a-mor ta-lo-ra

C   Son ver- - -gin vez-zo-sa in ve-sta— di— spo- sa

Act II

D   Qui la vo-ce sua so-a- ve mi chia-ma-va e poi spa-ri.—

E   Vien, di-let-to è in ciel la lu-na tut-to ta-ce

F   Il ri-val— sal-var tu de- i, il ri-val— sal-var,sal-var tu puoi—

G   Suo-ni la trom-ba,e in-tre-pi-do io pu-gnerò da— for-te

Act III

H   Vie-ni, vie-ni fra que-ste brac-cia, a-mor, de-li-zia e vi-ta,

La Sonnambula (opera)   **Act I**

I   Co- me per me se-re- - - - -no og-gi ri-na-cque il dì!

J   Pren-di l'a-nel- ti do- - - - -no che un dì,che un dì re-ca-

K   Sov-ra il sen la— man mi po-sa, pal-pi-tar,bal-zar,

L   Vi rav-vi-so O luoghi a- me- - - - -ni in cui lie-ti,

M   Tu non sa- i con quei be-gli oc-chi, co- me dol-ce il cor

N   A fos-co cie-lo, a not-te, bru-na, al fio-co rag-gio d'in-cer-ta lu-na

O   Son ge-lo-so del ze- - - - -fi-ro er-ran- - - - -te, che ti scher-za

P   D'un pen-sie- ro, e d'un ac-cen-to, rea non so-no,

Act II

Q   Ah! non cre-dea mi rar- - - - -ti si pre-sto es-tin-to O fio- - - - -re

R   Ah! non giun-ge u-man pen-sie-ro, al con-ten-to ond'io son pie-na

L'Abbandono (song)

S   Il so- spi-ro a me sol li-ce che do-len-te ed in-fe-li-ce

40
BELLMAN, Carl Michael (1740-1795)

Blasen nu alla (Ulla's Trip to the Deer Park) (Fredmans Epistel No. 25)
Blow one and all, hear the thun-der's call, and the surg-ing sea;

Fjäriln vingad syns pa Hoga (Butter-flies at Haga) (Fredmans Sang No. 64)
But-ter-flies at Ha-ga soar-ing, Through the fog and dew-y mists,

Hör klokorna med ängsligt dan (Fred-mans Sang No. 6)
Hör Kloc-kor-na med äng-sligt dan nu ringa för en Bacchi son

Joachim uti Babylon (Joachim at Babylon) (Fredmans Sang No. 41)
Jo-a-chim of Ba-by-lon, Had a wife Su-san-na,

Sa lunka vi sa smaningom (Fredmans Sang No. 21)
Sa lun-ka vi sa sman-ing-om fran bacchi buller ach tu-mult

Ulla min Ulla (The Little Fishing Town) (Fredmans Epistel No. 71)
Ul-la, my Ul-la, say, do you like my of-fer of straw-ber-ries

Villa vid denna Källa (Fredman's Fare-well to Ulla) (Fredmans Epistel No. 82)
Come, love, and rest a while now, our break-fast we shall spread 'neath leaf-y

BEMBERG, Henri (1861-)

Un Ange est venu
Un ange est ve-nu dans ma so-li-tu-de

Chant Hindou
Brahma, Dieu des croy-ants, Maî-tre des ci-tés sain-tes

Il a quit-té ce mon-de, m'ai-mant quand je l'ai-mais

Chant Vénitién
Le vent souf-fle et no-tre gon-do-le Sur l'eau s'en-vo-le

Il Neige
Il nei-ge, il nei-ge De gros flo-cons com-me du co-ton

Nymphes et Sylvains
L'air est lé-ger, la bri-se est pu-re, un frais par-fum

Mar-quez la dan-se Bien en ca-den-ce

BENEDICT, Sir Julius (1804-1885)

The Lily of Killarney (opera): Eily Mavourneen
Ei-ly Ma-vour-neen, I see thee be-fore me, fair-er than ev-er

Act I Duet
The moon has rais'd her lamp a-bove to light the way to thee,

La Capinera (The Wren)

Col ri-tor-nar___ Del dol ce_a-pril___ Tu tor-ni pur,

Carnevale di Venezia (Carnival of Venice)

O me be- a----ta Ri- tor- na in Ciel. l'al-bo- re

La bru-na gon- do- let-ta ap- pres-ta_o Bar- ca-rol

The Gypsy and the Bird

A gyp- sy roam- ing through the mead- ows,___ Spied a lin-net

BENJAMIN, Arthur (1893-   )

Calm sea and mist

The slow___ heave of the sleep-ing sea, with pulse like mo-tion swells_and falls

Hedgerow
Copyright 1925, Arthur Benjamin

The win- try winds are white; the wind seems fro-zen

The Wasp
Copyright 1925, Arthur Benjamin

Where the ripe pears droop heav- i- ly The yel- low wasp hums loud and long

BENNET, John (16th-17th cent.)

All Creatures Now

All crea-tures now are mer- ry. mer- ry, mer- ry mind- ed

Thyrsis, sleepest thou?

Thyr- sis, sleep- est thou? sleep-est thou? sleep-est thou?sleep-est thou

BERCHEM, Jachet Van (16th Cent.)

O Jesu Christe

O___ Je- su Chris- te, mi-se-re-re me- i, quum do- lo- re___

BERG, Alban (1885-1935)

Sieben frühe Lieder 1. Nacht
By permission Associated Music Publishers, Inc.

Däm- mern Wol- ken ü- ber Nacht und Thal

2. Schilflied

Auf ge-hei- men Wal- des-pfa- de schleich ich gern im A - - -bend-schein

3. Die Nachtigall

Das macht, es hat die Nach- ti- gall die gan- ze Nacht ge- sun- gen;

4. Traumgekrönt

Das war der Tag der wei- ssen Chry- san- the- men,

5. Im Zimmer

Herbst-son-nen-schein___ Der lie- be A-bend blickt so still her- ein

Sieben frühe Lieder
6. Liebesode

Im Arm der Lie- be schlie- fen wir se- lig ein___   A

7. Sommertage

Nun zie- hen Ta- ge ü- ber die Welt, ___   B

Wozzeck (opera) Op. 7
(Three selections) I
By permission Associated Music
Publishers, Inc.

Sol- da- ten, Sol- da- ten sind schö- ne Bur- - - - schen   C

II

Han- sel spann dei- ne sechs Schimmel an, Gib sie zu fressen auf's neu___   D

III

Rin- gel, Rin- gel Ro- sen- krantz, Rin - - - - - - gel-reihn!   E

BERLIOZ, Hector (1803-1869)

L'Enfance du Christ, Op. 25 (oratorio)
Part I. O misère des Rois

O mi- sè- re des Rois! Ré- gner___ et ne pas vi-vre!   G

Part II. L'Adieu des Bergers

Il s'en va loin de___ la ter- re Où dans l'é- table il vit___ le jour   H

Le Repos de la Sainte Famille

Les Pé- le- rins é-tant ve- nus En un lieu de bel- le ap-pa-ren- ce   I

Les Nuits d'Été, Op. 7 (Songs)
No. 1 Villanelle

Quand vien-dra la sai-son nou- vel- le, Quand au- ront dis- pa- ru   J

No. 2 Le Spectre de la Rose

Sou- le- ve ta pau- piè- re clo- se Qu'effleu- re un son- ge   K

No. 4 L'Absence

Re-viens, re-viens___ ma bien ai- mé- e comme un- e fleur___   L

La Damnation de Faust, Op. 24 (opera)
Part II. Chanson de la Puce

U- ne pu- ce gen- til- le chez un prin- ce lo- geait   M

Air de Roses

Voi-ci des ro-ses de cet-te nuit é- clo- ses, Sur___ ce lit en-bau-mé   N

Part III.

Au- tre-fois un roi de Thu- lé Qui jusqu'au tom-beau fut fi- dè- le   O

Mer- ci, doux cré- pus- cu- le! Oh! sois le bien- ve- nu!   P

Sérénade de Méphistophélès

De- vant la mai- son De ce- lui___ qui___ t'a- do - - - - re,   Q

Part IV. Romance

D'a- mour l'arden- te flam- me Con- su- me- mes beaux jours.   R

Invocation à la nature

Na- ture im- men- se, in- pénétrable et fiè- re   S

Les Troyens (Opera)
Act III. Scene I

Chers Ty- ri-ens,   tant de no-bles tra- vaux____   **A**

Act V. Scene II

A- dieu fiè- re ci- té   qu'un gé- né-reux ef-fort   **B**

I- nu- ti-les re-grets   je dois quitter Car-tha- ge   **C**

En un der-nier nau-fra- ge   Ah! puis-se_ je pé- rir   **D**

Requiem
1. Requiem aeternam

Re- qui-em_ ae- ter - - - - nam,   re- qui-em ae-ter-nam do-na e-is,   **E**

Te de- cet hym-nus, De- us in Si- on,____   **F**

2. Dies Irae

Di- es i- rae, di- es il- la, sol-vet sae- clum,   **G**

Et____ i- te- rum____ ven- tu- rus est cum glo- ri-a   **H**

3. Quid sum miser

Quid_ sum_ mi- ser____ tunc dic- tu- - - - rus   **I**

4. Rex tremendae

Rex! Rex! O rex tremendae ma-jes-ta-tis, rex tremendae ma-jes- ta- tis   **J**

5. Quaerens me

Quaerens me se-dis-ti las - - sus quae- rens me,   **K**

6. Lacrymosa

La - - - - - - cry- mo- sa di- es il - - - - - - - la,   **L**

7. Offertorium

Do - - mi- ne, Do - - -mi- ne Je- su Chris-te!   **M**

N

Accompaniment

9. Sanctus

Sanc- tus,____ Sanc- tus, Sanc- tus, Sanc- tus,____   **O**

Ho- san- na in ex- cel- sis, ho- san- na in ex- cel- sis,   **P**

10. Agnus dei

Ag- nus de- i, qui tol-lis pec-ca-ta mun-di, do- na e- is____   **Q**

BERNARD, Paul (1827-1879)

Ça fait peur aux oiseaux

Ne par- lez pas tant, Li- san- dre, Quand nous ten-dons nos fi- lets;   **S**

BEYDTS, Louis (1895-   )

C'est moi
Copyright 1944, Pierre Noel, Paris

Si ta marche at-tris-té- e   S'é-gare au fond d'un bois,   B

Un cri

Hi- ron-delle, hi-ron-delle, Hi-ron-delle! Est-il au   monde un coeur fi-dè- le?   C

En Arles A

Dans Arle, où sont les A- lis- cams,   Quand l'ombre est rou- ge   D

B

Theme in accompaniment (popular Fr. theme)   E

La Lyre et les Amours (Song Cycle)
No. 1 Le Bracelet
By permission Heugel & Cie, Paris,
copyright owners

A- mour en soit bé- ni!___   Le su-jet de mes voeux   F

No. 3 La belle esclave More

Beau mons- tre de na- tu- re,   il est vrai, ton vi-sage est noir   G

No. 4 Les Baisers de Dorinde

La douce ha- lei-ne des zé- phirs   Et ces eaux qui se pré- ci- pi- tent   H

BILLINGS, William (1746-1800)

Chester

Let   ty- rants shake their   i- ron___   rod And slav- 'ry clank___   J

The dying Christian's last farwell

My   friends, I am   go-ing a- long jour- ney__ nev- er__ to_ re- turn   K

Judea

A   Vir- gin   un- spot- ted by   Proph- et fore- told   L

New Plymouth

O Lord our fa- thers oft have told, In__ our at- ten- tive ears___   M

Psalms and Fuguing Tunes:
Be Glad then, America

Be glad then A- mer- i- ca, be glad then A- mer- i- ca, shout, shout, shout   N

Creation

When   I with__ pleas-ing won- der stand, and all___ my frame___ sur-vey,   P

When Jesus wept

When Je- sus wept___ the fall-   ing tear in mer- cy flowed__ be-yond   P

The Shepherd's Carol (Shiloh) A

Me- thinks I see an heav'n-ly Host of__ an- gels on the wing;   Q

B

Let all__ your fears__ be ban- ished hence, Glad tid-ings I pro- claim,   R

BIMBONI, Alberto (1882-   )

Sospiri miei
By permission Galaxy Music Corporation, N. Y.

So- spi- ri mie- i an- da- te o- ve vi man- do   A

BINCHOIS, Gilles (1400-1460)

A Solis Ortu Cardine (motet)

A so- lis or- - - - tu car- - - di- - - ne_____   C

De Plus en Plus (rondeau)

De plus en plus_____ se re- nou- - - - vel- le   D

Files a marier

Fi- les a ma- ri- er, ne vous ma- ri- ez ja ne vous ma- ri- ez ja,   E

Inter Natos Mulierum

In-   F

Je lce amours

Je loe a- mours et ma- da- me mer- cy- - - - - - - - - - - - - e   G

Sanctus

San- - - - - - - - - ctus San- - - - - - - - - - ctus_____ Do- mi- nus   H

BISHOP, Sir Henry (1786-1855)

Bid me discourse

Bid me dis- course I will_ en- chant_ thine_ ear   J

The Dashing White Sergeant

If_ I_ had a beau, for a sol- dier who'd go,   K

Echo Song (arr. Frank LaForge)
Copyright 1940, G. Schirmer, Inc.

A   Some spir- it seems - - - - to play, Some spir- it seems to play!_   L

B   Still_____ I hear_____ the change- ful_ strain   M

Home Sweet Home, from Clari, or the Maid of Milan (opera)

Mid plea- sures and pal- a- ces, Though_ we may roam,   N

Lo, Here the Gentle Lark

Lo here the gen- tle lark_____ wea- ry_ of_ rest   O

Love has eyes

Love's blind they say,_ O nev- er, nay_ Can words_ love's_ grace_ im- part_____   P

My Pretty Jane (The Bloom is on the Rye)

My pret- ty Jane, my pret- ty Jane - - - - Ah!_ nev- er, never look so shy   Q

Pretty Mocking Bird

A   Liv- - - ing e- - - - cho, liv- ing e- cho, bird_ of_ eve,_____   R

B   Pret- ty mock- ing bird, pret- ty mock- ing bird, pret- ty pret- ty, pret- ty   S

Should he upbraid

Should he up- braid, I'll own that he pre- vail

BIZET, Georges (1838-1875)

Carmen (opera) Act I

Sur la pla- ce Cha-cun pas-se, Cha- cun vient, cha- cun va,

Children's Chorus

A- vec la gar- de mon- tante, Nous ar- ri-vons, Nous voi- là!

Chorus of Cigarette Girls

Dans l'air nous sui-vons des yeux La fu- mé- e, La fu- mé- e

Habanera

L'a-mour est un oi- seau re- bel-le Que nul ne peut ap- pri-voi- ser.

L'a-mour est en- fant de Bo- hême, Il n'a ja- mais, ja-mais con-nu de loi.

Parle moi de ma mère (Duet Soprano and Tenor)

Tu vas, m'a-t- elle dit t'en al- ler a la vil- le:

Et tu lui di-rás que sa mè- re Songe nuit et jour

Ma mè- re je la vois! Oui, je re- vois mon vil-la- ge

Seguidille

Pres des ram- parts de Sé- vil- le,

Act II Chanson Bohème

Les tring-les des sistres tin- taient A- vec un é- clat

Toreador Song

Vo- tre toast je peux vous le ren- dre, Se- ñors, se-ñors

To- ré- a- dor, en gar- de! To- ré- a- dor

Quintet

Nous a- vons en tête une af- fai- re.

Quand il s'a- git de trom- pe- ri- e, De du- pe- ri-e,

Carmen's Dance

La la la la La la la la

Flower Song

La fleur que vous m'avais je- té- e, Dans ma prison

Là- bas, là- bas dans la mon- ta- gne, Là-bas, là-bas

Carmen (opera)

Act III March of the Smugglers — A
No-tre métier ___ no-tre metier est bon; ___ mais pour le faire il faut a-voir,

Card Trio A — B
Mêlons! Mêlons! Coupons! Coupons! Bien!_ C'est ce- la!

B — C
Et main- te- nant par-lez_ mes bel- les, De l'a- ve- nir

Card Song — D
En vain pour é- vi- ter les ré- pon-ses a- mères,

Michaela's Aria — E
Je dis___ que rien ne m'é-pou-van- te, Je dis_ hé-las!

Act IV — F
Les voi- ci! Voi- ci la quad-ril-le, La quad- ril- le des To- re-ros!

Duet Escamillo and Carmen — G
Si tu m'ai- mes, Car- men, ___ si tu m'ai-mes, Car- men

La Jolie Fille de Perth (The Fair Maid of Perth (Opera) Act II — H
Quand la flam- me De l'amour Brûle l'â- me nuit et jour

I
A la voix___ D'un a-mant fi- dè- - le___ Ah! ré-ponds ma bel- le___

Les Pêcheurs de Perles (opera) Act I — J
Au fond du tem- ple saint pa- ré de fleurs et d'or

K
Je crois___ en-tendre en- co- - - - re ca-ché sous les pal- miers___

L
O Dieu Brah- ma _____ O mai- tre sou-ve-rain

Act II — M
Comme autre- fois_ dans la nuit som- bre Ca-ché_ sous le feuil-lage

one theme — N
De mon a- mi- e, Fleur en-dor- mi- - - - - - - - e___

O
Au fond du lac___ si- len- - - - ci- eux___

Act III L'Orage s'est calmé — P
O Na- dir,___ tendre a- mi de mon jeune â- ge

Songs: Adieu de l'hôtesse arabe, Op. 21, No. 4 — Q
Puis-que rien ne t'ar- rête en___ cet_ heu- reux pa- ys,

Agnus Dei — R
A- gnus De- i! Qui tol-lis pec-ca- ta mun-di

Chanson d'Avril, Op. 21, No. 1 — S
Lè- ve- toi! lè- ve toi! le prin-temps vient de naî- tre!

Songs:
Ouvre ton coeur (Spanish Serenade)

La Mar- gue-rite____ a fer- mé sa co- rol - - - le

Pastorale

Un jour de prin-temps____ Tout le long d'un ver-ger___

Vieille Chanson

Dans les bois l'a-mou-reux Myr- til A-vait pris fau- vet- te lé- gè- re

BLAND, James A. (1854-1911)

Carry me back to old Virginny
Copyright by E. B. Marks
Music Corp., N. Y.

Car- ry me back to old Vir-gin- ny There's where the cot- ton

BLANGINI, F. (1781-1841)

Care pupille

Ca- re___ pu- pil- le tra mil- le e mil___

Per valli, per boschi

Per val- li, per bo- schi cer- can-do di ni- ce sol l'- co

BLOCH, Ernest (1880-   )

Poèmes d'Automne
I. La Vagabonde
Copyright 1918, G. Schirmer, Inc.

Elle a pas- sé dans le vent d'au-tom-ne El- le che- mi-nait

II. Le Déclin

Dans le ver- ger pai- si- ble, bor- dé là- bas de peu-pli- ers

III. L'abri

J'é- cou- te la voix de mon rêve Pour al- ler à toi,

IV. Invocation

Les co- lon- nes du tem- ple s'a- ni- ment d'u- ne pa-leur plus chaude

Psalms
No. 22 (baritone and orchestra)
Copyright 1919, G. Schirmer, Inc.

E- lo- him! E- lo- him!___ Why hast thou thus for-sa- ken me?

No. 114

Snatched a- way by Jah- veh___ from the land where they served___

No. 137

Re-clined_ by the wa-ters of Ba- bel,_ Our harps were hung up-on the wil-lows

BLOW, John (1649-1708)

The Self Banished

It is not that__ I love you less,_ Than when_ be- fore___

BOATNER, Edward (1897-   )

Oh, What a beautiful city! (arr.)

Oh, what a beau-ti-ful ci-ty, Oh, what a beau-ti-ful ci-ty   A

BODENSCHATZ, Erhard (1576-1636)

Joseph, lieber Joseph mein (14th century German traditional Christmas song)

Jo-seph, lie-ber Jo-seph mein, hilf mir wie-gen mein Kin- de-lein,   C

BÖHM, Karl (1894-   )

Still wie die Nacht, Op. 326, No. 27
By permission Associated Music Publishers, Inc.

Still wie die Nacht, tief wie das Meer,__ soll dei-ne Lie- be sein!__   E

Was i hab

Schö- ne Lied- le, ja die kenn i grad' drei an der Zahl   F

BOIELDIEU, François (1775-1834)

La Dame Blanche (Opera)
Act I

Ah quel plai-sir d'ê-tre sol- dat___ Ah quel plai-sir d'ê- tre sol- dat   H

Act II

Dé- jà la_ nuit, dé- jà la nuit plus som-bre sur nous ré- pand,   I

Viens gen-til- le da - - - me, viens_ gen-til- le da - - - me,   J

Act III Song of Georges Brown (Reverie)

Al- lons_ gai- ment_ re-ce-vons leur hom-ma-ge de mon nou-vel é- tat   K

BOITO, Arrigo (1842-1918)

Mefistofele (opera) Prologue
Copyright by G. Ricordi & Co., Inc.

1

A- ve Si- gnor,__ si-gnor de-gli an-ge- - li   M

2

Sal- ve Re-gi- na! s'in-nal-zi un e-co dal mon-do cie-co   N

Il bel gio-va- net- to sen vie- ne al- la fes- ta   O

Da- i cam- pi, da- i pra- ti che in-non-da- la_ not- te,   P

Act I

Son_ lo Spi- ri- to_ che ne-ga sem-pre tut- to; l'a- stro, il fior   Q

(Duet) A

Se tu mi do- ni un' o- ra di ri- po- so,   R

B

Fin da sta not- te, fin da sta not- te nel-l'or-gie ghiotte del mio mes-ser   S

BOND, Carrie Jacobs (1862-   )

BORDES, Charles (1863-1909)

BORODIN, Alexander (1833-1887)

BORODIN

Prince Igor (opera)
Prologue

Au so- leil_ bril-lant gloi- re! gloi- re! Au noble I- gor, no-tre prin-ce A

Act I

Je hais l'en-nui, je veux vi-vre gai-ment; I-gor pré-fè-re les ha-sards B

Si l'on me trou- vait bien di- gne D'ob-te-nir l'hon-neur_ in-si- gne C

Duet: Jaroslavna and Galitsky

Ah, peu m'importe à moi! Puis est-ce ton af-fai-re? J'ai pris ce qui m'a plu; D

Act II

O_ fleur_ fa - - né - - - - - - ê_ fleur_ ti - - - mi - - - - - de E

Vladimir's Cavatina

Ah! viens, ah! viens! Viens,_ re- ponds au ten-dre ap- pel, F

Igor's Aria

Hé- las! mon âme est triste A-dieu le doux re-pos En proie à mon cha-grin G

Tendre é- pou- se_ bien ai- mé- e, Comme_ à_ toi va_ H

Konchak's Aria

À la Kai- a- la fut bat- tu- e Ta brave ar-mée un jour I

I- gor, pour moi n'est qu'un guerrier que j'ai- me: Un cap-tif n'est jamais J

Polovetsian Dance with Chorus

Va sur l'aî- le_ des doux_ zé- phirs, A- é- ri- en- ne, va,_ chan-son, K

Hon-neur au Khan, au chef puis-sant Ah!_____ L

Act IV Duet: Jaroslavna and Igor

Ah! c'est toi que j'em-bras-se. Oh! pour moi tout s'ef-fa-ce! Rê- ves, M

J'ai_ cru rê- ver! mon_ Dieu, mer- ci! Est- il bien vrai qu'ils soit i- ci? N

SONGS:
A Dissonance

Thy lips say "I love thee, be-lieve me," And yet in the sound of thy voice O

Flowers of Love

Where tears of my passion have fal-len, Full man- y a flow- er has sprung P

The Sea

The sea toss- es and raves,_ While flinging heav'n-ward Q

The Sea Queen

Ah come, wea- ry one, make haste, it is eve; Thy heart is throbbing for me; R

The Sleeping Beauty

Sleep, deep in fo- rest gloom, Sleep, prin- cess, ful- fil thy doom S

SONGS: The Sleeping Princess

Hush! Hush! with love- ly eyes Closed in sleep, the Prin- cess lies,

Song of the Dark Forest

Thro' the for- est's— moan, thro' the for- est's— sigh

BORTNIANSKY, D. S. (1751-1825)

Cherubim Song

Let— us, who fig - - - - - ure forth— the Cher- u- bim,

Cherubim Song (No. 7)

Like— a choir of— an- gels glo - - - - rious gath-'ring soft- ly

BOUGHTON, Rutland (1878-   )

Faery Song, from The Immortal Hour (opera)
Copyright by Stainer & Bell, Ltd., London;
Galaxy Music Corporation, N. Y.,
U. S. Agents

How beau- ti- ful they are,— The lord- ly ones— Who dwell in the hills—

BOURGAULT-DUCOUDRAY, L. A. (1840-1910)

Chansons de Basse-Bretagne: L'Angelus

La clo- che son- ne l'an- gé- lus— La terre a donc un jour— de plus.

Dimanche à l'aube

Di- manche à l'aube, en me le- vant, Ho- ren drenn drenn Ho- la

Silvestrik

Saint Mi- chel en Grè- ve mon fils est— en- ga- gé—

BOURGEOIS, Louis (1510-1561)

Old Hundred

Praise God from whom all bless-ings flow, praise Him all creatures here be- low,

BOYCE, William (1710-1779)

The Song of Momus to Mars

Thy sword with- in the Scabbard keep, and let Man- kind— a- gree;

Tell me, lovely shepherd

Tell— me love- ly— shep- herd where, where, tell— me where thou feed'st

BRAGA, Gaetano (1829-1907)

Angel's Serenade

What sounds are those that wak- en me, Sweet ac- cents low and ten- der,

(Violin obbligato to above solo)

(violin obligato to above solo)

BRAHAM, John (1774-1856)

The Death of Nelson

O'er Nel-son's tomb with si-lent grief op-prest Bri-tan-nia mourns

'Twas__ in Tra-fal-gar's bay we saw the foe-men lay

BRAHE, May H.

Bless this House
By permission Boosey & Hawkes, Inc.,
copyright owners

Bless this house, O Lord we pray Make it safe by night and day

Down Here
By permission Boosey & Hawkes, Inc.,
copyright owners

Oh! it's quiet down here, yes as quiet as a mouse,

BRAHMS, Johannes (1833-1897)

Chorus and Solo Quartet: Songs for Women's Chorus, 2 Horns and Harp, Op. 17
No. 1. Es tönt ein voller Harfenklang

Es tönt ein vol-ler Har-fen-klang,den Lieb und Sehn-sucht schwel-len

No. 2. Lied von Shakespeare (Come away, death!)

Komm her-bei, Komm her-bei, Tod! Und ver-senk in Cy-pres-sen

No. 3. Der Gärtner

Wo-hin ich geh und schau-e, in Feld und Wald und Tal,____

No. 4. Gesang aus Fingal

Wein' an den Fel-sen der brau-sen-den Win-de, wei-ne, O Mäd-chen

Der Gang zum Liebchen, Op. 31, No. 3 (Quartet)

Es glänzt der Mond nie-der, Ich soll-te doch wie-der

Ein Deutsches Requiem, Op. 45 (A German Requiem) No. 1

Se-lig sind, Se-lig sind, die da Leid tra-gen,

No. 2

Denn al-les Fleisch es ist wie Gras und al-les Herr-lich-keit

So seid nun ge-dul-dig, lie---ben Brü-der,

Die Er-lö-se-ten des Herrn wer-den wie-der kom-men

No. 3

Herr, leh-re doch mich, dass ein En-de mit mir ha-ben muss,

Der Ge-recht-en See-len sind__ in__ Got-tes Hand

No. 4

Wie lieb-lich sind dei-ne Woh-nun-gen, Herr Ze - - - - - ba-oth,

BRAHMS

Ein Deutsches Requiem, Op. 45 (A German Requiem)

Rhapsody Op. 53, for Alto, Male Chorus and Orchestra

Schicksalslied, Op. 54, for Chorus and Orchestra (Song of Destiny)

O Heiland, reiss die Himmel auf, Op. 74, No. 2 (motet)

Nänie, Op. 82, for Chorus and Orchestra

Gesang der Parzen, Op. 89, for Chorus and Orchestra (Song of the Fates)

Zigeunerlieder, Op. 103

No. 4 — Wie lieb - - - - - - - - - lich sind dei - - ne Woh - nun- gen,

No. 5 — Ihr - habt nun Trau - - - - - - rig - - keit, Trau-rig-keit,

Ich will euch trö - sten wie ei - nen sei- ne Mut - - - ter

No. 6 — Denn wir ha - ben hie kei - - - - - - ne blei- ben- de Statt

Denn es wird die Po - sau - - - ne schal - - - len und die To - ten

Herr, du bist wür - dig zu neh- men Preis und Eh - - - re und Kraft

No. 7 — Se - - - - lig sind die To - ten, die in dem Her - ren ster - - - - - - ben,

Dass___ sie ru - - hen von ih - rer Ar - - - beit

Ach,__ wer hei-let die Schmer- zen des, dem Bal- sam zu Gift ward?

Ist auf dei - nem Psal- ter, Va- ter der Lie - - - be, ein Ton

Ihr wan-delt dro - - ben im Licht auf wei- chem Bo - den

Doch uns ist ge - ge- ben, Auf kei- ner Stät - - - - te zu ruhn.

O Hei-land reiss die Him- mel auf, her-ab, her- auf vom Him- mel lauf,

Auch das Schö - - - ne muss ster - - - - - - - - - - - - - - - ben,

A - ber sie steigt aus dem Meer mit al - len Töchtern des Ne- reus

Es fürch- te die Göt- ter das Men- schen-ge- schlecht!

Es wen- den die Herr-scher ihr seg-nen-des Au- ge von gan- zen Ge-schlechtern

No. 1 — He, Zi- geu- ner, grei- fe in die Sai- ten ein___

No. 2 — Hoch- ge- türm- te Ri- ma-flut, wie bist - - - du so trüb,

Zigeunerlieder, Op. 103

No. 3

Wisst ihr wann mein Kind- chen am al- ler- schönsten ist?

No. 4

Lie- ber Gott, du weisst, wie oft be- reut ich hab

No. 5

Brau- ner Bur- sche führt zum Tan- ze sein blau- äug- ig schö- nes Kind,

No. 6

Rös- lein drei- e in der Rei- he blühn so rot

No. 7

Kommt dir manch- mal in den Sinn, mein sü- sses Lieb

No. 8

Horch, der Wind klagt in den Zwei- gen trau- rig sacht;

No. 9

Weit und breit schaut Nie- mand mich an, und wenn sie mich has- sen,

No. 11

Ro- te A- bend- wol- ken ziehn am Fir- ma- ment

Sandmännchen (The Little Sandman, or, The Little Dustman), from 14 Volkskinderlieder, No. 4

Die Blü- me- lein sie schla- fen schon längst im Mon- den- schein

Songs and Duets:
Liebestreu, Op. 3, No. 1

O ver-senk, o ver-senk dein Leid, mein Kind, in die See, in die tie- fe See!"

In der Fremde, No. 5

Aus der Hei- mat hin- ter den Bli- tzen rot, da kom- men die Wol- ken her

Spanisches Lied, Op. 6, No. 1

In dem Schat- ten mei- ner Lo- cken schlief mir mein Ge- lieb- ter ein

Juchhe! No. 5

Wie ist doch die Er- de so schön, so schön! Das wis- sen die Vö- ge- lein,

Nachtigallen schwingen, No. 6

Nach- ti- gal- len schwin- gen lus- tig ihr Ge- fie- der

Treue Liebe, Op. 7, No. 1

Ein Mägd- lein sass am Mee- res- strand und blick- te voll Sehn- sucht ins Wei- te

Anklänge, No. 3

Hoch ü- ber stil- len Hö- - - hen stand in dem Wald ein Haus;

Heimkehr, No. 6

O brich nicht, Steg, du zit- terst sehr, o stürz nicht, Fels, du dräu- est schwer

Vor dem Fenster, Op. 14, No. 1

Soll sich der Mond nicht hel- ler schei- nen

Ein Sonett, No. 4

Ach könnt' ich, könn- te ver- ges- sen sie, ihr schö- nes, lie- bes

Songs and Duets:
Der Schmied, Op. 19, No. 4

Ich hör' mei-nen Schatz den Ham-mer er schwin-get, das rau-schet,

An eine Aeolsharfe, No. 5

An- ge-lehnt an die E- pheu-wand die-ser al-ten Ter-ras-se

Ihr kom-met, Win- de, fern her- ü-ber, ach von des Kna-ben,

Die Meere (Soprano and Alto
Duet) Op. 20, No. 3

Al- le Win- de schla-fen auf__ dem Spie- - -gel der Flut;

Duets for Alto and Baritone,
Op. 28
No. 1 Die Nonne und der Ritter

Da die Welt zur Ruh ge- gan-gen, wacht mit Ster- nen

No. 2 Vor der Tür

Tritt auf, tritt auf, den Rie- gel von der Tür

No. 3 Es rauschet das Wasser

Es rau- schet das Was- ser, und blei- bet nicht stehn;

No. 4 Der Jäger und sein Lieb-
chen

Ist nicht der Him- mel so blau?__ Steh am Fen- ster und schau!

Nicht mehr zu dir zu gehen, Op.
32, No. 2

Nicht mehr zu dir zu ge- hen, be-schloss ich und beschwor ich

Bitteres zu sagen denkst du No. 7

Bit-te-res zu sa-gen denkst du; a-ber nun und nim- mer kränkst du;

Wie bist du, meine Königin No. 9

Wie bist du, mei- ne Kö- ni- gin, durch sanf-te Gü- te wonne- voll!!

Magelone Romanzen, Op. 33
No. 3. Sind es Schmerzen, sind
es Freuden

Sind es Schmer-zen, sind__ es Freu-den, die durch mei-nen Bu- - - sen ziehn?

No. 4. Liebe kam aus fernen
Landen

Lie- be kam aus fer- nen Lan-den und__ kein We- sen__ folg-te ihr,

No. 5. So willst du des Armen

So willst__ du des Ar- men dich gnä- dig er- bar- men?

No. 8. Wir müssen uns trennen

Wir müs- sen uns tren-nen, ge-lieb-tes Sai-ten-spiel, Zeit ist es,

No. 9. Ruhe, Süssliebchen

Ru- he, Süss- lieb- chen, im Schat- ten der grü- nen,

No. 11. Wie schnell ver-
schwindet

Wie schnell ver- schwin-det so Licht__ als Glanz, der Mor- gen__ fin- det

No. 12. Muss es eine Trennung
geben

Muss__ es ei- ne Tren-nung ge- ben, die__ das treu- e Herz__ zer-bricht

No. 14. Wie froh und frisch

Wie froh und frisch mein Sinn sich hebt, zu- rück bleibt al- les__

BRAHMS

Songs

Magelone Romanzen, Op. 33, No.
15 Treue Liebe

Treu- e Lie- be dau- ert lan- ge ü- ber- le- bet man- che, man- che Stund   A

Von ewiger Liebe, Op. 43, No. 1

Dun- kel, wie dun- kel in Wald und in Feld! A- bend schon ist es,   B

Die Mainacht, No. 2

Wann der sil- ber- ne Mond durch die Ge- sträu- che blinkt   C

An die Nachtigall, Op. 46, No. 4

Geuss nicht so laut der lieb- ent- flamm- ten Lie- der ton- rei- chen Schall   D

Botschaft, Op. 47, No. 1

We- he, Lüft- chen lind und lieb- lich um__ Wan- - ge der Ge- lieb- ten   E

Sonntag, No. 3

So hab ich doch die gan- ze Wo- che mein fei- nes Lieb- chen   F

O liebliche Wangen, No. 4

O lieb- li- che Wan- gen, ihr macht mir Ver- lan- gen   G

Der Gang zum Liebchen, Op. 48, No. 1

Es glänzt der mond nie- der, ich soll- te doch wie- der   H

Der Überläufer, No. 2

In den Gar- ten wol- len wir ge- hen, wo die schö- nen Ro- sen   I

Am Sonntag Morgen, Op. 49, No. 1

Am Sonn- tag Mor- gen zier- lich an- ge- tan wohl weiss ich   J

Sehnsucht, No. 3

Hin- ter__ je- nen dich- ten__ Wäl- dern weilst du,   K

Wiegenlied (Cradle Song), No. 4

Gu- ten A- bend, gut Nacht mit Ro- sen be- dacht__   L

Wenn du nur zuweilen lächelst, Op. 57, No. 2

Wenn du nur zu- wei- len lä- chelst, nur__ zu- wei- len   M

Es träumte mir, No. 3

Es träum- te mir, ich sei dir teu - - - er doch zu er- wa- chen   N

Ach, wende diesen Blick, No. 4

Ach, wen- de die- sen Blick, wen- de dies An- ge- sicht!   O

Die Schnur, die Perl an Perle, No. 7

Die Schnur, die Perl an Per - - le um dei- nen__ Hals__   P

Blinde Kuh, Op. 58, No. 1

In Fin- stern geh ich su- chen, mein Kind, wo steckst du wohl?   Q

O komme, holde Sommernacht, No. 4

O kom- me, hol- de Som- mer- nacht, ver- schwie- gen;   R

Schwermut, No. 5

Mir ist so weh ums Herz, mir ist, als ob ich wei- nen möch- te vor Schmerz   S

BRAHMS
Songs

In der Gasse, Op. 58, No. 6

Ich bli-cke hin-ab in die Gas- se dort drü- ben hat sie ge-wohnt

A

Serenade, No. 8

Lei- se, um_ dich nicht zu we-cken, rauscht_ der Nacht-wind, teu- re Frau!

B

Dämm'rung senkte sich von oben, Op. 59, No. 1

Dämm- rung senk-te sich_ von o- ben, schon ist al- le Nä- he fern

C

Auf dem See, No. 2

Blau- er Him- mel, blau- e Wo- gen, Re- ben-hü- gel

D

Regenlied, No. 3

Wal- le, Re- gen, wal- le nie- der, we- cke mir

E

Agnes, No. 5

Ro- sen-zeit, wie schnell vor-bei, schnell vor-bei, bist du doch ver- gan- gen!

F

Eine gute, gute Nacht, No. 6

Ei- ne gu- te, gu-te Nacht pflegst du mir_ zu sa- gen

G

Mein wundes Herz, No. 7

Mein wun-des Herz ver-langt nach mil- der Ruh, O hau-che sie ihm ein

H

Dein blaues Auge, No. 8

Dein blau- es Au- ge hält so still, ich bli- cke bis zum Grund

I

Erinnerung, Op. 63, No. 2

Ihr wun- der-schö- nen Au- gen-blicke, die Lieb- lich-ste

J

An die Tauben, No. 4

Fliegt nur aus, ge- lieb- te_ Tau-ben! Euch als Bo- ten send_ ich_ hin

K

Meine Liebe ist grün, No. 5

Mei-ne Lie - - - be ist grün_ wie die Flie- der-busch,

L

O wüsst ich doch den Weg zurück, No. 8

O wüsst ich doch den Weg zu-rück, den lie- ben Weg_

M

Klage I, Op. 69, No. 1 (from the Bohemian)

Ach mir fehlt, nicht ist da, was mich einst süss be- glückt;

N

Klage II, No. 2 (Slovak)

O Fel- sen, lie- ber Fel- sen was stürz-test du nicht ein,

O

Des liebsten Schwur, No. 4

Ei, schmoll- te_ mein_ Va- ter nicht_ wach_ und im Schlaf,

P

Tambourliedchen, No. 5

Den Wir- bel schlag ich gar so stark, dass euch er-zit-tert

Q

Über die See, No. 7

Ü- ber die See, fern ü- ber die See ist mein Schatz ge- zo- gen,

R

Salome, No. 8

Singt mein Schatz wie ein Fink, sing ich Nach-ti-gal-len-sang;

S

Songs BRAHMS

Mädchenfluch, Op. 69, No. 9

Ruft die Mut- ter, ruft die Toch- ter ü- ber drei Ge- bir- - ge:

Gä- be Gott im hel- len Him-mel dass er sich er- hän- - - ge

Lerchengesang, Op. 70, No. 2

Ae- the-ri-sche fer- ne Stim-men, der Lerchen himm-li-sche Grü-sse,

Es liebt sich so lieblich im Lenze, Op. 71, No. 1

Die Wel- len blin-ken und flie-ssen da- hin, es liebt sich so lieb- lich

An den Mond, No. 2

Sil- - - ber- mond, mit blei-chen Strahlen pflegst_ du Wald und Feld zu ma-len

Geheimnis, No. 3

O Früh- lings-a- bend-däm- me-rung! O lau- es lin- des Wehn,

Willst du dass ich geh? No. 4

Auf der Hei- de weht der Wind, her- zig Kind, her- zig Kind

Minnelied, No. 5

Hol- der klingt der Vo- gel- sang, wenn die En- gel- rei- - ne,

Alte Liebe, Op. 72, No. 1

Es kehrt_ die dunk- le Schwal- be aus fer- nem Land_ zu-rück

O kühler Wald, No. 3

O küh- ler Wald wo rau- schest du, in dem mein Lieb-chen geht?

Verzagen, No. 4

Ich sitz am Stran- de der rau-schen-den See_ und su-che dort_ nach Ruh,

Sommerabend, Op. 84, No. 1

Geh schla-fen, Toch- ter, schla- fen! Schon fällt der Tau aufs Gras,

Der Kranz, No. 2

Mut- ter, hilf mir ar- men Toch- ter, sieh nur, was ein Kna- be tat

Vergebliches Ständchen, No. 4

Gu- ten A- bend, mein Schatz,_ Gu- ten A bend, mein Kind,

Mondenschein, Op. 85, No. 2

Nacht liegt auf den frem-den We- gen, Kran- kes Herz und mü- de Glie-der

Mädchenlied, No. 3

Ach, und du mein küh- les Was- ser! Ach, und du mein ro-tes Rös-lein!

In Waldeseinsamkeit, No. 6

Ich sass zu dei- nen Fü- ssen in Wal- des-ein- sam-keit;

Therese, Op. 86, No. 1

Du milch- jun- ger Kna- be, wie schaust du mich an?

Feldeinsamkeit, No. 2

Ich ru- he still im ho-hen grü- nen Gras und sen- de lan- - ge

Songs
Über die Heide, Op. 86, No. 4

Ü- ber die Hei- de hal- let mein Schritt, dumpf aus der Er- de wan- dert es mit.

Todessehnen, No. 6

Ach, wer nimmt von mei- ner See- le die ge- hei- me, schwe- re Last,

Two Songs for Alto, Viola and Piano, Op. 91,
No. 1 Gestillte Sehnesucht
(also theme of viola)

In gold- nen A- bend- schein ge- tau- chet, wie fei- er- lich

No. 2 Geistliches Wiegenlied
(Viola theme; old German folk tune)

Was lis- - - peln die Win- de, die Vö- - ge- - lein?

Jo- sef, lie- ber Jo- sef mein, hilf mir wieg'n mein Kind- lein fein

Die ihr schwe- bet um die- se Pal- men in Nacht und Wind

Mit vierzig Jahren, Op. 94, No. 1

Mit vier- zig Jah- ren ist der Berg ge- stie- - - gen, wir ste- hen still

Steig auf, geliebter Schatten, No. 2

Steig auf, ge- lieb- ter Schat- ten, vor mir in to- ter Nacht

Sapphische Ode, No. 4

Ro- sen brach ich Nachts mir am dunk- len Ha- - - ge;

Kein haus, keine Heimat, No. 5

Kein Haus, Kei- ne Hei- mat, kein Weib und kein Kind,

Das Mädchen, Op. 95, No. 1

Stand das Mäd- chen, stand am Ber- ges- ab- hang, wi- der- schien der Berg

Bei dir sind meine Gedanken, No. 2

Bei dir sind mei- ne Ge- dan- ken und flat- tern, flat- tern

Der Jäger, No. 4

Mein Lieb ist ein Jä- ger, und grün ist sein Kleid,

Vorschneller Schwur, No. 5

Schwor ein jun- - ges Mäd- chen: Blu- men nie zu tra- gen,

Mädchenlied, No. 6

Am jüngsten Tag ich auf- er- steh und gleich nach mei- nem Lieb- sten seh

Schön war, das ich dir weihte, No. 7

Schön war, das ich dir weih- te, das gol- de- ne Ge- schmei- de

Der Tod, das ist die kühle Nacht, Op. 96, No. 1

Der Tod, das ist die küh- le Nacht, Das Le- ben ist der schwü- le Tag

Wir wandelten, No. 2

Wir wan- del- ten, wir zwei zu- sam- men Ich war so still

Es schauen die Blumen, No. 3

Es schau- en die Blu- men al- le zur leuch- ten- den Son- ne hin- auf;

A
B
C
D
E
F
G
H
I
J
K
L
M
N
O
P
Q
R
S

Songs

Meerfahrt, Op. 96, No. 4   A
Mein Lieb-chen, wir sa-ssen bei-sa-men trau- lich

Nachtigall, Op. 97, No. 1   B
O Nach-ti-gall, dein sü-sser Schall, er-drin-get_ mir

Auf dem Schiffe, No. 2   C
Ein Vö-ge-lein fliegt ü-ber den Rhein und wiegt_ die Flü-gel

Dort in den Weiden, No. 4   D
Dort in den Wei-den steht ein Haus, da schaut die Magd zum Fen-ster 'naus!

Komm bald, No. 5   E
Wa-rum denn war-ten von Tag zu Tag? Es blüht im Gar-ten was blü-hen mag.

Wie Melodien zieht es mir, Op. 105, No. 1   F
Wie Me-lo-di - - en_ zieht es mir lei- se durch den Sinn

Immer leiser wird mein Schlummer, No. 2   G
Im- mer lei-ser wird mein Schlum- mer nur wie Schlei- er

Auf dem Kirchhofe, No. 4   H
Der Tag ging re- gen-schwer und sturm-be- wegt, ich war

Verrat, No. 5   I
Ich stand in ei-ner lau-en Nacht an ei-ner grü-nen Lin- de

Ständchen, Op. 106, No. 1   J
Der Mond steht ü- ber dem Ber- ge, so recht für ver-lieb-te

Es hing der Reif, No. 3   K
Es hing der Reif im Lin-den-baum, wo-durch das Licht

Meine Lieder, No. 4   L
Wenn mein Herz be-ginnt_ zu klin-gen und den Tö- nen

Ein Wanderer, No. 5   M
Hier_ wo sich die Stra-ssen_schei-den, wo_ nun gehn die We- ge_ hin?

Das Mädchen spricht, Op. 107, No. 3   N
Schwal- be,_ sing mir_ an 'Ist's dein_al-ter_ Mann

Maienkätzchen, No. 4   O
Mai-en-kätz-chen er-ster Gruss, ich bre-che euch und ste-cke euch

Mädchenlied, No. 5   P
Auf die Nacht in den Spinn-stubn, da_ sin-gen die Mäd-chen,

Vier ernste Gesänge (Four serious songs) Op. 121, No. 1   Q
Denn_ es_ ge-het dem Men- - schen_ wie dem Vieh,

No. 2   R
Ich wand- te mich, und sa- he an al- le,

No. 3   S
O Tod, O Tod, wie bit - - - ter, wie bit - - ter bist du

BRAHMS
Songs and Duets:
Vier ernste Gesänge (Four serious songs) Op. 121, No. 4

Wenn___ ich mit Men-schen und mit En-gel-zun-gen re-de-te,

Wir se-hen jetzt durch ei-nen Spie-gel in ei-nem dun-keln Wor-te

Deutsche Volkslieder (voice and piano)
Book I, No. 2

Er-lau-be mir, feins Mäd-chen, in den Gar-ten zu___ gehn,

No. 5

Die___ Son-ne scheint nicht mehr so schön, als wie vor-her,

No. 6

Da___ un-ten im Ta-le läufts Was-ser so trüb___

Book II, No. 12

Feins-lieb-chen, du sollst mir nicht bar-fuss gehn,

No. 14

Ma-ri-a ging aus wan-dern, so fern ins frem-de Land

Book III, No. 15

Schwes-ter-lein, Schwes-ter-lein, wann___ gehn___ wir nach Haus?

No. 16

Wach auf mein Her-zens schö-ne, zart Al-ler-lieb-ste mein

Book IV, No. 25

Mein Mä-del hat ei-nen Ro-sen-mund, und wer ihn küsst,

Book V, No. 33

Och mod'r ich well en Ding han! Wat för en Ding,

No. 34

Wie komm ich denn zur Tür her-ein, sag du, mein Lieb-chen, sag?

Book VI, No. 39

Schö-ner Au-gen schö-ne Strah-len, schö-ner ro-ter Wan-gen

No. 41

Es steht ein Lind in je-nem Tal, ach Gott, was tut sie da?

No. 42

In stil-ler Nacht, zur er-sten Wacht, ein Stimm be-ginnt zu kla-gen,

Deutsche Volkslieder "Altes Minne-lied" Vol. II, No. 17

Ich fahr da-hin wenn es muss sein, ich scheid mich von der Lieb-sten mein,

14 Deutsche Volkslieder No. 6

Ach lie-ber Her-re Je-su Christ, weil du ein Kind

Liebeslieder Waltzes for Vocal Quartet and Piano (4 hands) Op. 52, No. 1

Re-de, Mäd-chen all-zu lie-bes, das mir in___ die Brust,

No. 2

Am Ge-stei-ne rauscht die {Flut Ge-stei-ne rauscht die Flut
                                Am

Liebeslieder Waltzes, Op. 52, No. 3

O die Frau- en   O die Frau- en   wie sie Won- ne,   **A**

No. 4

Wie des A- bends schö- ne Rö- te   möcht ich ar- me   **B**

No. 5

Die grü- ne Hop- fen- ran- ke, sie schlän- gelt auf der Er- de hin__   **C**

No. 6

Ein klei- ner, hüb- scher Vo- gel nahm den Flug zum Gar- ten hin,   **D**

No. 7

Wohl schön be- wandt war es vor- e- he mit mei- nem Leb- en   **E**

No. 8

Wenn so lind dein Au- ge mir__ und so lieb - - - lich schau-et,   **F**

No. 9

Am Do- nau- stran- de,   Da steht ein Haus,__   **G**

No. 10

O__ wie sanft die Quel- le sich durch die Wie- se__   **H**

No. 11

Nein, es ist nicht aus- zu- kom- men mit den Leu- ten;   **I**

No. 12

Schlos- ser auf! Schlos- ser auf, und ma- che Schlös- ser,   **J**

No. 13

Vö- ge- lein__ durch-rauscht die Luft, durch- rauscht__ die Luft,   **K**

No. 14

Sieh, wie ist die Wel- le klar, blickt der Mond her- nie- der   **L**

No. 15

Nach- ti- gall, sie singt__ so schön, wenn die__ Ster- ne   **M**

No. 16

Ein dun- ke- ler Schacht ist Lie- be, ein gar zu ge- fahr- li- cher Bron- nen;   **N**

No. 17

Nicht wand- le, mein licht;__ dort au- ssen im Flur- be- reich!   **O**

No. 18

Es be- bet das Ge- sträu- che, ge- streift hat es im Flu- ge   **P**

BRETON, Tomás (1850-1923)

Jota, from La Dolores (opera)

Gran- de co- mo el mis- mo sol__ Es la jo- ta   **R**

BREWER, A. Herbert (1865-1928)

The Fairy Pipers
By permission Boosey & Hawkes, Inc., copyright owners

When all the birds are gone to sleep and all the pi- pers still,

Come out! Come out! Lis- ten on the air! Up there! Down there!

BRIDGE, Frank (1879-1941)

Love Went A-Riding
Copyright by Boston Music Co.

Love_____ went a- ri - - - -ding, Love_____ went a- ri - - - ding

O That It Were So

BRITTEN, Benjamin (1913-   )

The Ash Grove (arr.)
By permission Boosey & Hawkes, Inc., copyright owners

Down yon- der green val- ley where stream- lets__ me - an- der

Folk Songs:
By permission Boosey & Hawkes, Inc. copyright owners
La Belle est au jardin d'amour

La belle est au jar - din d'a - mour

The Bonny Earl o Moray

Ye Hie-lands and ye Low-lands,-- O where hae ye been? They hae slain the Earl

Come you not from Newcastle

Come you not from New- cas- tle?__ Come you not there a- way?__

The foggy, foggy dew

When I was a bach-elor I lived all a-lone and worked

Heigh ho, heigh hi!

Oh I lived with my dad- dy, an ap- prent- ice was I,

Little Sir William

Eas- ter day was a ho- li- day of all days in the year

Oliver Cromwell

Ol- i- ver Crom- well lay bur-ied and dead, Hee- haw

The Plough Boy

A flax- en head- ed cow- boy, as sim-ple as may be,

Le Roi s'en va-t-en chasse

Le roi s'en va t'en chas- se, dans le bois des Bour- bons__

The Sally Gardens

Down__ by the__ Sal- ly__ Gar- dens my__ love and I did meet,

Serenade for Tenor, Horn and Strings, Op. 31, No. 1 Pastoral (Cotton)
By permission Boosey & Hawkes, Inc., copyright owners

The Day's grown old; the faint- ing Sun Has but a lit- tle way__

Serenade for Tenor, Horn and Strings, Op. 31,
No. 2 Nocturne (Tennyson)   A

The splen - - dour falls_ on cas-tle walls_ and snow-y sum-mits

No. 3 Elegy (Blake)   B

O Rose, 'thou art sick; The in-vi-si-ble worm That flies_ in the night,

No. 4 Dirge (anon. 15th cent.)   C

This ae nighte, this ae nighte e - ver- y night and alle,

No. 5 Hymn (Ben Jonson)   D

Queen and hunt-ress chaste and fair_ Now the sun is laid to sleep

No. 6 Sonnet (Keats)   E

O soft_ em-balmer of the still mid-night, Shutting with care-ful fin-gers

Seven Sonnets of Michelangelo, Op. 22   Sonetto XVI
By permission Boosey & Hawkes, Inc., copyright owners   F

Si co - me nel la pe - na e nell' in - chio stro

XXIV   G

Spir - to ben na - to, in cui si spec-chia e ve- de

XXX   H

Veg- gio co' bei_ vo- stri oc-chi un dol- ce lu- me_

XXXI   I

A che più debb' io mai l'in-ten-sa vog- lia. Sfo- gar con pian ti

XXXII   J

S'un casto a-mor, s'u- na pie- tà su-per-na, S'u- na for-tu- na

XXXVIII   K

Ren- de-te a gli oc-chi miei, O fon-te o fiu-me,_ ren-de-te_

LV   L

Tu sa' ch'io so, si- gnior mie, che tu sai_ Ch'i ven - - ni

BRUCH, Max (1838-1920)

Odysseus, Op. 41, No. 8
By permission Associated Music Publishers, Inc.   N

Ich wob_ dies Ge- wand mit Thrä- nen am Ta- ge

BRUCK, Arnold Von (16th Cent.)

Aus tiefer Not (4-part chorus)   P

Aus tie- fer Not schrei ich zu dir, Herr Gott, er- hör

BRUCKNER, Anton (1824-1896)

Ave Maria (chorus)
By permission Associated Music Publishers, Inc.   R

A- ve Ma- ri- a gra-ti-a ple- na Do- mi-nus te- cum

Herbstlied (chorus)   S

Durch die Wäl-der streif' ich mun-ter, wenn der Wind die Stäm- me rüt-telt,

Mass in E Minor
No. 1 Kyrie

Ky- ri- e e- le- i- son Ky- ri- e e- le- i- son — A

No. 2 Gloria in Excelsis Deo

Et in ter- ra pax ho- mi- ni- bus bo- nae vo- lun- ta- tis — B

No. 3 Credo in unum Deum

Pa- trem o- mni- po- ten- tem, fa- cto- rem coe- li et ter- rae, — C

Et in- car- na- tus est de Spi- ri- tu san- cto, — D

No. 4 Sanctus

San- ctus, san- ctus, san- ctus — E

No. 5 Benedictus

Be- ne- di- ctus, Be- ne- di- ctus be- ne- di- ctus — F

No. 6 Agnus Dei

Ag- nus De- i, qui tol- lis pec- ca- ta mun- di — G

No. 7 Tota Pulchra es Maria
(Antiphon) (chorus)

To- ta pul-chra es Ma- ri- a. To- ta pul-chra es Ma- ri- a — H

BRUNEAU, Alfred (1857-1934)

Adieu forêt profonde, from L'Attaque
du Moulin, Op. 22 (opera)
Copyright by Choudens fils, Paris

A -dieu,— fo-rêt pro-fon- de, a- dieu,— géante a- mi- e,— — J

BUCK, Dudley (1839-1909)

Fear ye not, O Israel

Fear— ye not, O Is- ra- el,— nei-ther be thou still dis-may- ed — L

My Redeemer and my Lord
Copyright by John Church Co.
Used by permission

My Re- deem- er, My Re- deem- er and my Lord — M

Sunset, Op. 76, No. 4

Look off dear love a- cross the sal- low sands, — N

The Virgin's Lullaby
Copyright 1895, G. Schirmer, Inc.

Sleep, my Je- su sleep, my best,— In thy lone- ly man- ger rest— — O

BULL, Ole (1810-1880)

Saeterjendens Söndag (The Herdgirl's
Sunday)

I gaze on the sun, it mounts in the sky, The hour soon for mass — Q

BULLARD, Frederic Field (1864-1904)

The Stein Song
Copyright by Oliver Ditson Co.
Used by permission

Give a rouse, then, in the May- time for a life that knows no fear — S

The Stein Song

For it's al-ways good wea-ther, when good fel-lows get to-geth-er,

Winter Song
Copyright by Oliver Ditson Co.
Used by permission

Ho, a song by the fire!__ Pass the pipes, pass the bowl!

BUNGERT, August (1846-1915)

**Ich hab' ein kleines Lied erdacht,
Op. 49, No. 9**

Ich hab ein klei-nes Lied er-dacht und hab' es ge-sun-gen

BUONONCINI, Giovanni (1640-1703)

Deh piu a me non v'ascondete

Deh più a me nom v'as-con-de-te lu-ci va-ghe del mio sol,

Per la gloria d'adorarvi

Per____ la glo - - - - ria d'a - - - - do-rar - - - vi

Pupille nere

Pu-pil-le ne-re, Se voi guar-da-te, Ce-der voi fa-te,

Vado ben spesso

Va-do ben spes-so can-gian-do__ lo-   co,

BURLEIGH, Harry Thacker (1866-   )

**Arrangements of Negro Spirituals:
By an' By**
Copyright by G. Ricordi & Co., Inc.

Oh by__ an' by by__ an' by, I'm goin' to lay down dis heavy__ load

Deep River

Deep_____ riv-er, my home is o-ver Jor-dan____

Go down, Moses

When Is-rael was in E-gypt's lan' Let my peo-ple go,

Go down, Mo-ses, way down to E-gypt's lan'

Hard Trials

Been a-lis'-nin' all de night long, Been a-lis'-nin' all de day

Now ain't dem hard tri-als Great trib-u-la-tion,

Heav'n, Heav'n (I got a robe)

I got a robe, You got a robe, All of God's chil-dren got a robe

I don't feel no-ways tired

I am seek-in' for__ a ci-ty, Hal-le-lu - - - - - ja!

Lord,__ I don't feel no ways tir-ed, Chil-da-ren! Oh,____ Glo-ry

BURLEIGH—BUXTEHUDE

Arrangements of Negro Spirituals:
I want to be ready

A — I want__ to be read-y I want__ to be read-y

Nobody Knows de Trouble I've Seen

B — No-bod-y knows de trou-ble I've seen, No-bod-y knows but Je-sus

Oh, Didn't It Rain

C — Fo'-ty days fo'-ty nights when de rain kept a-fall-in

Oh, Peter, Go ring-a dem bells

D — Oh, Pe-ter, go ring-a dem bells, Pe-ter, go ring-a dem bells.

Sinner, please doan let dis Harves' Pass

E — Sin-ner, please doan let dis har-ves' pass;__ Sin-ner please

Swing Low Sweet Chariot

F — Swing low sweet char-i-ot,__ Com-ing for to car-ry me home

Were You There?

G — Were you there when they cru-ci-fied my Lord?__ Were you there

BUSCA, Padre Ludovico (17th Cent.)

Bionda, bionda Clori

I — Bion-da,bion-da Clo-ri bion-da Clo-ri che nel vol-to hai rac-col-to

Occhi belli

J — Oc-chi bel-li, non ful-mi-na-te,non ful-mi-na - - - - - - - - - te,

BUTTERWORTH, George (1885-1916)

A Shropshire Lad
By permission of Augener, Ltd., London

L — With rue my heart__ is lad-en For gold-en friends__ I had,

M — When the lad for long-ing sighs, Mute__ and dull of cheer and pale,

N — Oh fair e-nough are sky and plain but I know fair-er far

Bredon Hill

O — In sum-mer-time on Bre-don the bells they sound so clear;__

P — Love-liest of trees, the cher-ry now is hung with bloom a-long the bough

Q — Is my team plough-ing, That I was used to drive,

BUXTEHUDE, Dietrich (1637-1707)

CANTATAS:
Aperite mihi portas justitiae
(Ugrino No. 71)

(tenor)   (alto)

S — A-pe-ri-te, a-pe-ri-te, a-pe-ri-te, a-pe-ri-té

CANTATAS:

Aperite mihi portas justitiae (Ugrino No. 71)

Be- ne-dic- tus, qui ven- it, qui ve- nit qui ve- nit

Jubilate Domino (Ugrino No. 19)

Ju- bi- la- te, Ju- bi- la- te, Ju- bi- la- te Do- mi- no,

O fröhliche Stunden (Ugrino No. 12)

O fröh-li- che Stun-den, o fröh-li- che Zeit, es hat ü- ber wun-den,

Singet dem Herrn (Ugrino No. 16)

Sin - - - - - get, Sin - - - - - get dem Her-ren— ein— neu-es Lied

Was mich auf dieser Welt betrübt (Ugrino No. 71)

Was mich auf die- ser Welt be-trübt, das wäh-ret kur- ze Zeit,

Missa Brevis (Ugrino No. 42)
Kyrie

Ky- ri- e- e-lei - - - - - - - - - - - son

Gloria

Et in ter- ra pax ho- mi - - - - ni- bus

BUZZI-PECCIA, A. (1853-1943)

Colombetta

La bel- la Co- lom- bet- ta Al cal- do si ri- po- sa,

Lolita

A- mor, a- mor che lan- gue il cor,

BYRD, William (1543-1623)

MADRIGALS:

I thought that love had been a boy (5-part madrigal)

I thought that love had been a boy, I thought that love had— been a boy

Lullaby, my sweet little baby

Lul- la, lul- la, Lul- la, lul- la- by, lul- la- by—

Though Amaryllis Dance

Though A- ma- ry- lis dance in green, like fai- ry Queen

This sweet and merry month

This sweet and mer-ry, mer-ry month, and mer-ry, mer-ry month of— May

Mass (five voices)
I Kyrie Eleison

Ky- ri- e e- lei - - - - - son

II Gloria in excelsis

Et in ter- ra pax ho- mi - - - - - - ni-bus

III Credo

Pa- trem om- ni- po- ten- tem, fac- to- rem coe - - - - li et ter-rae

IV Sanctus

Sanc - - - - - - tus, Sanc - - - - - tus, sanc - - - - - -tus,

Mass (five voices)
V Benedictus

Be- ne- dic- tus qui ve- nit

VI Agnus Dei

Ag- nus de- i qui tol- lis pec- ca- - - - ta mun- - - - - - di,

MOTETS:
Ave Verum Corpus

A- - - - ve ve- - - - rum cor- - - - pus

Justorum Animae

Ju- sto- - - - rum a- ni- mae in ma- - - nu De- - - - - - i sunt

Non Vos Relinquam Orphanos

Non vos re- lin- quam or- pha- nos Al- le- lu- - - - - - - - - ja

O Mistress Mine

O mis- tress mine, where are you roam- ing O_____ mis- tress mine,

Sacerdotes Domini

Sa- cer- do- tes Do- - - - - - - - mi- ni in- cen- - - sum

CACCINI, Giulio (1548-1618)

Amarilli, mia bella

A- ma- ril- li mi a bel- la, non cre- di_o del mio cor

Dovrò dunque morire

Do- vrò dun- que mo- ri- - - re, Pria che di nuo- vo_io mi- ri

Non piango e non sospiro,
from Euridice (opera)

Non pian- go, e non so- spi- ro O mia ca- ra_Eu- ri- di- ce

Fere selvagge

Fe- re sel- vag- ge Che per mon- ti_er- ra- te, il piè fer- ma- te

Occhi Immortali

Oc- chi im- mor- ta- li, D'a- mor glo- ria_e splen- do- - re;

Tu, ch'hai le penne amore

Tu ch'hai le pen- ne, A- mo- re, E sai spie- gar- le_a vo- lo,

CADMAN, Charles Wakefield (1881-)

At Dawning, Op. 29, No. 1
Copyright by Oliver Ditson Co.
Used by permission

When the dawn flames in the sky I love you;

Far Off I Hear a Lover's Flute

Far off I hear a lo- ver's flute A- cry- ing thro' the gloom;

Four American Indian Songs,
Op. 45, No. 1
Copyright by White Smith Co.

From the Land of the Sky- blue Wa- ter,_____ They brought a cap- tive maid;_____

No. 2

The white dawn_ is steal- ing a- bove the dark ce- dar trees

Four American Indian Songs, Op. 45, No. 4

The moon drops low that once soared high as an ea-gle   A

A Moonlight Song, Op. 42, No. 2
Copyright 1933, G. Schirmer, Inc.

The moon-light shim-mers thro' the vine___ That to___ my___ porch   B

CALDARA, Antonio (1670-1736)

Come raggio di sol

Co- me rag-gio di sol   mi- te e se- re- no   D

Mirti, Faggi

Mir- ti,   fag- gi   tron- chi e fron- de   E

Selve amiche, ombrose piante

Sel- ve a- mi- che, om- bro- se pian- te, fi- do al- ber- go   F

CALLCOTT, Dr. (1766-1821)

To all you ladies now at land

To all you La- dies now at land We men at sea in- dite   H

Ye Mariners of England

A

Ye Ma- ri- ners of___ Eng- land that guard our na- tive seas   I

B

While the storm- y winds do blow,___ While the storm-y winds do blow___   J

CAMPBELL-TIPTON, Louis (1877-1921)

The Crying of Water
Copyright 1907, G. Schirmer, Inc.

O wa- ter,___ voice of my heart___ cry- ing in___ the sand,   L

A Spirit Flower
Copyright 1908, G. Schirmer, Inc.

A

My heart was fro- zen e- ven as the earth___   M

B

Down through the win- ter sun- shine snow flakes came, All shim-m'ring   N

CAMPION, Thomas (1567-1620)

The Cypress curtain of the night

The cy- press cur- tain of the night is spread   P

Follow thy fair sun

Fol- low thy fair sun, un- hap- py sha- dow. Though thou   Q

Follow your saint

Fol- low your saint, fol- low with ac- cents sweet;   R

My Sweetest Lesbia

My sweet-est Les- bia, let us live and love And though the sag- er sort

When to her lute Corinna sings

When to her lute Co- rin- na sings, her voice re- vives

Never weather-beaten sail

Nev- er weath- er beat- en sail more will- ing bent to shore,

What if a day, or a month, or a year

What if a day, or a month or a year, crown thy de- lights

CAMPRA, André (1660-1744)

Charmant papillon, from Les Fêtes Vénitiennes

Char- mant pa- pil- lon dont l'ai - - - - le d'or pas- se

CANTELOUBE, Joseph (1879-   )

Chants d'Auvergne:
Series I,
No. 2 Baïlèro
By permission Heugel & Cie, Paris, copyright owners

Pas- tré, dè dè- laï l'a- ïo, a gaï-ré de boun tèn dio lou baï- lè- ro

No. 3 (a)   L'aïo de Rotso

L'a- ïo dè rot- so te fo- ro mou- rir fi- lho- to,

(b) Ound' onoren gorda?

Ound' o- no- ren gor- da pit- chou no droou- lè- to?

(c) Obai din lou Limouzi

O- bal din lou Li- mou- zi, pit-choun' o- bal din lou Li- mou- zi

Series II,
No. 2 L'Antouèno (L'Antoine)

Quond o- no- rèn o lo fiè- ïro, ié! Quond o- no- rèn

No. 5 (a) Je n'ai pas d'amie

N'aï pas ïèu dè mi- o, soui qu'un pas- tou- rel

(b) Lo Calhé (La Caille)

E, dio mè tu, lo cal- hé, ound as toun nïou?

Series III,
No. 1 Lo Fiolaire (La Fileuse)

Ton qu'è- rè pit-chou- nè- lo Gor- da- vè loui mou- tous,

No. 2 Passo pel prat

Lo lo lo lo lo lo lo lo lo lo lo lo lo

Pas- so pel prat bè- lo- to Jeu pos- so- raï

No. 4 Brezaviola (Berceuse)

Soun, soun, bè- ni, bè- ni, bè- ni, soun, soun, bè- ni, bè- ni doun,

No. 5 Malurous qu'o uno fenno

Ma- lu- rous qu'o u- no fen- no, Ma- lu- rous qué n'o cat!

CAPLET, André (1878-1925)

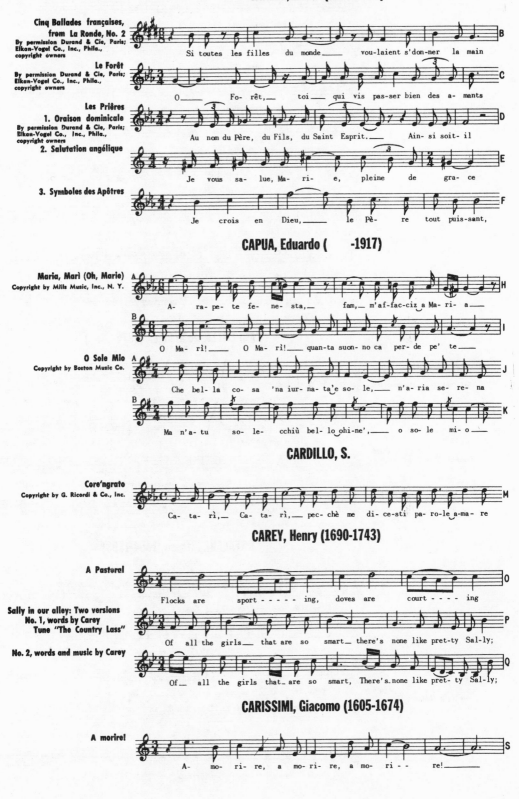

Cinq Ballades françaises,
from La Ronde, No. 2
By permission Durand & Cie, Paris;
Elkan-Vogel, Inc., Phila.,
copyright owners

Si toutes les filles du monde____ vou-laient s'don-ner la main

Le Forêt
By permission Durand & Cie, Paris;
Elkan-Vogel Co., Inc., Phila.,
copyright owners

O____ Fo-rêt, toi____ qui vis pas-ser bien des a-mants

Les Prières
1. Oraison dominicale
By permission Durand & Cie, Paris;
Elkan-Vogel Co., Inc., Phila.,
copyright owners

Au nom du Père, du Fils, du Saint Esprit.____ Ain-si soit-il

2. Salutation angélique

Je vous sa-lue, Ma-ri-e, pleine de gra-ce

3. Symboles des Apôtres

Je crois en Dieu,____ le Pè-re tout puis-sant,

CAPUA, Eduardo (-1917)

Maria, Marì (Oh, Marie)
Copyright by Mills Music, Inc., N. Y.

A- ra-pe- te fe- ne- sta, fam, m'af-fac-ciz a Ma-rì- a

O Ma-rì!____ O Ma-rì! quan-ta suon-no ca per-de pe' te

O Sole Mio
Copyright by Boston Music Co.

Che bel-la co- sa 'na iur-na-ta'e so- le, n'a-ria se- re- na

Ma n'a-tu so- le- cchiù bel-lo ohi-ne',____ o so-le mi-o

CARDILLO, S.

Core'ngrato
Copyright by G. Ricordi & Co., Inc.

Ca- ta- rì,— Ca- ta- rì,— pec-chè me di-ce-sti pa-ro-le a-ma-re

CAREY, Henry (1690-1743)

A Pastoral

Flocks are sport - - - - - ing, doves are court - - - - ing

Sally in our alley: Two versions
No. 1, words by Carey
Tune "The Country Lass"

Of all the girls____ that are so smart____ there's none like pret-ty Sal-ly;

No. 2, words and music by Carey

Of____ all the girls that____ are so smart, There's none like pret-ty Sal-ly;

CARISSIMI, Giacomo (1605-1674)

A morire!

A- mo- ri- re, a mo- ri- re, a mo- ri- - re!____

CARPENTER, John Alden (1876-   )

CATALANI, Alfredo (1854-1893)

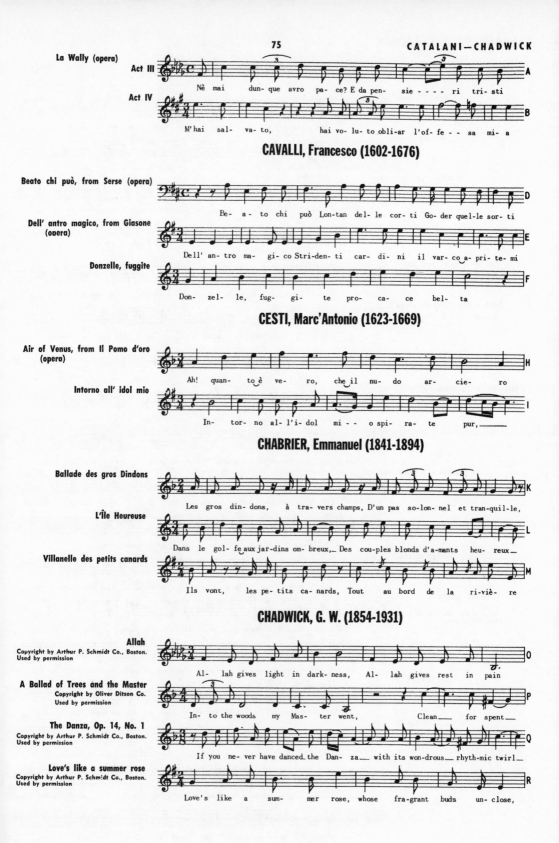

La Wally (opera)

Act III

Nè mai dun- que avro pa- ce? E da pen- sie- - - -ri tri- sti

Act IV

M'hai sal- va- to, hai vo- lu- to obli- ar l'of- fe- - - sa mi- a

CAVALLI, Francesco (1602-1676)

Beato chi può, from Serse (opera)

Be- a- to chi può Lon- tan del- le cor- ti Go- der quel- le sor- ti

Dell' antro magico, from Giasone (opera)

Dell' an- tro ma- gi- co Stri- den- ti car- di- ni il var- co a- pri- te- mi

Donzelle, fuggite

Don- zel- le, fug- gi- te pro- ca- ce bel- ta

CESTI, Marc'Antonio (1623-1669)

Air of Venus, from Il Pomo d'oro (opera)

Ah! quan- to è ve- ro, che il nu- do ar- cie- ro

Intorno all' idol mio

In- tor- no al- l'i- dol mi- o o spi- ra- te pur, ____

CHABRIER, Emmanuel (1841-1894)

Ballade des gros Dindons

Les gros din- dons, à tra- vers champs, D'un pas so-lon- nel et tran-quil- le,

L'Île Heureuse

Dans le gol- fe aux jar-dins om- breux,__ Des cou-ples blonds d'a-mants heu- reux__

Villanelle des petits canards

Ils vont, les pe- tits ca- nards, Tout au bord de la ri- viè- re

CHADWICK, G. W. (1854-1931)

Allah
Copyright by Arthur P. Schmidt Co., Boston.
Used by permission

Al- lah gives light in dark- ness, Al- lah gives rest in pain

A Ballad of Trees and the Master
Copyright by Oliver Ditson Co.
Used by permission

In- to the woods my Mas- ter went, Clean__ for spent__

The Danza, Op. 14, No. 1
Copyright by Arthur P. Schmidt Co., Boston.
Used by permission

If you ne- ver have danced the Dan- za__ with its won-drous__ rhyth-mic twirl

Love's like a summer rose
Copyright by Arthur P. Schmidt Co., Boston.
Used by permission

Love's like a sum- mer rose, whose fra-grant buds un- close,

CHAMINADE, Cécile (1857-1944)

L'Anneau d'Argent

Le cher an-neau d'ar-gent que vous m'a-vez don-né,

Chanson Slave

Dans mon beau pa-ys j'a-vais un a-mi

Si J'Étais Jardinier
Copyright 1894, G. Schirmer, Inc.

Si j'é-tais jar-di-nier des cieux, Je te cueil-le-rais des é-toi-les!

CHARLES, Ernest (1895-   )

Let my song fill your heart
Copyright 1936, G. Schirmer, Inc.

Let my song fill your heart with its mel-o-dy oh so di-vine

When I Have Sung my Songs
Copyright 1934, G. Schirmer, Inc.

When I have sung my songs to you, I'll sing no more.

CHARPENTIER, Gustav (1860-   )

A Mules (after "Impressions d'Italie")

Les yeux, la belle, hé-las! tes yeux fa-rou-ches

C'est l'heu - - - re où l'amant nous con-te fol-le-ment

La Chanson de Chemin

Qu'est-ce qui bril-le? Une au-ber-ge Ah! Ah!

La route est lon-gue, lon-gue, bon pé-le-rin.

Les Chevaux de bois

Tour-nez, tour-nez, bons che-vaux de bois, Tour-nez cent tours,

Louise (opera)
Act I
By permission Heugel & Cie, Paris,
copyright owners

O coeur a-mi! O coeur pro-mis! Hé-las! si loin, si près!

De-puis long-temps j'ha-bi-tais cet-te cham-bre, sans me dou-ter, hé-las!

Act II Scene II

Oh! moi quand je suis dans la ru-e, tout mon êt-re prend com-me feu!

Act III

De puis le jour où je me suis don-né-e,

Act IV

Les pau-vres gens peu-vent-ils être heureux? a qui le bon Dieu

Voir naître une en-fant, la fleur-ir des ca-res-ses,

Nocturne, Op. 8, No. 1

La nuit é-tait pen- sive et té- né- breu- se — A

Nos Souvenirs, Op. 8, No. 4

Nos sou- ve- nirs tou- tes ces cho- ses Qu'à tous les vents — B

Les Papillons, Op. 2, No. 3

Les pa- pil- lons cou-leur de nei- ge vo- lent par es- saims — C

Printemps triste, Op. 8, No. 3

Nos sen- tiers ai- més s'en vont, re- fleu- rir — D

Sérénade italienne, Op. 2, No. 5

Par- tons en bar- que sur la mer Pous pas- ser la nuit — E

Serres chaudes, Op. 24
No. 1 Serre chaude
Copyright by Salabert, Paris, N. Y.

O serre an mil-lieu des fo-rêts Et vos por-tes à ja-mais clo-ses! — F

No. 2 Serre d'ennui

O cet en-nui bleu dans le coeur a- vec la vi- si-on — G

No. 3 Lassitude

Ils ne sa- vent plus où se po- ser ces bai-sers,Ces lè-vres — H

No. 4 Fauves las

O les pas- si- ons en al- lées, Et les ri- res et les san-glots! — I

No. 5 Oraison

Vous sa- vez,Sei- gneur ma mi- sè- re! Voy-ez ce que je vous ap-por- te, — J

Les Temps de Lilas

Le temps des li- las et le temps des ro- ses — K

CHERUBINI, Maria Luigi (1760-1842)

J'ai vu disparaître l'espoir,
from Les Abencerrages (opera)

J'ai vu dis- pa- raî- tre L'és- poir dont j'o- sais me nour- rir — M

Guide mes pas, from Les Deux
Journées (opera)

Gui- de mes pas, ô pro- vi- den- ce! d'mon plan se- con- de — N

O Salutaris Hostia

O sa- lu- ta- ris, O sa- lu- ta- ris hos- ti- a qual coe- li —

CHOPIN, Frédéric François (1810-1849)

Polish Songs, Op. 74
No. 1 The Maiden's Wish

Were I a sun, so high in Heav'n out- beam- ing,

Accompaniment Theme

No. 2 In Spring

Thro' the dew- y val- ley mur- mur brooks mé- an- d'ring

Polish Songs
No. 3 Troubled Waters
Tell me an- gry flow-ing tor- rent, why so tur- bid is thy cur-rent?   A

No. 4 Bacchanal
Boys, be jol- ly, grief is fol- ly, Drink then while you can!   B

No. 5 What a young maiden loves
Stream- let lov-eth the sedg- es, bird- ling lov-eth the hedg- es,   C

No. 6 Go Thou, and haste Thee
"Go thou, and haste thee!" I mute- ly o- bey thee   D

No. 7 The Messenger
Rills are bright-ly glit-t'ring, green the banks they__ fol- low   E

No. 8 My Sweetheart
When an eye like fire glow-ing, And a heart no guile__ know- ing,   F

No. 9 A Melody
Mute and re-sign'd, for pi- ty ne'er ap- peal- ing,__   G

No. 10 The Trooper before the Battle
Why so rest- ive, so un- stead- y, Thou, my trust- y steed?   H

No. 11 Two Corpses
Fond were the lov- ers, Yet ne'er their love was plight- ed   I

No. 12 My Joys
When for a mo- ment thou dost speak, my dar- ling,   J

No. 13 Melancholy
Dew in the mead - - - - ow, mist in the val- ley   K

No. 14 The little Ring
Yet a child__ wert thou, O maid- en, when our faith__ we plight- ed   L

No. 15 The Return Home
Stran- ger in the storm swept for- est, Haste thee on, O Ri- der!   M

No. 16 Lithuanian Song
O- ver the mead- ow and home- ward I hied me,   N

No. 17 Poland's Dirge
By the storm they breast- ed Ev- 'ry leaf is wrest- ed   O

CIAMPI, Legrenzo Vincenzo (1719-1762)

Tre giorni son che Nina (2 different versions) (said to be by Pergolesi also)

1 Tre gior-ni son che Ni- na, che Ni- na in let- to se ne sta__   Q

2 Tre__ gior-ni son che Ni- ra, che Ni- na, che Ni - - na   R

CILEA, Francesco (1866-　　)

Adriana Lecouvreur (opera)
Copyright by Sonzogno, Milan

Act I — I- o son' l'u- mi- le an-cel-la del Ge-nio cre-a- tor___ — **B**

La dol- cis- si-ma ef-fi-gie sor- ri-den- te — **C**

Act II — O va- bon- da stel-la d'O- ri- en- te non tra- mon- tar, — **D**

L'a- ni-ma ho stan-ca, e la mè- ta è lon- ta- na: — **E**

I- o son___ su- a per l'a-mor___ ch'è più for- te del-la sor- te, — **F**

Act IV — Po- ve-ri fio- ri,___ gem- me de' pra- ti, pur ie- ri na- ti, — **G**

No, la mia fron- - te, che pen-sier non___ mu- ta, — **H**

L'Arlesiana (opera)
Copyright by Sonzogno, Milan

Act I — Co- me due tiz- zi ac- ce- si, dal-l'al- to del di- ru- po — **I**

Act II — Vie- ni con me sui mon- ti, go- drai va- sti o-riz-zon- ti — **J**

Anch' i- o vor- re- i dor-mir co- sì,___ nel son-no al- men — **K**

Act III — Ho da- to moglie al pa-dre del- lo spo- so e l'ho da- ta — **L**

Sa- i che gli ho da- to a bra- ni a bra- ni l'a- ni- ma___ — **M**

CIMARA, Pietro (1887-　　)

Canto di Primavera
Copyright by Forlivesi, Florence

A- pri- te tut- te le fi- ne-stra al So- le — **O**

Fiocca la neve
opyright by C. W. Homeyer, Boston

Len- ta la ne- ve fioc- ca, fioc- ca, fioc- ca — **P**

Scherzo
Copyright by F. Bongiovanni, Bologna

U- na notte al da- van-za- le e- ro so- la o pur non e- ro? — **Q**

Stornellata Marinara
Copyright by G. Ricordi & Co., Inc.

Ah! Al- ga di ma- - re!___ Quan- do m'af- fo-sca qual-che gran do-lore — **R**

Stornello
Copyright by F. Bongiovanni, Bologna

Son co-me i chic- chi del- la me- lo- grana___ — **S**

CIMAROSA, Domenico (1749-1801)

Il Matrimonio Segreto (opera)

U- di- te, tut- ti u-di- te le or- rec- chie spa- lan- ca- te

È ve- ro che in ca- sa io so- no, io son la pa- dro- na,

Pria che spun- ti in ciel___ l'au- ro- ra in ciel___ l'au- ro- ra

Bril- lar mi sen- to il co- re, mi sen- to___ giu- bi- lar

Per- do- na- te, sig-nor mi- o, se vi lascio e fo___ par- ten- za

Se non___ ven-di- ca - - - ta con- ten- ta___ già___ so- no

CLARIBEL (1830-1896)

Come Back to Erin

Come back to Er- in, Ma- vour- neen, Ma- vour- neen

I cannot sing the old songs

I can- not sing the old songs I sang long years a- go,

CLARKE, Rebecca (1886-   )

The Seal Man
By permission Boosey & Hawkes, Inc.,
copyright owners

And he came by her ca- bin to the west of the road, call-ing

Shy One
By permission Boosey & Hawkes, Inc.,
copyright owners

Shy one, shy one, shy one of my heart, She moves___

CLARKE, Robert C. (1879-1934)

The Blind Ploughman

CLAY. Frédéric (1838-1889)

Gipsy John

The gipsy fires are burn- ing, The ket- tle sings a song,

So dip your fin- gers in the stew, and drink a cup to me

I'll sing thee songs of Araby

I'll sing thee songs of A- ra- by___ and tales of fair Cash- mere___

The Sands o' Dee

Oh! Ma-ry go,   and call the cat-tle home, and call the cat-tle home   A

CLEMENS, Non Papa (1510-1555)

Aymer est ma vie

Ay- mer est__ ma vi- e   Ay--mer est ma__ vi- e____   C

COATES, Eric (1886-   )

Bird Songs at Eventide

I heard you singing

Tell me where is fancy bred
By permission Boosey & Hawkes, Inc.,
copyright owners

Tell   me   where   is   fan- cy bred, Tell   me   where   is   fan- cy bred   G

COLERIDGE-TAYLOR, Samuel (1875-1912)

Eleȧnore, Op. 37, No. 6
Copyright by Novello & Co., Ltd., London

The for-est flow'rs   are   fad-ed   all,   The   winds   com-plain,   I

Life and Death

To look for thee, cry   for thee, sigh for thee, un-der   my breath,____   J

Onaway! Awake, beloved!
from Song of Hiawatha, Op. 30

"On-a- way!   A- wake,_ be- lov- ed!__   Thou the wild-flow'r of the forest   K

She rested by the Broken Brook
Copyright by Oliver Ditson Co.
Used by permission

She__ rest-ed by the Bro-ken Brook, She drank of Wear-y Well__   L

COOKE, Thomas Simpson (1782-1848)

Love's Ritornella

Gen-tle Zi- tel-la, whi-ther a- way?   Love's Ri-tor-nel-la, list while I play   N

Over Hill, Over Dale

O- ver hill,   o- ver dale Tho-rough brush   tho-rough brier   O

COQUARD, Arthur (1846-1910)

Haï luli
Copyright 1899, G. Schirmer, Inc.

A Je   suis   tris- te   je m'in- qui- è- te, Je ne sais plus   Q

B Ha- ï lu- li!   Ha- ï lu- li!   Ha- ï lu- li!   R

CORNELIUS, Peter (1824-1874)

Ave Maria
A - - ve, a - - ve, Ma - ri - a! Gra - ti - a ple-na

Der Barbier von Bagdad (The Barber
of Bagdad) (comic opera)
Act I
Ach,____ das Leid hab ich er-tra-gen wie er-trag' ich nun das Glück?

San-fter Schlum-mer wiegt ihn ein, lin-dert mil-de je-de Pein

Act II
O, hol-des Bild in En-gel-schö-ne, oft____ wenn in Träu-men

So mag kein and'res Wort____ er-klin-gen, als das die blühnde Ro - - se

Ein Ton (The Monotone) Op. 3, No. 3
Mir klingt ein Ton so wun-der-bar in Herz und Sin-nen im-mer dar,

Accompaniment Theme

Weihnachtslieder, Op. 8
No. 1 Christbaum
Wie schön geschmückt der fest-li-che Raum! Die Lich-ter fun-kehn

No. 2 Die Hirten
Die Hir-ten wa-chen Nachts in Feld;so still und dun-kel liegt die Welt,

No. 3 Drei Könige
Drei Kön'-ge wan-dern aus Mor-gen-land, Ein Stern-lein führt sie

COSTELEY, Guillaume (1531-1606)

Allon, gay, gay, gay, Bergères
(madrigal)
Al- lon, gay, gay, gay, Ber-ge-res, Al- lon, gay, al- lon, gay

Mignonne, allon voir si la Roze
Mi- gnon- ne al-lon voir si la Ro-ze, Mignon-ne al-lon voir

COTTRAU, Teodoro (1827-1879)

Addio a Napoli
Ad-dio mia bel-la Na-po-li, ad-di-o, ad-di- - -o!

Santa Lucia (Neapolitan)
Sul ma-re lu-ci-ca l'a-stro d'ar-gen-to

Ve- ni-te al l'ag-gi-le Bar-chet-ta mi-a.

COUILLART (16th Cent.)

Viri Galilaei

Vi- ri Ga- li- lae- i, vi- ri Ga- li- - lae- - i

COUPERIN, François (1668-1733)

Air Serieux (Mars 1697)

Qu' on ne me di- se plus que c'est la seule ab- sen- ce

Air Serieux (Août 1701)

Doux li- ens de mon_____ coeur, Ai- ma- bles pei- nes,

Brunete (Décembre 1711)

Ze- phi- re, mo- de- re en ces lieux L'ar- deur dont tu ca- res- - se

Ostende nobis domine, from Motets du Roy

O- sten- - - - - - - - - - - - de O-sten- de no-bis, Do- mi- ne,

Quatre versets d'un Motet 1.

A- dole- - scen- - tu- lus sum e- go et con- tem- ptus

2.

I- gni-tum e- lo- quium tu- um ve-he-men- - - - - - - - - - ter

3.

Ju- sti- ti- a tu- a Ju-sti-ti- a tu- a Ju-sti-ti- a in aeter- - num

4.

Qui dat ni- vem si- cut la- nam ne- - - - bulam si- cut_ ci- ne-rem

Venite exultemus Domino (motet)

Ve- ni- te e- xul- te- mus Do- mi- no ju-bi- le-mus De- o

COWARD, Noel (1899-   )

**Bittersweet (operetta):
I'll see you again**
Copyright 1929 by Chappell & Co., Ltd.
Harms, Inc. Publisher and Owner of all
rights for the U. S. and Canada

I'll see you a- gain when- ev- er spring breaks through a- gain

Zigeuner
Copyright 1929 by Chappell & Co., Ltd.
Harms, Inc. Publisher and Owner of all
rights for the U. S. and Canada

Play to me be-neath some sum- mer moon, Zi- geu- ner

**I'll follow my secret heart, from
Conversation Piece (operetta)**

COWLES, Eugene (1860-   )

Forgotten
Copyright by Oliver Ditson Co.
Used by permission

For- got-ten you? Well if for- get- ting Be think-ing all the day

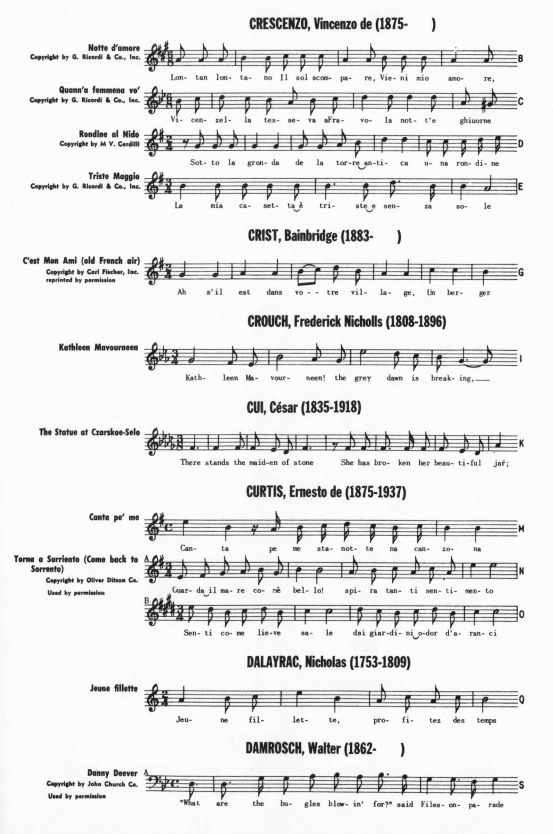

CRESCENZO, Vincenzo de (1875-   )

Notte d'amore
Copyright by G. Ricordi & Co., Inc.

Lon- tan lon- ta- no Il sol scom- pa- re, Vie- ni mio amo- re,

Quann'a femmena vo'
Copyright by G. Ricordi & Co., Inc.

Vi- cen- zel- la tes- se- va a Fra- vo- la not- t'e ghiuorne

Rondine al Nido
Copyright by M V. Cardilli

Sot- to la gron- da de la tor- re an- ti- ca u- na ron- di- ne

Triste Maggio
Copyright by G. Ricordi & Co., Inc.

La mia ca- set- ta è tri- ste e sen- za so- le

CRIST, Bainbridge (1883-   )

C'est Mon Ami (old French air)
Copyright by Carl Fischer, Inc.
reprinted by permission

Ah s'il est dans vo- tre vil- la- ge, Un ber- ger

CROUCH, Frederick Nicholls (1808-1896)

Kathleen Mavourneen

Kath- leen Ma- vour- neen! the grey dawn is break- ing,___

CUI, César (1835-1918)

The Statue at Czarskoe-Selo

There stands the maid-en of stone   She has bro- ken her beau- ti-ful jar;

CURTIS, Ernesto de (1875-1937)

Canta pe' me

Can- ta pe me sta- not- te na can- zo- na

Torna a Surriento (Come back to Sorrento)
Copyright by Oliver Ditson Co.
Used by permission

Guar- da il ma- re co- mè bel- lo! spi- ra tan- ti sen- ti- men- to

Sen- ti co- me lie- ve sa- le dai giar- di- ni o- dor d'a- ran- ci

DALAYRAC, Nicholas (1753-1809)

Jeune fillette

Jeu- ne fil- let- te, pro- fi- tez des temps

DAMROSCH, Walter (1862-   )

Danny Deever
Copyright by John Church Co.
Used by permission

"What are the bu- gles blow- in' for?" said Files- on- pa- rade

Danny Deever — For they're hang- in' Dan- ny Dee- ver, you can hear the Dead March play,

DARGOMIJSKY, Alexander (1813-1869)

I suffer — I suf- fer for I love thee from my in- most be- ing

The Lawyer's Clerk — There once was a clerk to a law- yer, So lit- tle and want- ing in grace,

The Miller — Said the mil- ler, home re- turn- ing Real- ly those are stran- ger's shoes

The Old Corporal — Chil- dren, keep step while you're march- ing! 'Ten- tion, your ri- fle hold fast!

Pretty Maiden — Oh,— pret- ty maid- en, see the Boy - - - ards are here!

Russalka (opera) Act I Miller's Aria — Hey, Hey, you young ones, Hey, you— pret- ty maid- ens, I'm on to all—

Act II Olga's Song — In our street it hap- pened that a hus- band asked his wife:

Act III Cavatina — Why am I drawn to these un- hap- py shores, What is their sec- ret?

All things here re- mind me of pleas- ures long o- - ver.

Wherefore? — So full— of grief, so waste— and worn? And none— who will help thee

The Worm — To my good wife I'm much in- debt- ed She taught me to be- come

DAVID, Félicien (1810-1876)

Lalla Roukh (opera) Romance de Noureddin — Ma mai- tresse a quit- té la— ten - - - te; Est elle al- lée

Couplets de Mirza — Si vous ne sa- vez plus— char- mer Ne vous en pre- nez—

La Perle du Bresil (opera) Couplets de Mysoli — Char- mant— oi- seau qui sous— l'om- bra- ge

DEBUSSY, Claude (1862-1918)

Cantatas
La Damoiselle Élue
By permission Durand & Cie, Paris; Elkan-Vogel Co., Inc., Phila., copyright owners
— La Da- moi- selle E- lue s'ap- puy- ait sur la bar- riè- re d'or du Ciel

87 DEBUSSY

DEBUSSY
88

Ariettes Oubliées
VI Aquarelles (Spleen)

Beau Soir
By permission Durand & Cie, Paris;
Elkan-Vogel Co., Inc., Phila.,
copyright owners

Lorsque au so-leil cou-chant les ri-viè-res sont ro-ses

La Belle au Bois Dormant

Des trous à son pour-point ver-meil, Un che-va-lier va_ par la

Chansons de Bilitis
I La Flûte de Pan
By permission Jean Jobert, Paris;
Elkan-Vogel Co., Inc., Phila.,
copyright owners

Pour le jour des Hy-a-cin-thies_ il m'a don-né u-ne sy-rinx

II La Chevelure

Il m'a dit: "Cet-te nuit, j'ai rê-vé J'a-vais ta che-ve-lure

III Le Tombeau des Naïades

Le long du bois cou-vert de gi-vre, je mar-chais;

Cinq Poëmes de Baudelaire
By permission Durand & Cie, Paris;
Elkan-Vogel Co., Inc., Phila.,
copyright owners
I Le Balcon

Mè-re des sou-ve-nirs maî-tres-se des maî-tres-ses

II Harmonie du Soir

Voi-ci ve-nir les temps où vi-brant sur sa ti-ge

III Le Jet d'Eau

Tes beaux yeux sont las_ Pauvre a-man-te!

IV Recueillement

Sois sa-ge Ô_ ma dou-leur, et tiens toi plus tran-quille

V La Mort des Amants

Nous au-rons des lits pleins d'o-deurs lé-gè-res, Des di-vans pro-fonds

Deux Romances (words by P. Bourget)
By permission Durand & Cie, Paris;
Elkan-Vogel Co., Inc., Phila.,
copyright owners
1. (a) Romance
   (b) Romance

L'âme é-va-po-rée et souf-fran-te L'âme dou-ce, l'âme a-do-ran-te

Voi-ci que le prin-temps, ce fils lé-ger d'A-vril

2. Les Cloches

Les feuil-les s'ou-vraient sur le bord des bran-ches Dé-li-ca-te-ment

Fêtes Galantes:
First Series
1. En Sourdine
By permission Jean Jobert, Paris;
Elkan-Vogel Co., Inc., Phila.,
copyright owners

Cal-mes dans le de-mi jour Que les bran-ches hau-tes font

2. Fantoches

Sca-ra-mouche et Pul-ci-nel-la Qu'un mau-vais des-sein ras-sem-bla

3. Clair de Lune

Votre âme est un pa-y-sa-ge choi-si Que vont char-mant mas-ques

Second Series
1. Les Ingénus
By permission Durand & Cie, Paris;
Elkan-Vogel Co., Inc., Phila.,
copyright owners

Les hauts ta-lons lut-taient a-vec les lon-gues ju-pes

2. Le Faune

Un vieux fau-ne de ter-re cui-te Rit au cen-tre des bou-lin-grins,

DEBUSSY

Fêtes Galantes:
Second Series
3. Colloque sentimental
Dans le vieux parc so- li- taire et gla- cé — A

Mandoline
By permission Durand & Cie, Paris; Elkan-Vogel Co., Inc., Phila., copyright owners
Les don-neurs de sé- re- na- des et les bel- les é- -couteu- ses — B

Noël des enfants qui n'ont plus de maisons
By permission Durand & Cie, Paris; Elkan-Vogel Co., Inc., Phila., copyright owners
Nous n'a-vous plus de mai-sons! Les en-ne-mis ont tout pris, — C

Nuit d'Étoiles
By permission Durand & Cie, Paris; Elkan-Vogel Co., Inc., Phila., copyright owners
Nuit d'é- toi- - -les, Sous— tes voi- - -les — D

Le Promenoir des deux amants
No. 1
By permission Durand & Cie, Paris; Elkan-Vogel Co., Inc., Phila., copyright owners
Au- près de cet-te grot- te som- bre Où l'on res-pire un air si doux, — E

No. 2
Crois mon con-seil, chè-re Cli- mè- ne, pour laisser ar- ri-ver le soir, — F

No. 3
Je trem- ble en voyant ton vi-sa- ge Flot- ter a-vec-que mes dé- sirs, — G

Proses Lyriques
No. 1 De Rêve
By permission Jean Jobert, Paris; Elkan-Vogel Co., Inc., Phila., copyright owners
La nuit a des dou-ceurs de fem- me Et les vieux ar-bres, — H

No. 2 De Grève
Sur la mer les cré-pus- cu-les tom-bent, Soie blanche ef-fi-lé- - e. — I

No. 3 De Fleurs
Dans L'ennui si dé-so- lé-ment vert de la ser- re de dou-leur — J

No. 4 De Soir
Di- man-che sur les vil- les, Di- man-che dans les cœurs! — K

Trois Ballades de François Villon:
No. 1 Ballade de Villon à s' amye
By permission Durand & Cie, Paris; Elkan-Vogel Co., Inc., Phila., copyright owners
Faul- se beau-té, qui tant me couste cher, Rude en effect, — L

No. 2 Ballade que Villon fait à la requeste de sa mère pour prier Nostre-Dame
Da- me du ciel, re-gen-te ter-ri- en-ne, Em-pe-riè- re des in-fer-naulx pa- lux — M

No. 3 Ballade des femmes de Paris
Quoy qu'on tient belles lan-ga- giè- res Flo-ren- ti-nes, Ve- ni-cien-nes, — N

Trois Chansons de France
No. 1 Rondel
By permission Durand & Cie, Paris; Elkan-Vogel Co., Inc., Phila., copyright owners
Le temps a lais- sié son man- teau De vent, de froiduré et de pluy- e, — O

No. 2 La Grotte
Au- près de cet- te grot- te som- bre Où l'on res-pire un air si doux, — P

No. 3 Rondel
Pour ce que Plai-sance est mor-te Ce may, suis ves- tu de noir; — Q

Trois Mélodies
No. 1
By permission J. Hamelle Music Publishers, Paris
La mer est plus bel- - le Que les ca- té- dra- les, — R

No. 2
Le son du cor s'af- fli- ge vers les bois D'une dou-leur — S

90

Trois Mélodies

No. 3 — L'é- che- lon- ne- ment des haies Mou- tonne à l'in- fi- ni, A

DEIS, Carl (1883-   )

Come down to Kew
Copyright 1916, G. Schirmer, Inc.

Go down to Kew in li- lac time, in li- lac time C

DELANNOY, Marcel (1898-   )

Le Galant Jardinier
By permission Heugel & Cie, Paris,
copyright owners

Je vais mon- ter sur la mon- ta- gne Là, j'é- lè- ve- rai un grand mur E

DELBRUCK, Alfred

Un Doux Lien
Copyright 1902, G. Schirmer, Inc.

Un doux li- en nous en- la- çait tous deux, Ton bras au mien G

DELIBES, Léo (1836-1891)

Arioso

Ô mer, ou- vre- toi, Lin- ceul du monde, mer pro- fon- de I

Bonjour, Suzon

Bon- jour, Su- zon, ma fleur des bois! Es- tu tou- jours la plus jo- li- e? J

Les Filles de Cadix (Bolero)

Nous venions de voir le tau- reau, Trois gar- çons trois fil- let - - - - - - - tes, K

Lakmé (opera)

Act I

A l'heure ac- cou- tu- mé- e Quand la plaine em- bau- mé- e L

Blan - - - - che Dour- ga, Pâ - - - - le Si- va M

Dô- me é- pais le jas- min A la ro- se s'as- sem - - - ble, N

Sous le dome é- pais où le blanc jas- min a la ro- se s'as- sem - - - ble, O

Quintet

Ah beaus fai- seurs de sys- te- mes, A- moureux du chan- ge- ment P

Leur ver- tu bi- zar- re man- que d'ap- par- at Q

Fan- tai- si- e aux div- ins men- son- ges Tu re- viens m'é- garer encore R

Pour- quoi dans les grands bois ai- mé- je a m'é- ga- rer pour y pleu- rer? S

Lakmé (opera)

Act I Duet — A — Ou-bli-er que je t'ai vu-e, Te re-dres-sant toute é-mu-e

B — C'est le Dieu de la jeu-nes-se, C'est le Dieu du prin-temps,

Act II — C — Lak-mé, ton doux re-gard se voi-le, Ton sou-ri-re s'est at-tris-té

Bell Song — D —

E — Où va - - la jeune In-dou-e Fil-le des Pa-ri-as,

F — Là-bas dans la fo - - -ret plus som-bre

G — Ah! Ah! Ah! Ah! Ah! Ah! Ah! Ah! Ah! Ah! Ah! Ah! Ah!

Duet — H — Dans la fo-rêt près de nous, Se ca-che tou-te pe-ti-te,

I — Ah! c'est l'amour en-dor-mi Qui de son ai - - le l'ef-fleu-re,

Act III — J — Sous le ciel tout é-toi-lé Le ra-mier blanc au loin s'en est al-lé

K — Ah! Viens, dans la fo-rêt pro-fon-de L'aile de l'amour a pas-sé

L — Tu m'as don-né le plus doux rê-ve Qu'on puisse a-voir sous notre ciel

M — Qu'au-tour de moi tout som-bre Je ne veux pas une om-bre

DELIUS, Frederick (1862-1934)

Appalachia (Variations on an old Slave Song) (chorus and orchestra)
By permission Boosey & Hawkes, Inc., copyright owners

O — Af-ter night has gone comes the day, the dark sha-dows will fade a-way

Cradle Song (Slumber Song)
By permission of Augener, Ltd., London

P — Das Kind-lein schlief ein Da schweb-te her-ein von En-geln

Hassan (closing chorus)
By permission Boosey & Hawkes, Inc., copyright owners

Q — We take the gold-en road to Sa-mar-kand

Indian Love Song
By permission Oxford Univ. Press, London, copyright owners

R — I a-rise from dreams of thee in the first sweet sleep of night,

Irmeline Rose
By permission Boosey & Hawkes, Inc., copyright owners

S — There was a king in days of old and a-mongst his man-y gems

Love's Philosophy
By permission Oxford Univ. Press, London, copyright owners

The foun-tains min-gle with the riv- er, and the riv-ers with the O-cean   **A**

The Nightingale
By permission of Augener, Ltd., London

Sing, sing, Nach-ti-gall Du, sing mir ein Lied-lein le- ben- dig   **B**

To the Queen of My Heart
By permission Oxford Univ. Press, London, copyright owners

Shall we roam, my love, To the twi - - light grove, When the moon is ris-ing   **C**

DEL LEUTO, Arcangelo (16th Cent.)

Dimmi, amor

Dim-mi a - mor, dim - - mi che fa la mia ca - -ra li-ber - - - tà?   **E**

DENZA, Luigi (1846-1922)

Funiculi, Funicula
Copyright by G. Ricordi & Co., Inc.

Some think___ the world is made for fun and frol-ic___ and so do I   **G**

Hark- en! Hark- en Mu- sic sounds a- far ___   **H**

A May Morning

Si vous l'aviez compris
Copyright by G. Ricordi & Co., Inc.

Rien qu'au re- voir___ mur-mu- ré tout bas, En me___ ser-rant   **J**

Pour- quoi ___ n'a- vez vous pas sur- pris mon se- cret   **K**

DIAZ, Eugéne (1837-1901)

Arioso, from Benvenuto Cellini (opera)

De l'art___ splen-deur im-mor- tel-le Ray- ons___ à peine en-tre-vus___   **M**

DIBDIN, Charles (1745-1814)

Tom Bowling

Here a sheer hulk, lies poor Tom___ Bowl-ing, the dar-ling of our___ crew,___   **O**

DOBSON, Tom (1890-1918)

Cargoes
Copyright 1920, G. Schirmer, Inc.

Quin- qui-reme of Nin- e-veh___ from dis- tant O- phir___   **Q**

DOHNÁNYI, Ernest Von (1877-)

Hungarian Folk Songs: Azok, Azok

Rain I thought it was that ran down drop by drop   **S**

Hungarian Folk Songs:
Szérettelek álnok lélek

Love I gave you, troth I gave you, Cru-el faith-less maid!   A

Valaki jár udvaromon

Some one I hear prowl-ing a-round knock-ing to come in.   B

DONATO, Baldassare (16th Cent.)

Chi la gagliarda (madrigal)

Chi la Gagliar-da chi la Gagliar-da Don-ne vo impa-ra-re   D

DONAUDY, Stefano (1879-)

Ah, mai non cessate
Copyright by G. Ricordi & Co., Inc.

Ah, mai non ces-sa-te dal vo---stro par-lar,   F

Amorosi miei giorni
Copyright by G. Ricordi & Co., Inc.

A-mo-ro-si miei gior-ni, chi vi po-trà mai più scor-dar,   G

Cuor mio, cuor mio non vedi
Copyright by G. Ricordi & Co., Inc.

Cuor mio, cuor mio non ve-di che, quan-do a-mor ti co-glie,   H

Freschi luoghi, prati aulenti
Copyright by G. Ricordi & Co., Inc.

Fre-schi luo-ghi,_ pra-ti au-len-ti, ri-ma-ne--te sem-pre in fior;   I

Luoghi sereni e cari
Copyright by G. Ricordi & Co., Inc.

Luo-ghi se-re-ni e ca-ri, Io vi ri-tro---vo   J

O bei nidi d'amore
Copyright by G. Ricordi & Co., Inc.

O bei ni-di d'a-mo-re, oc-chi a mi si ca-ri,   K

O del mio amato ben
Copyright by G. Ricordi & Co., Inc.

O del mio a-ma-to ben per-du-to in-can---to!   L

Quando ti rivedrò
Copyright by G. Ricordi & Co., Inc.

Quan-do ti ri-ve-dro, in-fi-da-a-man-te che mi fo-sti si ca-ra?   M

Se tra l'erba
Copyright by G. Ricordi & Co., Inc.

Se tra l'er-ba un ris no-vel-lo bal-za e cor-re ver-so il ma-re,   N

Spirate pur, spirate
Copyright by G. Ricordi & Co., Inc.

Spi-ra-te pur,_ spi-ra-te___ at--tor-no a lo--mio be-ne,   O

Vagliessima sembianza
Copyright by G. Ricordi & Co., Inc.

Va-ghis-si-ma sem-bian-za d'an-ti-ca don-na a-ma----ta,   P

DONIZETTI, Gaetano (1797-1848)

Don Pasquale (opera)
Act I

Bel-la sic-co-me un an-gelo in ter-ra pel-le gri-no,—   R

Ah,___ un fo-co in so-li-to mi sen-to ad-dos-so, o-mai re-sis-sti-re   S

DONIZETTI

94

Don Pasquale (opera)
Act I
So-gno so- a-ve e ca-sto de miei prim' an- ni, ad- di- - - o A

Quel guar-do il ca- va- lie-re in mez-zo al cor tra-fis- - - - - - se B

So anch' io la vir- tù ma- gi-ca d'un guar-do a tem-po e lo-co C

Pron- ta io son pur ch'io non man-chi all' a- mor D

Va- - - - do co- - - - - ro, sì va- do co- - - ro E

Act II
Cer- che-rò lon-ta- na terra, do-ve ge- mer sco- no- sciu-to, F

E se fia- che ad al- tro og-get- to tu ri- vol-ga G

Act III
Via ca- ro spo-si- - no non far-mi il ti- ran- - -no, H

(chorus)
Che in- ter- mi- na- bi- le an- di- ri vie-ni, I

(serenade)
Com' è gen- til la not-te a mez-zo a- pril, J

Tor- na mi a dir, che m'a- mi, dim- -mi, che mio tu se- - i, K

Rondo-finale
Bra- vo, bra-vo, Don Pas-qua-le, la mo-ra-le mol- to bel-la. L

La mo- ra- le e mol-to bel-la, bel-la, bel- la, bel- la, bel-la, M

Deserto in terra, from Don Sebastiano
(opera) Act II
De- ser-to in ter- ra che più m'a van-za! N

L'Elisir d'Amore (opera)
Act I
Quan- to è bel-la! quan-to e ca- ra! più la ve- -do e più mi_ pia-ce, O

Più tem- po, oh Dio non per-de-re, vo-la-no i gior-ni e l'o-re, P

U- di- te! u- di-te! o ru-sti- ci; at-ten-ti, non fia-ta- te! Q

Co- sì chia-ro e co-me il so- le che a cia-scu- no che, lo vuo- le, R

Ob- bli- ga- to, ah! sì ob-bli-ga-to! son fe- li-ce, son con- ten-to, S

DONIZETTI

L'Elisir d'Amore (opera)

Act I — A — A-di-na, cre-di-mi, te ne scon-giu-ro

B — Co-me Pa-ri-de vez-zo-so por-se il po-mo al-la più bel-la!

Act II — C — Io son ric-co e tu sei bel-la, io du-ca-ti e vez-zi hai tu

D — Ven-ti scu-di! E ben so-nan-ti. Quan-do? A-des-so?

E — U-na fur-ti-va la-gri-ma negl' occhi suoi spun-tò

F — Pren-di, pren-di, per me sei li-be-ro

La Favorita (opera)

Act I — G — U-na ver-gi-ne, un an-giol d'a-mo-re al Si-gno-re

H — An-giol ca-ro, so-a-ve, be-a-to, deh tu ve-glia

I — Bei rag-gi lu-cen-ti, bell' au-re be-a-te,

J — Ah! mio be-ne mio te-so-ro, il Cie-lo t'in-vi-a, vie-ni a vien

K — Fia ve-ro? la-sciar-ti! e tu il chie-di a me?

Act II — L — Vien, Leo-no-ra, a pie-di tuo-i, ser-to e so-glio il cor,

M — De' ne-mi-ci tuoi lo sde-gno di-sfi-dar sa-prò per te,

N — Quan-do le so-glie pa-ter-ne var-ca-i de-bil fan-ciul-la

O — In que-sto suo-lo a se-re-nar tuo cu-ra

Act III — P — A tan-to a-mor Leo-no-ra il tuo ri-spon-da

Q — O mio Fer-nan-do, del-la ter-ra il tro-no

R — Scrit-to è in ciel il mio do-lor, su, ve-ni-te ell'è u-na fe-sta,

Act IV — S — Splen-don più bel-le in ciel le stel-le, ma lut-to or-ren-do

DONIZETTI

La Favorita (opera)
Act IV

Preghiera

La Fille du Regiment (The Daughter of the Regiment) (opera) Act I

Act II

Linda di Chamounix (opera)
Act I

Love duet

Prayer

Spir- to gen-til, ne' so-gni mie— i bril las-ti un dì, ma ti per-dei

Pie- to— so al par del Nu- mi, pie- to— so_ su per me

Vie-ni_ah vien,_ io m'ab-ban- do— no_ al- la gio— ja_ che m'innebria

Au bruit de la guer- re j'ai re- çu le jour_

Cha- cun le sait, cha-cun le dit le re- gi-ment_ par ex- cel- len-ce

Il est là, il est là, il est là, mor- bleu,

De-puis l'in-stant où dans mes bras je vous re- çus_tou-te trem-blan- te

De cet a- veu si ten- dre non_ mon coeur en ce jour

Il faut par-tir_ mes bons com-pag- nons d'ar-mes

Par le rang et_ par l'o- pu- len-ce en vain l'on a cru m'é-blou-ir

Sa— lut à la Fran- ce à mes_ beaux_ jours_

Tous les trois ré- u- nis,quel plai-sir, mes a-mis,quel bon-heur,quel bon-heur,

Pour me rap- pro-cher_ de Ma- ri- e, je m'en-rô- lai pau- vre sol- dat

Am- bo na- ti in que— sta_ val- le

O lu- ce di quest' a— ni- ma de- li-zia a-mo-re e vi— ta

Per sua ma-dre an-dò una fi- glia mi-glior sor-te_a rin-trac- ciar;

Da quel dì, che t'in- con-tra- i ad a- mar_ quel dì_im-pa- ra- i

A con- so-lar mi_af-fre-ti- si tal gior-no de- si-a- to

O tu che re- go-li gli u-ma- ni_e-ven — — — ti,

Linda di Chamounix (opera)
Act II

Se tan-to in i-ra a-gli uo-mi-ni è___ l'a-mor no-stro,   A

Mad scene (duet)

No non è ver, men-ti-ro-nò tra-dir___ tu non mi puo___   B

Act III

Di tue pe-ne spar-ve il so-gno al-le gio-je a-mor ti___ de-sta   C

Lucia di Lammermoor (opera)
Act I

Cru-da, fu-ne-sta sma-nia___ tu m'hai sve-glia-to in pet - - to   D

Huntsmen's Chorus

Co-me vin-ti da_stan-chez-za, do-pa lun-go er-ra-re in-tor-no   E

La pie-ta - de in suo fa-vo-re Mi-ti sen-si in-van mi det - ta   F

Re-gna-va nel_si-len-zio al-ta la not-te e bru - - na   G

Quan-do ra-pi-to in e-sta-si del più co-cen-te ar-do-re   H

Sul-la tom-ba che rin-ser-ra il tra-di-to ge-ni-to-re,   I

Ver-ran-no a te sul l'a-u-re i miei so-spi-ri ar-den - - ti,   J

Act II

Sof-fri - - va nel pian-to, lan-gui - - a nel_do-lo-re,   K

Se tra-dir-mi tu po-tra-i la mia_sor-te e già com-pi-ta;   L

Per te d'im-men-so giu-bi-lo tut-to s'av-vi va in-tor - no   M

Sextet

Chi mi fre-na in tal mo-men-to? Chi tron-cò del-l'i-re il cor - so   N

E - - - sci,___ fug - - gi il fu-ror___ che m'ac-cen-de   O

Act III

Qui del pa-dre an-cor___ re-spi-ra l'om-bra i-nul-ta e par che fre - - - ma   P

O so-le più rat-to a sor - ger t'ap-pre-sta,   Q

Dal-le stan-ze, o-ve Lu-ci-a trat-ta a vea col suo con-sor-te   R

Oh qual fu-ne-sto av - - ve - ni - men - to!   S

Lucia di Lammermoor (opera)
Act III (Mad Scene)

Al- fin__ son tu- - - -a al- fin__ sei mi- - - - o,

Spar- gi d'a- ma- ro pian- to il mio ter- re-stre ve- - - - lo,

Fra po- co a me ri- co- ve- rò da- rà ne- glet-to a ve- - lo__

Tu che a Dio spie- ga- sti l'a- li o bel- l'al-ma in-na-mo- ra- ta,

Lucrezia Borgia (opera)
Prologue

Com' è bel- lo qua-le in-can- to In quel vol- to o- nesto e al- te- ro,

Di pe- sca-to- re i- gno- bi- le Es-ser figliuol cre- de- - - - i

Act I

Vie- ni! la mia ven- det- - - -ta È me-di-ta-ta e pron- ta

Act II

Il se- gre- to per es- ser fe- li- - - - - - ci

M'o- di, oh! m'o- di, Io non t'im- plo- ro Per vo- ler__

Fra l'erbe, from La Zingara (opera)

Fan- ciul- la sui grep-pi le ca-pre e-mu- la- - - - - - - - - - i

Un gior- - - no la ma- - - no mi por- - - se un don- zel- lo

DOURLEN, Victor Charles (1780-1864)

Je sais attacher des rubans,
from Le Frère Philippe (opera)

Je sais at- tach- er des ru- bans, Je sais com-ment viennent

DOWLAND, John (1563-1626)

First Book of Ayres:
Awake, sweet love

A- wake, sweet love, thou art re- turned. My heart, which long

Come again! Sweet love

Come a- gain! Sweet love doth now in-vite Thy grac- es, that re-frain

Come, heavy sleep

Come, hea- vy Sleep the im- age of true Death

Go, crystal tears

Go, crys- tal tears, like to the__ morn- ing showers,

Second Book of Ayres:
Fine knacks for ladies

Fine knacks for la- dies cheap, choice, brave and new! Good pen- ny worths!

Second Book of Ayres:
Flow, my tears

A — Flow, my tears, fall from your springs. Ex-iled for-ev-er let me mourn

Now cease, my wandering eyes

B — Now cease, my wan-d'ring eyes, strange beau-ties to ad-mire,

Shall I sue?

C — Shall I sue? Shall I seek for grace? Shall I pray? Shall I prove?

Now, o now I needs must part

D — Now, o now I needs must part, Part-ing though I ab-sent mourn

Say love, if thou didst ever find

E — Say love, if ev-er thou didst find a wo-man with a con-stant mind

Weep you no more, sad fountains

F — Weep you no more, sad foun-tains, What need you flow so fast

DUFAY, Guillaume (1400-1474)

Adieu m'amour

H — A-----dieu m'a--mour, a-----dieu ma joy-----e

Alma redemptoris mater

I — Al-------------------------------ma

Ave, maris Stella

J — A--ve,--------Ma---------ria Stel----la--------

Bon Jour, bon Mois

K — Bon jour, bon mois, bon an et bonne es-trai----ne

Flos Florum

L — Flos-------------------------flo-----rum,

Le Jour s'endort

M — Le jour s'en-dort, aus----si fait la sai-son

Kyrie, from Mass (4 voices) "Se la face ay pale"

N — Ky-ri-e e-ley-son, Ky-ri-e-----e-ley----son

Vergine bella

O — Ver-gi-ne bel-la, che di sol ves-ti-------------ta

DUKAS, Paul (1865-1935)

Ah! ce n'est pas encore, from Ariane et Barbe-Bleue Act II
By permission Durand & Cie, Paris; Elkan-Vogel Co., Inc., Phila., copyright owners

Q — Ah! ce n'est pas en-co-re la clar-té vé-ri-ta-ble

DUNHILL, Thomas (1877-)

The Cloths of Heaven, Op. 30, No. 3
Copyright Stainer & Bell, Ltd., London; Galaxy Music Corporation, N. Y., sole U. S. Agents

S — Had I the heaven's em-broid-ered cloths, En-wrought with gol-den

To the Queen of Heaven
Copyright 1926, T. F. Dunhill

Queen of heav-en, bless'd may thou be, for God- ës Son born

DUNSTABLE, John (15th Cent.)

Quam pulchra es

Quam___ pul - - chra és, et quam de-cor-ra, ca-ris-si-ma,

DUPARC, Henri (1848-1933)

Au pays où se fait la guerre
Copyright by Salabert, Paris, N. Y.

Au pa- ys où se fait la guer - - - - re mon bel a- mi

Chanson Triste
Copyright by Salabert, Paris, N. Y.

Dans ton coeur dort un clair de lu- ne, un doux clair de lu- ne

Élégie
Copyright by Salabert, Paris, N. Y.

Oh! ne mur-mu- rez pas___ son nom! qu'il dor-me dans l'om-bre,

Extase
Copyright by Salabert, Paris, N. Y.

Sur un lys pâ- le mon coeur dort D'un som-meil doux comme la mort___

L'Invitation au Voyage
Copyright by Salabert, Paris, N. Y.

Mon en- fant,___ ma sœur Songe___ a la dou-ceur D'al-ler là- bas

Lamento
Copyright by Salabert, Paris, N. Y.

Con- nais-sez vous la blan-che tom- bé Où flotte a-vec un son plain- tif

Le Manoir de Rosamunde
Copyright by Salabert, Paris, N. Y.

De sa dent soudaine ___ et vo- ra- ce Comme un chien l'amour___

Phidylé
Copyright by Salabert, Paris, N. Y.

L'herbe est molle___ au sommeil___ sous les frais peupliers,___

Re- po- se ___ ô Phidy- lé

Sérénade Florentine
Copyright by Salabert, Paris, N. Y.

É- toi- le dont la beau- té luit___ comme un di- a- mant dans la nuit,

Soupir
Copyright by Salabert, Paris, N. Y.

Ne ja-mais la voir ni l'en-ten- dre, Ne ja-mais tout haut la nom- mer,

Testament
Copyright by Salabert, Paris, N. Y.

Pour que le vent te les ap- por- te Sur l'ai-le noi-re d'un re-mord,___

La Vague et la Cloche
Copyright by Salabert, Paris, N. Y.

U- ne fois, ter-ras-sé par un puis- sant___ breu- va- ge J'ai rê-vé___

La Vie Antérieure
Copyright by Salabert, Paris, N. Y.

J'ai long- temps ha-bi- té sous de vas- tes por-ti- ques

DUPONT, Gabriel (1878-1914)

Mandoline
Copyright 1946, G. Schirmer, Inc.

Les don-neurs de sé- ré- na- des Et les bel- les é- cou-teu-ses

DURANTE, Francesco (1684-1755)

Danza, danza, fanciulla gentile

Dan- za,__ dan-za, fan- ciul- la,__ al__ mi- o can- tar,

Vergin, tutta amor

Ver- gin, tut-ta a-mor,__ O Ma-dre di bon- ta-de, O Ma-dre pi- a,

DVOŘÁK, Antonin (1841-1904)

The Devil and Kate, Op. 112 (opera)
Act III The Countess's Aria

Wie trau-rig rings-um öd' die Hal- len, wo-rin einst Freu- de

Dimitrij Op. 64 (opera)
Act II Dimitrij's Aria

Zdi- voké- ho ži- tí vi- ru du-še mo-je stou-hou spě- la

Act III Dimitrij's Aria

Vi- děl jsem je Xe-ni- i jsem zrel, my- slí ti-chým blahem o- po-je nou

Rusalka (opera)
Act I O lovely moon (Rusalka's Song)

Glei-ten- der Mond du, so sil-ber-zart,__ Sendest weit-hin deine Blik-ke__

Act I A strange vision (Prince's Air)

Weiss, dass ein Trug-bild du, dass wohl schwindet, wie vor der Nacht

Act II

Was im saal, in je- dem Stüb-chen heut' im Schloss für Mord- ru - - mor?

Act II Alas, alas

Hast du dir als Theil er-ko-ren,__ Im-mer wird dir Lust, nim-mer Lust und Schmerz__

Act II White flowers along the way

Blü- me-lein weiss am Wie-ges-rand, blüh-ten wohl still be- schei-den,

Act III I have golden hair

Mein, mein gold' nes Haar ist mein, mein, mein gold' nes Haar ist mein

The Sly Peasant, Op. 37 (opera)
Act I Prince's Song

Wer kann's mit Wor- ten sa- gen auch, was drinn im Her- zen

Biblical Songs, Op. 99 (duets)
No. 1 Clouds and darkness are round about
By permission Associated Music Publishers, Inc.

Clouds and dark-ness are round a-bout Him Right-eous-ness and judgment

No. 2 Lord, thou art my refuge

Lord, thou art my re-fuge and my shield, and in thy word put I my trust

No. 3 Hear my prayer, O Lord

Hear my__ prayer, O Lord, my__ God O hide__ not thy face

Biblical Songs:
No. 4 God is my Shepherd — God is my shep - - - herd, I want for no - thing. **A**

No. 5 I will sing Jehovah's praises — I will sing new songs of glad-ness, I will sing Je-ho-vah's prai-ses **B**

No. 6 Hear my prayer, O Lord — Hear my prayer O Lord ___ give ear un - to my ___ cry! **C**

No. 7 By the Waters of Babylon — By the wa-ters of Ba-by-lon, ___ there we sat us down ___ and wept **D**

No. 8 Turn Thee to Me — Turn Thee to me and have ___ mer - cy for I am de - so - late **E**

No. 9 I will lift mine eyes up to the mountains — I will lift mine eyes up to the moun - tains, **F**

No. 10 Sing ye a joyful song — Sing ye a joy - ful song un - to the Lord ___ **G**

Goin' Home, from New World Symphony, Op. 95, Largo (arr. William Arms Fisher)
Copyright 1922, Oliver Ditson Co. Used by permission. — Go - in' home, go - in' home, I'm a - go - in' home **H**

Gypsy Songs, Op. 55
No. 1 Mein Lied ertönt — Mein Lied er-tönt, ein Lie - bespsalm, be - ginnt der ___ Tag zu ___ sin - ken, **I**

No. 2 Ei, wie mein Triangel — Ei, wie mein Tri - an - gel wun - der - herr - lich läu - tet! **J**

No. 3 Rings is der Wald so stumm — Rings ist der Wald so stumm und still, das Herz schlägt mir so ban - - ge, **K**

No. 4 Als die alte Mutter (Songs my mother taught me) — Als die al - te ___ Mut - - - ter mich noch lehr-te ___ sin - - - gen, **L**

No. 5 Rein gestimmt die Saiten! — Rein ge - stimmt die Sai - ten! Bur - sche, tanz' im Krei - se! **M**

No. 6 In dem weiten, breiten (Freer is the gypsy) — In dem wei - ten, ___ brei - ten, ___ luft' gen Lei - nen - klei - de ___ **N**

No. 7 Darf des Falken Schwinge Tatra (Cloudy heights of Tatra) — Darf des Fal - ken Schwin-ge Tat - ra - höh'n um - rau - - - schen **O**

Lasst mich allein (Leave me alone) Op. 82, No. 1 — Lasst mich al - lein in mei - nen Träu-men geh'n, stört mir die Wol-lust nicht **P**

The Mower, Op. 73, No. 2 — Nah bei ___ Te - mes - var, dem Städt-chen mah - te ___ Gras ein her - zig Mäd-chen **Q**

Thirteen Moravian Duets, Op. 31, No. 1 The Fugitive — Where blue the Danube flows, far will I fly from thee Where blue the Danube flows **R**

No. 2 Speed thee, Birdie — Speed thee, bir - die, fly a - cross the pur - ple moun-tain **S**

Moravian Duets
No. 3 The Slighted Heart

Oh that now I held the scythe well sharpen'd, and the grass were wav-ing high   A

No. 4 Parting without sorrow

Gai- ly as I met thee, let us part to- mor- row, fear not that I e'er forget thee   B

No. 5 The pledge of love

Dost thou see the stars shi-ning yon-der? Thus are we and joy a-sun - - der   C

No. 6 Forsaken

Lo, the dove from her cot hath flown, sits on the al-der and makes her moan,   D

No. 7 Sad of heart

By the for-est sha-dy flows a brooklet clear, thither lead my steed, thou damsel young   E

No. 8 The modest maid

Swee- ter than the vio-let is my gen-tle mai- den, with the_ ro-se's dawning_blushes   F

No. 9 The Ring

Let us sing to day joy- ous roun- de- lay! Let us sing to- day   G

No. 10 Omens

Thrive and grow, thou come-ly grass, thrive on the sun-ny_ mea- dows!   H

No. 11 The Maid imprisoned

Mai- den journeys forth a- mow- ing, by the vineyard stands and pon-ders.   I

No. 12 Comfort

Thou fo- rest dear, fare- well, ah, who will tend thee now?   J

No. 13 The Wild Rose

Forth went a come- ly lass mov-ing the Au- tumn grass;   K

EAST, Michael (17th Cent.)

How Merrily We Live

How mer- ri- ly we live that shep- herds be, we live   M

EDWARDS, Clara (Contemporary)

By the Bend of the River
Copyright 1927, G. Schirmer, Inc.

The gold- en moon- light,_ the gloam, My thoughts re- turn-ing   O

By the bend of the riv- er_____ Where rush- es are grow- ing   P

Into the Night
Copyright 1939, G. Schirmer, Inc.

Si- lent- ly in- to the night I go, In- to the fra-grant night,   Q

EDWARDS, Richard (c.1523-1566)

In going to my naked bed

In go- ing to my nak- ed bed as one that would have slept   S

ELGAR, Sir Edward (1857-1934)

As torrents in summer, from King Olaf, Op. 30
By permission Novello & Co., Ltd., London

As tor-rents in sum-mer, Half dried in their chan-nels___ **B**

The Dream of Gerontius
By permission Novello & Co., Ltd., London

Sanc-tus for-tis, Sanc-tus De-us De pro-fun-dis o-ro te **C**

Praise to the ho-li-est in the height, and__ in the depth be praise; **D**

O lov-ing wis-dom of our God___ When all was sin and shame, **E**

Soft - - - - ly and__ gen-tly___ dear-ly ran-somed soul___ **F**

Lament, from Caractacus, Op. 35
By permission Novello & Co., Ltd., London

O my war-ri-ors, tell me tru-ly___ O'er the red groves where ye lie, **G**

The Light of Life, Op. 29 (oratorio)
By permission Novello & Co., Ltd., London

Be not ex-treme, O Lord,___ to mark_a-miss those se-cret sins **H**

As a spi-rit didst thou pass be-fore mine eyes, I saw thee not, **I**

Thou on-ly hast the words__ of life!___ Be__ pro-phet to my heart, **J**

I am the good Shep-herd, and know my sheep, and am known by them **K**

The Pipes of Pan
By permission Boosey & Hawkes, Inc.,
copyright owners

When the woods are gay___ in the time__ of June with the chest-nut flow'r and fan, **L**

Pleading, Op. 48, No. 1
By permission Novello & Co., Ltd., London

Will you come home-ward from the hills of Dream-land, Home in the dusk, **M**

Sea-Pictures, Op. 37
No. 1 Sea Slumber Song
By permission Boosey & Hawkes, Inc.,
copyright owners

Sea-birds are a-sleep,___ The world for-gets to weep___ **N**

No. 2 In Haven

Close-ly let me hold thy hand,__ Storms are sweep-ing sea and land; **O**

No. 3 Sabbath Morning at Sea

The ship went on with so-lemn face:___ To meet the dark-ness on the deep, **P**

No. 4 Where Corals Lie

The deeps have mu-sic soft and low___ When winds a-wake the air-y spry, **Q**

No. 5 The Swimmer

With short, sharp, vi-o-lent lights made vi-vid, To south-ward **R**

Coronation Ode, Op. 44, No. 6 (Trio of Pomp and Circumstance, No. 1)
By permission Boosey & Hawkes, Inc., copyright owners

Land of hope and glory Moth - - er of the free,

The Sun goeth down, from The Kingdom, Op. 51, No. 4 (oratorio)
By permission Novello & Co., Ltd., London

The sun go-eth down; Thou mak-est dark-ness, and it is night:

ERLEBACH, Philipp Heinrich (1657-1714)

Ihr Gedanken

Ihr Ge-dan-ken, Ihr Ge-dan-ken, quält mich nicht!

Nur getrost

Nur ge-trost nur ge-trost, lass al-les ge-hen,

Schwaches Hertz

Schwa-ches Hertz, du bist be-sie-get, du bist be-sie-get,

EULENBURG, Philipp zu (1847-1921)

Rosenlieder (song cycle)
No. 1 Monatsrose

Aus des Nach-bars Haus trat mein Lieb hin-aus, hielt ein Rös-lein in der Hand

No. 2 Wilde Rose

Bei dem Wal-des-saum im Wie-sen-hang stand am Ro-sen-strauch

No. 3 Rankende Rose

Sagt, ihr weis-sen Rank-rö-se-lein, Was treibt ihr am Hau-se des Lieb-chens mein?

No. 4 Seerose

Der a-bend ist still und dun-kel der See, im Schil-fe leuch-ten

No. 5 Weisse und rothe Rose

Mein Schatz der liegt auf der Tod-ten-bahr, hat weis-se Ro-sen

FALCONIERI, Andrea (c. 1600-1650)

Bella porta di rubini

Bel-la por-ta di ru-bi-ni ch'a-pri il var-co ai dol-ci ac-cen-ti,

Non più d'amore (villanella)

Non più d'a-mo-re, Non più d'ar-do-re, Pe-ne e tor-men-ti,

O Bellissimi capelli

O bel-lis-si-ma ca-pel-li, miei dol-cis-si-mi di-let-ti,

Occhietti amati

Oc-chietti a-ma-ti che m'in-cen-de-te per-chè spie-ta-ti o-mai più sie-te

Segui, segui dolente core

Se-gui, se-gui, do-len-te co-re, gli cc-chi fon-ti del vi-vo ar-do-re;

Vezzosette e care

Vez-zo-set-te e ca-re pu-pi-let-te ar-den-ti, chi v'ha fat-to a-va-re

FALLA, Manuel De (1876-1946)

El Amor Brujo (ballet)
Canción del amor dolido
By permission J. & W. Chester, Ltd., London,
copyright owners

Yo no sé — qué sien-to, ni sé qué me pa-sa,

Canción del fuego fatuo

Lo mis-mo que es fue-go fa-tuo, lo mis-mi-to es er-que-ré.

Danza del juego de amor

Tú e-res a-quel mal gi-ta-no

Quien lo ha-bi-a de de-ci que con o-tra la ven-di-as!

Las Campanas del Amanecer

Ya es-ta des pun-tan-do el dí-a! Can-tad, cam-pa-nos, can-tad,

Les Colombes
Copyright by Salabert, Paris, N. Y.

Sur le co-teau, là-bas où sont les tom-bes

Seguidilla
Copyright by E. B. Marks Music Corp., N. Y.

Un ju-pon ser-ré sur les han-ches Un pegne é-norme à son chi-gnon

Seven Popular Spanish Songs
No. 1 El paño moruno
By permission Associated Music
Publishers, Inc.

Al pa-ño fi-no en la tien-da, Al pa-ño fi-no en la tien-da,

No. 2 Seguidilla Murciana

Cualquie-ra que el te-ja-do ten-ga de vi-drio.

No. 3 Asturiana

Por ver si me con-so-la-ba, A-rri-me-me à un pi-no ver-de

No. 4 Jota

Di-cen que no nos que-re-mos

No. 5 Nana (Berceuse)

Duér-me-te, ni-ño, duer-me, Duer-me, mi al-ma,

No. 6 Canción

Por trai-do-res, tus o-jos, Voy á en-te-rrar los;

No. 7 Polo

Guar-do u-na — "A — y!" Guar-do u-na "A — y!"

Soneto a Córdoba
By permission Oxford Univ. Press, London,
copyright owners

Oh ex-cel-so mu-ro, oh to-rres co-ro-na-das De ho-nor

Tus Ojillos Negros

Yo no sé qué tie-nen tus o-ji-llos ne-gros

Mas, por o-tra par-te, son tan em-bus-te-ros

La Vida Breve
By permission Associated Music
Publishers, Inc.

Vi-van los que ri-en! Mue-ran los que llo-ran!

FARMER, John (c. 1565-c. 1600)

Fair Phyllis I saw sitting all alone

FARNABY, Giles (c. 1560-c. 1600)

Simkin said that Sis was fair

Some time she would

FAURÉ, Gabriel (1845-1924)

Dans les ruines d'une abbaye, Op. 2, No. 1
By permission J. Hamelle, Paris

Seule! Op. 3, No. 1
By permission J. Hamelle, Paris

Sérénade Toscane, No. 2

Chanson du Pêcheur, Op. 4, No. 1
By permission J. Hamelle, Paris

Lydia, No. 2

Chant d'Automne, Op. 5, No. 1
By permission J. Hamelle, Paris

L'Absent, No. 3

Tristesse, Op. 6, No. 2
By permission J. Hamelle, Paris

Sylvie, No. 3

Après un rêve, Op. 7, No. 1
By permission J. Hamelle, Paris

Barcarolle, No. 3

Au bord de l'eau, Op. 8, No. 1
By permission J. Hamelle, Paris

La Rançon, No. 2

Ici-Bas! Op. 8, No. 3 — A

I- ci-bas! tous les li-las meu-rent, Tous les chants des oi-seaux sont courts

Nell, Op. 18, No. 1
By permission J. Hamelle, Paris — B

Ta ro-se de pour-pre a ton clair so-leil O juin, é-tin-celle en-i- vré- e,

Le Voyageur, No. 2 — C

Voy- a- geur, où vas tu, mar- chant dans l'or vi- brant

Automne, No. 3 — D

Au- tom- - - ne au ciel bru-meux aux ho- ri-zons na-vrants,____

**Poèmes d'un Jour Op. 21
No. 1 Rencontre**
By permission J. Hamelle, Paris — E

J'é-tais triste et pen- sif quand je t'ai ren-con-tré- - - e,

No. 2 Toujours — F

Vous me de-man-dez de me tai- re, De fuir loin de vous pour ja-mais,

No. 3 Adieu — G

Com- me tout meurt vi- te, la ro- se dé- clo- se,

Les Berceaux, Op. 23, No. 1
By permission J. Hamelle, Paris — H

Le long du Quai__ les grands_vaisseaux, Que la houle in-cli-ne en si-len-ce__

Notre Amour, No. 2 — I

Notre a-mour est cho-se lé-gè- re, Com-me les par-fums que le vent prend aux

Le Secret, No. 3 — J

Je veux que le ma-tin l'i-gno-re Le nom que j'ai dit à la nuit,

La Fée aux Chansons, Op. 27, No. 2
By permission J. Hamelle, Paris — K

Il é-tait u- ne Fé- e D'her- be fol- le coif- fé- e,

Aurore, Op. 39, No. 1
By permission J. Hamelle, Paris — L

Des jar-dins de la nuit s'en-vo-lent les é- toi- - les__

Fleur jetée, No. 2 — M

Em- por- te ma fo- li- e au gré du vent Fleur en chan-tant cueil-li- e

Les Roses d'Ispahan, No. 4 — N

Les ro- ses d'Is- pa- han dans leur gaî- ne de mous- se,

Noël, Op. 43, No. 1
By permission J. Hamelle, Paris — O

La nuit de-scend du haut des cieux, le givre au toit suspend ses fran- ges

Nocturne, No. 2 — P

La nuit, sur le grand mys- tè- re, entr'-ou-vre ses é- crins bleus:

**Clair de Lune, Op. 46, No. 2
(Menuet)** — 1 — Q

Vo- tre â-me est un pa- y- sa-ge choi-si qui vont char-mant mas-ques

2 — Accomp. theme — R

**Requiem, Op. 48
I Kyrie**
By permission J. Hamelle, Paris — S

Ky- ri- e, Ky- ri- e, Ky- ri- e e- le- i- son Ky- ri-e e- le- i-son

La Bonne Chanson, Op. 61

No. 3 — La lu-ne blan-che luit dans les bois___ de cha-que bran-che___ A

No. 4 — J'al-lais___ par des che-mins per-fi- des___ B

No. 5 — J'ai presque peur,___ en ve-ri- té, Tant je sens ma vie en-la-cé- e C

No. 6 — A- vant que tu ne t'en ail-les pâle é-toi-le du ma-tin___ D

No. 7 — Donc, ce se-ra par un clair jour d'é- té,___ E

No. 8 — N'est-ce pas? nous i-rons, gais et lents,___ dans la voie mo-des- te F

No. 9 — L'hi- ver___ a ces- sé, la lu-miè - -re est tiè-de,___ G

La Parfum Impérissable, Op. 76, No. 1
By permission J. Hamelle, Paris

Quand la fleur___ du so-leil, la ro- se de La-hor,___ H

Arpège No. 2

L'â- me d'u-ne flû-te sou-pi- re Au fond du parc I

Prison Op. 83, No. 1
By permission J. Hamelle, Paris

Le ciel est, par dessus le toit si bleu, si cal- me, J

Soir No. 2

Voi-ci que les jar-dins de la nuit vont fleu- rir. K

Dans la Forêt de Septembre, Op. 85, No. 1
By permission J. Hamelle, Paris

Ra- mu - -re aux rumeurs a-mol-lies,___ Tronc so-no-res que l'â- ge creuse, L

Le plus doux chemin, Op. 87, No. 1

A mes pas le plus doux che-min Mè-ne à la por-te de ma bel- le M

Mirages, Op. 113
No. 1 Cygne sur l'eau
By permission Durand & Cie, Paris;
Elkan-Vogel Co., Inc., Phila.,
copyright owners

Ma pen-sé-e est un cy-gne har-mo-ni- eux et sa- ge N

No. 2 Reflets dans l'eau

É- ten-du- e au seuil du bas-sin, dans l'eau plus froi- de O

No. 3 Jardin Nocturne

Noc-tur- ne jar-din tout rem-pli de si-len- ce P

No. 4 Danseuse

Soeur___ des soeurs tis-seu- ses de vi-o- let-tes, Q

L'Horizon Chimérique, Op. 118, No. 1
By permission Durand & Cie, Paris;
Elkan-Vogel Co., Inc., Phila.,
copyright owners

La mer est in-fi-ni - - - - - -e et mes rê-ves sont fous. R

No. 2

Je me suis em-bar-qué sur un vaisseau qui dan- se et rou- le S

L'Horizon Chimérique, Op. 118, No. 3

Di-a-ne, Sé-lé-ne lu-ne de beau métal,____ Qui re-flé-tes vers nous,   A

No. 4

Vais-seaux, nous vous au-rons ai-més en pu-re per-te;   B

En Prière
By permission J. Hamelle, Paris

Si la voix d'un en-fant peut mon-ter jus-qu'a Vous, Ô mon Pè-re   C

FAURE, Jean Baptiste (1830-1914)

Charité

Voi-ci l'hi-ver et son tris-te cor-tè-ge, Les malheur-eux souffrent beaucoup,   E

Va,____ cha-ri-té____ vier-ge pu - - re et fé-con-de,   F

Crucifix! (duet)
By permission Heugel & Cie, Paris,
copyright owners

Vous qui pleu-rez, ve-nez à ce Dieu, car il pleu-re   G

Les Rameaux (The Palms)

Sur nos che-mins les ra-meaux et les fleurs____   H

Ho-san-na! Gloire au Seigneur! Bé-ni ce-lui qui vient sauver le mon - - - -de!   I

Sancta Maria

J'ai vu les Sé-ra-phins en son-ge Chanter dans leurs divins con-certs____   J

Vi-brez en-cor, sainte har-mo-ni-e, Vi-brez en-cor, hymne é-ternel!   K

FERRABOSCO, Alfonso (The Younger) (c. 1557- 1628)

Come, my Celia

Come, my Ce - - - lia, let us prove, while we may,   M

O eyes, o mortal stars

O eyes, O mor-tal stars, The au-thors of my harms,   N

FERRARI, Gustav (1872-   )

Le Miroir
Copyright 1949, G. Schirmer, Inc.

L'o-deur de vous flot-tait dans l'air si-len-ci-eux   P

FEVRIER, Henry (1875-   )

Elle avait trois couronnes d'or
By permission Heugel & Cie, Paris,
copyright owners

Elle a-vait trois cou-ron-nes d'or.____ A qui les don-na-t-el-le?   R

L'Intruse
By permission Heugel & Cie, Paris,
copyright owners

Elle est ve-nu-e vers le palais Le soleil se le-vait   S

FIBICH, Zdenko (1850-1900)

My Moonlight Madonna
(Words by Paul Webster)
Copyright by Carl Fischer, Inc.
reprinted by permission

Where are you____ beau-ti-ful moon-light Ma-don-na____ Like the dew

Sarka, Op. 51 (opera) Act I

Ja- ko bla- hý o-hlas do- by za- šlé vdu- še zvu- čí slo- va

Act II

Jsi krás-ná, ja-ko let- ní noc, jíž hvězd- ná zdo-ba v kšti-ci pla- ne!

(duet)

Jak jsi krás- na Cé- tiš žár jenž z na- der šle- há?

Act III

Já ne-le-kám se, smr- ti chlad- ná, muk- ni sti- nů____ tvých

FIELITZ, Alexander Von (1860-1930)

**Eiland, Op. 9,
No. 1 Stilles Leid**
Copyright 1910, G. Schirmer, Inc.

Ei- ne stil- le Zel- le an____ blau- er Wel- le

No. 2 Frauenwörth

Das war ein Tag' voll Mai- en-wind, da ist____ auf blau- en

No. 3 Rosenzweige

Wohl man-chen Ro- sen- zweig brach ich von Pfa- de

No. 4 Heimliche Grüsse

O Ir- men-gard, wie schön bist du hold- - - se- li- ger ist Kei- ne

No. 5 Am Strande

Mein Lieb- ling ist ein Lin- den-baum der steht am Strand;

No. 6 Kinderstimmen

Mit un- sern Fi-schern war ein Kind ge- kom- men

No. 7 Mondnacht

Ich lieg'____ an mei-nes La- gers End' und lug'____ in stille Ster-ne

No. 8 Wanderträume

O, der Al- pen blan- ke Ket- te, wie sie glänzt

No. 9 Anathema

Nun ist wohl San- ges En- de! Wie hart ich da- von schied,

No. 10 Ergebung

Ge- hor- chen ist das Er- ste! Ich hab' mich stumm ge- neigt,

Die stille Wasserrose, Op. 18, No. 1

Die stil- le Was- ser-ro- se steigt aus dem blau- en See

Frülingslied, Op. 26, No. 1

Und ein Duf- ten zieht ü- ber die Er- den- welt,

FINCK, Heinrich (1445-1527)

Ach herzigs Herz

Ach her-zigs Herz, mein Schmerz er - ken-nen tu, ich hab kein Ruh

FISCHER, Ludwig (1745-1825)

Im tiefen Keller

In tie-fen Kel-ler sitz' ich hier auf ei-nem Fass voll Re-ben,

FLÉGIER, Ange (1846-1927)

Le Cor
Copyright 1898, G. Schirmer, Inc.

J'ai-me le son du cor, le soir au fond des bois,

Que de fois seul dans l'om-bre à mi-nuit de-meu-ré,

FLOTOW, Friedrich Von (1812-1883)

Martha (opera)
Act I (duet)

So- lo, pro- fu- go, re- jet- to, Di mia vi- ta sul mat- tin

Act II

Siam giun- ti o gio- vi- net- te, al nos- tro ca- so- lar!

The Last Rose of Summer

Qui so- la ver- gin ro- sa, come puoi tu fio- rir

Goodnight Quartet

Dor- mi pur, ma il mio ri- po- so, tu m'hai tol- to in-gra- to- cor

Che vuol dir cio? l'of-fen- do, son col- mo di stu-por!

Pres- to, pres- to an- diam pren-de- te roc- ca e fu- so

Di ve- der- lo ah - - - - - - - - - - - -

Act III Porter's Song

Chi mi di- rà di che il bic- chier col-ma - - - to va,

M'ap- pa- ri tutt' a - - mor, il mio squar-do l'in-con - - tro;

Ah! che a voi per- do ni Id- dio-O, la mia pena il mio do- lor:

Act IV (This number not in Italian edition)

Den Theu- ren zu ver- söh- nen durch wah-re Reu, durch wah-re Reu,

Martha (opera) Act IV
Il mio Lio- nel pe- ri- ra___ Se a mico il ciel non a- vrà ___

Alessandro Stradella (opera) Act I, No. 2 Serenade
Horch! Lieb- chen, horch. es singt der Trau- te in Lieb' ___ er- glüht,

Act II
Al- les thei- le un- ser Glück; freund- lich wei- le Früh- lings- blick!

No. 5
Seid mei- ner Won- - - - ne stil- - le ___ Zeu- gen

Finale
Tief in den A- bruz- zen da lau- ert im Moos

Act III, No. 12
Wie freund- lich strahlt der Tag, die bunt- ge- schmuck- te Men- ge

Finale (Kymn)
Jung- frau Ma- ri- a, himm- - - - - lisch Ver- klär- - - te,

FONTENAILLES, H. de

Sais-tu?
Copyright by Salabert, Paris, N. Y.
Sais- tu qu'en ces jours tis- sus d'or ___ Que l'é- té vêt

Les Deux Coeurs
By permission Durand & Cie, Paris; Elkan-Vogel Co., Inc., Phila., copyright owners
Le coeur que tu m'a- vais don- né Ma douce a- mie, en ga- ge

Obstination
By permission Durand & Cie, Paris; Elkan-Vogel Co., Inc., Phila., copyright owners
Vous au- rez beau faire et beau di- re! ___ L'ou- bli me se- rait o- di- eux,

FOOTE, Arthur (1853-1937)

I'm wearing awa'
Copyright by Arthur P. Schmidt Co., Boston. Used by permission
I'm wear- ing a- wa', Jean, like snow when it's thaw, Jean; I'm wear- ing a- wa'

An Irish Folk-Song
Copyright by Arthur P. Schmidt Co., Boston. Used by permission
You'll wan- - der far and wide, dear, but you'll come back a- gain,
Ah - - - - - - -

FORD, Thomas (1580-1648)

Since first I saw your face
Since first I saw your face I re- solved to hon- our and re- nown ye,

There is a lady sweet and kind
There is a la- dy sweet and kind, was nev- er face so pleased my mind

FOSTER, Stephen (1826-1864)

Nelly was a lady
Down in de Mis-sis-sip-pi float-ing, Long time I trab-ble on de way

Oh boys, carry me 'long
Oh! car-ry me 'long;___ Der's no more trouble for me___

Oh, boys, car-ry me 'long; Car-ry me till I die___

Oh, Lemuel
Oh Lem-u-el, my lark, Oh, Lem-u-el, my beau

Go down to de cot-ton-field! Go down I say!

Oh, Susanna
I___ come from Al-a-ba-ma wid my ban-jo on my knee

Old Black Joe
Gone are the days when my heart was young and gay

I'm com-ing I'm com-ing, for my head is bend-ing low

Old Dog Tray
The morn of life is past And ev'-ning comes at last

Old dog Tray's ev-er faith-ful Grief can-not drive him a-way

Old Folks at Home
Way down up-on de Swa-nee Rib-ber, Far, far a-way

Open thy lattice, love
O-pen thy lat-tice, love, lis-ten to me! The cool bal-my breeze is a-broad

Ring, ring de banjo
De time is neb-ber drea-ry, If de dar-key neb-ber groans;

Ring, ring de ban-jo, I like dat good old song

Some folks like to sigh
Some folks like to sigh Some folks do, some folks do

Sweetly She Sleeps
Sweet-ly she sleeps,__ my Al-ice fair, Her cheek on the pil-low pressed__

Uncle Ned
There was an old dar-key, his name was Un-cle Ned,

The Village Maiden
The vil-lage bells are ring-ing, and mer-ri-ly they chime

FOURDRAIN, Felix (1880-1923)

La Belle au Bois Dormant
Copyright by G. Ricordi & Co., Inc.

Comme elle avait dor- mi cent ans Dans son lit fleu- rant la bruyère,

Carnaval
Copyright by G. Ricordi & Co., Inc.

Car- na- val!_ joy-eux Car- na- val! On s'é-lan- ce

Chanson Norvégienne
Copyright by G. Ricordi & Co., Inc.

Je suis pri-se d'u- ne tris- tes- se Qui pè- se, pè- se lour- dement

Le papillon
Copyright by G. Ricordi & Co., Inc.

Gai_ pa- pil-lon, pa - - - pil- lon d'or Qui t'en-vo- les rapide

FOX, Oscar J. (1879-   )

The Hills of Home
Copyright by Carl Fischer, Inc.
reprinted by permission

My prai-rie home is beau-ti-ful, but oh,_ I miss the bro-ken sky-line

The hills_ of home, the hills_ of home_

FRANCHETTI, Alberto (1860-   )

Germania (opera)
Prologue
Copyright by G. Ricordi & Co., Inc.

Stu- den-ti! U- di- te,o voi,an- ti-chi e no-vi,a- mi- ci

Act I

No, non chiu- der gli oc- chi va-glie ci-le-stri-ni_ co- me la-ghi,

Fe-ri- to prigio- nier, vol- li fug- gir per non mo-rir fra col-tri

FRANCK, César (1822-1890)

L'Ange Gardien

Veil- lez_ sur moi quand je m'é- veil-le Bon an- ge, puis-que Dieu_ l'a dit

Les Béatitudes (oratorio)
No. 4 Heureux les coeurs

Puis- que par- tout où nous en- traîne_ un sort fa- tal

Heu- reux les coeurs al- té- rés de jus- ti- ce

No. 8 Mater dolorosa

Moi du Sau- veur_ je suis la mè- - re; Sept glai-ves

Les Cloches du Soir

Quand les clo- ches du soir dans leur len- te vo- lé- e,

Lied

Pour moi sa main cueil- lait des ro- ses A ce buis- son_

Le Mariage des Roses — Mi-gnon-ne, sais tu com-ment S'é-pou-sent les ro-ses? — A

Ninon — Ni-non! Ni-non! que fais tu de la vi-e? — B

Nocturne — O frai-che nuit, Nuit transpar-en-te, Mys-te-re sans obscu-ri-té — C

Panis Angelicus, from Messe Solonnelle, Op. 12 — Pa-nis an-ge-li-cus Fit pa-nis ho-mi-num Dat pa-nis coe-li-cus — D

La Procession — Dieu s'a-vance à tra-vers les champs! par les lan-des, les_ prés — E

Psalm 150 — Lou-ez le Dieu ca-ché dans des saints ta-ber-na-cles — F

La Terre a tressailli, from The Redemption — La terre a tres-sail-li d'une ex-ta-se pro-fon-de — G

S'il est un charmant gazon — S'il est un char-mant ga-zon que le ciel ar-ro-se — H

Souvenance — Com-bien j'ai dou-ce sou-ve-nan-ce Du jo-li lieu — I

Le Vase Brisé — Le vase où meurt cet-te ver-vei-ne D'un coup d'even-tail fut fé-lé — J

La Vierge à la Crêche — Dans les lan-ges blancs fraîche-ment cou-sus, La_ Vierge ber-çait — K

FRANCK, Johann Wolfgang (17th Cent.)

Auf, auf zu Gottes Lob — Auf, auf zu Got-tes Lob, ihr hol-den Che-ru-bim — M

Jesus neigt sein Haupt und stirbt — Je-sus neigt_ sein_ Haupt und_stirbt,seht am Kreu-ze ihn ent-schlafen — N

Sei nur still — Sei nur_ still, sei nur_ still und harr' auf_ Gott,er weiss alles — O

FRANCK, Melchior (1573-1639)

Ach treuer Gott, Herr Jesus Christ — Ach, treu-er Gott, Herr Je-su Christ,der du al-lein mein Hei-land bist; — Q

FRANZ, Robert (1815-1892)

Er ist gekommen, Op. 4, No. 7 — Er ist ge-kom-men in Sturm_ und Re-gen — S

Aus meinen grossen Schmerzen, Op. 5, No. 1

Aus mei- nen gros- sen Schmer- zen mach' ich die klei- nen Lie- der

A

Liebchen ist da! No. 2

Blüm- lein im Gar- ten, schaut euch doch um, steht nicht so trau- rig;

B

Auf dem Meere, No. 3

Aus den Him- mels- au- gen dro- ben fal- len zit- ternd lich- te Fun- ken

C

Mädchen mit dem rothen Mündchen, No. 5

Mäd- chen mit dem ro- then Münd- chen, mit dem Äug- lein

D

Gute Nacht, No. 7

Die Höh'n und Wäl- der schon stei- gen im- mer tie- fer in's A- - bend- gold,

E

Vergessen, No. 10

O ban- ger Traum, was flat- terst du mit schwar- zem Flü- gel

F

Wie des Mondes Abbild, Op. 6, No. 2

Wie des Mon- des Ab- bild zit- - tert in den wil- den Mee- res- wog- en

G

Bitte, Op. 9, No. 3

Weil auf mir, du dunk- les Au- ge, ü- - be

H

Für Musik, Op. 10, No. 1

Nun die Schat- ten dun- keln, Stern an Stern er- wacht.

I

Stille Sicherheit, No. 2

Horch, wie still es wird im dun- keln Hain, Mäd- chen, wir sind sicher

J

Mutter, o sing' mich zur Ruh! No. 3

Mut- ter, O sing' mich zur Ruh', wie auch in schö- ne- ren Stun- den,

K

Umsonst, No. 6

Des Wal- des Sän- - ger sin- gen, die ro- the Ro- se blüht,

L

Abschied, Op. 11, No. 1

Wie schie- nen die Stern- lein so hell, so hell

M

Am leuchtenden Sommermorgen, No. 2

Am leuch- ten- den Som- - mer- mor- - gen geh' ich im Gar- ten her- um

N

Zwei welke Rosen, Op. 13, No. 1

Zwei wel- ke Ro- sen träu- men im San- de zum letz- ten Mal

O

Widmung, Op. 14, No. 1

O dan- ke nicht für die- se Lie- der Mir ziemt es dank- bar Dir zu sein;

P

Du liebes Auge, Op. 16, No. 1

Du lie- bes Au- ge willst dich tau- chen in mei- nes Aug's

Q

Abends, No. 4

A- bend- lich schon rauscht der Wald aus den tief- sten Grün- - den

R

Ständchen, Op. 17, No. 2

Der Mond ist schla- fen gan- gen, die Ster- ne blin- zeln blind

S

Im Herbst, Op. 17. No. 6

Die Hai- de ist braun, einst blüh- te sie roth;___ die Bir- ke ist kahl,

A

Marie, Op. 18, No. 1

Ma- rie, am Fen- ster sit- zest du, du lie- bes sü - - - sses Kind___

B

Im Rhein, im heiligen Strome, No. 2

Im Rhein, im hei- li- gen Stro- me, da spie- gelt sich in den Well'n___

C

Die blauen Frühlingsaugen, Op. 20, No. 1

Die blau- en Frül- lungs- au - - gen schau'n aus dem Gras her- vor

D

Das macht das dunkelgrüne Laub, No. 5

Das___ macht das dun- kel- grü- ne Laub, dass der Wald so schat- tig ist;

E

Im wunderschönen Monat Mai, Op. 25, No. 5

Im wun- der- schö- nen Mo- nat Mai, als al- le Knos- pen spran- gen

F

Lieber Schatz, sei wieder gut mir, Op. 26, No. 2

In dem Dornbusch blüht ein Rös- lein, ist ein Lust, es an- zu- sehn___

G

Sterne mit den gold'nen Füsschen, Op. 30, No. 1

Ster- ne mit den gold'- nen Füss- chen wan- deln dro- ben

H

Wonne der Wehmut, Op. 33, No. 1

Trock- net nicht,___ trock- net nicht___ Thrä- nen der e- wigen Liebe

I

Es ragt in's Meer der Runenstein, Op. 39, No. 2

Es ragt in's Meer der Ru- nen- stein, da sitz' ich

J

Wandl' ich in dem Wald des Abends, No. 4

Wandl' ich in dem Wald___ des A- bends, in dem träu- me- ri- schen Wald

K

Die helle Sonne leuchtet, Op. 42, No. 2

Die hel- le Son- ne leuch- tet auf's___ wei- te Meer her- nie - - - der

L

Es hat die Rose sich beklagt, No. 5

Es hat die Ro- se sich___ be- klagt___ dass gar zu schnell

M

Ach Elslein, liebes Elselein

Ach Els- lein, lie- bes El- se- lein mein, wie gern wär' ich bei dir!

N

Dich meiden

Dich mei- den nein,___ ach nein!

O

Es taget vor dem Walde

Es ta- get vor dem Wal- de; stand auf Kä- ther- lein___

P

FRASER-SIMSON, Harold (1878-1944)

Vespers (Christopher Robin is saying his prayers)
Copyright 1924, E. P. Dutton & Co., Inc., N. Y.

Lit- tle boy kneels at the foot of the bed, Drops on the lit- tle hands

FRESCOBALDI, Girolamo (1583-1643)

Non mi negate, ohimè
Non mi_____ ne- ga- te, ohi- mè, Lu- - mi se-re- ne,

Se l'Aura spira
Se l'Au- ra spi- ra tut-ta vez - - - zo-sa, La fres-ca Ro- sa ri-den- te_____ stà

Voi partite mio Sole
Voi par- ti- te mio So- le   E por-ta il vo-stro lu-me al tro-ve il gior- no;

FRIML, Rudolf (1881-   )

L'Amour-Toujours-l'Amour
Copyright 1922, Harms, Inc.
L'a-mour_____ tou-jours_____ l'a-mour,_____   Love, now at last, you've found me_____

Giannina Mia, from The Firefly (operetta)
Copyright 1912, G. Schirmer, Inc.
In my gon-do-la, love, let us glide_____ O'er the drow- sy blue la-goon_____

For_____ I a-dore,_____ I a-dore you Gian- ni- na mi- a

Give me one hour, from The White Eagle (operetta)
Copyright by Mills Music Inc., N. Y.
Give me one hour whose pas-sion re- pays   The death of   power,

Rose Marie (operetta)
Copyright 1924 Harms, Inc.
Indian Love Call
When I'm call- ing you - - - - -   oo - -   oo - - - - oo -oo- oo!

Rose Marie
O Rose Ma- rie, I   love you_____ I'm al- ways dream- ing of you

Vagabond King (operetta)
Only a Rose

Song of the Vagabond

FUENLLANA, Miguel de (16th Cent.)

Paseábase el Rey moro
Pa- se- á- ba- se el rey mo- - re   Por la ciu- dad

GABRIELI, Giovanni (1557-1612)

Benedictus
Be- - ne- di- ctus qui ve- nit, Be- ne- di- ctus

Jubilate Deo
Ju- bi- la- te De- o om - - - - - nis ter - - - - - - - - - ra,

GADE, Niels W. (1817-1890)

Elverskud (The Erl-King's Daughter)
(cantata)
Part I Oluf's Ballade

When- e'er I ride through the ten- der grove, A- glow with the sun- beams

Part III The sun now mounts
the eastern sky

The sun now mounts_ the eas- tern sky, To clouds bright hues he lends

Farvel, Lille Grete

Ak, kjae- re- ste, Hr. Guld- smed jeg har kun Sorg og Saon

Knud Lavard

Herr Mag- nus han stir- ren i Vin- ter- nat- ten ud:

GALUPPI, Baldassare (1706-1785)

Adriano in Siria (opera)

E in- gra- to, lo veg- gio, ma sie- de nel so- glio, ma sie- de nel so- glio,

Pri- gio- ni- e- ra, ab- ban- do- na- ta,

Son troppo vezzose, from Enrico
(opera)

Son trop- po vez-zo- se Del vol- to le ro- se, Son ca- re

GANZ, Rudolph (1877-)

A Memory
Copyright 1919, G. Schirmer, Inc.

Some- how I feel that thou_ art near, Though there is naught a-round;

GARNIER, François (16th Cent.)

Resveillez-moy

Res- sveil-lez moy, re- sveil- lez moy mon bel a- my.

GASPARINI, Francesco (1668-1727)

Adoramus Te, Christe (wrongly
ascribed to Mozart)

Ad- o- ra - - - - - - mus te, Chri - - - ste, et be- ne-di- ci - mus

Caro laccio, dolce nodo (cantata)

Ca- ro lac- cio, dol-ce no- do, che le- ga- sti, le- ga- sti

Lasciar d'amarti

Lasciar d'a- mar- ti per non pe- nar, ca- ro mio be- ne,

GASTOLDI, Giovanni Giacomo (1550-1619)

Maidens fair of Mantua's city

Mai-dens fair of Man-tua's ci- ty, none so grace-ful, none so pret- ty

GEEHL, Henry E.

For you alone
Copyright by Schubarth Music Pub.
Co., Inc., N. Y.

Take thou this rose, this lit-tle ten-der rose;—

GENTIAN, (16th Cent.)

La Loy d'Honneur

La loy d'hon-neur qui nous dict et com-man-de,

GERMAN, Edward (1862-1936)

Charming Chloe
Copyright by Novello & Co., Ltd., London

It was the charm-ing month of May— When all— the flow'rs were fresh

Merrie England (opera)
Act I

The Yeomen of England

Act II The English Rose

Rolling Down to Rio
Copyright by Novello & Co., Ltd., London

I nev-er sailed the A-ma-zon, I've nev-er reached— Bra - zil;

Waltz Song, from Tom Jones
(operetta)

Who'll buy my lavender?
By permission Boosey & Hawkes, Inc.,
copyright owners

La- dies fair, I— bring to you La-ven- der with spikes of— blue

GERSHWIN, George (1897-1937)

Porgy and Bess (opera)
Act I, Scene I Summertime

A woman is a sometime thing

Act I, Scene II My man's gone
now

Act II, Scene I It takes a long
pull to get there

Porgy and Bess (opera)
Act II, Scene I It takes a long
   pull to get there

I got plenty o' nuttin'

Buzzard Song

Bess, you is my woman now

Scene II, It ain't necessarily so

There's a boat dat's leavin' for
   New York

Act III, Scene III Oh, Bess, oh
   where's my Bess

Oh Lawd, I'm on my way

GESUALDO, Carlo (Prince of Venosa) (1560-1613)

Dolcissima mia vita

Io tacerò

Moro lasso (madrigal)

Resta di darmi noia (madrigal)

GHERARDELLO, da Firenze (15th Cent.)

Tosto che l'alba; caccia

GHIZEGHEM, Hayne Van (15th Cent.)

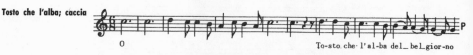

Les grans regrets

GIANNINI, Vittorio (1903-)

Tell me, Oh blue, blue Sky
Copyright by G. Ricordi & Co., Inc.

Sum- mer has flown, the leaves are fall-ing, I hear a voice

GIBBONS, Orlando (1583-1625)

Ah, dear heart (madrigal)

Ah,____ dear heart__ why do you rise? The light that shines comes from your__ eyes

Dainty fine bird

Dain- ty fine Bird, that art en- cag- ed there

Hosanna to the son of David

Ho- san- na to the Son of Da- vid, of____ Da- vid

The Silver Swan (madrigal)

The sil- ver swan, who, liv- ing, had no note, when death ap-proached

What is our life? (madrigal)

What is our life?__ our____ life? A play of__ pas- sion

GIBBS, Cecil Armstrong (1889-)

Five Eyes, Op. 9, No. 3

In Hans' old mill his three black cats Watch the bins

Padraic the fidiler
Copyright 1931, A. Gibbs

Pod-raic sits in the gar- den In un- der the bright new moon____

Take heed, young heart
Copyright 1926, A. Gibbs

Take heed, young heart, to Time How soft his foot- fall is

To One Who Passed Whistling
Through the Night
Copyright 1921, A. Gibbs

Some- thing hath called me, Called me from far dreams____

Ah

GILBERT, Henry F. (1868-1928)

Pirate Song
Copyright by Novello & Co., Ltd., London

Fif-teen men on the dead man's chest, Yo! ho! ho and a bot-tle of rum

GIORDANI, Giuseppe (1744-1798)

Caro mio ben

Ca- ro mio ben, cre-di-mi al- men, sen-za di te lan - - gui-sce il cor____

GIORDANO, Umberto (1867-   )

Andrea Chenier (opera)

Act I

Act II

Act III

Act IV

Fedora (opera)

Act I

Act II

Act III

Brilla sulla mia fronte, from Il Re (opera) Act 3
Copyright by Sonzogno, Milan
A — Bril - la sul - - la mia fron - - - te,_ ri - splen - de

Siberia (opera)
Act I
Copyright by Sonzogno, Milan
B — T'in - con - trai per via! L'occhio pen-so-so_e gra-ve è pe-ne- tra-to

C — Nel suo_a-mo - re ri-a-ni - ma - ta la co - scien - za

Act II
D — Or - - - ri - de step - - pe! Tor - ri - da l'e-sta - - te!

Act III
E — Non o - di là il mar - tir d'an-go-scia fie - ra?

GLAZOUNOV, Alexander (1865-1936)

Romance
G — Wenn ich in dei-ne Au - gen seh', so schwindet all' mein Leid

Romance Orientale
H — Dans le sang brû - - - - - le ar - den - te flam - - me

GLIÈRE, Reinhold (1875-   )

Ah, twine no blossoms (Oh, do not wreathe) Op. 18, No. 7
J — Ah_twine no blos-soms fair and frag-rant To weave a-new my crown of woe,

Over the Depths of the Sea, Op. 59
Copyright 1923, G. Schirmer, Inc.
K — O-ver- hang-ing the fath-om-less o-cean, a cliff tow-ers high

GLINKA, Michael (1804-1857)

A Life for the Czar (Ivan Sussanin) Act I Introduction
A — M
Fou - - dre_et vent gron - - dent en vain,_ Le_ fau - con_ fran - chit

B — N
Le_ doux prin - temps pa - rait_ Le_ beau prin - temps re - nait_

Rondo of Antonida
O — Au vil - la - ge sur la ri - viè - re, L'on at - tend l'ai - mé,

Act IV Bogdan Sobinjin's Aria
A — P
Frè - res, le froid, l'hor - - - - - reur des_ bois pro - fonds,

B — Q
Tris - te et_ dans_ l'an - gois - se,_ la fil - le at - tend_ cher_coeur!

Sussanin's Aria
R — Pâle au - ro - re,_ tu vien - dras Bai - gner_ mes yeux_ las - sés

Russlan and Ludmilla Act I Song of the Bard
S — Dort, gen Mit - ter - nacht liegt ein wüs - tes_ Land

Russian and Ludmilla (opera)
Act II Farlaf's Rondo

Nah ist die Stun-de schon mei-nes Tri-umph's und Russ-lan der ge-hass-te

Russlan's Aria

Gieb, o Kriegs-gott, mir ein Schwert nach mei-ner Hand

O Lud-mil - - - la! bald wird uns die Freu-de

Act III Persian Chorus

Schon deckt die Fel - - -der dunk - - -le Nacht.

Gorisslava and Chorus

O mein Rat-mir, dich seh' ich wie-der hier! vereint auf's neu' mit dir

Cherubin Song

Like glad Cher-u-bim in heav'n-ly cho-rus,

Doubt

Be si-lent de-spair of af-fec-tion, Oh heart without hope

In my blood the fire of desire burns
(Now am I all with fever shaken)

Now am I all with fe-ver sha-ken, Grief in my soul

I remember

The mo-ment I re-mem-ber clear-ly Thou didst ap-pear

The Lark

High o'er earth in Hea - - - -ven, floats the sound of sing-ing

Midnight Review

When mid-night is strik-ing the hour The drum-mer from grave-yard

The North Star

'Neath a mar-vel-lous roof man-y man-sions a-rise

Venetian Night (Barcarolle)

Fann'd by South-ern winds that chast-en, In the balm-y sum-mer night

GLUCK, Christoph Willibald (1714-1787)

Alceste (opera)
Act I

Grands Dieux! du des-tin, qui m'ac-ca-ble sus-pen-dez du moins

Pa-rez vos fronts des fleurs nou-vel - -les, ten-dres a-mants,

Di-vi-ni-tés du Styx, di-vi-ni-tés du Styx,

Non! ce n'est point un sac-ri-fi - -ce!

Act II

Ban-nis la crainte et les a - - lar - - -mes

GLUCK

Iphigénie in Aulis (opera)

Act II, No. 20 — A
Par la crainte et par l'es-pé-rance, Ah, que mon coeur est tour-men-té!

No. 24 — B
Chan-tons, cé-lé-brons no-tre Rei-ne! L'hy-men,— qui sous— ses lois

No. 31 — C
Par son pè-re cru-el á la mort con-dam-né— — — e

No. 37 — D
O toi, l'ob-jet le plus ai-ma-ble, que tant de ver-tus font ché-rir

Act III, No. 40 — E
Il faut de mon de-stin— su-bir la loi su-prê— — me,

No. 42 — F
A-dieu, con-ser-vez dans— votre â-me le sou-ve-nir

No. 44 — G
Cal-chas, d'un trait mor-tel bles-sé se-ra ma pré-mie-re vic-ti-me

No. 47 — H
Ju-pi-ter, lan-ce ta fou-dre, lan-ce, lan-ce ta fou-dre

No. 53 — I
Heu-reux guer-riers, vo-lez à la vic-toi-re

Iphigénie en Tauride (opera)

Act I — J
O toi, qui pro-longe-as mes jours,— re-prends—un bien que je dé-tes-te,

Act II — K
Dieux qui me pour-sui-vez, Dieux, au-teurs de mes cri-mes

— L
U-nis dès la plus ten-dre en-fan-ce nous n'a-vions qu'un mê-me de-sir,

Act III — M
D'une i-mage hé-las! trop ché-ri-e j'aime en-core à m'en-tre-te-nir,

— N
Ah! mon a-mi,— j'im-plo-re ta pi-tié

— O
Di-vi-ni-té des gran— — des â-mes A-mi-tié

Act IV — P
Je t'im-plo-re,et je trem-ble, ô Dé-es-se im-pla-ca-ble!

Orfeo ed Euridice (Orpheus) (opera)

Act I, No. 1 — Q
Ah! se in-to-no a quest'— ur-na fu-ne-sta

No. 7 — R
Chiamo il mio ben— co-sì, Quan-do si mo-stra il di—

No. 13 — S
Dal-la ce-tra tua dol-ci tuo-ni ar-mo-ni-ci— fa ri-so-nar;

feo ed Euridice (Orpheus) (opera)
Act I, No. 15 — A
Gli squar- di trat- tie - - ni, af- fre - na gli ac- cen - ti,

No. 17 — B
Ad- dio, ad- dio, o miei so- spi- ri, han spe-me i miei de- si- ri;

No. 19 and 21 (chorus) — C
Chi mai dell' E- re-bó fra le ca- li- gi- ni sull' or-me d'Er-co- le

Act II, No. 22 — D
Deh pla- ca- te- vi con me! Fu- rie, No, Fu- rie, No,

No. 23 — E
Mi- se- ro gio- va- ne, che vuoi, che me- di- ti

No. 24 — F
Mil- le pe- - - ne om- bre sde- gno- - - se

No. 25 — G
Ah! qua-le in- cog- ni- to af- fet- to fle- bi- le

No. 26 — H
Men ti- ran- ne, voi sa- re- ste al mio pian- to, al mio do- lor -

No. 32 — I
È quest' a- si- lo a- me-no e gra- to del ri- po- so il ter-ren, -

No. 33 — J
Che pu- ro ciel! che chia-ro sol! che mio va luce

No. 34 — K
Vie- ni a re- gni del ri-po- - so, grande E- ro- e, te- ne- ro spo- so

Act III, No. 39 Duet — L
Su e con me vie- ni, ca- ro su e con me vie- ni,

No. 41 A — M
Che fie- ro mo- men- - - to che bar- ba- ra sor- - - te

B — N
Av vez-zo al con- ten- to d'un pla- ci- do ob- bli- o

No. 43 — O
Che fa- ró sen-za Eu- ri- di- ce, do-ve an-dró sen-za il mio ben!

A — P
Tri- on-fi A-mo- re, e il mon-do ser-va in-tie-ro all' im-pe-ro del-la bel- ta

B — Q
Tal di- spe- ra, tal af- fan- na d'u-na ti- ran- na

A — R
Gau- dio, gau- dio son al cuo- re que-ste pe- ne dell' a- mor -

B — S
Qual pia-ce- - re, qual dol-cez- za l'a-mor ci ren-de,

Paris et Helena (opera)

O del mio dol-ce ar- dor___ bra-ma-to og-get- - - - to,

Spiag- ge a- ma- te, o- ve ta-lo-ra l'I-dol mi- o

Un ruisselet, bien clair, from La Rencontre Imprévue (opera)

Un ruis- se- let, bien clair, bien net, Qui dans la plai-ne ri- an-te

Vieni, che poi sereno, from La Semi- ramide (opera)

Vie- ni che poi se-re - - - - -no, al- ta tua bel-la in son - - - - no

GODARD, Benjamin (1849-1895)

Nous allons partir, from Dante (opera) Act IV, Scene II

Nous al- lons par- tir___ tous deux, Par- tir___ tous deux

Berceuse, from Jocelyn (opera)

Ca- chés dans cet a- sile où Dieu nous a con- duits

Oh! ne t'é- veille pas en- cor___ Pour qu'un bel an-ge de ton rê- ve

La Vivandière (opéra-comique)

Viens a- vec nous pe-tit,___ Viens a-vec nous, viens!

(The Letter)

Mon p'tit gars,___ si nous t'é- cri-vons C'est pour te bien di-re sans ces-se

Chanson de Florian

Ah! s'il est dans vo-tre vil- la - - ge Un ber- ger sen-si-ble

Embarquez-vous!

Em- bar- quez- vous! qu'on se dé- pè - - - - - che;

Te souviens-tu? Op. 19, No. 6

Le souviens-tu de ta pro- mes - - se? Te souviens-tu des ans pas- sés?

GOETZ, Hermann (1849-1878)

Die Kraft versagt, from The Taming of the Shrew (opera)

Die Kraft ver- sagt des Kam- pfes des Kam-pfes bin ich mü- de

Es schwei- ge die Kla- ge In De-muth es tra - - - ge,

GOLDMARK, Carl (1830-1915)

The Queen of Sheba (opera) Act I

Der Freund ist dein,___ der Freund ist dein___ der un-ter Ro- - sen wei-det,

Act II

Lift thine eyes to worlds a- bove thee, to the throne___ of God most high

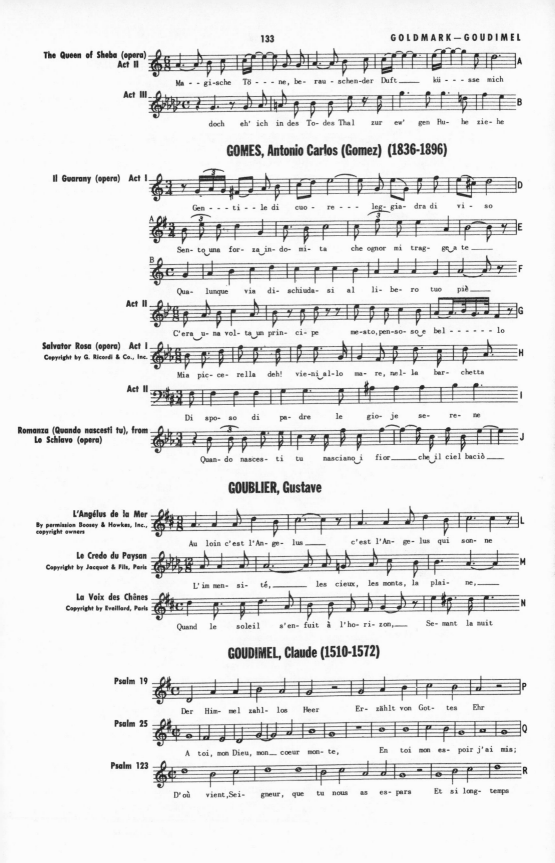

The Queen of Sheba (opera)
Act II
Ma - gi-sche Tö - - ne, be- rau -schen-der Duft___ kü - - sse mich   **A**

Act III
doch eh' ich in des To- des Thal zur ew' gen Ru- he zie-he   **B**

GOMES, Antonio Carlos (Gomez) (1836-1896)

Il Guarany (opera) Act I
Gen - - ti - le di cuo - re - - - leg- gia-dra di vi - so   **D**

Act II
Sen- to una for- za in-do- mi- ta che ognor mi trag- ge a te___   **E**

Qua- lunque via di-schiuda- si al li- be- ro tuo piè___   **F**

Act II
C'era u- na vol- ta un prin- ci- pe me-sto,pen-so- so e bel - - - - - lo   **G**

Salvator Rosa (opera) Act I
Copyright by G. Ricordi & Co., Inc.
Mia pic- ce- rella deh! vie-ni al-lo ma- re, nel- la bar- chetta   **H**

Act II
Di spo- so di pa- dre le gio- je se- re- ne   **I**

Romanza (Quando nascesti tu), from Lo Schiavo (opera)
Quan- do nasces- ti tu nasciano i fior___ che il ciel baciò___   **J**

GOUBLIER, Gustave

L'Angélus de la Mer
By permission Boosey & Hawkes, Inc., copyright owners
Au loin c'est l'An- ge- lus___ c'est l'An- ge- lus qui son- ne   **L**

Le Credo du Paysan
Copyright by Jacquot & Fils, Paris
L'im men- si- té,___ les cieux, les monts, la plai- ne,___   **M**

La Voix des Chênes
Copyright by Eveillard, Paris
Quand le soleil s'en- fuit à l'ho- ri- zon,___ Se- mant la nuit   **N**

GOUDIMEL, Claude (1510-1572)

Psalm 19
Der Him- mel zahl- los Heer Er- zählt von Got- tes Ehr   **P**

Psalm 25
A toi, mon Dieu, mon___ coeur mon- te, En toi mon es- poir j'ai mis;   **Q**

Psalm 123
D'où vient, Sei- gneur, que tu nous as es- pars Et si long- temps   **R**

GOUNOD, Charles François (1818-1893)

Messe Solennelle (St. Cecilia Mass)
Agnus Dei — Ag - - - nus De- i, Ag - - nus De i qui tol-lis, qui tol-lis

Benedictus — Be-ne-dic-tus qui ve - - nit____ in no - - mi- ne Do - - - - mi-ni

Credo — Cre- do____ in u-num De- um Pa-trem____ o- mni- po- ten-tem

Sanctus — Sanc- tus, sanc- tus,____ sanc-tus Do - mi- nus____ Sanc-tus, sanc- tus,____

Mors et Vita (oratorio)
Hosanna — Ho- san- na in ex - cel- sis De - - - - - - o,

Judex — Se- den- ti in Thro- no et Ag - - no,____ be- ne- dic - ti- o

Faust (opera)
Act I — Sa- lut! ô mon der-nier ma- tin!____ Sa- lut! ô mon der-nier ma-tin!

Pa- res- seu- se fil- le Qui som- meille en- co- re,____

À moi____ les plai-sirs, les jeu - - - nes maî - tres- ses!

Act II Kermesse — Vin ou biè- re, Bière ou vin, que mon____ ver- re soit____ plein!

Cavatina — A- vant de quit- ter ces lieux,____ Sol na- tal de mes a- ieux____

The Golden Calf — Le veau d'or____ est tou-jours de-bout! On en-cen- se sa puis-san - - - - - ce,

De l'en- fer qui vient é-mous-ser nos ar- mes;

Chorale — C'est u - ne croix qui de l'en- fer nous gar- de,

Waltz — Ain- si que la brise le- gè- re Sou- lève en é-pais tour-bil-lons,

(accompaniment theme)

Act III Flower Song — Fai- tes-lui mes a- veux Por-tez mes voeux! Fleurs é-closes près d'el- le

Cavatina — Sa- lut! de-meu- re chaste et pu- re, Sa- lut! de-meu- re chaste et pu- re,

Mireille (opera)
Act II Chanson

Voi- ci la sai- son, mi- gnonne, Voi- ci la sai- son

Mon coeur ne peut chan-ger!___ Sou-viens-toi que je t'ai-me!

A toi mon â- me Je suis ta fem-me! Mal-gré leur blâ - - - me

Si les fil- les___ d'Ar- les sont rei- nes

Act IV Scene II

Le jour se lève Et fait pa- lir la som- bre nuit!

Heu- reux pe- tit ber- ger! Heu- reux pe- tit ber- ger!

Act V Chorus of Sainte-Marie

Vous qui du haut des cieux___ Vo- yez les pleurs de nos yeux___

An- ges du pa- ra- dis cou- vrez- la de votre ai- le___

La foi, de son flam-beau di- vin, Gui- dait par le che- min,

Philémon et Baucis (opera)
Act I

Ah, si je re-de- ve-nais bel- le, Si son front pou-vait ra-jeu-nir,___

Au bruit des lourds mar-teaux d'ai-rain___ Au sombre é- clat

Que les songes heu- reux___ pla- nant sur votre tê- te

Act II

Phi- lé- mon m'aimerait en- co- re, J'aime- rais en-core Phi- lé- mon,

Ô___ ri- an- te na- tu- re Ô jar-dins em- bau- més___

Polyeucte (opera)
Act II

À Ves- ta, por-tez vos of-fran-des; Devant el- le je vais m'in-cliner

Nym - - - - - phes at- ten- ti - - ves___ Dans les ro- seaux!

Act IV

Sour- ce dé- li- ci- eu- se en mi- sé - res fé- con- de

La Reine de Saba (Queen of Sheba)
(opera)

Sous les pieds d'u- ne fem - - me A-bais-sant de___ son â- me

Act II

In-spi-rez moi, ra-ce di- vi - - - ne! no-bles a-ieux___ en qui j'ai foi!

GOUNOD

La Reine de Saba (Queen of Sheba) (opera) Act III — A
Plus grand, dans son ob-scu-ri- té,__ Qu'un roi pa- ré du di-a-dè- me

Roméo et Juliette (opera) Act I Ballade of Queen Mab — B
Mab, la rei- ne des_ men-son- ges, Pré-side aux son- ges,

"Waltz song" — C
Je veux vi- - - vre dans le rê- - - ve__

Madrigal — D
Ange a- do- ra-ble, ma main cou-pa- ble Pro-fane, en l'o-sant tou-cher__

— E
Al- lons! jeu-nes gens__ Al- lons! bel- les da- mes

Act II Cavatina — F
Ah! lè- ve- toi, so- leil!__ fais pa- lir les é- toi- les

Act III — G
Que fais tu, blan-che tour- te- rel- le, Dans ce nid de vau- tours?__

Act IV Love duet — H
Nuit d'hy- mé- né- - - e!__ Ô dou- ce nuit d'a-mour!

— I
Que l'hym- ne nup- ti- al__ suc- cède aux cris d'a-lar- mes

— J
C'est- là qu'après un jour vo- tre corps et votre â- me

— K
A- mour,__ ra-ni- me mon cou- ra-ge, Et de mon coeur chas- -se l'ef-froi__

O ma lyre immortelle, from Sappho (opera) — L
O ma lyre im-mor- tel- le Qui dans les tris- tes jours__

Aimons-nous! — M
Au fleuve le ruisseau se mêle Et le fleuve à la mer!__

Au Printemps — N
Le printemps chas-se les hi-vers Et sou-rit dans les ar- bres verts

Au Rossignol — O
Quand ta voix cé- les- te pre-lude au si- len-ce des bel-les nuits__

Ave Maria (Meditation on Bach Prelude in C, Well-tempered Clavichord, Book I, No. 1) — P
A- ve Ma-ri- a__ Gra- ti-a ple-na, Do- - minus te- - cum

Ce que je suis sans toi — Q
Ce qu'est le lier-re sans l'or-meau. Qui fut l'ap-pui de son en- fan- ce

Le Ciel a visité la terre — R
Le ciel a vi-si-té la ter- re, mon bien ai- mé re-pose

Entreat me not to leave thee — S
En- treat me not to leave thee, En- treat me not to leave thee

Envoi de Fleurs — Si l'on veut sa- voir qui m'en- voi- - - - e ces bel- les fleurs,

La Glu — Y a- vait un fois un pauv' gas et lon lon lon lair- e e lon

Hymne à la Nuit — Viens, lorsque dans l'a- zur les as- tres ra- di- eux

Medjé (Chanson Arabe) A — O Medjé, qui d'un sou- ri- re En- chainas ma li- ber- té

B — La voix de l'a- mour mê- me De- vrait te dé- sar- mer

Nazareth — Né dans u- ne crê- che, Di- vin Ré- - demp- teur

Oh, That We Two Were Maying — Oh, that we two were may- ing O- ver the fra- - grant grass

O ma belle rebelle — O ma bel- le re- bel- le, Las que tu m'es cru- el- le

Où voulez-vous aller (Bacarolle) — Di- tes la jeu- ne bel- le où vou- lez vous al- ler?

Repentir (O Divine Redeemer) A — Ah! ne re- pous- se pas mon â- me pé- che- res- se!

B — O Di- vin Ré- demp- teur O Di- vin Ré- demp- teur

Ring out, wild bells — Ring out, wild bells, to the wild sky The fly-ing cloud,

Sérénade — Quand tu chan- - - tes ber- cé- e le soir, en-tre mes bras

Le Soir — Le soir ra- mè- ne le si- len- ce, As- sis sur ces ro-chers dé-serts,

There is a green hill far away (Le Calvaire) A — There is a green hill far a- way, With- out a ci-ty wall

B — There was no oth- er good e- nough To pay the price

Le Vallon A — D'i- ci je vois la vi- e à tra-vers un nu- a- ge

B — Re- po- se- toi, mon â- me, en ce der- nier a- - si- le

Venise — Dans Ve- ni- - se la rou- ge, Pas un bateau qui bou- ge;

GRAENER, Paul (1872-1944)

Philantropisch, Op. 43 b, No. 6
Ein ner-vö-ser Mensch auf ei-ner Wie-se   Wä-re bes-ser oh-ne sie

Palmström, No. 7
Palm-ström steht an ei-nem Tei-che und ent-fal-tet gross ein rotes Taschentuch

Der Page sprach, Op. 49, No. 1
Mei-ne wun-der-schö-ne Kö- ni-gin, du sollst wis- sen

Der alte Herr, No. 3
Kennst du nur den al-ten Her- ren der zur sel-ben Mit-tag-stunde

Der König, Op. 71, No. 3
By permission Associated Music
Publishers, Inc.
Das war der jun-ge__ Kö-nig, der Kö-nig oh- ne__ Land,

Verspruch, No. 9
Wir sind ein-an-der zu- ge-sellt für al-le E- wig-keit,

GRAINGER, Percy (1882-   )

Brigg Fair (arr.)
Copyright by Percy Grainger
It was on the fift'__ of Au- gust, er the wea-ther fine and fair

GRANADOS, Enrique (1867-1916)

Amor y odio
Copyright by Union Musical Española
Pen-se que yo sa- bri-a o-cul-tar la pe- na mi-a

Callejes
Copyright by Union Musical Española
Dos ho-ras ha que ca-lle-je--o, pe-ro no ve--o

Las Currutacas modestas
Copyright by Union Musical Española
De- cid__ que da-mi se--las se ven por a-hí__ que luz-can a-si

El Majo discreto
Copyright by Union Musical Española
Di- cen que mi ma- jo es fe--o, Es po-si-ble__ que si

La Maja Dolorosa, No. 1
Copyright by Union Musical Española
¡Oh__ muer-te cruel ¿Por-qué tu á trai-ción

No. 2
¡Ay ma-jo de mi vi- da, no no, tu no has muer-to;__

No. 3
De a-quel ma-jo a-man-te que fué mi 'glo-ria guar-do an-he- lan-te

La Maja de Goya
Copyright by Union Musical Española
Yo no ol-vi--da-re en mi vi-da de Go-ya la i-ma-gen

The Maiden and the Nightingale,
from Goyescas (opera) (La Maja
y el Ruiseñor)
Copyright 1915, G. Schirmer, Inc.
Por-qué en-tre som-bras el rui-se-ñor en-to-na su ar-mo-nio-so can-tar?

El Majo Olvidado
Copyright by Union Musical Española
Cuan- do re-cuer-des los di-as pa- sa- dos piensa—- en mi;

El Majo Tímido
Copyright by Union Musical Española
Lle- ga á mi re-ja y me mi- ra por la no-che un ma-jo

El Mirar de la Maja
Copyright by Union Musical Española
Por-que es en mis o- jos   tan hon-do el mi- rar

El Trá-lá-lá y el Punteado
Copyright by Union Musical Española
Es en bal- de ma-jo mi- o que si-gas ha- blan-do

GRENON, Nicolas (15th Cent.)

Je ne requier de
Je ne re- qui- er de ma— dame et ma mi

Nova vobis gaudia
No- va vo- bis gau-di- a — re- fe- ro

GRETCHANINOV, Alexander (1864-   )

The Wounded Birch, Op. 1, No. 2
By the hatch-et wound-ed, See the birch-tree lan-guish;

My Native Land (My Country) No. 4
Home— land mine, my na- tive land! Beat-ing hoofs of hors- es,

Berceuse (Cradle Song)   No. 5
Sleep, my dar- ling sleep, my star-ling, Bye, my ba- by, bye—

Over the Steppe, Op. 5, No. 1
Sad lies the Steppe— in its sol- i-tude Night comes on shad- ow-y wings;

Night   No. 2
Stil- - le Schlaf und nächt-lich Dun- kel al- les zau-be-risch

Hushed the song of the Nightingale, Op. 20, No. 2
Copyright by Oliver Ditson Co.
Used by permission.
Hushed the song of the night-in-gale, Yon-der star fall-ing trails thro' the blue

The Captive   No. 4
Je suis dans ma ca- ge dans l'om- bre gla- cée

(Children's Songs), Op. 47, No. 1 Snowflakes
By permission Associated Music Publishers, Inc.
We-het, weht ihr Flock-en-ster- ne, uns nur bleibt hübsch fer - - - ne!

No. 9 The Snowdrop
Im Wal- de wo Bir-ken sich drän- gen zu Hauf,

Death (La Morte), Op. 48, No. 5
By permission Associated Music Publishers, Inc.
O mort vieux ca- pi- tai- ne, il est temps! le- vons— l'an-cre

Ob ich gehe, ob ich stehe, Op. 120, No. 2
By permission Associated Music Publishers, Inc.
Ob ich ge- he, ob ich ste- he ob-ich ge- he, ob ich ste- he,

GRETRY, André (1741-1813)

Jugement de Midas (opera) — Doux char-me de la vi - e, Di-vi-ne mé-lo-di-e   B

Par___ u-ne grâ - - - ce tou-chan-te u-ne mine in-té-re-san-te   C

Naissantes fleurs, from Céphale et Procris (opera) — Nais - - san-tes fleurs,___ ces - - - - sez d'é-clo - re   D

Plus de dépit, plus de tristesse, from Les Deux Avares (opera) — Plus de dé-pit,___ plus de tris - tes-se   E

Qu'il est cruel d'aimer, from Les Évènements Imprevues (opera) — Qu'il est cru-el d'ai-mer,___ D'ai-mer sans o-ser di - re,   F

Richard Coeur-de-Lion (opera) Act I, No. 2 — La dan-se n'est pas ce que j'ai-me, Mais c'est la fille   G

Duet — U-ne fiè-vre brû-lan - - te Un jour me terras-sait   H

Je crains de lui par-ler la nuit, J'é-cou-te trop tout ce qu'il dit   I

Song of Blondel — O Ri-chard, ô mon Roi! L'u-ni-vers t'a-ban-don-ne   J

Si l'u-ni-vers en-tier m'ou-bli-e S'il faut i-ci pas-ser ma vi-e   K

Serenade, from L'Amant Jaloux (opera) — Tan-dis que tout_ som-meil-le dans l'om-bre de_ la nuit___   L

Vous étiez ce que vous n'êtes plus, from Le Tableau Parlant (opera) — Vous é-tiez ce que vous n'ê-tes plus, Ce que vous n'ê-tes___ plus___   M

Zémiré et Azor (opera) — Ah, quel tour-ment d'ê-tre sen-si - - - ble, D'a-voir un_ coeur   N

Du mo-ment qu'on ai-me, L'on de-vient___ si_ doux___   O

La fau-vet-te a - - - vec ses pe-tits___   P

Ro-se ché-ri - - e, Ai-ma-ble fleur! Ro-se ché-ri - - - e   Q

GRIEG, Edvard Hagerup (1843-1907)

To brune Øjne, Op. 5, No. 1 (Two Brown Eyes) — To bru-ne Øj-ne jeg ny-lig saa, i dem mit Hjem   S

Ich liebe dich (I Love Thee), Op. 5, No. 3

Du mein Ge-dan-ke, du mein Sein und Wer-den!

Vuggesang, Op. 9, No. 2

Sov min Søn, o slum-re sødt end-nu gar din Vug-ge blødt

Ausfahrt (Outward Bound), No. 4

Es war ei-ne däm-mern-de Som-mer-nacht, ein Schiff am U-fer lag,

Love, Op. 15, No. 2

The sun like vi-sions of love doth glow; he cool-eth his face

The Poet's Last Song, Op. 18, No. 1

Thou Gi-ant Death O hear me high, To Spi-rit land swift fly-ing!

Vandring i skoven No. 2

Min sø-de Brud, min un-ge Vio, min kjaer-lif hed, mit Liv

Hytten No. 3

Hvor Bel-gen hejt mod ky-stens slaar en gan-ske lil-le

Herbststurm (Autumn Storm) No. 4

Im Som-mer wie war da so grün der Wald, als Zwit-schern von je-dem Zweig

Erstes Begegnen (First Meeting), Op. 21, No. 1

Des er-sten Se-hens Won-ne ist wie der Duft im Wal-de

Dein Rat ist wohl gut (Your Advice is Good) (Thanks for the Rede) No. 4

Dein Rat ist wohl gut, der mich warnt vor der Flut,

Kvad, Op. 22, No. 1

Nor-rø-na fol-ket det vil fa-re, det vil fa-re

Peer Gynt (drama with music) Solveig's Song, Op. 23, No. 1

Der Win-ter mag schei-den, der Früh-ling ver-geh'n, der Früh-ling ver-geh'n,

Ah -

Solveig's Slumber Song, No. 2

Schlaf', du theu-er-ster Kna-be mein! Ich will wie-gen mein Kind

Ein Schwan (A Swan), Op. 25, No. 1

Mein Schwann, mein stil-ler, mit wei-ssem Ge-fie-der, dei-ne wonnigen

Glücksbote mein, No. 3

Glücks-bo-te mein, so nannt ich dich, ver-glich dich einem Ster-ne

Mit einer Wasserlilie, No. 4 (With a Water-Lily)

Sieh, Ma-rie, was ich dir brin - - - - ge:

Am schonsten Sommerabend war's (It was a lovely summer eve) Op. 26, No. 2

Am schön-sten Som-mer- a-bend war's, ich ging durch ein ein-sam Thal,

Hoffnung (Hope), Op. 26, No. 3 — Ich möchte ju-beln in al-le Win-de doch fasst ihr wohl   A

Mit einer Primula Veris (With a Primrose), No. 4 — Mag dir, du zar-tes Früh-lings-kind, dies er-ste Blüm-chen from-men   B

Den store hvide Flok (The Great White Host), Op. 30, No. 10 (baritone and male quartet) — Den_ sto-re hvi-de Flok_ vi-se, som_ tu-sind Bjer-ge_ fuld of Sne,   C

Landkjending (Landsighting), Op. 31 — Og det war O-lav Tryg-va-son, staevned o-ver Nords-jö fram_   D

Der Frühling (Springtide), Op. 33, No. 2 — Ja, noch ein-mal könnt den Win-ter ich seh'n dem Früh-lin-ge wei-chen,   E

Der Verwundete (The Wounded Heart), No. 3 — Mein Her-ze war mit in des Le-bens streit und Wun-den hat es   F

An einem Bache (At the Brookside), No. 5 (Langs en Å) — Du wald, der sich her-ü-ber biegt und küsst den schwar-zen Bach   G

Auf der Reise zur Heimat (On the Road Home), No. 9 — So seh aufs neu ich je-ne Berg und Ta-le,   H

Vom Monte Pincio (from Monte Pincio), Op. 39, No. 1 — A-bend wie mil-de! Son-ne wie roth! Al-les er-füllt sich   I

Greeting, Op. 48, No. 1 — Ten-der mu-sic, from my soul_ pour_ with sweet persistence;   J

Ein Traum (A Dream), No. 6 — Mir träum-te einst ein schö-ner Traum: mich lieb-te ei-ne blon-de Maid;   K

Vug, o Vove, Op. 49, No. 2 — Vug, o Vo-ve, med var-som Haand Baa-den, hvor-i   L

Spring Showers, No. 6 — Sweet strains from fai-ry in-stru-ments are sound-ing   M

Til Norge (To Norway), Op. 58, No. 2 — Du er min mor, jeg el-sker dig, der-med er al-ting sagt!_   N

Margeretlein Lein, Op. 60, No. 1 — Mar-ga-ret-lein sass spät_ am A-bend, der Kuckuck rief in dem grünen Tann,   O

Moderen synger No. 2 — Gret-chen lig-ger i Ki-ste dybt i den sor-te Muld_   P

Im Kahne (In the Boat), No. 3 — Mö-ven, Mö-ven in weis-sen Flo--cken! Son---nen-schein!   Q

Der skreg en Fugl No. 4 (There screamed a Bird) — Der skreg en Fugl o-ver ö-de Hav, langt_ fra Lan-de   R

Zur Johannisnacht (St. John's Eve), Op. 60, No. 5
Ei- ne We-ste wünsch ich von Sei-de mir, ja,— ja, von Sei-de— mir. — A

Fisher's Song, Op. 61, No. 4
Ere day-light a-wak-eth, the fi-sher-man tak-eth his boat on the main — B

Haugtussa, Op. 67, No. 1 Det syng (Det synger)
Og vad du den Dröm og vad du den Sang sä vil du To-ner-ne gemme— — C

No. 2 Veslemöy (Ungmöen)
Hun er ma-ger og mörk og myg med bru-ne og re- ne Drag,— — D

No. 3 Blåbaer-Li (I Blåbaer-Tuerne)
Nei se, hvor det blå-ner her! Nu vil en Hirl vi os ta- ge! — E

No. 4 Møte (Møde)
En stil- le Sön- dag sid-der hun i Li;____ det strömmer på — F

No. 5 Elsk (Elskoe)
Den vil-de Gut-ten mit Sind har då- ret, som Fugl i Sna-ren jeg sid-der sa-ret; — G

No. 6 Killingdans (Kiddenes Dans)
A hipp og hop-pe og tipp og top-pe på den- ne— Dag; — H

No. 7 Vond Dag (Ond Dag)
Hon toel-ler Dag og Stund og se- ne kvoeld til Sön-dags- tid — I

No. 8 Ved Gjaetle-Bekken (Ved Gjatle-Bakken)
Du ris- len-de Boek, du heis-len-de Boek, her lig-ger i Sol du så klar — J

A Boat on the Waves is Rocking, Op. 69, No. 1
A boat on the waves is rock- ing, There sit-ting a- lone on board____ — K

Eros, Op. 70, No. 1
Hört mich, ihr frö- sti-gen Her - - - - zen im Nord, — L

Lichte Nacht (Radiant Night), No. 3
Sank nicht die Son-ne kaum erst zum Meer in duf-ti-ger däm_mernder Fer-ne, — M

GRIFFES, Charles Tomlinson (1884-1920)

In a Myrtle Shade, Op. 9, No. 1
Copyright 1918, G. Schirmer, Inc.
To a love-ly myr-tle bound, Blos-soms_show-'er-ing all a- round — O

Waikiki No. 2
Warm per-fumes like a breath from vine and tree — P

An Old Song Re-Sung, No. 4
I saw a ship a sail-ing, a- sail- ing, a- sail-ing, — Q

Sorrow of Mydath, No. 5
Wear - - - y the cry____ of the wind____ is — R

A Feast of Lanterns, Op. 10, No. 5
Copyright 1917, G. Schirmer, Inc.
In Spring for sheer de-light__ I set the lanterns swinging through_the trees — S

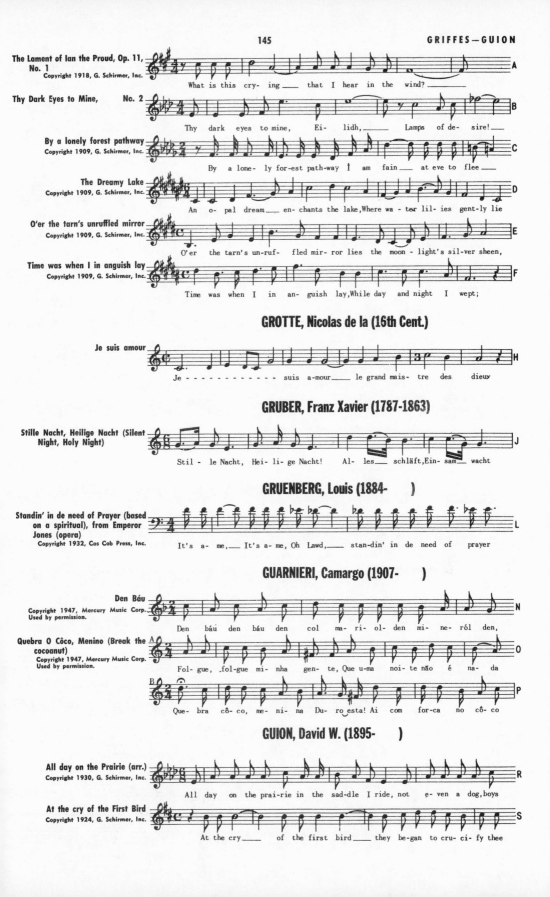

The Lament of Ian the Proud, Op. 11, No. 1
Copyright 1918, G. Schirmer, Inc.

What is this cry- ing____ that I hear in the wind?____

Thy Dark Eyes to Mine,   No. 2

Thy dark eyes to mine, Ei- lidh,____ Lamps of de- sire!____

By a lonely forest pathway
Copyright 1909, G. Schirmer, Inc.

By a lone- ly for-est path-way I am fain__ at eve to flee_

The Dreamy Lake
Copyright 1909, G. Schirmer, Inc.

An o- pal dream__ en- chants the lake, Where wa- ter lil- ies gent-ly lie

O'er the tarn's unruffled mirror
Copyright 1909, G. Schirmer, Inc.

O'er the tarn's un-ruf- fled mir- ror lies the moon- light's sil-ver sheen,

Time was when I in anguish lay
Copyright 1909, G. Schirmer, Inc.

Time was when I in an- guish lay, While day and night I wept;

GROTTE, Nicolas de la (16th Cent.)

Je suis amour

Je - - - - - - - - - - - - - suis a-mour____ le grand mais- tre des dieux

GRUBER, Franz Xavier (1787-1863)

Stille Nacht, Heilige Nacht (Silent Night, Holy Night)

Stil - le Nacht, Hei- li- ge Nacht! Al- les schläft, Ein- sam wacht

GRUENBERG, Louis (1884-)

Standin' in de need of Prayer (based on a spiritual), from Emperor Jones (opera)
Copyright 1932, Cos Cob Press, Inc.

It's a- me,__ It's a- me, Oh Lawd,____ stan-din' in de need of prayer

GUARNIERI, Camargo (1907-)

Den Báu
Copyright 1947, Mercury Music Corp.
Used by permission.

Den báu den báu den col ma- ri- ol- den mi- ne- ról den,

Quebra O Côco, Menino (Break the cocoanut)
Copyright 1947, Mercury Music Corp.
Used by permission.

Fol- gue, fol-gue mi- nha gen- te, Que u-ma noi- te não é na- da

Que- bra cô- co, me- ni- na Du- ro esta! Ai com for-ca no cô- co

GUION, David W. (1895-)

All day on the Prairie (arr.)
Copyright 1930, G. Schirmer, Inc.

All day on the prai-rie in the sad-dle I ride, not e- ven a dog, boys

At the cry of the First Bird
Copyright 1924, G. Schirmer, Inc.

At the cry____ of the first bird____ they be- gan to cru- ci- fy thee

HAHN

Ciboulette (operetta) — A

Nous a-vous fait un beau voy-a- ge Nous a-vons fait un beau voy-a- ge!

C'est sa banlieue — B

Y'a des ar-bres,__ des mai-sons__ Y'a l'é-glise et la mai- ri- e__

Valse — C

A- mour qui meurs, a- mour qui pas-ses, A- mour fra-gi- le,

Cimetière de Campagne
By permission Heugel & Cie, Paris, copyright owners — D

J'ai re-vu le ci-me-tiè- re du beau pa-ys d'Am-bé- rieux

Les Cygnes
By permission Heugel & Cie, Paris, copyright owners — E

Ton âme est un lac d'a-mour Dont mes dé- sirs sont les Cy- gnes

La Dernière Valse (Une Revue)
By permission Heugel & Cie, Paris, copyright owners — F

Les feuilles tom-bent, c'est l'au-tom- ne. Tu pars, tout est fi-ni

D'une prison
By permission Heugel & Cie, Paris, copyright owners — G

Le ciel est par des-sus le toit, si bleu, si cal- -me

L'Énamourée
By permission Heugel & Cie, Paris, copyright owners — H

Ils se di-sent, ma co-lom- be que tu rê-ves,morte en-co- re,

En sourdine
By permission Heugel & Cie, Paris, copyright owners — I

Cal- -mes dans le demi jour que les branches hautes font__ Pé-né-trons bien

Les Étoiles
By permission Heugel & Cie, Paris, copyright owners — J

Les cieux__ res-plen-dis- sants d'é-toi- les Aux ra- di-eux

Fêtes Galantes
By permission Heugel & Cie, Paris, copyright owners — K

Les don-neurs de sé-ré-na- - - des Et les bel-les é-cou-teu- - -ses,

Fumée
By permission Heugel & Cie, Paris, copyright owners — L

Com-pa-gne de l'é-ther,__ in-do-len- te fu- mé- - -e,

L'Heure Exquise
By permission Heugel & Cie, Paris, copyright owners — M

La lu-ne blan-che luit dans les bois; de cha-que bran-che Part une voix

L'Incrédule
By permission Heugel & Cie, Paris, copyright owners — N

Tu crois au marc de ca-fé,__ Au pré sa- ges, aux grands jeux__

Infidélité
By permission Heugel & Cie, Paris, copyright owners — O

Voi-ci l'or-me qui ba-lan- ce Son om- - -bre sur le sen-tier,

Je me metz en vostre mercy
By permission Heugel & Cie, Paris, copyright owners — P

Je me metz en vos-tre mer-cy,__ Tres bel- -le, bon- ne

Lydé
By permission Heugel & Cie, Paris, copyright owners — Q

Viens, c'est le jour d'un Dieu, Pui-sons a-vec lar-gesse

Mai
By permission Heugel & Cie, Paris, copyright owners — R

De-puis un mois,chère ex- i-lé- e, Loin de mes yeux tu t'en al-las,__

Mozart (operetta) Act I
By permission Heugel & Cie, Paris, copyright owners — S

Etre a-do-ré! Pren-dre les coeurs Et les sen-tir tous qui se li-vrent,

Mozart (operetta)
Act II Letter Song
De-puis ton dé- part, mon a-mour,__ De-puis, hé-las, de si longs jours

Act III Air des Adieux
Sois cou-ra-geu-se, O ma maî-tres-se, Pen-dant que je te dis a-dieu

Nocturne
By permission Heugel & Cie, Paris, copyright owners
Sur ton sein pâ- le, mon coeur dort D'un som-meil doux__ com-me la mort.

Offrande
By permission Heugel & Cie, Paris, copyright owners
Voi- ci des fruits, des fleurs, des feuilles et des branches Et puis voi-ci mon coeur

Paysage
By permission Heugel & Cie, Paris, copyright owners
A deux pas de la mer qu'on en- tend bour-don- ner,

Paysage Triste
L'om- bre des ar- bres dans la ri-viere em-bru- mé__ meurt

Phyllis
By permission Heugel & Cie, Paris, copyright owners
De-puis neuf ans et plus dans l'am- pho-re scel-lé- - e

Le Plus Beau Présent
By permission Heugel & Cie, Paris, copyright owners
Tu m'as don-né un cous-sin de soi- e, Un brû-le-par-fum d'un art per- san;

Le Printemps
By permission Heugel & Cie, Paris, copyright owners
Te voi-là, __ ri- re du Prin-temps__ Les thyr-ses des li-las.

Quand je fus pris au pavillon
By permission Heugel & Cie, Paris, copyright owners
Quand je fus pris au pa-vil-lon de ma da-me très gente et bel - - le

Rêverie
By permission Heugel & Cie, Paris, copyright owners
Puisqu'i-ci vas toute â-me Donne à quel-qu'un Sa mu-si-que, sa flamme

Le Rossignol des Lilas
By permission Heugel & Cie, Paris, copyright owners
O pre-mier ros-si- gnol qui viens dans les li-las, sous ma fe- nê-tre,

Seule
By permission Heugel & Cie, Paris, copyright owners
Dans un bai-ser, l'onde, au ri- va- ge, Dit ses dou- leurs__

Si mes vers avaient des ailes
Mes vers fui-raient doux et frêles vers vo-tre jar-din si beau,

Le souvenir d'avoir chanté
By permission Heugel & Cie, Paris, copyright owners
Le sou-ve-nir d'a-voir chan- té Au so-leil, sous l'a-zur cé- les- -te,

Sur l'eau
By permission Heugel & Cie, Paris, copyright owners
Je n'en-tends que le bruit de la rive et de l'eau__

Tyndaris
By permission Heugel & Cie, Paris, copyright owners
O__ blan- che Tyn- da- ris, les Dieux me sont a- mis

HALÉVY, Jacques François (1799-1862)

La Juive (opera)
Act I
Si la ri-gueur et la ven- gean-ce leur font ha- ir__ la sain-te loi

La Juive (opera)

Act II — O Dieu, Dieu de nos pè- res, par- mi nous dé- scends!

Si tra- hi- son ou per- fi- di- e o- sait se glisser par- mi nous,

Cavatine — Dieu, que ma voix trem- blan- te s'é- lè- - - - ve jusqu'aux cieux,

Il va ve- nir! et d'éf- froi je me sens fré- mir

Act III — Vous qui du Dieu vi- vant ou- tra- gez la puis- san- ce

Act IV — Ra- chel, quand du Seig- neur la grâ- ce tu- té- lai- re

HAMMERSCHMIDT, Andreas (1612-1675)

Sei nun wieder zufrieden — Sei nun wie- der zu- frie- den, mei- ne See- le,

HANDEL, George Frederick (1685-1759)

Arioso (cantata con stromenti) (Questionable authenticity) — Dank _____ sei Dir, Herr, Dank _____ sei Dir, Herr Du hast Dein

O come, let us worship, from Chandos Anthem — O come, _____ let us wór- ship, let us wor- ship and fall down, _____

Di Cupido impiego — Di Cu- pi- - do im- pie- go i van- - - - - ni

Nel dolce dell' oblio (cantata for solo voice—secular) Aria — Giacchè il son- no a lei di- pin- ge la sem- bian- za del suo be- - ne,

Aria — Ha l'in- gan- no il suo di- let- to se i pen- sier mos- si _ d'af- fet- to

Praise of Harmony — Look down, look down, har- mo- - - - - - - - - - - nious Saint,

Süsse Stille — Sü- sse _____ Stil- le, sanf- te Quel- le _____ ru- - - - hi- ger

Te Deum (Dettingen) — Vouch- safe, O Lord! Vouch- safe, O Lord! to keep us this day with- out _ sin

When thou took- est up- on thee to de- li- - ver man

ODES: Alexander's Feast — Bac- chus e- ver fair and _____ young, drink- ing days did first or- dain

Alexander's Feast: Revenge, Timotheus cries

Re- venge, re-venge, re-venge, Ti-mo-theus cries, re-venge, Ti-mo-theus cries

L'Allegro

But, oh! sad vir- gin that thy power might raise Mu-sae - us from his bower!

Come and trip__ it as__ you go, on the light fan-tas-tic toe, trip it, trip it

Come, come, thou god-dess__ fair and free, fair__ and free in heav'n yclep'd Eu-phro-sy-ne,

Come with na- tive lus-tre shine, Mo- de- ra- tion, grace di- vine

Hide me__ from day's gar-ish__ eye, While the bee with hon - -ied__ thigh

Let me wan - -der not__ un- seen, by hedge-row elms on hill-locks green.

Or let the mer- ry bells ring round, And the jo-cund re-beck's__ sound

Mirth, ad --mit me of thy crew, Mirth, ad-mit me of thy crew, Mirth, ad-mit me,

Mirth, ad-mit me of thy crew!__ Mirth, admit me of__ thy crew, Mirth, admit me,

Oft on a plat of ris-ing ground I hear the far off cur- few__ sound

Sweet bird,__ Sweet bird, that shun'st the noise of folly,

Ode to St. Cecilia

But oh!__ What art can teach, what hu- man voice__ can reach

The soft com- plain - - - - - ing Flute in dy- ing notes dis-co - -vers

OPERAS
Admeto

Can-gio d'aspet- to il cru-do fa-to e nel mio pet-to

Lu- ci ca-re, ad-di- o, po-sa-te! Lu-ci ca-re, ad- di- o,

Si- gnor, lo cre-di a me: ti ser-ba a- mo - -re e fè

Spe - - ra, si, mio ca- ro__ be - ne, ch'io per te__

Quan- to god-rà, al- lor-che mi ve-drà l'a-ma-to spo-so mi-o,

OPERAS
Atalanta

Di ad I- re- ne,_ ti- ran- na in- fe- de- le,

La- scia_ ch'io par- ta so- lo, e tu ri- man- ti, oh bel- la,

M'al- lon- - - - ta- no, sde- gno- - se pu- pil- le,

Ri- por- tai,_ glo- rio- - sa pal- ma,

S'è tuo_ pia- cer, ch'io mo- ra va- do a mo- rir, I- re- - ne

Sof- fri in pa- ce il tuo do- lo- re, se il mio a- mor tu di- sprez- za- sti

Berenice

Si, tra i cep- pi e le ri- tor- te La mia fè ri- splen- de- rà,_

No, sof- frir non può il mio a- mo- re, che non re- gni tua bel- tà,

Caro amor, from Il Pastor
Fido Act II

Ca- ro A- mor, Ca- ro A- mor, sol per mo- men- - - ti

Deidàmia

Due bell' al- me in- na- mo- ra- te, ca- re, fi- de a- man- ti

Nel ri- po- so e nel con- ten- to Go- do e sen- to Lie- ve il pe- so

Ezio

Se pen- si a- mor tu so- lo per vez- zo e per_ bel- ta

Na- sce al bos- co in roz- - za cu- na un fe- li- ce pa- - - sto- rel- la

Quan- to mai fe- li- ce sie- te, in- no- cen- ti pas- to- rel- le,

Se un bell' ar- di- - - - re Può in- na- mo- rar- ti

Flavio

Vi fi- - - da lo spo- - - so, vi fi- da il re- gnan- te,

A- mor, nel mi- o pe- nar_ deg- - gio spe- - rar,

L'ar- - mel- lin_ vi- ta non cu- ra se d'of- fen- de- re ha_ ti- mo- re

Chi può mi- ra- re e non_ a- - ma- re, e non a- a- ma- re

153

HANDEL

OPERAS
Flavio

Quan- to dol- ci, quan- to ca- re son le gio- je nel mio sen,

Floridante

Al - - - ma mi - a, sì, sol tu se- i la mia glo- ria, il mio di- let- to,

A- mor com- man- da o- no- re in- vi- ta, più bel im- pe- gno

Fin- che lo stra- le non giun- ge al se- gno, pen- sier re- ga- le, no, non si sa

Non las- ciar Op- pres- sa del- la sor- te Pe- rir quell' al- ma for- te

Se dol - - ce m'e- ra gia vi- ver, cor mio, con te,

Giulio Cesare (Julius Caesar)

Da tem- pe - - - - ste il le - - gno in- fran - - - - - - - to,

Dal ful- gor di que- sta spa - - da

Pian- ge- rò, pian- ge- rò la sor- te mi - a,

Se pie- tà di me non sen- ti giu- sto ciel, io mo- ri- rò,

V'a- do- ro, pu- pil- le, sa- et - - - te d'a- mo - - re,

Lotario

Già mi sem- bra al ca - - - ro av- vin- to Trar l'au- da- ce,

Per sal- var- ti, i- do- lo mi- o so ben i - - o,

Lusinghe più care, from Alessandro

Lu- sin- ghe più ca- re d'A- mor ve- ri dar- di

Muzio Scevola

Pu- pil- le sde- gno- se! sa- re- ste pie- to- se,

Vo- la- te più dei ven- ti, mo- men- ti che scor- re- te,

Nel mondo e nell' abisso, from
Riccardo

Nel mon- do e nell' a- bis- so io non pa- ven - - - - - - - - to

Orlando

La- scia A- mor, e sie- gui Mar- te, va! com- bat- ti, com- bat- ti

Sor- ge in- fau sta u- na pro- cel - la, Che o- scu- rar fa il cie- lo e il ma- re

OPERAS
Orlando
Va- ghe pu- - pil- le, no, non pian-ge- te,__ no, [A]

Ottone
Af- fan- ni del pen- sier, un sol mo-men-to da-te-mi pa-ce almen [B]

Ah! tu non sai, quant'_ il mio cor so- spi- ra,e_ sen- te [C]

Del mi- nac-ciar del ven- - - - - - - - - - - - - - - - - to [D]

Un di-sprez-za-to af- fet- to, un mi- se- ro so-spet-to [E]

Io spe- - - - - ra- i, io spe-rai tro-var ri- po- so [F]

S'io dir po-tes-si al mio cru-de- le la tua fe-de- le [G]

La spe-ran- za e giun- - - - - -ta,in por- to [H]

Ve - ni,o fi - - -glio! ve- ni,o fi - - -glio, e mi con-so- la, [I]

Partenope
Fu- ri- bon- - - - - - - - - - - - - - - - - -do spi-ra,il ven-to [J]

Sei mia__ gio-ja sei_mio be- ne, sei mia pa-ce e mia spe- ran-za [K]

Qual far- fal- let- ta__ gi- ra,a quel__ lu- me, [L]

Poro
Chi vi-ve,a man-te sai che de- li- ra, sai che de-li- ra, [M]

E prez- zo leg-gie- ro D'un sud- di- - to il san-gue [N]

Son con-fu-sa pa- sto- rel- la, che__ nel__ bo-sco,a notte,o-scu-ra, [O]

Radamisto
Ca- ra spo- sa,a-ma- to be- ne pren-di spe-ne [P]

Già che mo-rir non pos-so: fu- rie che cie-co,a-bis- so [Q]

Om - - bra ca- ra, Om - - - - -bra ca- ra di_ mia spo- sa [R]

Per- fi-do! per- fi- do, di a quell' em- pio ti- ran- no [S]

HANDEL

OPERAS
Radamisto — A
Qual na - - ve smar-ri - ta trà sir-ti,e tem-pe-sta,

B
Quan-do mai spie-ta - ta sor-te, spie-ta - - ta sor-te,

C
Som - mi De - i, som - mi De - i, che scor-ge-te

Rinaldo — D
Ca - - - - - ra spo-sa, a-man-te ca - ra, Do-ve se - i?

E
Del vostro E- re-bo sull' a - ra, Col-la fa-ce del mio sdegno

F
Las - cia ch'io pian-ga mia cru - da sor - - te,

G
Il Tri-cer-bero hu-mi-lia-to al mio bran-do ren-de-rò

H
Vò far guer-ra, e vin-cer vo-glio,e vin-cer vo-glio

Rodelinda — I
Con-fu-sa si mi-ri l'in-fi-da con-sor-te,

J
Con rau-co mor--mo-ri o Pian-go-no al pian-to mi-o

K
Do- -ve se- i, a-ma-to be-ne? Vie-ni, l'al-ma

L
L'em- - pio ri-gor del fa-to vi le non po - trà far-mi

M
Ho per- - -du-to il ca - ro spo-so,

N
Mio ca - ro be-ne! ca-ro, ca-ro! mio ca-ro be-ne!

O
Mor-rai sì, l'em-pia tua te-sta, già m'ap-pre--sta

P
Om-bre, pian-te ur-ne fu-ne-ste! Voi sa-re-ste

Q
Pa-sto-rel-lo d'un po-ve-ro ar-men-to pur dor-me con-ten-to

R
Pri-gio-nie-ra hò l'al-ma in pe-na mà si bel-la

S
Ri- tor- na,oh ca- ro,e dol- ce mio te-so- ro,

OPERAS

Rodelinda

A — Scas - cia - ta dal suo ni - do sen__ vo - la in al-tro li - do,

B — Spieta- ti, Io vi giu-rai, se al mio fi-glio il cor do-na- i,

Rodrigo

C — Al- lor-chè sor-ge____ a- stro lu- cen-te,

D — Begl' oc - - - - - chi begl' oc-chi del__ mio ben,

E — Il dol - ce fo - co mi - o, il dol-ce fo - co mi - o

Scipione

F — Dim- mi, ca - ra dim-mi tu dei mo-rir," mà oh ca-ra, non mi dir:

G — Ge- ne - ro - so chi sol bra - ma quel che pia-ce al ben ch'e-glia-ma

H — Par- to, fug- go, re- sta, e godi de tue fro-di

I — Pen - - - - sa oh__ bel- la, al- la mia__ spe- me

J — Se mor-mo- ra ri-vo o fron-da, su-sur-ran ven-ti- - cel-li

K — Son pel- le-gri- no che d'al-to ve-de il con-fi-ne del suo cam-mi-no

L — Tut- ta rac-col-ta an-cor nel pal-pi-tan-te cor tre-man- te ho l'al-ma,

**Sento che un giusto sdegno,
from Faramondo**

M — Sen- to che un gius-to sde- gno mi spro-na a ven-di- car- mi,

Serse (Xerxes)

N — Ca- ro voi sie-te all' al- ma, dol- ce voi sie-te al cor,

O — Del mio ca- ro ba- co a-ma- bi- le nell' im-pe- ro suo

P — Di- rà che a-mor per me pia- ga- to il cor non gli ha

Q — Nè men con__ l'om-bre d'in-fe-del- tà vo-glio tra-di- re l'a-ni-ma

R — Non so se sia la spe- me, che mi so-stie-ne in vi - - ta

(accompaniment)

S — Om - - - - - bra mai__ fu____ Di ve-ge - ta-bi-le

OPERAS
Serse (Xerxes)

A — Quel- la che tut- ta fè per me lan-guia d'a-mo-re

B — Va go----den-do vez-zo-so e bel-lo quel ru-scel-lo la li-ber-ta

Siroe

C — Ch'io mai vi pos-sa la-sciar d'a-ma-re

D — Deg-gio mo-ri- re o stel-le, nè all in-no-cen-za mi a

E — Ge- li- do, in o-gni ve-na scor-rer mi sen-to il san-gue:

F — Mi la-gne-rò ta-cen-do del mio de-sti-no a-va- ro,

G — Non vi piac-que in-giu-sti De- i, ch'io na-sces-si pa-sto-rel-la;

H — La sor-te mia ti-ran-na far-mi di più non può

I — Tor- ren-te cre-sciu-to per tor- bi-da pie- na,

Sosarme

J — Ren-di'l se-re-no al ci----glio, Ma-dre, non pian-ger più,

K — Si, si, si, si, mi-nac-cia, e vin-ta l'i-ra in si gran pe-ri-glio

Tamerlano

L — A suoi pie-di pa-dre e san-gue la su- per-ba mi ve-drà,

M — Bel-la A-ste- ria, bel-la A-ste-ria il tuo cor mi di-fen-da,

N — Cor di pa-dre e cor d'a-man-te, Sal-da fe-de o-dio co-stan-te,

O — Deh! la-scia-te-mi il ne-mi-co, se to-glie-ste a me l'a-man-te

P — Em- pio, em-pio, per far-ti guer-ra, dal re-gno di sot-ter-ra

Q — Fi-glia mi-a, non pian-ger, no, no, fi-glia, no, non pianger,

R — For-te e lie-to a mor-te an-drei, se ce-las-si ai pen-sier mie-i

S — Nò, nò, il tuo sde-gno mi pla----co,

OPERAS

Tamerlano — Par che mi na-sca in se--no un__ rag-gio di spe-ran--za,

Teseo — Più non cer-ca li-ber-ta,__ mà l'a-mor, la fe-del-tà,

Ri-cor-da-ti, oh bel--la, che tu__ sol sei quel-la per cui__ pe-nail cor

Vie-ni, tor--na, i-do-lo mi----o, que-sto cor__ a con-so-lar!

Tolomeo — Non lo di-rò col lab-bro, che tan-to ar-dir non ha

Stil-le a-ma---re, gia vi sen-to tut-te in se-no, la mor-te a chiamar

Voi dol-ci au-ret-te al cor, mo-stra-te o-ve s'ag-gi-ra,

Vado a morir, from Arminio — Va-----do, va-do a mo-rir va-do a mo-rir vi la-scio

Zweier Augen Majestät from Almira — Zwei-er__ Au-gen-Ma-je-stät zwei-er__ Au-gen__ Ma-je-stät

ORATORIOS

Acis and Galatea — As when__ the__ dove__ la--ments__ her__ love,

Love in her eyes sits play-ing, and sheds__ de-li--cious death;

Love sounds th'a-larm,__ love sounds th'a-larm, and fear is__ a__ fly-ing

O rud-dier than the cher-ry o sweet-er than the ber-ry,

Would__ you gain__ the ten-der crea-ture, soft--ly, gent--ly, kind--ly

Alexander Balus — Con-vey me to some peace-ful shore, where no tu-mul-tuous billows roar,

Here a-mid__ the sha-dy woods Frag-rant flow'rs and crys-tal floods,

Sub-tle__ love with fan---cy view-ing, rapt'-rous joys on__ joys ensu-ing,

Athalia — Gen-tle airs me-lo-dious strains,__ Call for rap--tures out of woe

Oh__ Lord Oh Lord whom__ we a--dore, whom we a--dore

ORATORIOS
Athalia — A — Will God, whose mer-cies ev-er flow Ex-pose his chil-dren's youth to woe?

Belshazzar — B — Great God! who yet but dark-ly known___ Thus far hast deigned my arms to___

C — O sa- - - - -cred,__ sa-cred o-ra-cles of__ truth,

D — Thus saith the Lord to Cy-rus his a-noint-ed Whose right hand I have holden

Deborah — E — All dan-ger dis-dain-ing, all dan-ger dis-dain-ing for bat-tle I glow

F — Impious mor-tal, cease to brave_us, Great Je-ho-vah soon_ will save_us,

G — In___ the bat-tle fame___ pur- su- ing

H — Tears, tears such as ten-der fa-thers shed

Esther — I — Al-le-lu-ja, al-le-lu- - - - - - - - - - - - - - - ja

J — O beau-teous Queen un-close_those eyes, My fair-est shall_not bleed,

K — Pluck root and branch from out the land: Shall I the God of Is-rael fear,

L — Sing songs of praise,__ bow down the knee, bow down the knee,___

M — Turn not, O Queen, thy face___ a- way___

Hercules — N — From ce-les-tial_seats de-scending, joys di-vine a-while sus- pend- ing

O — My fa-ther! ah! me-thinks I see the sword inflict the deadly_wound

P — The smil-ing hours___ a joy-ful___ train,

Q — The world when__ day's ca- - - -reer___ is__ run

Israel in Egypt
Part I, No. 10 — R — But as for his peo-ple, but as for his peo-ple,

Part II, No. 17 — S — Mo-ses and the chil-dren of Is-rael sung this song un-to the Lord

The Lord shall reign for e- ver and e- ver,

No. 39

Sing ye to the Lord, for He hath tri- umph- ed glo- rious- ly;

The e- ne- my said: I will pur- sue I will o- ver take,

The Lord is a man of war, the Lord, the Lord is a__ man of war

Thou_shalt bring_them in and plant them in the moun - - - - - - tain

Jephtha
Recitative A

Deep- er and deep-er still thy good-ness, child, Pier-ceth a fa-ther's bleeding heart,

Aria B

Waft her, an- gels, through the skies, Far a- bove yon a- zure plain

A

Fare- well, fare- well, ye lim - - - pid springs__ and floods,

B

Bright-er scenes I seek a - bove In_the realms of peace and love____

In gen - tle_ mur-murs will__ I mourn, As mourns____ the mate

Pour forth no more un- heed- ed prayers To i-dols deaf and vain

The smi - ling__ dawn____ of hap- py days Pre - - sente a prospect clear,

Joseph

The pea- sant tastes_the sweets of life,___ un - - wound- ed by its__ cares

What's sweet- er than the new - - blown rose or bree- zes from the new mown close?

Joshua

Aw- ful pleas-ing Be-ing, say, If from heav'n thou wing'st

Hark, hark! 'tis the lin-net and the thrush, In dul - cet_ notes

He-roes, when with glo- ry__ burn- ing, all their toil with plea-sure bear

Oh, had I Ju- bal's lyre, or Mi - riam's__ tune-ful__ voice:

See the ra-ging flames a- rise _____

HANDEL

ORATORIOS
Joshua — A
Shall I in Mam-re's fer-tile plain the remnant of my days re-main

Judas Maccabeus
No. 2 — B
Mourn, mourn, mourn, ye af-flict-ed chil-dren, the re-mains

No. 9 — C
Oh Fa - - - ther, whose al-might- -y pow'r

No. 11 b — D
We come, we come, we come, in bright ar-ray, in bright ar-ray,

No. 22 — E
Pi-ous or - - -gies, pi-ous airs, de - - -cent sor-row,—

No. 23 — F
Fall'n is the foe Fall'n is the foe; so fall thy foes

No. 26 — G
Zi-on now her head shall raise, tune your harps,

No. 28 — H
Hail, hail, hail Ju-de-a, hap-py land, Ju-de-a, hap-py land,

No. 35 — I
Arm, arm ye brave! arm, arm ye brave! a no - -ble cause, a no - -ble cause

No. 43 — J
Call forth thy pow'rs, my soul, and dare the con-flict, the con-flict

No. 45 — K
Sing un-to God and high af-fec-tions raise,

No. 46 — L
Oh li-ber-ty thou choicest treasure, seat of virtue source of pleasure!

No. 51 — M
'Tis li - - - - - -ber-ty, dear li-ber-ty a-lone

No. 52 — N
Hal-le-lu-jah, A-men, a-men, Hal-le-lu-ja, a-men

No. 54 — O
Come, e-ver smil-ing li-ber-ty, come, smil-ing li-ber-ty, and with thee bring

No. 66 — P
No, no un-hal-low'd de-sire our breasts shall in-spire,

No. 92 — Q
So ra-pid thy course is, not num-ber-less for-ces

No. 110 — R
From might- -y kings he took the spoil, and with his acts made Judah

No. 120 — S
How vain is man who boasts in fight

Judas Maccabeus
No. 132 — The Lord work-eth won - ders — A

No. 136 — Sound an a-larm, sound an a-larm! your sil-ver trum-pets sound, — B

No. 148 — With pi-ous hearts and brave as pi-ous, Oh Si-on, we thy call at - - tend; — C

No. 152 — Wise men, flat - t'ring, may de - - - - ceive us — D

No. 172 — Fa-ther of Heav'n! from Thy e-ter-nal throne, From Thy e-ter - nal throne — E

No. 178 — So shall the lute and harp a-wake, and sprightly voice sweet descant run, — F

No. 186 — See, the con-qu'ring he - - - - ro comes! sound the trum-pets, — G

No. 199 — With ho-nour let de-sert be crown'd the trum-pet ne'er in vain shall sound, — H

No. 210 — Oh love-ly peace, with plen-ty crown'd, oh, love-ly love-ly peace — I

Messiah
No. 2 — Com-fort ye, Com - - - fort ye my peo-ple, — J

No. 3 — Ev'-ry val - ley, ev'-ry val - ley shall be ex-alt-ed — K

No. 4 — And the glo-ry, the glo-ry of the Lord, And the glo-ry, the glory of the Lord — L

No. 6 — But who may a-bide the day of his com-ing, — M

For he is like a re-fi - - - - - - ner's fire — N

No. 7 — And he shall pu-ri-fy, and he shall purify — O

No. 9 — O, thou that tell-est good tid-ings to Zi-on, — P

No. 11 — The peo - - ple that walk - - ed in dark - - - - - ness, — Q

No. 12 — For un-to us a child is born, un-to us a son is giv-en, — R

No. 18 — Glo-ry to God, Glo-ry to God in the high-est, — S

ORATORIOS
Messiah
No. 19

Re- joice, re- joice, re- joice _____ great- ly

No. 21

He shall__ feed his flock like a shep - - - - - - - - herd

No. 22

His yoke___ is ea - sy

No. 23

Be- hold the Lamb of God be - - hold the Lamb of God, the Lamb of God

No. 24

He was des- pis- ed, des- pis- ed_ and re-ject-ed

No. 25 A

Sure- ly, sure- ly He hath borne our griefs, and carried our sorrows

B

And with his stripes we are heal - - - - ed,

No. 26

All we like sheep, All we like sheep have gone a-stray, _____

No. 28

He trust-ed in God that he would_ de- li-ver him; let him de- li-ver him

No. 30

Be- hold and_ see, be-hold and_ see if there be an- y sor-row

No. 32

But Thou didst not leave his soul in_ Hell, but Thou didst_ not_ leave

No. 33

Lift up your heads O ye_ gates and be ye lift up, ye ev-er-lasting doors,

No. 36

Thou art gone up on high, Thou art gone up on high

No. 38

How beau- ti-ful are the feet_ of them that preach_ the gospel of peace,_

No. 39

Their sound is gone out in-to all lands, Their sound is gone out

No. 40

Why do the na- tions so fu-rious- ly rage_ to - -geth-er?

No. 41

Let us break their bonds a- sun - -der, let_ us break,

No. 43

Thou shalt break them, Thou shalt break them with a rod_____ of i-ron;

No. 44 "Hallelujah" Chorus

Hal- le- lu- jah! Hal- le- lu- jah! Hal-le- lu- jah! Hal-le- lu-jah!

ORATORIOS
Messiah
No. 45

I know that___ my Re-deem----er liv-eth

No. 48

The trum-pet shall sound____ and the dead shall_be__ raised

No. 50

O death, o death,where, where is thy sting? O death,where is thy sting?

No. 51

But thanks__ but thanks,thanks,thanks be to God, but thanks,thanks,thanks,

No. 52

If God___ be for us, who can be a-gainst us?

No. 53

Wor-thy is the lamb that was slain, and hath re-deem-ed us to God

Amen Chorus

A- - - - - - - - - -men,A - - - - - - - - - - - men, A - - - - - - - - - - - - -men

Occasional Oratorio

His sceptre is the rod of righteousness, his sceptre is the rod

Je-ho-vah, to my words_give ear, To my words_give_ear,

Then will I___ Je-ho- -vah's praise ac-cord-ing_to his jus-tice_raise,

Samson

A- wake the trum-pet's loft-y sound, A- wake, a-wake

Honour and arms____ scorn such a foe,scorn such_a foe

How will-ing_my pa-ter-nal_love the weight_to share_of fil-ial care,

Let the bright Se-ra-phim in burn- - - -ing row,

Re-turn, re-turn, Oh_ God___ of hosts! oh God re- -turn,

Thus when the sun from's wa- -t'ry_bed all cur-tain'd_with_a clou- -dy red,

Thy glo-rious deeds in-spir'd_my_tongue,whilst airs of joy from_ thence_did flow

To-tal e-clipse! No sun, no moon, all dark,____ all dark____

Why does the God of Is-rael sleep? A-rise with dread-ful sound,

ORATORIOS
Samson

A — Ye sons of Is-rael, now la - ment; your spear is _ broke, your_ bow's un - bent

Saul

B — Brave Jo - na - than his bow ne'er_ drew. but wing'd with death,

C — Fell rage and black des-pair_ pos- sessed, with hor-rid sway the mon-arch's breast,

D — Oh_ god-like youth!_ by all_ con-fess'd of hu-man race _____ the pride!

E — Oh Lord, whose mercies num-ber-less o'er all thy works _____ pre-vail,

F — Sin not, O King, a- gainst the youth   Who ne'er_ of-fend - - - ed_ you,

Semele

G — End- less plea - - sure   End- less plea - sure, endless love

H — Hence, hence, I- ris, hence a- way,   I- ris, hence a-way, a - way,

I — Hy-men, haste,   Hy-men, haste! thy torch prepare! Love al-read-y his has lighted,

J — Leave_ me,   leave me, loath - some light! re-ceive me, re - ceive me,

K — Oh _____ sleep,   Oh_ sleep why dost thou leave_me?

L — Where 'er you_walk, cool gales shall fan the glade; trees, where you sit, shall crowd

Solomon   Chorus

M — May no rash in- tru- der dis- turb their soft hours;

N — What though I trace each herb and_ flow'r that drinks the morning dew,

O — With thee th'un-sheltered moor I'd_ tread, nor once of fate_com- plain,

Susanna

P — Ask if yon damask rose_ be sweet, that scents the_ am- bient air?

Q — Be- neath the cy- press gloom- y shade where silver lil-lies paint the glade

R — Crys-tal_ streams in mur - murs_ flow - ing in mur- murs_ flow - - ing,

S — If guiltless blood be your in - - tent, I here re- sign it all

ORATORIOS
Susanna

The parent bird in search of food a-while de-serts her cal-low brood,

When first__ I saw my love-ly maid, be-neath__ the cit-ron's shade

Ye ver-dant hills, ye balm-y vales bear wit-ness of my pain

Theodora

An-gels e-ver__bright and__fair, an-gels e-ver__bright and fair,take,oh,take me,

As with ro-sy steps the morn ad-vanc-ing,drives the shades of night

De-fend her, Heaven,let an-gels spread_____

Lord, to__thee,each__night and__day, strong in hope we sing and__pray

The Triumph of Time and Truth

False, de-struc-tive ways of__ pleasure Leave, and court a no-bler__treasure

Loath-some urns,__ dis-close your treas-ure,Pride and pleasure Un-veil to me

HANDL, Jacob (1550-1591)

Adoramus te, Jesu Christe

A- do- ra- mus te, Je- su Chris- te

Ecce quomodo montur justus

The right- eous, the right-eous per - -ish-eth, per- ish-eth

HANSON, Howard (1896-   )

Oh, 'tis an earth defiled, from Merry
Mount (opera)
(pseud., Helen Guy Rhodes)

Oh,'tis an earth de- filed where-on we live!There is no leaf- y bow'r,

HARDELOT, Guy d' (1858-1936)

Because

I know a Lovely Garden

Sans Toi

HARRISON, Annie Fortescue (d. 1944)

In the Gloaming — In the gloam-ing o my dar-ling! When the lights are dim and low

HARTMANN, Johann Peter (1805-1900)

Flyv, Fugl, Flyv — Flyv, Fugl, flyv o-ver Fu-re-søens Vo-ve!

Frøjas Stjerne (choral) — Kun een er Frej-as Stjer-ne, men rundt den sen-der sin Glans

Jaegersang (choral) — Snart er Nat-ten svun-den, Da-gen bry-der frem

Jeg synge skal en Vise — Jeg syn-ge skal en Vi-se; vel-an jeg er be-red

Laer mig! — Laer mig, Nat-tens Stjer-ne, at ly-de fast og ger--ne

Mindnesang over de faldne — Slum-rer sødt i Sles-vigs Jord, dy-re-købt den blev ved e-der!

Rejsen til Vinlandene (choral) — Vort Dag-waerk er til En----de; som fri og mun-tre Sven-de

Sange af "Ambrosius" — Den ked-som Vin-ter gik sin Gang, den Dag saa kort, den Nat saa lang

Studentersang (choral) — Vi er et ly-stigt Fol-ke-faerd fra al-le Ver-dens Kan-ter

Ved Jaegerhuset — Du, som har Sorg i Sin-de gak ud i Mark og Lund,

HARTY, Hamilton (1879-1941)

My Lagan Love (arr.)
By permission Boosey & Hawkes, Inc., copyright owners — Where Lagan stream sings lull-a-by There blows a li-ly fair:

Three Irish Folksongs (arr.)
1. The Lowlands of Holland
By permission Oxford Univ. Press, London, copyright owners — The first night I was mar-ried, a hap-py hap-py bride

2. The Faery King's Courtship — On the first day of May at the close of the day

3. The Game Played in Erin-go-Bragh — In London one day as I walked up the street, An im-pu-dent fel-low

HASSLER, Leo (1564-1612)

Feinslieb, du hast mich g'fangen

Feins-lieb, du hast mich g'fan-gen mit dein zwei Aüg-lein schon — B

Jungfrau, dein schöne G'stalt

Jung-frau, dein schö-ne G'stalt er-frent mich sehr je länger je mehr — C

Mein Lieb' will mit mir kriegen

Mein Lieb' will mit mir krie-gen, hat sich ge-rist zur Schlacht — D

Tanzsen und Springen

Tan-zen und Sprin-gen, Sin-gen und Klin-gen, fa la la la — E

HATTON, John L.

Goodbye, sweetheart, goodbye

The bright stars fade, the morn is break-ing, The dew-drops pearl — G

Simon the Cellarer

Old Si-mon the Cel-lar-er keeps a rare store. — H

HAYDN, Franz Josef (1732-1809)

The Apothecary (opera)

Al-le Ta-ge, Al-le Ta-ge klop-fen, rei-ben — J

Sitzt Ei-nem hier im Kopf das Weh' so neh-men wir von die-sem Thee — K

Wo Lie-bes-göt-----ter lach-ten, stürmt Hass auf Hass — L

Es kam ein Pa-scha aus Tür-ken-land — M

Die-se Püpp-chen sind nicht zu er-grün-den, sind nicht zu er-grün-den — N

Wie Schlei--er seh' ichs nie--der schwe-ben — O

Mass No. 11 (Nelson Mass)
I Kyrie

Ky-ri-e, Ky-ri-e e-lei-son Ky-ri-e e-lei-son — P

II Gloria

Glo-ri-a in ex-cel----sis De-o — Q

Lau-da-mus te, be-ne-di-ci-mus te — R

III Qui Tollis

Qui tol-lis, qui tol-lis pec-ca-ta — S

Mass No. 11 (Nelson Mass)
IV Quoniam Tu Solus — Quo- ni- am tu so- lus so- - - - - lus sanc- tus tu

V Credo — Cre- do in u- num De- - - - um, Pa- - - - trem om- ni- po- ten- 'tem

VI Et Incarnatus — Et in- car- na- tus est de Spi- ri- tu__ san- cto

VII Et Resurrexit — Et, et re- sur- rex- - it ter- ti- a di- - e

VIII Sanctus — Sanc- - - tus__ Sanc- - - tus,__ san- ctus Do- mi- nus

IX Benedictus — Be- ne- di- ctus qui ve- nit', be- ne- di- ctus qui ve- nit

X Osanna — O- san- na in ex- cel- - - - - - - - - - - sis,

XI Agnus Dei — A- gnus__ De- i qui tol- lis pec- ca- ta mun- di

XII Dona Nobis — Do- na__ no- bis pa- cem pa- - cem, pa- - cem,

The Creation (Die Schöpfung)
(oratorio) Part I, No. 6 — Roll- ing in foam- ing__ bil- lows up- lift- ed, roars the boist'rous sea

Soft- ly purl- ing,__ glides on through si- lent vales the lim- pid brook

No. 8 — With ver- dure clad the fields ap- pear de- lightful to__ the ra -vish'd sense__

No. 10 — Stimmt an die Sai- ten ergreift die Leier, lasst eu- er Lob- ge- sang

(Same theme, text in English) — A- wake the Harp, the lyre a- wake! In shout and joy your voi- ces

No. 13 — The hea- vens are tell- ing the glo- - ry of God__

Part II, No. 15 — On might- y__ pens up- - lift- ed__ soars__ the eagle a- loft

No. 18 — Most beau- ti- ful ap- pear, with__ ver- dure young a- dorn'd

No. 21 — The cattle in herds al- rea- dy seeks his food on fields and meadows green

No. 22 — Now heav'n in full- est glo- - - - - - - - - ry__ shone__

A B C D E F G H I J K L M N O P Q R S

The Creation (Die Schöpfung)
(oratorio)   Part II, No. 24

A — In na-tive worth and ho-nour clad, with beau-ty, cou-rage,— strength adorn'd

No. 28

B — A-chieved is the— glo-rious work. Our song let— be the praise of— God

Part III, No. 34

C — Sing the Lord, ye voi-ces all! Ut-ter, ut-ter thanks, ye all his works——

No. 30

D — By thee———— with bliss, o boun - - - - - - teous Lord,

No. 32

E — Grace - - ful con-sort At thy— side— softly fly the golden— hours——

The Seasons (Die Jahreszeiten)
(oratorio)
Spring No. 2

F — Come, gen-tle Spring!—— ae- the-real mild-ness come——

No. 4

G — With ea-ger-ness the hus-band-man his— till-ing work be-gins

No. 6

H — Be now— gra-cious O— kind hea-ven o- -pen thee, o-pen thee

No. 8

I — O what— num'rous charms un- fol-ding, shows the— coun-try now——

Summer No. 11

J — The— rea-dy swain is gath'ring now his bleat-ing flock— and lov-ing herd

No. 17

K — O what com-fort to the sen-ses! How re-lie-ved is— the heart!—

Autumn No. 25

L — Ye la-dies fine and fair o come, o come! and look, and look—

No. 27

M — Be-hold the wide ex-tend-ed meads Be-hold the— wide ex-tend-ed meads

Winter No. 34 Cavatina

N — Light and life— in sad - - ness lan-guish, vi-tal heat— and joy for-sake— us

No. 36

O — Here stands the Wand'- rer now un-cer-tain and per-plex'd

No. 40

P — An ho-nest coun-try-girl— there— was that plea-sed much her lord.

No. 42

Q — Be-hold, o weak and fool-ish man, the pic-ture of thy life be-hold!

No. 44

R — Then comes the great and glo-rious morn, the new cre-a-ted world a-wakes

The Seven Words of the Savior on the Cross (The Seven Last Words of Christ) No. 1

S — Va-ter im Him-mel! O sieh' her-nie-der vom e-wie-gen Thron—

HAYDN

The Spirit's Song
Hark! Hark! What I tell to thee no sor-row o'er the tomb

Un tetto umil
Un tet - - - to u- mil cui cinge il fag-gio e il pin,

The Wanderer
To wan-der a- lone__ when the moon faint-ly__ beam-ing

HEAD, Michael (1900-   )

Money, O!
By permission Boosey & Hawkes, Inc.,
copyright owners
When I had mon-ey,__ mon-ey O! I knew no joy till I went

A Piper
By permission Boosey & Hawkes, Inc.,
copyright owners
A pi- per in the streets today Set up and tuned, and started to play

Sweet chance, that led my steps abroad
By permission Boosey & Hawkes, Inc.,
copyright owners
Sweet chance that led my steps a- broad, Be-yond the town,

When I Think Upon the Maidens
By permission Boosey & Hawkes, Inc.,
copyright owners
When I think up-on the mai-dens whom I swore to love_ for__ aye

HEISE, Peter (1830-1879)

Ak, hvem der Havde en Hue
Ah__ who once wore a fine bon- net with plume and bro-cade so__ gay

Arnes Sang
Ör- nen löf- ter med stoer-ke Slag o- ver de hör- e Fjel-de

Dengang jeg var Kun saa (Helligtrekongersaften)
Den- gang jeg var kun saa stor som saa, saa stor som saa__

It Rises (Det Stiger)
It ri- ses, it ri- ses, it ri-ses so high Riv- er wanders 'gainst mountain

Jylland mellem tvende Have
Jyl-land mel-lem tven- de Ha- ve som en Bu- ne- stav er lagt,

Liden Karen
Hus- ker Du i Höst, da vi hjemod fra Mar- ken gik

Woodland Stillness
Through aisles_ of birch- - en for-est I led_ thee, coy_ but willing;

HENSCHEL, Sir George (1850-1934)

Morning Hymn, Op. 46, No. 1
Copyright by John Church Co.
Used by permission
Soon night will pass; Through field and grass What o-dors sweet

HERBERT, Victor (1859-1924)

Babes in Toyland (operetta) Act II, No. 13 Toyland
Copyright 1903, M. Witmark & Sons
Toy- land! Toy- land! Lit - - tle girl and boy- land,

The Fortune Teller (operetta)
Copyright 1898, M. Witmark & Sons
Gypsy Love Song
The birds of the for-est are call-ing for thee— and the shades, and the glades—

Slum- ber on, my lit-tle gyp-sy sweet-heart, Dream of the field and the grove

Romany Life
We have a home 'neath the for-est shade Nev- er an- y oth-er—

Kiss in the Dark, from Orange Blossoms (operetta)
Copyright 1922, M. Witmark & Sons
I re- call the mad de- light of a love- ly dance—

Oh that kiss in— the dark was— to him just— a lark,

Kiss Me Again, from Mlle. Modiste (operetta)
Copyright 1915, M. Witmark & Sons
Sweet sum-mer breeze, Whis-per-ing trees, Stars shining brightly a- bove

Naughty Marietta (operetta)
Copyright 1910, M. Witmark & Sons
Ah! Sweet Mystery of Life
Ah! sweet mys-ter-y of life at last I've found thee

I'm falling in love with someone
For I'm falling in love with some- one, some one girl;—

Italian Street Song
Oh! my heart is back in Na- po- li,— dear Na-po- li

Zing, Zing, ziz- zy, ziz-zy, zing, zing, Boom, boom aye, Zing, Zing

'Neath the Southern Moon
'Neath the South- ern moon, Oh, love so warm and ten- der

Tramp, Tramp, Tramp along the Highway
Tramp, tramp, tramp a-long the high-way, Tramp, tramp, tramp, the road is free

Neapolitan Love Song, from Princess Pat (operetta)
Copyright 1915, M. Witmark & Sons
Sweet one!— How my heart is yearn-ing— Ev-er— with you to be—

The Red Mill (operetta)
Copyright 1906, M. Witmark & Sons
Because You're You
Not that I am fair, dear, Not that I am true. Not my gold- en hair, dear

Isle of Our Dreams
In the beau-ti-ful isle of our dreams, dear, there is nev-er a sorrow or pain

The Streets of New York
In old New York! In old New York! The peach crop's al- ways fine—

Thine Alone, from Eileen (operetta)
Copyright 1917, M. Witmark & Sons
In thine arms en-fold me, my be- lov-ed! Lift thine eyes look fondly in-to mine

Waltz, from Sweethearts (operetta)
Copyright 1913, G. Schirmer, Inc.

Sweet-hearts make love their ver-y own, Sweethearts can live on love a-lone — A

When You're Away, from The Only Girl (operetta)
Copyright 1914, M. Witmark & Sons

When you're a-way, dear, how wear-y the lone-some hours — B

HERMANN, Hans (1870-1931)

Drei Wandrer, Op. 5, No. 4

Drei Wan-drer sind — ge-gan-gen, und als der A-bend fiel — D

HEROLD, Louis (1791-1833)

Le Pré aux Clercs (opera)
Act I. No. 2

Le ren-dez-vous de nob-le com-pa-gni-e se don-nent tous — F

Dans la prai-ri-e fraiche et fleu-ri-e da-me jo-li-e viendra — G

No. 3

O ma ten-dre a-mi-e — je suis près de toi — H

O toi — de qui l'ab-sen-ce tou-jours — me fait gé-mir — I

No. 5

Sou-ve-nir du jeune â-ge sont gravés — dans mon coeur — J

Act II, No. 6

Jours de mon en-fan-ce o — jours d'in-no-cen-ce — K

Oui Mar-gue-rite en qui j'es-pè-re pro-tège u-ne pauvre — L

Act III

À la fleur du bel â-ge — Geor-get-te cha-que jour di-sait — M

Perchè Tremar, from Zampa (opera)
Act III, No. 34

Per-chè — tre-mar per-chè? son — i-o che pre-go — N

HILDACH, Eugen (1849-1924)

Im Volkston

Was leuch-tet ihr Ster-ne so hell in der Nacht? — P

Der Lenz, Op. 19, No. 5

Die Fin-ken Schlagen, der Lenz ist da, und kei-ner kann sa-gen, — Q

Der Spielmann, Op. 15, No. 1

Du mit dei-ner Fie-del blei-be hier nicht stehn, — R

Wo du hingehst, Op. 8

Wo du — hin-gehst, da will — auch ich, auch ich hin-ge-hen — S

HIMMEL, Friedrich (1765-1814)

HINDEMITH, Paul (1895-)

Gebet während der Schlacht
Va-ter, ich ru-fe dich! Brül-lend um-wolkt mich der Dampf

Eight Songs, with piano, Op. 18, No. 2
By permission Associated Music Publishers, Inc.
Wie Sankt Fran-cis-cus schweb'ich in - der Luft mit bei-den Fü--ssen

No. 4
Auf der Trep-pe sit-zen mei-ne Öhr-chen wie zwei Kätzchen die die Milch

No. 8 Trompeten
Un-ter verschnit-te-nen Wei-den wo brau-ne Kin-der spie-len

Five songs on old Texts: Of Household Rule
By permission Associated Music Publishers, Inc.
Es ist_ ge--wiss ein from--mer Mann, ein from-mer Mann,

Lady's Lament
Nun heis-sen sie mich mei---------------den

The Devil a Monk Would Be!
Ein wolf, ein wolf_____ der Sün-den-angst be- wog,

True Love
Tris-tan muss--- te oh-ne Dank Treu-e wahr'n der Kö-ni-gin

Troopers' Drinking Song
Tum-mel dich, tum-mel dich, guts Wein-lein, tum-mel dich, tum-mel dich

Frisch_ auf,_ gut_ Gsell, lass rum-mer gahn,

Das Marienleben, Op. 27, No. 1 Geburt Maria
By permission Associated Music Publishers, Inc.
O was muss es die En-gel ge-ko--stet ha-ben,

Schwin-gend ver-schwie-gen sie sich und zeig-ten die Rich-tung

No. 5 Argwohn Josephs
Und der En-gel sprach_____ und gab sich Müh an dem Mann

No. 7 Geburt Christi
Hät-test du der Ein-falt nicht, wie soll-te die ge-schehn_

No. 11 Pieta
Jetzt wird mein E-lend voll und na-men-los er-füllt es mich

Six Chansons No. 1 The Doe
By permission Associated Music Publishers, Inc.
O thou doe,_ what vis-tas of sec-u-lar for-ests ap-pear in thine eyes

No. 2 The Swan
A swan is breast-ing the flow all in him-self_ en-fold-ed

Six Chansons
No. 3 Since all is passing

Since all is pass-ing, re- tain The mel- o- dies that wan-der by us

No. 4 Springtime

O song that from the sap art pour-ing and through the sounding board

No. 5 In Winter

With the win- ter, Death, gris-ly guest through the door-way steals in

No. 6 Orchard

The earth is no-where so real a pres-ence As mid thy branches, O orchard

HOLBROOKE, Joseph (1878-   )

Noden's song, from Children of Don (opera)
By permission Novello & Co., Ltd., London

Deep is my bon- dage and a dread-ful sleep__ the gods have set me

Sea King's Song, from Dylan (opera)
By permission Novello & Co., Ltd., London

The night that bounds my sub- ject spa-ces has no fierc- er gloom

HOLLMAN, J. (1852-1927)

Chanson d'Amour

Te sou- vient il des mar- ron-niers fleu- ris

HOLMÈS, Augusta (1847-1903)

Au pays
Copyright by L. Grus, Paris

Sur la route, Et gaie-ment, Sans u - - ne crou- te!

Noël

Trois an- ges sont ve- nus ce soir M'ap- por- ter de bien

HOLST, Gustave (1874-1934)

Four Songs for Voice and Violin, Op. 35,
No. 1
By permission J. & W. Chester, Ltd., London, copyright owners

Je- su Sweet, now will I sing to thee a song of love long- ing

No. 2

My soul has nought but fire and ice and my bo- dy earth and wood:

No. 3

I sing of a mai-den that match-less is: King of all Kings

No. 4

My Le- man is so true of love and full stead- fast

The Heart Worships
By permission Galaxy Music Corporation, N. Y., sole U. S. agents for Stainer & Bell, Ltd., London

Si- lence in Heav'n Si- lence on Earth Si- lence within

Hymn to the Waters (Choral Hymn, from the Rig-Veda)

Flow - - ing from the fir- ma- ment Forth to the o- cean.

I Love My Love (arr.)
Copyright 1917, J. Curwen
A- broad as—I was walk- ing one— eve-ning in the spring   A

Midwinter
By permission Oxford Univ. Press, London, copyright owners
Our God, heaven can- not hold Him nor— earth sus- tain   B

The Sergeant's Song
Copyright by Edwin Ashdown, London
When Law- yers strive to heal a breach, and Par- sons prac-tice   C

This Have I Done for My True Love
By permission of Augener, Ltd., London
To- mor- row shall be my danc-ing day, I would my true— love   D

Turn Back O Man (melody from the German Psalter, 124th Psalm)
By permission Galaxy Music Corporation, N. Y., sole U. S. agents for Stainer & Bell, Ltd., London
Turn back O Man, for- swear thy fool- ish ways. Old now is Earth   E

Wassail Song (arr.)
Copyright 1931, G. Holst
The was- sail, the— was- sail through- out all the world   F

HOMER, Sidney (1864-   )

Requiem, Op. 15, No. 2
Copyright 1904, G. Schirmer, Inc.,
Un- der the wide and star- ry sky Dig the grave and— let me lie.   H

A Banjo Song, Op. 22, No. 4
Copyright 1910, G. Schirmer, Inc.
I plays de ban- jo bet- ter now Dan him dat taught me do   I

Dearest, Op. 24
Copyright 1910, G. Schirmer, Inc.
Dear- est, when I am dead,— make one last song for me   J

Sheep and Lambs, Op. 31
Copyright 1914, G. Schirmer, Inc.
All in the A- pril morn- ing A- pril airs were a- broad   K

HONEGGER, Arthur (1892-   )

"Àlcools" Six Poèmes de G. Apolli-naire
No. 1. A la "Santé"
Copyright by Salabert, Paris, N. Y.
Que len-te-ment passent les heu-res Com-me passe un en-ter- re- ment   M

No. 2. Clotilde
L'a-nè-mone et l'an-co- li- e Ont poussé dans le jar- din   N

No. 3. Automne
Dans le brouillard s'en vont un pa- y- san ca- gneux et son boeuf   O

No. 4. Saltimbanques
Dans la plai-ne les ba- la- dins S'e- loi-gnent au long des jar-dins   P

No. 5. L'Adieu
J'ai cueil- li ce brin de bru- yè -re L'au-tomne est mor- te   Q

No. 6. Les Cloches
Mon beau tzi-ga-ne mon a-mant É- cou-te les clo-ches qui son-nent   R

Berceuse de la Sirène
Copyright by Salabert, Paris, N. Y:
Danse a- vec nous dans le bel o- ce- an   S

Judith (opera)
Act I, No. 3 Prière
Copyright by Salabert, Paris, N. Y.

A

Seigneur____ Dieu de mes pères, e- cou-te-moi et viens à mon se- cours

No. 4 Cantique funèbre

B

Ch Béthu-li- e Béthu- lie a-ban- don-né- e nous te tendons les mains

Act II, No. 6 Incantation

C

Is-tar____ Is-tar____ Dé-es- se des ba- tail-les Mar-douk__ Mardouk__

Act III, No. 11 Cantique de la bataille

D

Ho Ho Ho__ Ho_____ Ho Ho Ho__ Ho__ Ho

E

Je crie à toi__ dans le ba-taille__ Je crie à toi__ dans le dan-ger

No. 12 Cantinque des Vierges

F

Com- me le jour d'é-té met en fui- te la nuit l'É-ter-nel s'est levé

No. 13 Cantique de la victoire

G

Son non est Je- ho-vah____ c'est un vail-lant guerrier

H

Gloire au Dieu Tout Puis-sant Je- ho-vah des ar- mé- es

Mimaamaquim (Psalm 130)
Copyright by Salabert, Paris, N. Y.

I

Mi- ma- a- ma-quim que-ra-ti kha__ A- do - - - - - - - - nai

4 Chansons pour voix grave
No. 1 (Tchobanian)
Copyright by Salabert, Paris, N. Y.

J

La douceur de tes yeux peut gue- rir____ la plus mortel - - le

No. 2 (William Aguet)

K

Der- rière__ Marcie en fleurs je con-nais un che- min qui mè- ne jusqu'à toi

No. 3 (Verlaine)

L

Un grand som-meil noir tom- be sur ma vi- e: Dor-mez tout es- poir

No. 4 (Ronsard)

M

La ter- re les eaux va bu- vant L'ar-bre la boit par sa ra- ci- ne

Le Roi David (Symphonic Psalm)
No. 2 Cantique du berger David
Copyright by E. C. Schirmer, Boston

N

L'É- ter- nel est mon ber- ger. Je ne suis que son a- gneau

No. 3 Psalm

O

Lou- é soit le Sei-gneur plein de gloi- re Le Dieu vi-vant,

No. 4 Chant de Victoire

P

Vi- ve Da- vid, vain- queur des Philis- tins, L'E-ter-nel l'a choi-si;

No. 7

Q

Ah, si j'a-vais des ai- les de co- lom- be, Je vo- le-rais bien loin

No. 8 Cantique des Prophètes

R

L'hom- me né de la fem- me a peu de jours a vi-vre.

No. 11 Psalm

S

L'É- ter- nel est ma lu- mière____ in-fi- ni- e_____

Le Roi David (Symphonic Psalm)
No. 17 Cantique

De mon coeur jail- lit un can-ti-que Je dis, mon oeu- vre pour le Roi

No. 18 Chant de la Servante

Bien ai- mé, prends ma main, de- scen- dons la col- li- ne

No. 22 La Chanson d'Ephraim

O fo- rêt d'Eph- ra- im où tour- nent les cor- beaux

No. 24

Je t'ai- me- rai, Sei-gneur____ d'un a- mour ten- - dre

No. 27 La Mort de David

Dieu le dit: un__ jour vi- en- dra où u- ne fleur fleu- ri- ra

Al - - - - - - - le - - lui- a, Al - - - - - - - - le - - lui- a ____

Saluste du Bartas
No. 1 Le Château du Bartas
By permission Henri Lemoine, Paris; Elkan-
Vogel Co., Inc., Phila., copyright owners

Un Gas- con à mi- ne fiè- re É- crit de beaux vers pom-peux

No. 2 Toute le long de la Baïse

Tout le long de la Ba- ï- se C'est Sa-lus- te du Bar-tas

No. 3 Le Départ

A- vec sa bel- le pres- tan- ce Lè- vre rou- ge regard noir,

No. 4 La Promenade

Mar- gue- ri- te de Na- var- re Par un jour brû- lant d'é- té

No. 5 Nérac en Fête

Qu'est ce donc sur la ga- ren- ne Le peu- ple dan-se gai-ment

No. 6 Duo

La-mour auquel tout in- vi- te Va ré- u- nir à la fin

Six Poésies de Jean Cocteau
No. 1 Le Nègre
Copyright by Salabert, Paris, N. Y.

Le nè- gre mi-neur de l'a- zur que ja- mais pleu-voir ne mouille

No. 2 Locutions

Fraî- che comme u- ne ro- - se Sa- ge comme une i- ma- - - ge

No. 3 Souvenirs d'enfance

Pen-dant la nuit u- ne ro- se a- van- ce sous feux é- teints

No. 4 Ex-voto

Au- tour de la Sain- te Vi- erge il fait chaud ce sont les cier- ges

No. 5 Une danseuse

Le crabe sort sur ces pointes A- vec ses bras en cor- beil- le

No. 6 Madame

O Ma- da- - me voi- là ce qu'il fau-drait com- pren- - dre

Three Psalms: 1. Psalm 34
Copyright by Salabert, Paris, N. Y.

Ja- mais ne ces- se- rai De ma- gni-fi-er le Sei-gneur

Three Psalms: 2. Psalm 140 — O Dieu don-ne-moi dé-li-vran-ce de cet hom-me per-ni-ci-eux — A

3. Psalm 138 — Il faut que de tous mes es-prits Ton los et pris, — B

Trois Poèmes de Claudel No. 1 Sieste *Copyright by Salabert, Paris, N. Y.* — Deux heu-res a-près di-ner Il est temps de se re-po-ser — C

No. 2 Le Delphinium — Tou-te pu-re comme le ciel brû-lan-te com-me le feu — D

No.3 Le Rendez-vous — Fo-rêt pro-fon----de Il fait si som-bre — E

Trois poèmes de Paul Fort No. 1 Le Chasseur Perdu en Forêt *Copyright by Salabert, Paris, N. Y.* — Quand le son du cor s'en-dort, gai chas-seur ne tar-de — F

No. 2 Cloche du Soir — Ah! ce soir là vrai-ment tout é-tait si pai-si-ble — G

No. 3 Chanson de Fol — Les sor-ciers et les fées dan-----sent sur le cô-teau — H

HOOK, James (1746-1827)

Bright Phoebus — Bright Phoe-bus has mount-ed_ the_ char-iot of day — J

The Lass of Richmond Hill — On Rich-mond Hill there lives a_ lass, more bright than May-day morn,_ — K

Love's Call — Hi-ther, hi-ther, Ma-ry, hi-ther, hi-ther come — L

Mary of Allendale — Oh! have you seen the blush--ing_ rose_ — M

With a Mile of Edinboro' — 'Twas with-in_ a_ mile of_ Ed-in-bo-ro town — N

HOPKINSON, Frances (1737-1791)

Beneath a Weeping Willow's Shade — Be-neath a weep--ing wil-low's shade, She sat and sang a-lone,_ — P

Come, Fair Rosina — Come fair Ros-i-na, come_ a-way, Long since stern win---ter's storms_ — Q

My Days have been so Wondrous Free — My days have_ been so_ won--drous free, The lit-tle_ birds that fly — R

My Generous Heart Disdains — My_ gen'rous heart dis-dains the_ slave of love to be — S

O'er the Hills — A
O'er the hills far a-way at the birth of the morn, I heard the full tone

The Traveller Benighted — B
The trav-'ler be-night-ed and lost O'er the moun-tain pursues his lone way;

HORN, Charles Edward (1786-1849)

The Banks of Allan Water — D
On the banks of Al-lan wa-ter, when the sweet springtime did fall

Cherry Ripe — E
Cher-ry ripe, cher-ry ripe, ripe I cry;— Full and fair ones

I've Been Roaming — F
I've been roam-ing, I've been roam-ing Where the mea-dow dew is sweet

HORSMAN, Edward (1873-1918)

The Bird of the Wilderness — H
Copyright 1914, G. Schirmer, Inc.
My heart, the bird of the wil - der-ness

HUE, Georges (1858-   )

À des Oiseaux — J
Copyright by A. Leduc Music Publishers, Paris
Bon-jour, bon-jour les fau-vet-tes Bon-jour les joy-eux pin-sons

L'Âne Blanc — K
By permission Heugel & Cie, Paris, copyright owners
Je ne t'en-voie ni va-se, ni ro-ses ce soir, Mi-gnon-ne Mir-za

Les Clochettes des Muguets — L
Copyright by Salabert, Paris, N. Y.
Les clo-chet-tes des mu-guets, Fris-son-nan-tes sous la bri-se

La Fille du Roi de Chine — M
By permission Heugel & Cie, Paris, copyright owners
Je suis fou de la fil-le de roi de Chi-ne

Il a Neigé des Fleurs — N
Copyright by Salabert, Paris, N. Y.
Il a nei-gé des fleurs cet-te nuit; Les sen-tiers et les al-lées

J'ai Pleuré en Rêve — O
Copyright by A. Leduc Music Publishers, Paris
J'ai pleuré en rê-ve: J'ai rê-vé que tu é-tais mor-te

Sonnez les Matines — P
By permission Heugel & Cie, Paris, copyright owners
Pour-quoi ne me ber-cez-vous plus Ô chan-son de Ro-se Ma-ri-e?

Sur l'Eau — Q
By permission Heugel & Cie, Paris, copyright owners
Sur l'eau mu-si-ca-le qui pas-se U-ne ro-se se berce

Tête de Femme est Légère — R
By permission Heugel & Cie, Paris, copyright owners
Tê-te de femme est lé-gè-re Et tourne au-tant que plume au vent

HUGHES, Herbert (1882-1937)

ARRANGEMENTS:
By permission Boosey & Hawkes, Inc.,
copyright owners

A Ballynure Ballad (Antrim)
As I was goin' to Bal-ly-nure, the day I well___ re-mem-ber___ B

I know my love (Irish tune)
I___ know my love by his way o' walk-in and I know my love C

I know where I'm goin' (Antrim)
I know where I'm go-in, And I know who's go-in with me D

I will walk with my love (Dublin)
I once loved a boy and a bold I-rish boy who would come and would go E

The next market day (Ulster)
A maid goin' to Com-ber her mar-kets to larn, To sell for her mam-my F

The Old Turf Fire
Oh, the old turf___ fire and the hearth swept clean, There is no one G

She moved thro' the fair (Donegal)
My___ young love said to me___ "My mother won't mind and my father___ H

HUHN, Bruno (1871-   )

Invictus
Copyright by Arthur P. Schmidt Co., Boston.
Used by permission
Out of the night that cov-ers me, Black as the pit from pole to pole J

HULLAH, John Pyke (1812-1884)

Three Fishers Went Sailing
Three fish-ers went sail-ing out in-to the west L

HUME; Alexander (1811-1859)

Flow Gently, Sweet Afton
Flow gent-ly, sweet___ Af-ton, a-mong thy green braes N

HUMPERDINCK, Engelbert (1854-1921)

Hänsel und Gretel (opera) Act I
A Su-sy, lit-tle Su-sy, pray what is the news? P

B Cross-patch a-way, Leave me I pray! Just let me reach you Q

A Bro-ther come and dance with me, both my hands I of-fer thee R

B With your foot you tap, tap, tap, With your hand you clap, clap, clap S

Konigskinder (opera)

Act I

Va- ter! Mut- ter! Hier will ich knien!___ Bit-ten! Flehn!

Act III

Weisst noch das gro- sse Nest aus Moos und Laub ge-äst

Lie- ber Spiel-man, al- le Kin- der und ich, wir ha- ben ge- be-ten

Am Rhein

Wenn im son- - ni-gen Herb- ste die Trau- be schwillt___

Wiegenlied

Es schau-keln die Win- de das Nest in der Lin- de

HUMPHREY, Pelham (1647-1674)

I pass all my hours

I pass all my hours in a sha- dy old grove

O the sad day

O___ the sad___ day when men shall shake their heads and say

INDY, Vincent d' (1851-1931)

Madrigal dans le style ancien, Op. 4

Qui ja- mais fut de plus char-mant vi- sa- ge, De col plus blanc,

Mirage, Op. 56
By permission J. Hamelle Music
Publishers, Paris

De loin, tu pa-rais-sais très gran-de Et très grave aus-si___

ARRANGEMENTS:
Le Roy Loys, Op. 90, No. 1
Copyright by Salabert, Paris, N. Y.

Le Roy Lo- ys est sur son pont, Ten-ant sa fille en son gi-ron.

Le Vingt-cinq d'Août, Op. 100, No. 1
Copyright by Salabert, Paris, N. Y.

C'etait vers le vingt-cinq d'A- oût voi-ci ve- nir, sous l'vent à nous___

En Passant par la Lorraine, No. 2

En pas-sant par la Lor- rai-ne, a- vec mes sa- bots___

À La Pêche des Moules, No. 3

À la pê- che des mou-les, je ne veux plus al- ler, ma-man,

Gentil Coqu'licot, No. 4

Je des- cen- dis dans mon jar- din; Je des-cen- dis dans mon jar-din

Cadet Rousselle, No. 5

Ca- det Rous- selle a trois mai- -sons qui n'ont ni pou-tres ni che-vrons

Compère Guillery, No. 6

Il é- tait un p'tit hom- me, qui s'app'lait Guil-le- ry, ca-ra- bi,

Lied Maritime

Au loin dans la mer s'é- teint le so- leil___ et la mer est calme

IPPOLITOV-IVANOV, Michael (1859-1935)

Bless the Lord, O my Soul
Copyright by Boston Music Co.

Bless the Lord, O — my soul. Blessed art Thou, — O — Lord

Parting (Adieu)
By permission J. & W. Chester, Ltd., London, copyright owners

We've trod one road, long years in ev-'ry wea-ther

IRELAND, John (1879-   )

The Bells of San Marie
By permission of Augener, Ltd., London

It's plea-sant in Ho- ly Ma-ry By San Ma-rie la-goon,

The Heart's Desire
By permission Boosey & Hawkes, Inc., copyright owners

The boys— are up the woods_with day to fetch_the daf-fo-dils —

Hope the Hornblower
By permission Boosey & Hawkes, Inc., copyright owners

Hark ye, hark to the wind-ing horn, Sluggards, a-wake and front the morn! —

If there were dreams to sell
By permission Boosey & Hawkes, Inc., copyright owners

If there were dreams to sell,— What would you buy?

I have twelve oxen
By permission Boosey & Hawkes, Inc., copyright owners

I have twelve ox- en that be fair and brown

The Lent Lily
By permission of Augener, Ltd., London

'Tis spring; come out to ram-ble the hill- y brakes a- round,

The Salley Gardens
By permission Associated Music Publishers, Inc.

Down by the sal- ley gar-dens my love and I did meet

Sea Fever
By permission of Augener, Ltd., London

I must go down to the seas a-gain, to the lone- ly sea and the sky,

The Soldier
By permission Boosey & Hawkes, Inc., copyright owners

If I should die, think on- ly this of me: that there's some cor-ner

Vagabond
By permission of Augener, Ltd., London

Dun- no a heap a- bout the what an' why

We'll to the woods no more
By permission Oxford Univ. Press, London, copyright owners

We'll to the woods no more, The lau- rels are all cut

ISAAC, Heinrich (1450-c. 1517)

Innsbruck, ich muss dich lassen

Inns-bruck, ich muss dich las- sen, ich fahr da- hin mein Stra- ssen

IVES, Charles (1874-   )

Ann Street

Quaint name Ann - - street. Width of same_ ten feet Bar-num's mob —

Charlie Rutlage
Copyright 1932, Cos Cob Press, Inc.

An- oth-er good cow-punch-er has gone to meet his fate,

Evening
Copyright 1932, Cos Cob Press, Inc.

Now came still Eve-ning on, and Twi-light gray had in her so- ber liv-er-y

General William Booth enters into heaven
Copyright 1935, Charles Ives

Booth led bold- ly with his big bass drum (Are you washed in the blood

The Greatest Man

My teacher said us boys should write a- bout some great___ man___

Resolution

Walk- ing strong- er un- der dis- tant skies,

Two little flowers

On sun- ny days in our back yard, Two lit-tle flowers are seen

JACKSON, Marylou

Trampin' (Try'n a make Heav'n my home) (Negro spiritual) (arr.)

I'm tram- pin', tram- pin', try'n a make heav'n my home

JACOBSON, Myron

Chanson de Marie Antoinette (arr.)
Copyright 1927, Carl Fischer, Inc.
Used by permission

On dit que le plus fier c'est moi Moi pau- vre jar- di- nier

JACQUES-DALCROZE, Emile

Le Coeur de ma mie
Copyright by Jobin & Cie, Paris

Le coeur de ma mie est pe- tit, tout pe- tit, pe- tit;

JANACEK, Leos (1854-1928)

Jenufa (opera)
Act II, Scene 5
By permission Associated Music Publishers, Inc.

Co chví - - - - la co chví -la a já si mám - - -

Act III, Scene 12

O- de- sli Jdi ta- ke! Vsak'yčil vi- diš, že smým

JANNEQUIN, Clement (1529-1559)

A ce joly moys

A ce jo- ly moys, jo- ly moys, jo- ly moys de mays

L'Alouette

Or sus, or sus, vous dor- mez trop Ma- da- me Jo-li- et - - - - - - - - - - te

Au joly jeu

Au jo- - ly, jo-ly, jo- ly jeu du pous- se a- vant, du pous-se a-vant

Au premier jour du joly moys de may — A
Au premier jour du jo-ly moys de may

Au verd boys — B
Au verd boys je m'en i-ray je m'en i-ray seu-le, au verd boys,

La Bataille de Marignan (La Guerre) — C
É-cou-tez, é-cou-tez é-cou-tez tous_ gentils gal - - - - lois_

Ce moys de may — D
Ce moys de may, ce moys de may, Ce moys de may ma ver-te

Ce sont gallans — E
Ce sont gal - lans qui s'en vont res- jou- yr

Le Chant des Oiseaux A — F
Re-veil-lez- vous coeurs en-dor-mis Le_ dieu d'a-mour vous son- ne,

B — G
Les oi- seaux quand sont ra- vis, En leur chant font mer- veil- les.

Las, povre coeur — H
Las,_ po-vre coeur_ tant tu as de tri - - - - stes - - se

Petite Nymphe folastre — I
Pe- ti- te Nym-phe fo- la- stre, Nym-phet-te que l'i- do- la-stre

Quand j'ay esté — J
Quand j'ay es- té quinze heu- res a- vec vous

Quand je boy — K
Quand je boy du vin cla- ret, Tout tour_

JARNEFELT, Armas (1869-)

Sunnuntaina (Sunday) — M
Kau- nis Kir-kas_ nyt on aa- mu, Aa- mu ar-mas_ sun-nun-tain

JENSEN, Adolf (1837-1879)

Lehn' deine Wang', Op. 1, No. 1 — O
Lehn' dei- ne Wang an mei-ne Wang', dann flie-ssen die Trä-nen

Marie, No. 2 — P
Ma- rie, am Fen-ster sit-zest du, du lie-bes, sü-sses Kind,_

Waldesgespräch, Op. 5, No. 4 — Q
Es ist schon spät es wind schon kalt, was reit'st du ein-sam durch den Wald?

Murmuring Breezes, Op. 21, No. 4 — R
Mur - - - meln-des Lüft-chen, Blü-ten-wind,_ der die schö-ne Welt_

Am Ufer des Flusses, des Manzanares, No. 6 — S
Am U- fer des Flusses, des Man-za- na-res, Spült Lin-nen das Mäd-chen

Der Schmied, Op. 24, No. 6 — A
Ich hör mei- nen Schatz den Ham-mer er schwin- get, das rauschet, das klin-get,

Mein Herz ist im Hochland, Op. 49, No. 1 — B
Mein Herz ist im Hochland, mein Herz ist nicht hier! Mein Herz ist im Hochland

Wenn durch die Piazzetta, Op. 50, No. 3 — C
Wenn durch die Piaz-zet-ta die A- - -bendluft weht, dann weisst du

Leis' rudern hier, mein Gondolier! No. 4 — D
Leis' ru- dern hier, mein Gon-do- lier! Die Flut vom Ru-der sprühn

Wiegenlied, Op. 53, No. 2 — E
Süss und sacht, sach-te weh', Wind du vom west-li-chen Meer;

O lass dich halten, gold'ne Stunde — F
O lass dich hal- ten, gold'- ne Stun-de, die nie so schön

JOHN of Fornsete (13th Cent.)

Sumer is icumen in (Reading rota) — H
Sum-er is i-cum-en in, Loud now sing cuck- oo

JOHN IV, King of Portugal (1604-1656)

Crux fidelis — J
Crux fi- de- lis in- - -ter om- nes

JOMMELLI, Niccolo (1714-1774)

Chi vuol comprar — L
Chi vuol com-prar la bel- la ca- lan- dri- - - na

JONES, Robert (1597-1617)

Farewell, dear Love — N
Fare-well, dear love, since thou will needs be gone Mine eyes do show

Go to bed, sweet muse — O
Go to bed, sweet Muse, take thy rest, Let not thy soul be so op- prest

Love is a bable — P
Love, love, love, love, love is a ba- ble, love is a ba-ble

Love's god is a boy — Q
Love's god is a boy; None but cow-herds re-gard him; His dart is a toy

My love bound me with a kiss — R
My love bound me with a kiss That I should no long-er stay

What if I sped? — S
What if I sped where I least ex- pect- ed? What shall I say?

JOSQUIN, des Prés (c. 1445-1521)

Allégez moy (chanson 6 voices) — Al- le- gez moy,____ doul- ce plai- sant bru- net - - - - te

Ave Maria I — A- ve____ Ma- ri - - a   Gra — — ti- a ple - - - - - - 'na,

Ave Maria II — A- ve Ma- ri - - - - a, gra - - - - ti- a____ ple - - - - - - - - na

Ave verum — A- ve ve - - - rum,____ ve - - - - - - rum cor- pus na- tum____

Basies moy (chanson 6 voices) — Ba - - - - - sies moy,____ ba - - - - - - sies moy,

Coeur Langoreulx (chanson 5 voices) — Coeur lan- go- reulx   qui   ne fais que____ pen- ser

Incessament (chanson 5 voices) — In- ces- sa- ment____ in- ces- sa- ment____ li- vre suis

J'ay bien cause de lamenter (chanson 6 voices) — J'ay bien cau- se de____ la- men- ter

J'ay bien cau- se   de la - - - - - - - - men- ter

Je me complains (chanson 5 voices) — Je   me com- plains de mon____ a- my, de mon____ a- my

Kyrie of the Missa Hercules — Ky - - - - ri- e   e - - - - - le - - - - i - - son,

Ma bouche rit (chanson 6 voices) — Ma   bou- che rit, ma   bou- che rit et   mon coeur pleu - - - - - re

Miserere mei, Deus — Mi- se- re- re me- i, De - - - - - us,____

N'esse pas ung grant desplaisir (chanson 5 voices) — N'es- se pas   ung grant des - - - - - - - - - plai- sir,

O Domine Jesu Christe — O____ Do - - mi- ne Je- su Chri - - - - - ste

Parfons regretz (chanson 5 voices) — Par- fons re- gretz____ et la- men- ta- ble joi - - e,

Plaine de dueil (chanson 5 voices) — Plai- ne de dueil   et   de mé- lan- co- ly - - - e,

Se congié prens (chanson 6 voices) — Se   con- gié prens   de mes bel- les a- mours____

Stabat Mater

Part I

Sta- bat ma- ter do- lo- ro - - sa   Jux- ta- cru-cem

Part II

E- ia Ma - - - - - - ter   fons a - - - - mo - - - - - - - ris,

Tenez moy en voz bras (chanson 6 voices)

Te- nez moi en voz bras, Mon___ a- my, je suis___

Tu pauperum refugium

Tu   pau- pe- rum re- fu- gi- um,   Tu lan- - guo-rum

KAHN, Percy B.

Ave Maria
Copyright 1913, G. Schirmer, Inc.

A- ve Ma- ri - - a,   gra- - - ti- a__ ple- na

KENNEDY-Fraser, Marjory (1857-1930)

Songs of the Hebrides (arrangements)
By permission Boosey & Hawkes, Inc., copyright owners
Aillte

The Queen of Loch- lin of the brown   shields Deep love   gave,

An Eriskay Love Lilt

Bheir mi ò - - - - ro bhan   o Bheir mi ò - - - - ro bhan

The Bens of Jura

Like wa- ter- cress ga-ther'd fresh from cool streams Thy kiss,dear love,

Bloweth the West Wind

Lad down yon- der, Ho-i- o,   Keep'st thou watch_there? Ho-ro Yal- lo- vi,

A Fairy's Love Song

Why should I   sit and sigh,   Pu- in brack- en, pu- in brack-en,

Islay Reaper's Song

A day in the corn field I a reap- in' Cut-tin' my sheaf

Kishmul's Galley

High   from the Ben a Hay- ich   On   a day of days Sea-ward I_gaz'd

Land of Heart's Desire

Land of Heart's De-sire, Isle of Youth,dear Western   Isle, gleaming in sun-light!

The Mull Fisher's Love Song

O Mhairead og!___   Mhairead,my girl,___ Thy sea-blue eyes___

The Road to the Isles

A   far croon- in is   pull- in' me a- way

Sure, by Tummel and Lech Rannoch and Lock- a- ber I will go,

Sea Sorrow (arr. by Bantock)

Mouth of glad- ness! Mu-sic's laughter Sad that I am not be-side_thee.

Songs of the Hebrides (arrangements)
Skye Fisher's Song

Far the rug-ged mis-ty Isle The Isle of Skye__ doth show

Sleeps the Noon

Sleeps the noon in the deep blue sky While bright the sun shines on Co-na's steep__

The Wild Swan

Swan o' the West, Mate o' my heart, West-ward I'd fly toward Ju-ra

KERN, Jerome (1885-1946)

All the things you are, from Very
Warm for May

All through the Day, from Centennial
Summer (film)

I dream too much, from I Dream too
Much (film)

Show Boat:
Bill

Can't Help Lovin' Dat Man

Make Believe

Ol' Man River

Smoke gets in your eyes, from Roberta

The Song is you, from Music in the
Air

KIENZL, Wilhelm (1857-1941)

Der Evangelimann, Op. 45 (opera)
Act II
By permission Associated Music
Publishers, Inc.

O schö- - -ne Ju- gend-ta-ge mit eu?- rem stil-len Glück__

Se- lig sind, die Ver- fol- gung lei- den um der Ge- rech-tig-keit

Der Kuhreigen, Op. 85 (opera)
Act I
Copyright by Josef Weinberger, Ltd.,
London

Lug',Dursel, lug',__ der A-bend bricht her-ein.__ Lug' wie der Son-ne

Der Kuhreigen, Op. 85 (opera)
Act I

Zu — Stras-burg auf der Schanz', da — ging mein Trauern an;

KILPINEN, Yrjo (1892-)

Von zwei Rosen, Op. 59, No. 3
By permission Associated Music Publishers, Inc.

Von zwei — Ro-sen duf-tet ei-ne an-ders als die and-re Ro-se,

Siehe, auch ich—lebe, Op. 59, No. 5

Al- so ihr lebt noch, al- le, al- le, ihr, am Bach ihr Wei- den

Thalatta! Op. 59, No. 6

Es stür- zen der Ju- gend Al- tä- re zu- sam-men,

Lieder der Liebe, Op. 60, No. 1
By permission Associated Music Publishers, Inc.

Mein Herz ist leer, — ich lie - - - be dich nicht mehr —

No. 2

Es ist Nacht, und mein Herz — kommt zu dir, hält's nicht aus,

No. 3

Die - - se Ro - se von heim - li-chen Küs - - sen schwer

No. 4

Wir sit- zen im Dun-keln. Der Vor-hang rauscht lei - - se

No. 5

Wir sind zwei Ro- sen, dar- ü- ber der Sturm fuhr und — sie ab-riss.

Lieder um den Tod, Op. 62, No. 1 Vöglein Schwermut
By permission Associated Music Publishers, Inc.

Ein schwar- zes — Vög- lein — fliegt ü- ber die Welt,

No. 2 Auf einem verfallenen Kirchhof

Was — gehst du, ar- mer/ blei- cher Kopf, mich an Es ist kein Grund

No. 3 Der Tod und der einsame Trinker

Gu-ten A-bend, Freund! — Dein Wohl! Wie geht's? — Dein Wohl!

No. 4 Winternacht

Flok-ken-dich- te Win- ter- nacht — Heim-kehr von der Schen-ke

No. 5 Der Säeman

Durch die Lan- de auf und ab schrei- tet weit Bau - - er Tod

No. 6 Unverlierbare Gewähr

Ei- nes gibt's dar- auf ich mich freu - - - - en — darf

Vorfrühling, Op. 79, No. 3
By permission Associated Music Publishers, Inc.

Durch ho- he Tan- nen träu- felt schon in schwin-den- den Schnee — das Licht.

Venezianisches Intermezzo, Op. 79, No. 4

Durch al- te Mor- mor- hal- len streift weicher Wind von Meer

Marienkirche zu Danzig im Gerüst, Op. 79, No. 7

Du Trotz des Glau- bens! Du — be-helm- tes Haupt Burg Got-tes-

KJERULF, Halfdan (1815-1868)

Aftenstimmung (Twilight musing)
The prin-cess sat high in her loft-y bow'r, — B

Detvar da
Hear how the break-ers An-gri-ly lash the sand, — C

Ingrids Vise (Ingrid's Song)
The fox lay low neath the birchtree root By the hea-ther, by the heather — D

Laengsel (Longing)
Last night the night-in-gale woke me, When all the world was still, — E

Mit Hjerte og miss Lyre
I give thee all, I can no more, Tho' poor the off'-ring be, — — F

Sing, Sing!
Sing, sing Night-in-gale, sing, Sing as we watch to- geth-er, — G

Synnöve's Sang (Synnöve's Song)
Grate-ful am I for the hap-py time We two, from child-hood — H

KNIGHT, J. P. (1812-1887)

Rock'd in the cradle of the deep
Rock'd in the cra-dle of the deep, — I lay me down— in peace a- sleep; — J

KODALY, Zoltan (1882-   )

Hary Janos, Op. 15, (opera) No. 5
By permission Boosey & Hawkes, Inc.,
copyright owners
Sej! verd meg Is- ten, a ki ez- tet csi- nál- ta! — L

No. 6
La la la la la la la la la la la la la la la la la la — M

No. 7
Pi-ros al- ma le-e-sett a sár-ba Ki felve-szi nem e-sik hi- á-ba — N

No. 8
Óh, mely sok hal te-rem oz nagy Ba- la-ton bah- ha-rah-ha- ra — O

No. 9
Ti-szán in-nen Du-nán túl, túl a Ti szán, van egy csikós— nyá-jas- túl — P

No. 11
Ku- ku- ku-kus- kám, Szállj le hoz- zám madár- kám! — Q

No. 13
Ho-gyan tud- tál ró- zsám, i- de jön- ni? Ár- kot kel-tett né-ked — R

No. 14
Hej két ti- kom ta- va-li, há- rom har- mad- é- vi — S

KODALY

Hary Janos, Op. 15 (opera) No. 15 A

Sej, be- so- roz-tak, sej, be-so- roz-tak enge- met ka to- no-tak,

B

Nagy- a bony- ban csak kit to- rony lát szik

No. 21

Hagyj bé-két, vi- as-ko-dó, óh! Mi-don nem vagy hasz nos hó óh

No. 22

A- jo lo-vas ka-to-ná- nak, de jo va-gyon dol- ga

No. 23 A

Gyíy- tot- tam gyer-tyát a-vó- le gén-nek, Lát-tam sze- me-lit

B

Mar en- gem, mat kam, ti zen ké- ret-tek! Adj jó ta- ná-csot

No. 26

Á- bé- cé- dé, Raj-tam kez- dé, A nagy böl cses-sí- get,

No. 28

Sze- geny va- gyok, sze- gény- nek szü- let- tem,

No. 29

Fel- szán tom a csá- szár ud- va-rát, Be- le- ve- tem ha-zam

Hungarian Folksongs:
By permission Oxford Univ. Press, London,
copyright owners
(except where otherwise noted)

A Növérek (The Sisters)
Arról Alúl (Over Yonder)

Frei- er kam zum Schwester-lein: rei- cher Schneider Gün-ther,

O- ver yon-der clouds are spread-ing dull and grey, Where my sweet- heart sits

Aszszony, Aszszony (Woman,
Woman)

Wo- man, wo- man, out of your bed! From the drink-ing par-ty I'm back

A rossz feleség (The heartless
wife)

Come home quickly, mother dearest Fath-er on his deathbed's lying

Az hol én elményëk (I rove, I
look around)

I rove, I look a-round,__ See eve- ry tree weep-ing__

Akkor szep az erdö (Lovely is
the forest)

Love- ly is the for- est, forest green, Tur- tle doves a- woo-ing,

Apró alma lehulott (From the
tree an apple fell)

From the tree an ap-ple fell, high,dil- ly, He who finds it, picks it up,

Cigány nóta (Gypsy Song)

E- gész fa- lut ösz-sze- jár-tam, Még- is sem- mit sem Kop- hat-tam,

Elkiáltom magamat (Far across
the village green)

Far a- cross the vil-lage green There's my sweetheart passing, Ea-ger-ly I wave

Egy nagyórú böha (Long-nose
Flea)

Long__ Nose comes a- call- ing, Dai-ly comes a- call-ing, Comes to lunch,

hungarian Folksongs:
Egy kicsi madarka (Came a bird a-flying)

Came a bird a fly - - - - -ing To my flow - er gar - -den

Hej, a Mohi hegy borának (Hey! The wine of Mohi)
By permission Boosey & Hawkes, Inc., copyright owners

Hey! the wine of Mo-hi vin-tage___ now costs flo-rins twen-ty

Három Árva (The Three Orphans)

Trudged a-long the road___ three or-phans, Way-worn, wea-ry,___

Kitrákotty mese (Tale of the clucking)

Once I went to mar-ket with one groat to spend, And up-on a roos-ter

Kádár Kata (Dear Mother)

Gyu-la-i-né, é-des a-nyám!___ En-ged-je-meg___ azt az e-gyet,

Körtéfa (The Pear Tree)
By permission Boosey & Hawkes, Inc., copyright owners

Still you stand, O, Peartree, As of old, green Pear Tree! Once your spreading

Kocsi, szekér (Wheelcart, barrow)

Wheel-cart, bar-row wheelcart, sleigh, I'm a spin-ster, Fol-de-rol de rid-dle

Kádár István (Ballad of Stephen Kádár)
By permission Boosey & Hawkes, Inc., copyright owners

Once Pa-no-nia lay in dire dis-tress and pe-ril,___

Katona vagyok én (Called to serve

Called to serve my country all I love I'm leaving___ Sad-ly weeps my mo-ther

Kit Kéne elvenni (Which one should I marry)

Wise it were and time-ly ev-en now to mar-ry.

Labanc gúnydal a Kuruczra ("Labantz" mocking "Kurutz)
By permission Boosey & Hawkes, Inc., copyright owners

Look out, Ku-rutz, run a-way now, Rough haired Ger-mans

Megégett Rácország (All our homes)
By permission Boosey & Hawkes, Inc., copyright owners

All our homes___ charred ruins, Three a-lone scaped burning, One is our King's palace

Meghalok, Meghalok (Woe is me)

Woe is me, woe is me, so young and hale, I die, Let me for-e-ver sleep

Mónár Anna (Ballad of Annie Miller)

Come, my darling An-nie Mil-ler, Let us go forth, both to-gether,

No, I come not, reckless Mar-tin! I won't leave my home my hus-band

Most jöttem Erdélyböl (I've just arrived)

Bin e-ben an-ge-langt, Aus Sie-ben-bur-gen's Land,

Öreg vagyok már én (I am old now)
By permission Boosey & Hawkes, Inc., copyright owners

I am old and bold now I don't work at all now,

Puciné
By permission Boosey & Hawkes, Inc., copyright owners

One small loaf is all my liv-ing, This to Pu-ci-ne I'm giv-ing, Hey!

Rákoczi kesergöje (Rakoczi's Lament)
By permission Boosey & Hawkes, Inc., copyright owners

Hear-ken un-to me my Magyars! All my words are___ true,

Hungarian Folksongs:

Siralmas volt nekem (All my days are clouded)
By permission Boosey & Hawkes, Inc., copyright owners

All my days are cloud-ed___ Joy - - - less___ dawns___ each mor-row

Szölöhegyen keresztül (Through the vineyard)

Through the vine-yard fair Kit-ty With her bro-ther walk'd one day

Szomoru füzfänak (The weeping willow)

See the weep-ing wil-low's three and thir-ty bran-ches

Tölem a nap (Shades of eve)

Shades of eve are slow-ly fall-ing,___ No___ re-lief

Tücsök lakodslom (Wedding of the Cricket)

Gril-le ist ein ar-mer Wicht, Möch-te sich ver-mäh-len,

Vasárnap bort inni (Sit and drink all Sunday)
By permission Boosey & Hawkes, Inc., copyright owners

Sit and drink, all___ Sun-day, Id-le rest all___ Mon-day,

Verbunk (Recruiting)

All Hus-sars are splendid fellows Al-ways___ gay and___ chee-ry,

Virágos kenderem (All the hemp)

All the hemp lies wast-ed, far too long lay sleep-ing My be-loved

Zöld erdöben (In the forest)

Tief im Wal- de, auf der Hal- de, Tief im Wal-de auf der Hal-de

KOECHLIN, Charles (1867-   )

La Nuit
Copyright by Bordoux, Paris

Nous bé-nis-sons la dou-ce Nuit, Dont le frais bai-ser

Si tu le veux
Copyright by Boston Music Co.

Si tu le veux, ô mon a-mour, ce soir des que la fin du jour

Le Thé
Copyright by Boston Music Co.

Miss El-len, ver-sez-moi le thé Dans la bel-le tas-se chi-noise

Villanelle, Op. 21, No. 1
Copyright by Philippo, Paris

Le temps, l'é-ten-due et le nom-bre Sont tom-bés du noir fir-ma-ment

KOENEMAN, Theo (-1938)

When the King went forth to war, Op. 7, No. 6
By permission J. & W. Chester, Ltd., London, copyright owners

When the King went forth to war To a coun-try strange and far

KORBAY, F. (1846-1913)

Hungarian Folksongs (arrangements):
Had a horse

Had___ a horse, a fi-ner no one ev-er saw

But the she-riff sold him in the name of law.

Hungarian Folksongs (arrangements):
Rosebud, to the fields art going

Rose-bud, to the fields art go- ing Ten-der are thy hands for mow-ing   A

Shepherd, see thy horse's foaming mane

Shep-herd see thy hor-se's foam-ing mane Why dost ride so wild-ly   B

KORNGOLD Enrich (1897-   )

Die tote Stadt (The Dead City), Op. 12 (opera)
Act I Marietta's Song
By permission Associated Music Publishers, Inc.

Glück, das mir ver- blieb', rück zu mir, mein treu-es Lieb—   D

Marietta's Lute Song

O Tanz,— O Rausch!— Lust_ quillt aus mir, braust in mir, jagt den Puls   E

Act II Pierrot Song

Mein Seh-nen,— mein Wäh-nen,— es träumt sich zu- rück   F

Act III Ich werde sie nicht Wiedersehen

O Freund, ich wer-de sie nicht mehr wie-der-sehn—   G

Ich wer-de sie nicht mehr wie- der- sehn—   H

Ich ging zu ihm, from Das Wunder der Heliane (opera) Act II
By permission Associated Music Publishers, Inc.

Ich ging zu ihm der mor- gen-ster ben - - - - soll—   I

Doch schön war_ der Kna- be, schön wie ein Stern im Ver- ge-hen   J

DE KOVEN, Reginald (1859-1920)

At Parting
Copyright by John Church Co.
Used by permission

To-night the dew will kiss the rose— The song bird shel-ter on the tree—   L

Robin Hood (operetta) Oh, promise me

Oh prom-ise me that some day you and I will take our love to-geth-er   M

Act II, No. 10 Brown October Ale

And it's will ye quaff with me, my lads, And it's will ye quaff with me?—   N

So laugh, lads, and quaff, lads- 'Twill make you stout_ and hale—   O

Act III, No. 16 Armorer's Song

Let ham-mer on an-vil ring,— And the forge-fire bright- ly shine—   P

Clang! clang! clang! Then huz- zah for the an- vil, the forge and the sledge,   Q

KRAMER, J. Walter (1890-   )

The Last Hour
Copyright by John Church Co.
Used by permission

Sup-pose, be- lo- ved, that the gods should say: S

The Last Hour

And you should gaze deep down in my eyes ___

KREISLER, Fritz (1875-)

The Old Refrain
Copyright by Charles Foley, New York

I of-ten think of home, Dee-oo-lee-ay, When I am all a-lone

You are free, from Apple Blossoms
(operetta)
Copyright 1919, Harms, Inc.

Free as the birds in the air ___ Fly-ing with nev-er a care ___

Love is just a game we two are play-ing

KREMSER, Eduard (1838-1914)

Berg op Zoom (arr.)

Sieh,wel-che Macht sie ge-bracht uns zur Schlacht! Wie grim-me Lev'n

Wir treten zum Beten

Wir tre-ten zum Be-ten vor Gott, den Ge-rech-ten,

KŘENEK, Ernst (1900-)

Jonny spielt auf, Op. 45 (opera)
Swanee River Song
By permission Associated Music
Publishers, Inc.

Oh! ___ Das wur-de mir nun doch zu dumm! Das ist kein Le-ben

Triumphlied

Jetzt ist die Gei-ge mein, und ich will drauf spie-len,

KREUTZER, Konradin (1780-1849)

Das Nachtlager in Granada (opera)
Act I

Sei-ne from-me Lie-bes-ga-be ist auf e-wig nun da-hin

Ein Schütz bin ich in des Re-gen-ten Sold In Deutschlands Gau-en

No. 11

Schon die A-bend-glo-cken klan-gen, und die Flur

Act II

Für-wahr, für-wahr es ist ein A-ben-teu - er,das mir je mehr

Es zieht aus je-ner Welt von gold'nen hei-tern Ster-nen-zelt

Lei-se we-het, lei-se wal-let rings der Tau, rings der Tau,

No. 18

Tren-ne nicht das Band ___ der Lie-be,

Schäfers Sonntagslied

Das ist der Tag des Herrn, das ist der Tag des Herrn

Hobellied, from Der Verschwender
(Fairy opera) Act III

Da strei-ten sich die Leut her-um oft um den Wert des Glücks

KŘIČKA, Jaroslav (1882-)

L'Albatros, Op. 14, No. 1

Tout là-haut dans le ciel pro-fond au des-sus de la va-gue,

KRIEGER, Johann Philip (1649-1725)

Die Gerechten werden weggerafft

Die Ge-rech-ten wer-den weg-ge-rafft vor dem Un-glück,

KÜCKEN, Friedrich (1810-1882)

How Can I Leave Thee (Ach! Wie ist möglich dann)

How can I leave thee! How can I from thee part!

LA FORGE, Frank (1879-)

An einen Boten
Copyright 1909, G. Schirmer, Inc.

Wenn du zu mei'm Schat-ze kommst, sag':

Come unto these yellow sands
Copyright 1907, G. Schirmer, Inc.

Come un-to these yel - - - - - - - - - - - low sands

Hills
Copyright by G. Ricordi & Co., Inc.

I want my hills! Hills! The trail that scorns the hol-lows

Song of the Open
Copyright by Oliver Ditson Co. Used by permission.

To your soul is it wine, As it is to mine

Take, O take those lips away
Copyright 1909, G. Schirmer, Inc.

Take, o take those lips a-way that so sweet-ly were for-sworn

LALO, Edouard (1823-1892)

Ballade à la lune

C'é-tait dans la nuit bru-ne, sur le clocher jau-ni la lu-ne,

Guitare

Com-ment, disaient ils, a-vec nos na-celles fuir les al-gua-zils?

Oh, quand je dors

Oh quand je dors, viens au-près de ma cou-che!

Le Roi d'Ys (opera)
Act I (Breton theme)

Les guerres sont ter-mi-né-es, Voi-ci pour nous dé-sor-mais

Le Roi d'Ys (opera)
Act I   A

En si- len- ce pour-quoi souf-frir? Dans mon coeur___ é-pan-che ta pei-ne!

Act II   B

Le sa- lut nous est pro- mis, c'est à nos seuls en- ne- mis

C

Ah! si j'a- vais souf- fert de la mê- me tor- tu- re,

Act III Aubade   D

Vai- ne- ment___ ma bien ai- mé- e On croit me dé- ses-pé-rer

E

A l'au-tel j'al-lais rayon- nant___ mon amour é-tait ma pri-è- re___

L'Esclave   F

Cap- ti- ve et peut- ê-tre ou-bli- é- e je songe

LAMBERT, Constant (1905-   )

The Rio Grande
By permission Oxford Univ. Press, London,
copyright owners

A   H

By the Ri- o Grande___ they dance a sa-ra- bande___

B   I

But they dance in the ci- ty down the pub- lic squares

C   J

The Com- men- da- dor and Al- qua- cil___ are there on horse-back

D   K

The noi -- sy streets are emp- ty and hushed is the town___

E   L

Such a space of si- lence through the town___ to the ri-ver

LAMBERT, Frank

She is far from the land

LANDINO, (Landini) Francesco (1325-1397)

Benche ora piova   P

Ben- che o- ra___ pio- va___ pur buon tem-po

Gram piant'agli occhi   Q

Gram - - - - - - - - - - - - - piant' agl'___ oc- chi

LANG, Margaret Ruthven (1867-   )

Irish Love Song, Op. 22
Copyright by Arthur P. Schmidt Co., Boston.
Used by permission   S

O, the time is long Ma- vour-neen, Till I come a-gain,

LANGE-MÜLLER, Peter Erasmus (1850-1926)

Efteraar (Autumn), Op. 61, No. 3
Copyright by Oliver Ditson Co. Used by permission.

Skin ud, du Klare Solskin (Bright Sunshine), Op. 18, No. 4
Copyright by Oliver Ditson Co. Used by permission.

LASSEN, Eduard (1830-1904)

Allerseelen

Ich hatte einst ein schönes Vaterland

Mit deinen blauen Augen

LASSUS, Orlando de (1530-1594)

Chansons Françaises
A ce matin

Amour, donne moy payx

Bon jour, bon jour

Dessus le marché d'Arras

Guerir ma douleur

Hélas, quel jour

J'ay cherché la science

Margot, labourez les vignes

La nuit froide

O Mère des Amours

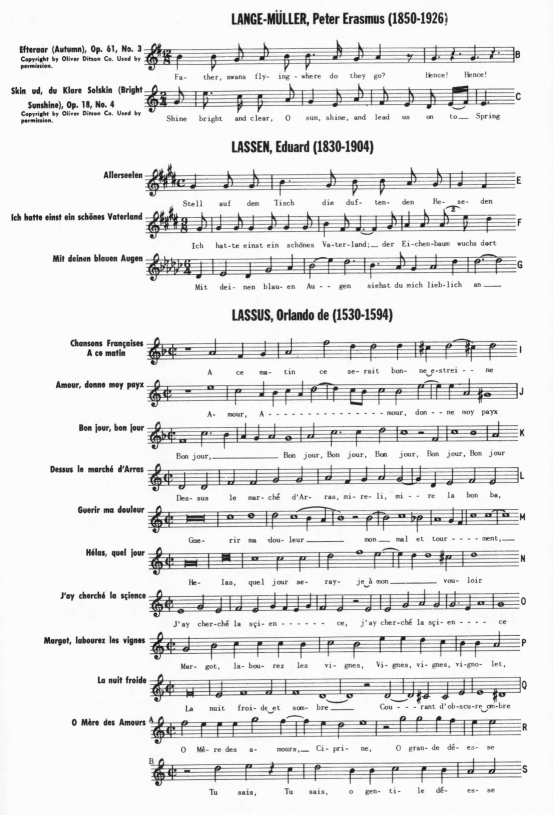

Chansons Françaises
O vin de vigne — A

O vin de vi-gne, gen-til jo-li vin de vi-gne, Vi-gnon, vi-gna

Quand mon mary vient de dehors — B

Quand mon ma-ry vient de de-hors Ma rente est d'e-stre ba-tu- e,

Le Rossignol plaisant — C

Le Ros-si-gnol plaisant et gra-ti- eux, Le Ros-si-gnol plaisant

Scais tu dir l'ave — D

Scais tu dir l'A- ve? di-soit il. Ou- y, di-soit il,

Susanne un jour — E

Su- san- ne un jour d'a-mour so-li-ci-té- e,

Toutes les nuitz — F

Tou- tes les nuitz que sans vous

Justorum Animae — G

Jus-to- rum a- ni-mae in ma-nu De-i- sunt,

Mass "Douce Memoire"
Sanctus — H

Sanc- tus, Sanc- tus

Benedictus — I

Be- ne-dic- tus qui ve- nit, Be-ne-dic- tus

Agnus Dei — J

A- gnus De- i, A-gnus De-i qui tol-lis pec-ca- ta

Mon coeur se recommande à vous — K

Mon coeur se re-com-mande à vous, mon coeur se re-com-mande

Matona mia cara — L

Ma-to-na mi a ca-ra mi fol-le-re can-zon

Nos qui sumus in hos mundo — M

Nos qui su-mus in- hoc mun-do

Ola, O che bon echo (madrigal from "Libro de Villanelle") — N

Hol-lah welch gu-tes E-cho! Ru-fet es an

Seven Penitential Psalms
Miserere mei Deus — O

Mi- se-re-re me-i De- us, se-cun-dum ma-gnam,

Miserere mei Domine — P

Mi- se-re-re me-i Do-mi-ne Mi-se-re-re me-i

Surrexit pastor bonus — Q

Sur- re- xit pas-tor bo- nus, sur-re-xit pa-stor bo- nus,

Tristis est anima mea — R

Tri- stis est a-ni-ma, tri-stis est a-ni-ma me-a

LEGRENZI, Giovanni (1626-1690)

Che fiero costume

Che fie- ro co-stu- me d'a- li- ge- ro nu- me, che a for-za di pe- ne

LEHÁR, Franz (1870-1948)

Friederike (operetta)
Act I

Sah ein Knab' ein Rös- lein stehn, Rös- lein auf der Hei- den

Act II

O Mäd- chen, mein Mäd- chen___ wie lieb ich dich!___

Wa- rum hast du mich wach ge- küsst? Hab nicht ge-wusst

Lie- - be, se- li-ger Traum___ aus himm- li-schen Höh'n, du kannst nicht vergehn

Giuditta (operetta)

Du bist mei- ne Son- ne,___ du bist ein Traum voll süs-ser Won- ne!

Freun- de, das Le- ben ist le- bens- wert

Mei- ne Lip-pen, sie Küs- sen so heiss_ Mei-ne Glie-der sind schmiegsam

Hab' ein blaues Himmelbett, from Frasquita (operetta) Act II

Schatz, ich bitt' dich, komm heut Nacht Al- les ist be-reit ge- macht___

Ein Glück dir winkt_ so wie noch nie,___ Kein Laut uns stört,_

Im heimlichen Dämmer, from Eva (operetta) Act I
Copyright 1912, G. Schirmer, Inc.

Im heim- li-chen Däm- mer___ der sil- ber-nen Am- pel,___

Wär' es auch nichts als ein Au- gen- blick, wär' es auch nichts

Das Land des Lächelns (The Land of Smiles)
Act I Immer nur lächeln

Ich tre- te ins Zim- mer, von Sehn- sucht durch- bebt.

Von Ap- fel-blü- ten ei- nen Kranz,___ ah___

Du bist das traum- süs- se Le- ben, Du al- lein

Act II

Wer hat die Lie-be uns ins Herz ge-senkt,___ uns den süs-sen Rausch

Dein ist mein gan- zes Herz! Wo du nicht bist, Kann ich nicht sein,

The Merry Widow
Act II Vilia Song
    Es lebt ei- ne Vil- ja, ein Wald- mäg- de- lein,

    Vil- ja, O Vil- ja, du Wald- mäg- de- lein, fass' mich und lass' mich

Act III
    Lip- pen schwei- gen, 'sflü- tern Gei- gen: Hab mich lieb

Paganini (operetta) Act II
    Gern hab' ich die Frau'n ge- küsst, hab' nie ge- fragt

    Lie- - - be, du Him- mel auf Er- den, e- - - wig be- steht

Waltz, from The Count of Luxemburg
(operetta)

Was ich längst erträumte, from Der
Göttergatte
    Was ich längst er- träum- te, was ich lang ver- säum- te

Wenn sich zwei lieben, from Der
Rastelbinder Act I
    Wenn sich zwei lie- ben, so steht's ge- schrie- ben, sind sie ein Herz,

Der Zarewitsch (operetta)
Act I
    Ei- ner wind Kom- men der wird mich be- geh- ren

    Mir ist so bang, als hielt mich ein Traum be- fan- gen

Volgalied
    Hast Du dort o- ben ver- ges- sen auf mich? Es sehnt doch mein Herz

Act II
    Hab' nur dich al- lein, die gan- ze Welt sollst du mir sein,

Act III Napolitana
    Wa- rum hat je- der Früh- ling ach nur ei- nen Mai

Zorika, kehre zurück, from Zigeuner-
liebe Act II
    Zo- ri- ka, Zo- ri- ka, keh- re zu- rück, lass uns zur Hei- mat

LEHMANN, Liza (1862-1918)

The Cuckoo
    The Cuc- koo sat in the old pear tree. "Cuc- koo"

Go, lovely Rose

In a Persian Garden (song cycle)
Ah, moon of my delight
    Ah, moon of my de- light that knows no wane

Alas! that Spring should
vanish with the rose
    A- las! That Spring should va- nish with the Rose

In a Persian Garden (song cycle)
Myself when young
Copyright by Boston Music Co.

.My- self when young did ea- ger- ly fre- quent Doc- tor and Saint

Magdalen at Michael's gate

There are Fairies at the Bottom of our Garden

LEJEUNE, Claude (1530-1600)

O occhi manza mia

O oc- chi man- za mi- a, o oc- chi man- za mia

Revecy venir du Printans

Re- ve- cy ve- nir du Prin- tans L'a- mou- reuz' et bel- le sai- son

LEMAIRE, Gaston (1854-1928)

Vous dansez, marquise (Gavotte des Mathurins)

Vous dan- sez, mar- qui- se, D'un pas si lé- ger

LEONCAVALLO, Ruggiero (1858-1919)

La Bohême (opera)
Act II
Copyright by Sonzogno, Milan

Io non ho che u- na po- ve- ra stan- zet- ta

Da quel suon so- a- - ve- men- te Già le poop- pie i- ne- bri- a- te

Act III

Tes- ta a- do- ra- ta, più non tor- ne- ra i,

Pagliacci (opera) Prologue
Copyright 1906, G. Schirmer, Inc.

Si può? Si può? Si- gno- re! Si- gno- ri! Scu- sa- te- mi

Poi- chè in iscena ancor le an- tiche ma- schere met- te l'au- to- re;

Un ni- do di me- mo- rie in fon- do a l'a- ni- ma can- ta- va un gior- no,

E voi, piut- to- sto che le no- stre po- ve- re ga- ba- ne

Act I

Un gran- - - de spet- ta- co- lo a ven- ti- tre o- - - - - - - - - re

Un tal gio- co, cre- de- te- mi è meglio non gio- car- lo con me,

Bell Chorus

Din, don, suo- na ve- spero, ra- ga- ze e gar- zon,

Ballatella

Stri- do- no las- sù, li- be- ra- men- te lan- cia- ti a vol,

Pagliacci (opera)
Act I Ballatella
Van- no lag- giù_____ ver- so un pa- e- se stra- no

Duet: Tonio and Nedda
So ben che dif- for- me, con- tor- to son i- o;

Hai tem- po a ri- dir- me- lo stas- se- ra, se bra- mi

Duet: Silvio and Nedda
De- ci- di il mio de- stin, Ned- da! Ned- da, ri- ma- ni

Non mi____ ten- tar! Vuoi tu per- der la vi- ta mia?

E al- lor per- che, di',____ tu m'hai stre- ga- to se vuoi la- sciar- mi

Tut- to - - - scor- diam!____ Tut- to scor- diam____

Vesti la giubba
Ve- sti la giub- ba e la fac- cia in fa- ri- na

Act II Serenade
O____ Co- lom- bi- na il te- ne- ro fi- do Al- lec- chin è a te vi- cin!____

Guar- do, amor mio, che splen- di- da ce- net- ta__ pre- pa- ai!

No! Pa- gliac- ci non son; se il vi so è pal- li- do,

Spe- rai tan- to il de- li- rio ac- ce- ca- to m'a- ve- va,

Zaza (opera)
Copyright by Sonzogno, Milan
Act II
Buo- na Za- za del mio buon tem- po, a- scol- ta:

Act III
O mio pic- co- lo ta- vo- lo in- gom- bra- to

Act IV
Za- za, pic- co- la zin- ga- ra, schia- va d'un fol- le a- mo- re

Mattinata
Copyright by G. Ricordi & Co., Inc.
A beau- ti- ful morn- ing is break- ing With won- der and light, now the sun____

LEROUX, Xavier (1863-1919)

Le Nil
Copyright 1905, G. Schirmer, Inc.
Les eaux du Nil____ tou- tes pâ- les, s'é- cou- lent____

Le bien ai- mé____ s'ac- cou- dant sur la prou- e

LEVERIDGE, Richard (c. 1670-1758)

The Beggar's Song — B

How jol-ly are we beg-gars Who nev-er toil for treas-ure

Black-ey'd Susan — C

All in the Downs the fleet was moor'd, The streamers wav-ing in the wind

When Dull Care — D

This great world is a trou-ble Where all must their for-tunes bear;

LIE, Sigund (1871-1904)

Sne (Snow) — F
Copyright by Oliver Ditson Co. Used by permission.

There is nought on earth so still as the snow

LIEURANCE, Thurlow (1878-)

By the Waters of Minnetonka (Indian Love Song) — H
Copyright by Theodore Presser Co. Used by permission.

Moon Deer How near your soul di - - - - vine

LILLIJEBJORN, H. (1797-1875)

When I Was Seventeen (När jag blef sjutton år) (arr.) — J

Four-teen years I had seem'd just to be Lit-tle maid-en so hap-py

LINLEY, William (1771-1835)

Lawn as white as driven snow, from "A Winter's Tale" — L

Lawn as white as dri-ven snow; Cy-press, black as a-ny crow;

LISZT, Franz (1811-1886)

Christus vincit, from Christus (oratorio) — N

Chris-tus vin-cit, Chris-tus reg-nat, Chris-tus im-pe-rat

Comment, disaient-ils — O

Com-ment, di-saient-ils, A-vec nos na-cel-les Fuir les al-gua-zils?

Die drei Zigeuner — P

Drei Zi-geu-ner fand ich ein-mal lie - - gen an ei-ner Wei-de

— Q

Hielt der Ei-ne für sich al-lein in den Hän-den die Fie-del,

Du bist wie eine Blume — R

Du bist wie-ei-ne Blu - - me, so hold so schön und rein

Es muss ein Wunderbares sein — S

Es muss ein Wun-der-ba-res sein Um's Lie-ben zwei-er See-len

Freudvoll und Leidvoll — Freud- voll und leid- voll ge- dan- ken voll sein, — A

Ich liebe dich — Ich lie - be dich weil ich dich lie- ben muss; — B

Im Rhein, im schönen Strome — Im Rhein, im schö- nen Stro- me, Da spie- gelt sich in den Wel- len — C

Die Lorelei — A — Ich weiss nicht, was soll's be- deu- ten, dass ich so trau- rig, — D

B — Die Luft ist kühl, und es dun- kelt, — E

Mignons Lied (Kennst du das Land) — Kennst du das Land, wo die Zi- tro- nen blühn, — F

Missa Choralis
I Kyrie — Ky- ri- e e- le- i- son e- le- i- son — G

II Gloria — Glo- ri- a in ex- cel- sis De- o Et in ter- ra pax — H

III Credo — Cre- do in u- num De- um Pa- trem om- ni- po- ten- tem — I

IV Sanctus — San- ctus, San- ctus, San- ctus Do- mi- nus De- us Sa- ba- oth — J

V Benedictus — Be- ne- di- ctus, be- ne- di- ctus — K

VI Agnus Die — A- gnus De- i qui tol- lis pec- ca- ta mun- di — L

Nimm einen Strahl der Sonne — Nimm ei- nen Strahl der Son- ne, vom A- bend- stern das Licht, — M

Oh! quand je dors — Oh! quand je dors, viens au- près de ma cou- che — N

O Lieb (original version of Liebestraum, No. 3) — O lieb', o lieb, so lang du lie- ben kannst — O

Wieder möcht' ich dir begegnen — Wie- der möcht' ich dir be- geg- nen, Wie- der schau- en dei- nen Blick; — P

LOEWE, Karl (1796-1869)

Edward, Op. 1, No. 1 — A — Dein Schwert, wie ist's von Blut so rot? Ed- ward, Ed- ward! — R

B — Ich hab' ge- schla- gen mei- nen Gei- er tot Mut- ter, Mut- ter! — S

Der Wirtin Töchterlein, Op. 1, No. 2 — A
Es zo- gen drei Bur- sche wohl ü- ber den Rhein

Erlkönig, No. 3 — B
Wer rei-tet so spät durch Nacht und Wind? Es ist der Va- - ter

Walpurgisnacht, Op. 2, No. 3 — C
Lie- be Mut-ter, heut Nacht heul- te Re- gen und Wind

Niemand hat's geseh'n, Op. 9, No. 4 — D
Die Trepp'_ hin- un-ter-ge-schwun- gen_ komm' ich_ in_ vol-'lem Lauf,

Hochzeitlied, Op. 20, No. 1 — E
Wir sin- gen und sa- gen vom Gra- fen so gern,

Die wandelnde Glocke, No. 3 — F
Es war ein Kind, das woll- te nie zur Kir- che sich be- que- men,

Des fremden Kindes heil'ger Christ, A, Op. 33, No. 3 — G
Es läuft ein frem- des Kind am A- bend vor Weih- nach- ten,

B — H
Du lie- ber heil-ger Christ, nicht Mut-ter und nicht Va-ter hab' ich

Heinrich der Vogler, Op. 56, No. 1 — I
Herr_ Hein-rich sitzt am_ Vo-gel-herd, recht froh und wohl- ge-muth;

Friedericus Rex, Op. 61 — J
Frie- de- ri- cus Rex, un- ser Kö- - - nig und Herr,

Süsses Begräbnis, Op. 62, No. 4 — K
Schäfer- in, ach,_ wie ha- ben sie dich so süss_ be- gra- - ben

Der heilige Franziskus, Op. 75, No. 3 — L
Fran- zis- kus einst, der Heil'- ge sass_ vor_ sei- ner Zell',

Prinz Eugen, Op. 92 — M
Zel- te, Po- sten, Wer-da-ru-fer! Lust- ge Nacht am Do- nau- u- fer!

Der Mohrenfürst auf der Messe, Op. 97, No. 3 — N
Auf der Mes- se, da zieht es, da stürmt_ es hin an

Des Glockentürmers Töchterlein, Op. 112a — O
Mein hoch- ge-bor-nes Schä-tze-lein, des Glo- - cken- tür-mers_Töch-ter-lein

Odins Meeresritt, Op. 118 A — P
Mei- ster O- luf, der Schmied auf Hel- - go- - land, ver-lässt dem Am- bos

B — Q
Her- aus, Her- aus, be-schlag' mir mein Ross, ich muss noch weit,

Die Uhr, Op. 123, No. 3 — R
Ich tra- ge, wo ich ge- he stets ei- ne Uhr bei mir;

Archibald Douglas, Op. 128 A — S
Ich hab' es ge-tra- gen sie-ben Jahr und ich kann_ es nicht tra-gen mehr,

Archibald Douglas, Op. 128

Denk' nicht an den al-ten Dou-glasneid, der trotzig dich be-kriegt,

Der Nöck, Op. 129, No. 2

Es tönt des Nö-cken Har-fen-schall

Tom der Reimer, Op. 135

Der Rei-mer Tho-mas lag am Bach, am Kie-sel-bach

Da sah er ei-ne blon-de Frau, die sass auf ei-nem weis-sen Ross

Canzonetta

War schö - - - - ner als der schön - - - - -ste Tag,

Das Erkennen

Ein Wan-der-bursch, mit dem Stab in der Hand, Kommt wie-der heim

Die nächtliche Heerschau

Nachts um die zwölf-te Stun-de ver-lässt der Tam-bour sein Grab

Der Zahn

Vic- to- ri- a! Vic- to- ri- a! Der klei- ne weis- se Zahn ist_ da,

LOGAN, Frederic Knight

Pale Moon
Copyright by Foster Music Co., Chicago

Out of my lodge at e-ven-tide_ 'Mong the sob-bing_ pine_

LORTZING, Gustav Albert (1801-1851)

Undine (opera)
Act II

Es wohnt am See ge-sta-de ein ar-mes Fis-cher-paar,_

Act III

Va- ter, Mut-ter, Schwes-tern, Brü-der, hab' ich auf der Welt nicht mehr

O kehr' zu-rück,_ mein ei-tel Seh-nen ist nun ge-stillt,

Act IV

Ich war in mei-nen jun-gen Jah-ren ein feu-ri-ges, ver-lieb-tes Blut,

Im Wein ist Wahr-heit nur al-lein, Im Wein ist Wahr-heit nur al-lein

Auch ich war ein Jüngling, from Der Waffenschmied (opera) Act III

Auch ich war ein Jüng-ling mit lo-cki-gem Haar,

Der Wildschütz (opera)
Act I Duet and Chorus

A B C D, der Jung-ge-sel-len-stand tut weh, E F G H,

Act II

Fünf- tau-send Tha-ler! Fünf- tau-send Tha-ler Träum o-der wach ich?

Der Wildschütz (opera)
Act II — Gret-chen, thrä-nen-voll, mich um Gott-tes wil-len bit-tet

Act III — Hei-ter-keit,und Fröh-lich-keit, ihr Göt-ter die-ses Le-bens

Zar und Zimmermann (opera)
Act I — Auf, Ge-sel-len,greift zur Axt und regt die nerv'-gen Ar-me

O Sanc-ta Ju-sti-tia, ich möch-te ra-sen, ich möch-te ra-sen

Die-se aus--drucks-vol-len Zü--ge, die-ses Aug',

Act II — Le-be wohl, mein flan-drisch Mäd-chen, wi-der Wil-len muss ich fort

Act III — Heil sei dem Tag an wel-chem Du bei uns er-schie-nen "Di-del-dum

O wie schön die Wor-te, wie schön die Wor-te flie-ssen,

Sonst spielt' ich mit Scep-ter mit Kro-ne und Stern

LOTTI, Antonio (1667-1740)

Crucifixus — Cru-ci-fi- - - - - - - - - - - - - - - xus, Cru-ci-fi-xus

Pur dicesti — Pur di- -ce-sti, o boc-ca boc-ca bel-la,

LULLY, Jean Baptiste (1632-1687)

Au clair de la lune — Au clair de la lu-ne, mon a-mi Pier-rot

Alceste (opera)
Prologue — Le Hé-ros que j'at-tends ne re-vien-dra-t-il pas?

Act IV — Il faut pas-ser tôt ou tard, Il faut pas-ser dans ma bar-que,

Amadis (opera)
Act II — Dans un piè-ge fa-tal son mau-vais sort l'a-mè-ne

Bois é-pais re-dou-ble ton om-bre: Tu ne sau-rais être

A-mour, que veux tu de moi? Mon coeur n'est pas fait pour toi,

Amadis (opera)   Act V

A — Fer- mez- vous pour ja- mais, mes yeux, mes tris- tes yeux

Armide (opera)   Act I

B — Al- lez, al-lez rem- plir ma pla- ce aux lieux d'où mon mal- heur

Act II

C — Plus j'ob- ser- ve ces lieux, et plus je les ad- mi- re

Act III

D — Ah! si la li- ber- té me doit ê- tre ra- vi- e

Act IV

E — Que vois-je? O spec-tacle effro- ya-ble O trop fu-nes- te sort

Cadmus et Hermione   Act II

F — A- mour, vois quels maux tu nous fais, où sont les biens que tu pro- mets?

Act V

G — Belle Her-mi- o- ne, He- las! He-las! puis-je être heu- reux sans vous?

Dormons tous, from Atys (opera)   Act III

H — Dor- mons dor-mons tous, ah! ah! Que le re-pos est

Persée (opera)   Act III

I — J'ai per- du la beau- té qui me ren- dit si vai- ne

J — Je por - - - te l'e- pou- vante et la mort en tous lieux.

Act V

K — Ô mort! Ve- nez fi- nir mon des-tin dé- plo- ra- ble

Thésée (opera)   Prologue

L — Re- ve- nez, re- ve- nez A- mours re- ve- nez Re- ve- nez, A- mours

M — Que rien ne trouble i- ci Vé- nus et les a- mours

Act V

N — Ah! Ah! faut- il me ven- ger, En per-dant ce que j'ai - - me!

LUTHER, Martin (1483-1546)

A mighty fortress is our God (Ein feste Burg)

P — A might- y fort-ress is our God, A bul-wark nev-er fail - - ing

Vom Himmel hoch

Q — Vom Him- mel hoch da Komm' ich her, ich bring' euch

MAC DOWELL, Edward (1861-1908)

Deserted, Op. 9, No. 1
Copyright by Arthur P. Schmidt Co., Boston.
Used by permission

S — Ye banks and braes o' bon- nie Doon, how can ye bloom sae fair!

The Blue Bell, Op. 26, No. 5 — In love_ she fell, My shy_ Blue-bell, With a stroll-ing Bum-ble-Bee

Cradle Hymn, Op. 33, No. 2
Copyright by Arthur P. Schmidt Co., Boston.
Used by permission
— Dor-mi Je-----su! dor-mi Je--su, Ma-ter ri-det

Menie, Op. 34, No. 1
Copyright by Arthur P. Schmidt Co., Boston.
Used by permission
— In vain to me the cow-slips blaw, In vain to me_ the vi-o-lets spring

Thy beaming eyes, Op. 40, No. 3
Copyright by Arthur P. Schmidt Co., Boston.
Used by permission
— Thy beam-ing eyes, Are Par-a-dise, to me, my love, to me,

The Sea, Op. 47, No. 7 — One sails_ a-way to_ sea, to_ sea, One stands on the shore_and cries_

Long Ago, Op. 56, No. 1
Copyright by Arthur P. Schmidt Co., Boston.
Used by permission
— Long a-go_____ sweet-heart_mine, Ros-es bloomed as ne'er be-fore,

The Swan bent low, No. 2 — The Swan bent low to the Lil-y, Mid wav'-ring shad-ows green_

A maid sings light, No. 3 — A maid sings light, And a maid sings low, With a mer-ry, mer-ry laugh

As the gloaming shadows creep, No. 4 — As the gloam--ing shad-ows creep Through_ the for-est deep_

Fair Springtide, Op. 60, No. 2
Copyright by Arthur P. Schmidt Co., Boston.
Used by permission
— Fair Spring-tide com-eth once a-gain____ Stirs_the sap in_lone-ly trees_

MAC GIMSEY, Robert (1898-   )

Shadrack
Copyright 1937, Carl Fischer, Inc.
Used by special permission.
— Thah was three chill-un frum nuh lan' uv Is-ri-el_ Shad--rack

MACHAUT, Guillaume De (c. 1300-1377)

De tout sui si confortée (Virelai) — De tout sui si con-for-té-e Que je-mais n'iert hoste-lé-e

Je puis trop bien (ballade) — Je-----------puis_trop_bien ma-------da-me com-pa-rer

Mass

1. Kyrie — Ky-ri-----e-----e-----

2. Qui propter nos — Qui pro-pter_____nos_____ho-mi-nes,_____

3. Agnus Dei — A-------------gnus De-------------i

A-------------gnus De-------i

Quant Theseus (ballade)

Quant The - - - - - se - - - us, Her - cu - - les et_ Ja - zon

Ne quier ve - - - - - oir la - - - beau-té_ d'Ab-sa- lon

Rose lys (rondeau)

Ro - se lys _ printemps ver-du-re

MAHLER, Gustav (1860-1911)

Blicke mir nicht in die Lieder

Blik- ke mir_ nicht in die Lie- der! Mei- ne_ Au- gen_

Ich atmet' einen linden Duft

Ich at - met' ei - nen lin- den Duft Im Zim- mer stand_

Ich bin der Welt abhanden gekommen

Ich bin der Welt_ ab - - - han - - den ge- kom- men

Kindertotenlieder (song cycle) No. 1
By permission Associated Music
Publishers, Inc.

Nun will die Sonn' so hell auf- geh'n als sei_ kein Un - glück,

No. 2

Nun seh' ich wohl war- um so dunk- le Flam- men

No. 3

Wenn dein Müt-ter-lein tritt zur Tür her-ein und den Kopf ich dre- he,

No. 4

Oft denk ich sie sind nur aus ge- gan- gen!

No. 5

In die-sem Wet- ter, in die-sem Braus, nie hätt' ich ge- sen- det

In die- sem Wet- ter, in die- sem Saus in_ die - - sem Braus,

Des Knaben Wunderhorn (song cycle)
Des Antonius von Padua Fisch-
predigt
By permission Boosey & Hawkes, Inc.,
copyright owners

An- to-nius zur Pre- digt die Kir- che findt_ le- dig!

Das irdische Leben

Mut- ter, ach Mut- ter, es hun- gert_ mich! Gib mir Brot,

Lob des hohen Verstandes

Einst- mal in ei-nem tie- fen Thal Ku- kuk und Nach- ti- gall

Rheinlegendchen

Bald_ gras' ich am Nek-kar,_ bald_ gras ich am Rhein,

Wer hat dies Liedlein erdacht?

Dort o- ben am Berg in dem hoh - - - en Haus, in dem Haus,

Wo die schönen Trompeten
blasen

Wer ist denn draussen und wer klop-fet an der mich_ so_ lei - - se,

Des Knaben Wunderhorn (song cycle)
Wo die schönen Trompeten blasen

Das ist der Herz- al- ler-lieb- ste dein, steh auf und lass_mich zu dir ein

Sieben Lieder aus letzter Zeit
Der Tamboursg'sell

Ich_ ar- mer Tam- bours- g'sell Man_ führt mich aus dem G'wölb—

Revelge

Des_ Mor- gens zwi- schen drei'n und_ vie- ren,

Ach Bru- der, ach Bru- der, ich kann dir nicht tra- gen

Liebst du um Schönheit

Liebst du um Schön-heit, O nicht mich lie- be! Lie- be die Son- ne

Das Lied von der Erde (song cycle)
By permission Boosey & Hawkes, Inc.,
copyright owners
No. 1 Das Trinklied vom Jammer der Erde

Schon winkt der Wein_____ im gold' - -nen Po- ka- le,

Dun- kel ist das Le- ben, ist der Tod

No. 2 Der Einsame im Herbst

Herbst- ne- bel wal- len bläu- lich ü- berm See

No. 3 Von der Jugend

Mit- ten_ in_ dem_ klei- nen Tei- che steht ein Pa- vil- lon aus grü- nem

In dem Häus-chen sit-zen Freun- de, schön ge-klei-det, trin-ken, plau-dern

No. 4 Von der Schönheit

Jun- ge Mäd- chen pflük- ken Blu- men, pflük- ken Lo-tos-blu- men_an dem_U-fer

No. 5 Der Trunkene im Frühling

Wenn nur ein Traum das_ Le-ben ist war- um denn Müh' und Plag'

der Lenz ist da, sei kom- men ü- ber Nacht!

No. 6 Der Abschied

Die Son- ne schei- det hin- ter dem Ge- bir- ge. In al- le Tä- ler

Lieder eines fahrenden Gesellen (song cycle)
No. 1

Wenn_ mein_ Schatz Hoch- zeit macht froh- li-che Hoch-zeit macht

No. 2

Ging heut' mor-gens ü- ber's Feld, Tau noch_ auf den Grä-sern hing;

No. 3

Ich hab ein glü-hend Mes- ser, ein Mes-ser in mei-ner Brust, O weh

No. 4

Die zwei blau- en Au- gen von mei-nem Schatz, die ha- ben mich

Symphony No. 2: 4th movement
"Urlicht"
By permission Boosey & Hawkes, Inc.,
copyright owners

Der Mensch liegt in gröss- ter Noth! Der Mensch liegt in grösster Pein

Symphony No. 2, 5th movement
(Chorus)

Auf- er- steh'n, ja_ auf- er- steh'n, wirst du, mein Staub, nach kur-zer_ Ruh!

Symphony No. 4, 4th movement
By permission Boosey & Hawkes, Inc.,
copyright owners

Wir ge-nie-ssen die himm - - - - - - - - - - - li-schen Freu-den

Jo- han-nes das Lämm- lein aus- las-set, der Metz-ger He- ro-des drauf pas-set

'Jm Mitternacht
By permission Boosey & Hawkes, Inc.,
copyright owners

·Um Mit - - ter-nacht hab' ich ge-wacht und auf-ge-blickt zum Him- mel

MAILLART, Louis (1817-1871)

Les Dragons de Villars (opéra-comqiue)
Act I No. 3

Ne par- le pas. Ro- se, je t'en sup-li- e, car me tra- hir

Act I No. 5

Grâce à ce vi- lain er- mi-te, a sa clo-che mau-di- - te,

Act III No. 13 bis
Soldatenart (this aria by Franz Abt)

Wenn mann beim Wein sitzt, wenn man beim Wein sitzt, was ist da das Bes-te

MALOTTE, Albert Hay (1895-)

The Lord's Prayer
Copyright 1935, G. Schirmer, Inc.

Our Father,___ Which art in heaven,___ Hal-low-ed be_ thy Name._

Song of the Open Road
Copyright by A B C Music Corp., N. Y.

What in the world could be so sweet, As the thun-der-ing clat- ter

MANA-ZUCCA (1890-)

I love life, Op. 83
Copyright by John Chuch Co.
Used by permission

I love life___ and I___ want to live___ and drink of life's full-ness

Rachem, Op. 60, No. !
Copyright by John Chuch Co.
Used by permission.

O- vi- nu mal- ke- nu O- vi- nu O- vi- nu A- do- nai- nu

Wie lang wet men ins_ stick-en, Wie lang wet men ins er- drick-en

MANNING, Katherine Lockhart

In the Luxembourg Gardens
Copyright 1925, G. Schirmer, Inc.

When sha- dows fall I wan- der thro' the gar- dens,

MANZOLO, Domenico (17th Cent.)

Quando tu mi guardi e ridi

Quando tu mi guar-di e ri- di, o mio be- ne, o mio co- re,

Se vedeste le piaghe

Se ve-de- ste le pia-ghe ch'io por- to nel cor,

MARCELLO, Benedetto (1686-1739)

Quella fiamma che m'accende
Recitative

Il mio bel fo- co o lon-ta no o vi-ci- no ch'es-ser pos-si- o

Aria

Quel- la_____ fiam- ma che m'ac - - - cen - de

MARENZIO, Luca (1550-1599)

Già torna

Già tor- na a ral- le- grar_____ l'a- ria e la ter- ra

O Rex Gloriae (O King of Glory)

O King of Glo- ry Lord_ of all_ pow- er, Lord_ of all_ pow'r,

Perche di pioggia

Per- che di piog - - - - - gia'l ciel non si de-stil - - - - - le,

Strider faceva

Stri- der fa- ce- va le zam- po- gne a l'au - - - - - ra,

MARSCHNER, Heinrich (1795-1861)

An jenem Tag, from Hans Heiling (opera) Act I

An je- nem Tag da du mir Treu - - - - e ver- spro- chen

O lass die Treu- e nie-mals wan-ken, o lass die Treu- e

MARSHALL, Charles (1887-1927)

I Hear You Calling Me
By permission Boosey & Hawkes, Inc., copyright owners

I hear you call-ing me. You call'd me when the moon had veil'd her light,

MARTIN, Easthope (1887-1925)

Come to the Fair
By permission Boosey & Hawkes, Inc., copyright owners

The sun is a shin-ing to wel-come the day_ Heigh- ho! come to the fair!_

MARTINI, Giovanni (1741-1816)

Plaisir d'Amour

Plai- sir d'a- mour_____ ne du- re qu'un_ mo- ment;_ cha- grin d'a-mour

MARX, Joseph (1882-   )

Ein junger Dichter denkt an die Geliebte
By permission Associated Music Publishers, Inc.

Der Mond steigt auf-wärts, ein ver-lieb-ter Träu-mer,

Hat dich die Liebe berührt
By permission Associated Music Publishers, Inc.

Hat Dich die Lie--be be-rührt, still un-ter lär-men-dem Vol-ke

Marienlied
By permission Associated Music Publishers, Inc.

Ich se-he dich in tau-send Bil-dern Ma-ri-a lieb-lich aus-gedrückt,

Nocturne
By permission Associated Music Publishers, Inc.

Süss duf-ten-de Lin-den-blü-te in quel-len-der Ju-ni-nacht,

Regenlied
By permission Associated Music Publishers, Inc.

Wo ich fer-ne des Mi-ka-ne ho-hen Gip-fel ra-gen seh,

Selige Nacht
By permission Associated Music Publishers, Inc.

Im Arm der Lie-be schie-fen wir se--lig ein

Und gestern hat er mir Rosen gebracht
By permission Associated Music Publishers, Inc.

Und ge-stern hat er mir Ro-sen ge-bracht, Sie ha-ben ge-duf-tet

Valse de Chopin
By permission Associated Music Publishers, Inc.

Wie ein blas-ser Trop-fen Blut's färbt die Lip-pen ei-ner Kran-ken

Venetianisches Wiegenlied
By permission Associated Music Publishers, Inc.

Ni-na ni-na-na, will ich Dir sin-gen Um Mit-ter-nacht

Waldseligkeit
By permission Associated Music Publishers, Inc.

Der Wald be-ginnt zu rau-schen, den Bäu-men naht die Nacht

MASCAGNI, Pietro (1863-1945)

L'Amico Fritz (opera) Act I
Copyright by Sonzogno, Milan

Son po-chi fio-ri, po-ve-re vio-le, Son l'a-li-to d'A-pri-le,

Noi sia--mo fi-glie ti-mi-de e pu-di-che di pri-ma-ve-ra

La-ce-re, mi-se-ri, tan-ti bam-bi-ni lan-guia-no qua

Per voi, ghiot-to-ni i-nu-ti-li, la vi-ta è nel go-der

Act II Duetto delle ciliege

Suzel, buon dì. D'un ga-io ro-si-gnuo-lo la vo-ce mi sve-glio

Han del-la por-po-ra vi-vo il co-lo-re, Son dol-ci e te-ne-re,

Tut-to ta-ce, ep-pur tut-to al cor mi par-la; que-sta pa-ce,

L'Amico Fritz (opera)
Act II Duetto delle ciliege

Tut-to il pra - - to d'un tap-pe-to s'è smal- ta- to,

Act III

O pal- li-da, che un gior-no mi guar- da-sti, in so-gno tor-na- mi!

O a- mo- re, o bel-la lu-ce del co-re, fiam-mel-la e- ter-na,

Non mi re- sta che il pian-to ed il do- lo- re,____

Cavalleria Rusticana (opera)
Siciliana: O Lola

O Lo- la, bian-ca co- me fior di spi-no,____

Opening Chorus

Gli a- ran-ci o- le za- no sui ver- di mar- gi- ni,

Tem- po è si mor- - mo-ri da o-gnu-no il te-ne-ro can- to

In mez- zo al cam-po tra le spi-che d'o-ro giun-ge il ru-mo-re

Il ca- val- lo scal-pi- ta i so-na-gli squil- la- no,

O che bel me-stie- re fa- re il car- ret- tie- re

Re- gi- na Coe - - - - - li, lae- ta- re (Al- le- lu- ja!)

In- neg- gia- mo il Si-gnor non è mor-to! Ei ful- gen-te ha di-schiu-so

In- neg- gia - - - mo il Si- gnor non è mor - - - - to

Voi lo sa- pete, o mam-ma, pri- ma d'an-dar sol- da- - to

Turriddu-Santuzza Duet

E sta-mat- ti-na al-l'al- ba t'han-no scor-to pres- so

Ba- da, San-tuz- za, schiavo non so-no di que- sta va- na

Lola's Ditty

Fior di giag- gio - lo____ gli an-ge-li bel-li stan-no a mille

Turiddu-Santuzza Duet (2nd part)

No, no, Tu- rid - - du, ri- ma- ni, ri- ma- ni an- co- ra

La tu- a San-tuz- za pian-ge e t'im-plo - - - - - ra____

Cavalleria Rusticana (opera)
Duet: Santuzza-Alfio
A

Tu - - rid- du, mi tol - - se, mi tol-se l'o - no - - - - - - - - - - ré,

Intermezzi
B

A - ve Ma - ri - - - - a___ Gra-tia ple - na

Chorus
C

A ca- sa, a ca-sa, a- mi - ci, o- ve ci a-spet-ta- no

Brindisi
D

Vi-va il vi no spu-meg-gian- te, nel bic-chie-re scin-til- lan- te

E

Vi-va il vi - no ch'è sin- ce- ro che ci al- lieta o- gni

Addio al mamma
(Turiddu's Farewell)
F

Voi do-vre-te fa- re da ma- - - - dre a San-ta,

Il Piccolo Marat (opera) Act II Duet
Copyright by Sonzogno, Milan
G

Va nel-la tua stan-zet- ta, Pre- - - ga ed a-spet- ta___

E sempre il vecchio andazzo, from
Guglielmo Ratcliff, (opera)
Act I
Copyright by Sonzogno, Milan
H

E sem-pre il vec-chio an -daz-zo. Vi si cor-re a ca- val-lo

Iris (opera)
Act I Inno al sole
Copyright by G. Ricordi & Co., Inc.
I

Son I- o! Son Io la Vi- ta! Son la Bel-tà in-fi - ni-ta

J

A-pri la tua fi- ne-stra!___For son i- o - - - che ven-go al tuo chia-mar,

K

In pu- re stil- le, ga- ie scin- til- le scen-de la vi- ta!

Act II
L

Io pin-go, pin-go, ma'il mio pen-nel-lo in-vano stendo in-tin-go

M

Un dì (e- ro pic-ci- na) al tem-pio vid'i un bon- zo

N

Or dam-mi'il brac- cio tu- o, brac-cio di ne- ve e a- vo- rio

Isabeau (opera)
Act I
Copyright by Sonzogno, Milan
O

Tu ch'odi lo mio gri- do scru-ta le vi- e del cie- lo___

P

Non co- lom-bel- le! Il do-no mi- o chiama- re vo-glio dal cie- lo

Act II
Q

Or so-lo in-tor- no i- na-ni-ma- te co- se

R

E pas-se- rà la vi-va cre- a- tu- ra entro il si- lenzio

Act III
S

Fu vi-le l'E- dit- to che vi li fè gli uo- mi- ni

Isabeau (opera) Act III
I tuo- i oc-chi! Gli a-per-ti oc-chi sol-tan-to col- pe— vo- li!

Lodoletta (opera) Act III
Copyright by Sonzogno, Milan
Ah! ri- tro- var-la nel-la sua ca- pan- na tut- ta pian- gen- te

Flam- men, per- do- na- mi non pian-ger più! Son i- o!

Il Canto del Lavoro
Quan- do la Pa- tria si chia-ma-va Ro- ma, I- ta- li- a- no,

Serenata
Co- me col ca- po sot- to la- la bian- ca

MASSÉ, Victor (1822-1884)

Les Noces de Jeannette (opera) No. 1 Air de Jean
Qu'un au- tre se ma- ri- e, moi, je re-prends ma foi,

No. 2 Romance
Par- mi tant d'a-mou- reux em- pressés à me plai- re,

No. 3
Ah! jar-ni-gué! Ca' n'est pas gai, le bon-homme est par- fois bru-tal.

No. 5
Cours, mon ai- guille, dans la lai- ne, ne te casse pas dans ma main!

Les voi- là, ces meubles joy-eux, les voi-là, ces meubles joy-eux

No. 6 Air du Rossignol
Au bord du che- min qui passe à ma por - - - - - - te

Voix lé- gè- re chan-son pas-sa- ge- re, ba- bil gra- ci- eux

Song of the Tiger, from Paul et Virginie (opera) Act I
Mid the thick li- a - - - - - - - - - - - - - - - - - na

MASSENET, Jules (1842-1912)

Le Cid (opera) Act I
O no-ble la - - me é-tin-ce- lan-te Pu-re comme un— re-gard

Act II
Plus de tour-ments— et plus de pei- ne au jour— at-ten- du

Act III
Pleu- rez! pleu- rez mes yeux— tom- bez tris- te ro- sé- e

O sou- ve-rain,— ô ju- ge, ô pe- re, Tou-jours voi- lé—

Don Quichotte (opera)
Act I

Quand la femme a vingt ans, La ma-jes-té su-prê - - - - me

Quand ap-pa-rais-sent les é-toi-les Et quand la nuit

Act V Morte de Don Quichotte

O mon maitre, ô mon Grand! dans des splen-deurs de son-ge

Prends cette i-le qu'il est tou-jours en mon pou-voir De te don-ner

Grisélidis (opera)
Prologue
By permission Heugel & Cie, Paris,
copyright owners

Ou-vrez-vous sur mon front, por-tes du pa-ra-dis!

Act I

Oi-seau qui pars à ti-re d'ai-le Qui là-bas me par-le-ra

Act II

Il par-tit au prin-temps Voi-ci ve-nir l'au-tom-ne

Je suis l'oi-seau que le fris-son D'hi-ver chas-se de la ra-mé-e

Hérodiade (opera)
Act I

Il est doux, il est bon, sa pa-role est se-rei-ne:

Sa-lo-mé! Sa-lo-mé! ah! reviens! je te veux!c'est ma voix qui t'implore

Ne me re-fu-se pas! Toi,mon seul bien! Pour qui j'ai tout quitté

Duet: Salomé and Jean

Ce que je veux te di - - re que je t'ai-me,

Act II

Vi - si-on fu - - gi-tive et tou-jours pour-sui-vi-e,

Act III

As-tres é-tin-ce-lants que l'in-fi-ni pro-mè-ne

De-mande au pri-son-nier qui re-voit la lu-miè-re,

Act IV

A-dieu donc, Vains ob-jets qui nous charment sur ter-re!

Quand nos jours s'é-tein-dront com-me une chas-te flam-me

Le Jongleur de Notre-Dame (opera)
Act I
By permission Heugel & Cie, Paris,
copyright owners

O Li-ber-té, m'ami - - - - e In-sou-ci-eu-se fé-e

Par son charme di-vin, tout me rit,tout m'en-chan - - - - te

MASSENET

224

Manon (opera)
Act III Scene 1

Par- don! mais j'é-tais là près de vous, à deux pas

Faut- il donc sa- voir tant de cho- ses? Que de- vien-nent

Scene 2

É- pou- se quel-que bra- ve fil- le, Di-gne de nous, di- gne de toi

Ah! fuy- ez, dou- ce i- ma- ge, à mon â- me trop chè- re

N'est-ce plus ma main que cet-te main pres- se? N'est-ce plus ma voix?—

Act IV

A nous les a- mours et les ro- - - - - -ses! Chan-ter, ai- mer,

Marie-Magdeleine (sacred drama)
Act I (La Magdaléenne à la fontaine)
By permission Heugel & Cie, Paris, copyright owners

C'est i- ci même en cet- te pla- - ce, C'est i- ci, Qu'il daigna m'apparaitre

Act III (La Magdaléenne à la croix)

O Bien- ai- mé, Ô Bien ai- mé, sous ta som- bre cou- ron- ne

Promesse de mon avenir, from Le Roi de Lahore (opera) Act IV
By permission Heugel & Cie, Paris, copyright owners

Pro- mes- se de mon a- ve- nir, O Si- tâ, rê- ve de ma vi- e,

Sapho (opera)
Act I
By permission Heugel & Cie, Paris, copyright owners

Ah!— qu'il est loin mon pa- ys! Ah!— qu'il est loin

Act II

Ce que j'ap- pel- le beau— c'est d'a-voir————— tes vingt ans,

Act IV

Pen-dant— un an— je fus ta femme,— et j'entends res-ter à toi

Thais (opera)
Act I
By permission Heugel & Cie, Paris, copyright owners

Hé- las!— en-fant en- co- re, a- vant qu'à mon coeur—

Voi-là donc la ter- ri- ble ci- té— A-le-xan-dri- e!

Act II

Qui te fait si se- vè- - re, et pour-quoi démens- tu la flam-me

Dis-moi que je suis bel-le et que je se- rai belle— é-ter- nel- le-ment!

L'a- mour— est un- e ver-tu ra- re, J'ai pé-ché non par lui,

Act III

O— mes-sa-ger de Dieu,— si bon dans ta ru-des- se, sois be-ni,

Bai-gne d'eau mes mains et mes lè- - vres, don-ne ces fruits, donne ces fruits,

MASSENET

Thais (opera) Act III — Te sou-vient-il_ du lu-mi-neux voy-a-ge, lors que tu m'as con-duite i-ci

Touraine est un pays, from Panurge (opera) Act I
By permission Heugel & Cie, Paris, copyright owners — Tou-raine est un pa-ys Au ciel bleu comme un re-gard ten-dre,

Werther (opera) Act I
By permission Heugel & Cie, Paris, copyright owners — O na-tu-re, plei-ne de grâ-ce, Rei-ne du temps et de l'es-pa-ce,

Quel-le pri-è-re de re-con-nais-sance et d'a-mour

Il faut nous sé-pa-rer. Voi-ci no-tre mai-son

Vous a-vez dit vrai!___ C'est que l'i-ma-ge de ma mère

Act II — J'au-rais_ sur ma poi-tri---ne pres-sé la plus di-vi-ne,

Lor-sque l'en-fant re-vient d'un voyage, a-vant l'heu-re

Act III — Wer-ther! Wer-ther! Qui m'au-rait dit la place que dans mon coeur

Des cris joy-eux d'en-fants mon---tent sous ma_ fe-nê-tre

Va!_ lais-se cou-ler mes lar-mes elles font du bien, ma ché-ri-e

Pour-quoi me reveiller, Ô souffle du prin-temps,_ pour-quoi me re-veiller?_

SONGS:
By permission Heugel & Cie, Paris, copyright owners

Chant provençal — Mireil-le ne sait pas en-co--re Le doux char--me de sa beau-té

Crépuscule — Comme un ri-deau---- sous la blan-cheur De leurs pé-ta-les

Elégie — Ô_ doux prin-temps d'autre-fois. Ver-tes saisons, Vous a-vez fui pour toujours!_

Noël Païen — No-ël!_ No-ël!_ Sous le ciel é-ton-né,_

Nuit d'espagne — L'air est em-bau-mé! la nuit est se-rei-ne,

Ouvre tes yeux bleus — Ou-vre tes yeux bleus, ma mi-gnon-ne: Voi-ci le jour

Pensée d'automne — U-ne chan-son d'a-dieu sort des sour-ces trou-blé-es;

Sérénade du Passant

Mi- gnon - - - ne, voi- ci l'A- vril! Le so- leil re- vient__ d'e- xil;   A

Si tu veux, Mignonne

Si tu veux, Mignonne,   au prin- temps Nous ver- rons fleu- rir   B

MAUDUIT, Jacques (1557-1627)

A la fontaine

A la fon- tai- ne je vou- drais a- vec ma bel-le al-ler jou- er,   D

En son temple sacré, Psalm 150

En son tem- ple sa- cré__ lou- ez le grand Dieu   E

Si d'une petite oeillade

Si d'u- ne pe- ti- te oeil-la- de tou- te d'a- mour et de- sir   F

MC GILL, Josephine (1877-1919)

Duna

By permission Boosey & Hawkes, Inc.,
copyright owners

When I was a lit- tle lad with fol- ly on my lips __   H

MEHUL, Etienne Henri (1763-1817)

Chant du Depart

La vic- toire en chan- tant nous ou- vre la bar- riè- re   J

La Ré- pub- li- que vous ap- pel- le, sa- chez vaincre ou sachez pé- rir,   K

Champs paternels, from Joseph
(opera)   Act I

Champs pa- ter- nels, Hé- bron, dou- ce val- lé- e, loin de vous   L

Romance du barde, from Ariodant
(opera)   Act II

Fem- me sen- sible, en- tends tu le ra- ma- ge de ces oi- seaux   M

MENDELSSOHN, Felix (1809-1847)

Elijah, Op. 70 (oratorio)

No. 4

If with all your hearts ye tru- ly seek me, ye shall e- ver sure- ly find me,   O

No. 9

Blessed are the men who fear him, they e- ver walk in the ways of peace   P

No. 14

Lord God of A- bra- ham, I- saac and Is- ra- el, this day let it be known   Q

No. 17

Is not His word__ like a fire?__ and like a ham- mer   R

No. 18

Woe, woe un- to them who for- sake Him! De- struction shall fall up- on them   S

Elijah, Op. 70 (oratorio)

No. 20 — Thanks be to God! He la-veth the thirsty land, the thirs - - ty land

No. 21 — Hear ye, Is- ra- el, hear what the Lord___ speak- eth!

I, I am he that com- fort- eth! Be not a-fraid,

No. 22 — Be not a-fraid, saith God the Lord, be not a- fraid; thy help is near

No. 26 — It is e- nough! O Lord, now take a- way my life___

No. 28 — Lift thine eyes, o lift thine eyes to the moun-tains whence com-eth

No. 29 — He, watch-ing o- ver Is- ra- el slum- bers not nor sleeps

No. 31 — O rest in the Lord, wait pa- tient- ly for Him

No. 37 — For the moun-tains shall_de-part___ and the hills, the hills be remo- ved

No. 39 — Then, then_shall the righteous shine forth as the sun in the heav'nly father's realm

No. 41 — O come, ev' - - ry one that thirst-eth, o come to the wa- ters,

St. Paul, Op. 36 (oratorio)

No. 7 — Je- ru- sa- lem, Je- ru- sa- lem, thou that kill - est the Pro-phets,

No. 11 — Hap- py and blest are they who have en- dur - - - - - - - - ed

No. 12 — Con- sume them all, Lord Sa- ba- oth, con- sume all these thine en-e- mies

No. 13 — But the Lord is mind-ful of His own___ He_ re- mem- bers His chil-dren

No. 15 — Rise! up! a- rise! rise, and shine,_ rise, and shine! Rise up! A- rise!___

No. 18 — O God, have mer- cy, have mer- cy up- on___ me,

No. 20 — I praise Thee O Lord___ my God, with all___ my___ heart___

No. 22 — O great is the depth of the rich- es of wis- dom and knowledge

St. Paul, Op. 36 (oratorio) No. 26 — A
How love- ly are the mes- sen- gers that preach us the gos- pel of peace

No. 27 — B
I will_ sing of Thy great mer- cies, O Lord, of Thy mer- cies, O Lord,

No. 35 — C
O be gra- cious, ye im- mor- tals, O be gra- cious, ye im- mor- tals!

No. 40 — D
Be_ thou faith- ful un- to death, and I will give to thee a_ crown of life_

Minnelied im Mai, Op. 8, No. 1 — E
Hol- der klingt der Vo- gel- sang, wenn die En- gel- rei- ne,

Erndtelied No. 4 — F
Es ist ein Schnit- ter, der heisst Tod, hat Ge- walt vom_ höch- sten Gott

Frühlingslied No. 6
(In Schwäbischer Mundart) — G
Jetzt kommt der Früh- ling, der Him- mel isch blau,_____

Maienlied No. 7 — H
Man soll hö- ren sü- sses Sin- gen in_ den Au- en ü- ber-all

Im Grünen No. 11 — I
Will- kommen im Grünen! Der Himmel ist blau, der Him- mel ist blau

Frühlingslied, Op. 19, No. 1 — J
In dem Wal- de sü- sse_ Tö- ne sin- gen klei- ne Vö- ge-lein

Das erste Veilchen No. 2 — K
Als ich das er- ste Veil- chen er- blickt, wie war ich von Far- ben und Duft

Neue Liebe No. 4 — L
In dem Mon- den- schein im Wal- de sah ich jüngst die El- fen rei - - ten,

Gruss No. 5 — M
Lei- se zieht durch mein Ge- müth lieb- li- ches Ge- läu- te

Reiselied No. 6 — N
Brin - - get des treu'_____ sten Her - - zens_ Grü- sse

Auf Flügeln des Gesanges (On Wings
of Song) Op. 34, No. 2 — O
Auf Flü- geln des_ Ge- san- ges, Herz- lieb- chen, trag' ich dich fort,

Frühlingslied No. 3 — P
Es bre- chen im schal- len- den Rei- gen die Früh- lings- stim- men los,

Zuleika No. 4 — Q
Ach um dei- ne feuch- ten Schwin- gen, West, wie sehr ich dich

Sonntagslied No. 5 — R
Ring- sum er- schallt im Wald und Flur viel fer- nes Glo- cken- klin- gen

Reiselied No. 6 — S
Der Herbst- wind rüt- telt die Bäu- me, die Nacht ist feucht und kalt;

MENDELSSOHN

Minnelied, Op. 47, No. 1
Wie der Quell so lieblich klin-get, und die Zar-ten Blu-men küsst,

Morgengruss No. 2
Ü-ber die Ber-ge steigt schon die Son-ne, die Läm-mer-heer-de läu-tet

Frühlingslied No. 3
Durch den Wald,_ den dun-keln, geht hol-de Früh - - ling-mor-gen-stun-de,

Volkslied No. 4
Es ist be-stimmt in Got-tes Rath, dass man von Lieb-sten

Der Blumenstrauss No. 5
Sie wan-delt im Blu-men-gar-ten und mus-tert den bun-ten Flor,

Bei der Wiege No. 6
Schlumm - - re! Schlumm-re und träu-me von kom-men-der Zeit

Der Jager Abschied, Op. 50, No. 2
Wer hat dich, du schö-ner Wald, auf-ge-baut so hoch da dro-ben?

Lobgesang (Hymn of Praise) Op. 52, No. 2
Al-les, Al-les, Al-les was O-dem hat Al-les, Al-les

No. 3
Er zäh-let uns'-re Thrä-nen in der Zeit der Noth,

No. 5
Ich har-re-te des Herrn, und er neig-te sich zu mir,

No. 6
Die Strich-e des Tod-es hat-ten uns emp-fan-gen,

Altdeutsches Lied, Op. 57, No. 1
Es ist in den Wald ge-sun-gen, wenn_ ich dir mein Lei-den sa-ge

Hirtenlied No. 2
O Win-ter, schlimmer_ Win-ter, wie ist die Welt so klein!

Suleika No. 3
Was be-deu-tet die Be-we-gung? bringt der Ost mir fro-he Kun-de?

O Jugend, O schöne Rosenzeit, No. 4
Von al-len schö-nen Kin-dern auf der Welt_ mir ei-nes doch am meisten

Venetianisches Gondellied No. 5
Wenn durch_ die Piaz-zet - - - ta die A-bend-luft weht,_

Abschied vom Wald, Op. 59, No. 3
O, Thä-ler weit o Hö-hen, O schö-ner grü-ner Wald,

Die Nachtigall No. 4
Die Nach-ti-gall, sie war ent-fernt, der Früh-ling lockt sie wie-der

Ich wollt' meine Lieb' ergösse sich, Op. 63, No. 1
Ich wollt'_ mei-ne Lieb'_ er-gös-se sich all'_ in ein ein-zig Wort,

Abschiedslied der Zugvögel, Op. 63, No. 2 — Wie war so schön_doch Wald und Feld! Wie ist so trau - rig jetzt die Welt! A

Gruss No. 3 — Wo- hin ich geh', und schau- e, in Feld und Wald und Thal B

Herbstlied No. 4 — Ach, wie so bald_____ ver- hal - - let_ der Rei- gen C

O säh' ich auf der Haide dort (O wert thou in the could blast) No. 5 — O säh' ich auf der Hai- de dort im Stur- me dich, im Stur- me dich! D

Festgesang, Op. 68, No. 2 (male chorus) (Hark the Herald Angels sing) — Va- ter- land, in dei- nen Gau - - en brach der gold'- ne Tag einst an E

Tröstung Op. 71, No. 1 — Wer- de hei- ter mein Ge- mü- the und ver- giss der Angst und Pein! F

An die Entfernte No. 3 — Die- se Ro- se pflück' ich hier in der wei- ten Fer - ne, G

Schilflied No. 4 — Auf dem Teich, dem re- gungs- lo- sen, weilt des Mon- des hol- der Glanz, H

Nachtlied No. 6 — Ver- gan- gen ist der lich- te Tag, von fer- ne kommt der Glo- cken Schlag; I

Lauda Sion, Op. 73, No. 6 — Ca - ro ci- bus, san- guis_ po- tus,_ ma- net ta- men Christus to- tus J

Der frohe Wandersmann, Op. 75, No. 1 — Wenn Gott will rech- te Gunst er- wei- sen, den schickt er in die Wei- te Welt K

Sonntagsmorgen, Op. 77, No. 1 — Das ist der Tag des Herrn, das ist der Tag des Herrn. Ich bin al- lein L

Lied aus Ruy Blas No. 3 — Wo- zu der Vög- lein Chö- re be- lau- schen fern und nah? M

Jagdlied Op. 84, No. 3 — Mit Lust thät ich aus- rei - - ten durch ei- nen grü - nen Wald_____ N

Die Liebende schreibt, Op. 86, No. 3 — Ein Blick von dei- nen Au- gen in die mei- nen O

Der Mond No. 5 — Mein Herz ist wie die dunk- le Nacht, wenn al- le Wi- pfel rau- schen; P

Neujahrslied, Op. 88, No. 1 — Mit der Freu- de zieht der Schmerz trau- lich durch die Zei- ten, Q

Heimkehr aus der Fremde, Op. 89, No. 4 (Son and Stranger) — Ich bin ein viel- ge- reis- ter Mann, der al- ler Län- der Tän- ze kann R

Concert Aria, Op. 94 (Infelice! Gia' del mio sguardo) — Ah,_ ri- tor- na_e- tà fe- li- ce quando_ac- can- to del mio be - - ne S

Die Lorely, Op. 98, No. 2 Ave Maria — A

Horch der A-bend-glo-cke Ton! A-ve Ma-ri-a!

Lieblingsplätzchen, Op. 99, No. 3 — B

Wisst ihr wo ich ger-ne weil' in der A-bend-küh-le?

Wenn sich zwei Herzen scheiden, No. 5 — C

Wenn sich zwei Her-zen schei-den,die sich der-einst ge-liebt,

Beati Mortui, Op. 115, No. 1 (male chorus) — D

Be-a-ti mor-tu-i in Do-mi-no mo-ri-en-tes,

Der Blumenkranz (By Celia's Arbour) — E

An Ce-lia's Baum in stil - - - ler Nacht

Drei Volkslieder (Three Folksongs)
No. 1 Wie kann ich froh — F

Wie kann ich froh und lus-tig sein? Wie kann ich geh'n mit Band und Strauss

No. 2 Abendlied — G

Wenn ich auf dem La-ger lie-ge, in Nacht ge-hüllt,

No. 3 Wasserfahrt — H

Ich stand ge-leh-net an den 'Mast, und zähl-te je-de Wel-le,

Hear My Prayer (Hymn) A — I

Hear my prayer O God, in-cline thine ear! Thy-self from my pe-ti-tion

B — J

O for the wings, for the wings of a dove! Far a-way

Two Songs after Eichendorff
1. Pagenlied — K

Wenn die Son-ne lieb-lich schie-ne wie in Wälsch-land,lau und blau

2. Das Waldschloss — L

Wo noch kein Wand-rer ge-gan-gen, hoch ü-ber Jä-ger und Ross

Warnung vor dem Rhein — M

An den Rhein, an den Rhein, zieh nicht an den Rhein,

MENOTTI, Gian-Carlo (1911-)

The Consul
The Empty-handed Traveler
Copyright 1950, G. Schirmer, Inc. — O

I'm not cry-ing for him not for us; but for John

Lullaby — P

I shall find for you shells and stars. I shall swim for you

Magda's Aria A — Q

To this we've come: that men with-hold the world from men

B — R

If to men, not to God, we now must pray, tell me,

W — S

What is your name? Mag-da Sor-el Age? Thir-ty three.

The Medium (opera)
Act I
Copyright 1947, G. Schirmer, Inc.

A — Where, oh, where___ is my new gol-den spin-dle and thread?

B — Mo-ther, mo-ther, are you there? Mo-ther, mo-ther, are you there?

Black Swan Song

C — The sun has fallen and it lies in blood, The moon is weav-ing

D — O black swan, where, oh, where___ is my lov-er gone

Act II

E — Up in the sky some one is play-ing a trom-bone and a gui-tar

F — Mon-i-ca, Mon-i-ca, dance the waltz, Mon-i-ca, Mon-i-ca, dance the waltz.

G — A-fraid, am I a-fraid? Madame Flo-ra a-fraid!

The Telephone
Copyright 1947, G. Schirmer, Inc.

H — Hel-lo! Hel-lo? Oh Margaret, it's you, I am so glad you called,

I — And how are you? And how is John? And how is Jean? You must tell them

J — It all be-gan on a Sun-day, when John and I went skat-ing

Duet

K — Hel-lo? Hel-lo? Where are you, my dar-ling? I'm ter-ri-bly near you

MESSAGER, André (1835-1929)

Fortunio (opera)
.Act II La Maison Grise
Copyright by Choudens fils, Paris

M — J'ai-mais la vieil-le mai-son gri--se Où j'ai gran-di

Act III Chanson de Fortunio

N — Si vous croy-ez que je vais di-re Qui j'ose ai-mer

Le jour sous le soleil béni, from
Madame Chrysanthème (opera)
Act III
Copyright by Choudens fils, Paris

O — Le jour, sous le so-leil bé-ni,___ La nuit, sous L'é-toi-le qui rê----ve,

Véronique (opéra-comique)
Act 1, No. 7
Copyright by Choudens fils, Paris

P — Pe-ti-te dinde: Ah! quel ou-tra-ge! Vrai-ment je suf-fo-que

Q — Ah Monsieur Flo-res-tan! A nous deux main-te-nant!

Act III, No. 20

R — Ma foi! pour ve-nir de pro-vin-ce Le tour n'est pas trop mal,

METCALF, John W.

Absent

Some-times be-tween long shad-ows on the grass

MEYERBEER, Giacomo (1791-1864)

L'Africaine (opera)

Act I   A-dieu, mon doux ri-va-ge, a-dieu mon seule a-mour!

Pour cel-le qui m'est chè-re qui m'est chè-re,

Act II   Sur mes ge-noux fils du so-leil, Vainqueur au champ d'a-lar-mes

Fil-le des Rois, à toi l'hom-ma-ge à toi l'hom-ma-ge

Je vois dans la gran-de î-le, en nos jours fortu-nés,

Act III   A-da-mas-tor, roi des va-gues pro-fon-des

Aux voi-les, aux cor-da-ges De van-cez les o-ra-ges

Act IV   Ô pa-ra-dis sor-ti de l'on-de

Con-dui-sez-moi vers ce na-vi-re Dont la voi-le bril-le à vos yeux

L'a-voir tant a-do-ré-e Et dans ce jour fa-tal

Dinorah (Le Pardon de Ploërmel) (opera)

Act II   De-puis lors, quand la nuit ga-gne Le vil-lage et la mon-ta-gne,

Om-bre lé-gè-re Qui suis mes pas Ne t'en va pas! non, non, non!

Act III   Le jour est le-vé, La pluie a la-vé Les cieux et la plai-ne,

Ah! mon re-monde te ven-ge De mon fol a-ban-don

L'Etoile du Nord (opera) Act I (Finale)

Veil-le sur eux tou-jours, Mè-re, mè-re,

O jours heu-reux de joie et de mi-sè-re

La, la, la, air ché-ri la, la, la la c'est lui,

Robert le Diable (opera)
Act I Ballade
Ja- dis régnait en Nor-man-di-e un prin-ce no-ble et va-leu-reux,

Romance
Va! Va! va! dit el - le, va, mon en - fant

qu'il eut la der-niè-re pen-sé-e, la der-niè-re pen-sé-e

Act III
Quand __ je quit-tai la Nor-man-di-e un__ vieil er-mi-te de cent ans,

Évocation
Non - nes qui re-po- sez sous cet-te froi- de   pier - re!

Act IV Cavatine
Ro- bert! Ro- bert! toi que j'ai - - me   et qui re- çus,

Grâ - ce, grâ-ce,__ pour toi mê - - me, pour toi mê - - me,

MEYER-HELMUND, Erik (1861-1932)

Dein gedenk' ich, Margaretha
Son- ne taucht in Mee -res-flu-then, Him-mel blitzt in letz-ten Glu-then

Das Zauberlied
Wenn   dein   ich denk', dann   sinn   ich oft

MIGNONE, Francisco (1897-   )

Cantiga de ninar
Copyright by E. B. Marks Music Corp., N. Y.
Can- to bai- xi- --nho U-ma ve- lha can- ção de ni-   nar

MILAN, Luis (c. 1500-c. 1561)

Durandarte
Du- ran- dar-te   du-ran-dar- te   Buen ca-ba- lle- ro

Perdida tengo la color
Per- di- da   ten- go la co- lor   Di- ze mi- nya

MILHAUD, Darius (1892-   )

L'Aurore
Copyright by Salabert, Paris, N. Y.
Quel-le   dou-ce   clar-té vient é-clai-rer l'O- ri-   ent!

Chants Populaires Hébraïques:
IV Berceuse
By permission Heugel & Cie, Paris
copyright owners
Dors, dors, dors, __   ton   pa-pa i- ra au vil-la- ge

VI Chant Hassidique
Que__ te di- rai-je et que   te ra-con-te-rai - - - - je

Cinq Chansons de Paul Vildrac:
I Les quatre petits lions
Par-tis d'u-ne mé-na-ge- rie un jour, quatr' tout pe-tits li- ons

Cinq Chansons de Paul Vildrac:
II Poupette et Patata

Au beau mi-lieu de l'i-le ver-te Il y a un cha-teau de bois — A

III La pomme et l'escargot

Il y a-vait u-ne pom-me A la ci-me d'un pom-mier — B

IV La Malpropre

Un fer-mier du voi-si-na-ge Qui boit plus que de rai-son — C

V Le Jardinier Impatient

Dans son po-ta-ger ma grand mè-re m'a ré-ser-vé un pe-tit coin — D

Poèmes Juifs
I Chant de Nourrice
By permission Associated Music
Publishers, Inc.

Dors, ma fleur, mon fils ché-ri pendant que je ba-lan-ce-rai ton ber-ceau; — E

II Chant de Sion

Ce n'est__ la ro-sée__ ni la pluie, ce sont__ mes__ lar-mes — F

III Chant du Laboureur

Mon es-pé-ran--ce n'est pas en-core per--due — G

IV Chant de la pitié

Dans les champs de Beth-le-em__ u-ne pier-re se dres--se — H

V Chant de resignation

Prends mon à----me fais en u-ne ly-re bril-lan-te — I

VI Chant d'amour

En mê-me temps que tous les bourgeons la Ro--se de mon coeur — J

VII Chant de forgeron

Près du Jourdain il y a u-ne mai-son de for-ge-ron — K

VIII Lamentation

Au ciel__ sept ché-ru- bins si-len-ci-eux com-me les rêves — L

La Tourterelle
By permission Durand & Cie, Paris;
Elkan-Vogel Co., Inc., Phila.,
copyright owners

Ma co-lom-be, Ô ma tour-te- rel-le, Est-ce vous dont j'entends — M

Tros Poèmes de Jean Cocteau
I Fumée
Copyright by Ed. de la Sirene, Paris

C'est per-mis de fu- mer__ ga--re L'e-cu-yer de Me-dra-no — N

II Fête de Bordeaux

La ma-nège a va-peur__ re-gar-de s'en al-ler__ — O

III Fête de Montmartre

Ne vous ba-lan-cez pas si fort le Ciel est à tout le mon-de — P

MILLOECKER, Karl (1842-1899)

The Beggar Student (Der Bettel-
student) (operetta)   No. 2

Yet this he- ro__ all vic- to-rious__ whom re- vere__ high and low — R

Noth-ing I have ev-er heard worse than that up-on my word, worse than that — S

No. 3

The world to soaring ge-nius ev-er Quick re-cog-ni- tion has re- fused — T

MONTEMEZZI, Italo (1875-   )

Son quarant' anni, from L'Amore dei tre re (opera)   Act I
Copyright by G. Ricordi & Co., Inc.

MONTEVERDE, Claudio (1567-1643)

Amor (Lamento della Ninfa)

A- mor Di- ce a- mor il ciel mi- ran-do il pie fer-mò

Ardo

Ar- do Ar- do Ar- do Ar - do e scoprir ahi_ lasso

Ardo si ma non t'amo

Ar- do si ma non t'a - - - - mo___ Da un si le-al a-man- te

Il Balletto delle Ingrate

Ahi trop - - po Ahi trop-po è du- ro cru- del sen-ten- za

Chiome d'oro

Chio-me d'oro bel the-so-ro tu mi leghi in mille mo- di_____

Ch'io t'ami

Ch'io t'a- mi e t'a-mi più de la mia vi - - - - ta

Cor mio mentre vi miro

Cor mio men- tre vi mi - - - - - ro

Ecco mormora l'onde (madrigal, 5-part)

Ec- co mor- mo-ra l'on- de e tre-mo-lar le ron- de

Hor ch'el ciel e la terra (madrigal, 6-voice)

Hor ch'el ciel e la ter-ra el ven-to ta- ce E le fe- re e gli angeli

Guer-ra è il mio sta- to Guer-ra guer-ra guer-ra guer-ra guer-ra guer-ra

Lagrime d'Amante al Sepolcro dell' Amata:

In - - ce-ne-ri- te spo-glie a- va-ra tom- - ba___

Di-te- lo o fiu-mi, o fiu- mi O fiu- mi O fiu-mi e voi che udeste

Da- rà la notte il sol lu- me alla ter- ra Splenderà Cin - - tia il dì

Ma te rac- co-glie o Nin fa ma te rac-co-glie o Nin- fa

O chio- me d'or ne - - ve gen-til ne - ve gen-til___ del se- no

Dun - - - que a- ma- te re- li-quie un mar di pian- to

Orfeo (opera)

Act II (Shepherds)

In que-sto pra-to a- dor-no___ o- gni sel-vag-gio nu- me___

Qui le Na- pee vez-zo-se schie- ra sem- pre fio- ri- ta

(Orfeo)

Vi ri- cor-da o bo-schi om-bro- si Vi ri- cor-da o bo-schi om-bro- si

Lament (Orfeo)

Tu___ sè mor- ta se' mor-ta mia vi- ta ed io re-spi- ro

(Chorus)

Ahi ca- so a-cer- bo, Ahi fat' em- - - pio e cru- de- le,

(Chorus)

Chi___ ne con-so-la ahi las- si O pur chi ne con- ce- de

Act III (Orfeo)

Pos-sen- - te spir- to e for-mi-da- - -bil nu- - me

(Orfeo)

Sol tu no- bi- le Dio puoi dar mi a- i- ta

(Orfeo)

Ahi sven-tu-ra-to a-man-te, sperar dun- que non li-ce ch'o- dan miei prie- ghi

(Chorus)

Nul-la im-pre- sa per huom si ten-ta in va - - - - - no

Act IV (Prosperina)

Si-gnor quel in- fe- li- ce che per queste di morte am- - pie cam-pa- gne

(Orfeo)

Qual ho- nor___ di te sia de- gno mia cetra on- ni- pò- ten- te,

(Chorus)

È la vir- tu- te rag-gio di ce- le- ste be-lez- za

Act V (Orfeo)

Que- sti i cam-pi di Tra-cia lo- ve pas- somm'il co- re

(Orfeo and Apollo)

Sa- liam,___ sa- liam___

(Chorus)

Van-ne Or-feo fe- li- ce a pie- no, a go- der ce- le-ste ho- no- re,

MORALES, Cristóbal de (c. 1500-1553)

O vos omnes

O___ vos o - - - - - - - - mnes___ qui tran si- tis___

MORLEY, Thomas (1557-c. 1603)

April is in my mistress' face — A-pril is in my Mis-tress' face, April is in my Mis-tress' face,

Dainty fine sweet nymph — Dain-ty fine sweet nymph de-light-ful, while the sun a-loft is mount-ing

Fire, fire — Fire fire, Fire, fire Fire, fire, Fire, fire, my heart

Hard by a crystal fountain — Hard by a Crys-tal fount - - - - - - - - - - - - - - - ain

I follow, lo, the footing — I fol-low, lo, the foot-ing I fol-low, lo, the foot-ing

It was a Lover and his Lasse — It was a lov-er and his lasse with a hey, with a hoe

My bonny lass she smileth — My bon-ny lass she smil-eth When she my heart be-guil-eth

Now is the gentle season — Now is the gen-tle sea-son fresh-ly flow'r-ing

Now is the month of Maying — Now is the month of May-ing when mer-ry lads are play-ing

Shoot, false love, I care not — Shoot false love I care not, spend thy shafts, and spare not,

Since my tears and lamenting — Since___ my tears and la-ment-ing, false love breed thy con-tenting

Sing we and chant it — Sing we and chant it, While love doth grant it, Fa la la la la la la la

Sweet nymph — Sweet Nymph, come to___ thy lo-ver, to___ thy lov-er,

MOZART, Wolfgang Amadeus (1756-1791)

Bastien and Bastienne (opera) K. 50
No. 1 — Mein lieb-ster Freund hat mich ver-lassen, mit ihm ist Schlaf___

No. 2 — Ich geh' jetzt auf die Wei-de be-täubt und___ ganz ge-dan-ken___ leer,

No. 4 — Be-fra-get mich ein zar-tes___ Kind um sein zu-künftges Glücke

No. 5 — Wenn mein Ba-stien einst___ im Scherze mir ein___ Blüm-chen___ sonst ent-wand

Bastien and Bastienne (opera) K. 50

No. 6 — A
Würd ich auch wie man- che Buh- le- rin- nen

No. 8 — B
Grossen Dank dir_ ab- zu- stat- ten, gro- ssen_ Dank, gro- ssen_ Dank

No. 10 — C
Dig-gi, dag-gi, schurry, murry, horum, harum, lirum,

No. 11 — D
Mei- ner_ Lieb-sten schö- ne_ Wan- gen will ich froh auf's neu-e seh'n

No. 12 — E
Er war mir sonst treu und er- ge- ben, mich lieb- te Bastien al- lein

No. 13 — F
Geh' hin! dein Trotz soll mich nicht schrecken; ich lauf auf's Schloss,

No. 16 A — G
Kinder! Kinder! seht, nach Sturm und Regen wird ein_ schöner Tag

B — H
Gebt euch die Hand! Knüpft die_ See- len und die_ Her- - zen!

Mass No. 3 in C major K. 66 — I
Et in_ Spi- ri- tum san - - - ctum_ Do- mi- num, et vivifi- can- tem,

Psalm 129 "De profundis" K. 93 — J
De pro- fun-dis cla- ma- vi ad te, Do- mi- ne, Do- mi- ne,

Regina Coeli K. 108 I 1 — K
Re- gi- na coe-li lae- ta- re,_ lae- ta- re Al- le- lu- ja,

II 2 — L
Qui- a quem me- ru- i - - - sti por- ta- re

III 3 — M
O- ra, o- - ra pro no- bis, o- -•- - - - - ra pro no- - bis

IV 4 — N
Al- le- lu- ja, Al- le- lu- ja Al- le- lu- ja

Ridente la calma K. 152 — O
Ri- den- te la cal- ma nell'_ al- ma_ si_ de - - - - sti,

Exsultate, jubilate K. 165 I 1 — P
Ex- sul- ta- te, ju- bi- la- te, o vos_ a- ni-mae be- a- tae

II 2 — Q
Tu vir- gi- num co- ro- na, tu no- bis_ pa- cem do- na,

III 3 — R
Al- le- lu- ja, al- le- lu- ja_ Al- le- lu- ja, al- le- lu- ja,

La Finta Giardiniera (opera) K. 196
Act I No. 4 — S
Noi don-ne po- ve- ri- ne, ta- pi- ne, sfor- tu- na- te,

Dans un bois solitaire K. 308
Dans un bois so-li- tai-re et som-bre je_ me pro-me-nais_

Popoli di Tessaglia K. 316
Io non_ chie-do e-ter-ni De-i, tut-to il ciel per me se-re-no

Mass in C ("Krönungs Messe")
(Coronation Mass) K. 317
Agnus Dei
A- gnus De- i, a- gnus De- i, qui tol- lis pec- ca- ta,

Adoramus te K. 327
Ad- o- ra - - - - - mus te, Chri- ste, et be-ne-dici - - mus_ ti-bi,

Vesperae solennes de confessor
K. 339 No. 5
Lau - - - - da - - - - - - te Do- mi-num o - - mnes gen- tes

Wiegenlied K. 350 (K.anh. 284 f)
(attributed to Mozart. Actually
by Bernard Flies, a contemporary
of Mozart)
Schlafe mein Prinzchen schlaf' ein, es ruh'n nun Schäfchen und Vö- ge- lein

Komm, liebe Zither K. 341
Komm, lie-be Zi- ther, komm, du Freund in stil- ler Lie- be,

Idomeneo (opera) K. 366 Act I
Pa- dre! Ger- ma-ni ad- di- o voi foste io vi per- de- i

A
Non ho col-pa e mi con- dan- ni e mi con- dan- ni

B
Col-pa è vos-tra o Dei_ ti- ran- ni è di pe- na

Tut- te nel cor vi sen- to, vi sen- to, vi sen- to

Ve- drom-mi in-tor- no l'om-bra do- len-te, l'om-bra, l'om-bra

Il Pa- dre_ ado- ra- to ri- tro-vo, e lo per-do

Act II
Se il tuo duol, se il mio de - - si- o s'in-vo-las _

Se il pa- dre per- de- i la Patria, il ri- po- so,

Fuor del mar ho un mar in sen-no che_ del pri-mo è più fu- nesto

I - - - dol_ mi- o se_ ri- tro-so al- tra A- man- te

Act III
Zef- fi- ret- ti lu- sin- ghie- ri

Se co - - - là nè fa- ti è scrit- to

Idomeneo (opera)   K. 366   Act III

A: D'O- re- ste, d'A- ja- ce ho in se- no i tor- men- ti D'O- re- ste

B: Tor - - - - na la pa- ce al co- re, al co- re,

Ma che vi fece, o stelle   K. 368

C: Spe- ra- i vi- ci- no, vi- ci- no il li- do,

D: Ma tra- por- tar mi sen- to,

Misera, dove son!   K. 369

E: Ah! non son io che par- lo, Ah, non son io che par- lo

F: Non cu- ra il ciel ti- ra- no l'af- fan no in cui mi ve- do

A questo seno deh vieni   K. 374

G: Or che il cie- lo a me ti ren- de, ca- ra par- te del mio cor,

Die Entführung aus dem Seraglio (The Abduction from the Seraglio) (opera)   K. 384   Act 1

H: Hier soll ich dich denn se- hen, Kon- stan- ze, dich, mein Glück-

I: Wer ein Lieb- chen hat ge- fun- den, das es treu und red- lich meint,

J: Sol- che her- ge- lauf'ne Laf - - - - - - - - - - - - - fen

K: O wie ängstlich, o wie feurig Klopft mein lie- be- vol- les Herz

L: Ach ich liebte, war so glücklich, kann- te nicht der Lie- be Schmerz

M: Doch wie schnell schwand mei- ne Freude, doch wie schnell schwand meine Freude!

Act II

N: Durch Zärt- lich- keit und Schmeicheln Ge- fäl- lig- keit und Scherzen

O: Ich ge- he, doch rathe ich dir, den Schurken Ped- ril- lo zu mei- den

P: Trau- rig- keit ward mir zum Lo- se, ward mir zum Lo- se,

Q: Mar- tern al- ler Ar- ten al- ler Ar- ten mö- gen mei - - ner war- ten,

R: Wel- che Won- ne, wel- che Lust regt sich nun in mei- ner Brust

S: Frisch zum Kampfe! Frisch zum Streite! Nur ein fei- ger Tropf verzagt,

Die Entführung aus dem Seraglio (The Abduction from the Seraglio) (opera)

K. 384 Act II Duet — A

Vi - vat__ Bac-chus! Bac-chus le-be! Bac-chus war ein bra-ver Mann.

— B

Wenn der Freu-de Thrä-nen fliessen, lä-chelt Lie-be__ dem Ge-liebten hold__

Act III (Romanze) — C

Ich bau - e ganz__ auf__ dei - ne Stär - ke,

— D

Im Moh-ren-land ge-fan-gen war__ ein Mäd-chen hübsch und fein,

— E

O! wie will ich tri-um-phi-ren, wenn sie euch zum Richt-platz füh-ren,

— F

Nie werd' ich dei-ne Huld ver-ken-nen, mein Dank bleibt e-wig dir ge-weiht.

Ich würd auf meinem Pfad K. 390 — G

Ich würd auf mei-nem Pfad__ mit Thränen oft hin zum fer-nen En-de

Sei du mein Trost K. 391 — H

Sei du__ mein Trost, ver-schwiegne Trau-rig-keit

Verdankt sei es dem Glanz K. 392 — I

Verdankt sei es dem__ Glanz der Gro-ssen, dass er mein Nichts mir deutlich zeigt,

Mia speranze adorata (recitative and concert aria) K. 416 — J

Ah, non sa-i, qual pe-na si-a il__ do-ver-ti.

No, no, che non sei capace (concert aria) K. 419 — K

No, no, no, che non sei ca-pa-ce di cor-te-sia, d'o-no-re,

Per pietà, non ricercate K. 420 A — L

Per pie-tà, non ri-cer-ca-te la ca-gion__ del mio tor-men-to,

B — M

Ah, tra l'i-re e tra gli sdegni del-la mia fu-ne-sta sorte

Mass in C minor K. 427 — N

Ky - ri-e e-lei-son, e-lei----son. Ky-ri-e e-leison

— O

Glo---ri-a in ex-cel--------------sis

— P

Lau-da--------mus__ te,__ be-ne-di-ci-mus te,__

— Q

Do-mi-ne De-us__ rex coe-le-stis, rex__ coe-le-stis,

— R

Qui tol--lis pec-ca-ta mun-di qui tol-lis pec-ca-ta,

— S

Quo-ni-am tu so----------lus sanc--tus,

Mass in C minor K. 427

A — Cum san - - - - cto spi-ri-tu in glo - - - - - - - - - - - - ri-a

B — Et in - car - na - tus est de spi - ri - tu san - - - cto

C — Et in Spi-ri-tum san-ctum, do-mi-num, et — vi-vi-fi - cantem

D — Cre-do, Cre-do in u-nam sanctam ca-tho-li-cam et a-posto-li-cam

E — Et vi-tam ven-tu-ri sae-cu-li, a - - - - - - - - - - - men,

F — Be-ne-di - - - ctus qui — ve-nit, Be-ne-di - - ctus qui — ve-nit

Cosi dunque tradisci K. 432

G — A- spri ri-mor-si a- tro-ci, a- spri ri-mor-si a- tro-ci

Warnung K. 433

H — Män-ner su-chen stets zu na-schen, lässt man sie al- lein —

Gesellenreise (Masonic Song) K. 468

I — Die ihr ei-nem — neu-en — Gra-de der Er-kennt-niss nun euch — naht —

Der Zauberer K. 472

J — Ihr Mäd-chen, flieht Damö- ten ja! als ich zum er-stenmal ihn sah,

Das Veilchen K. 476

K — Ein Veil-chen auf der Wie-se stand ge- bückt in sich und un-be-kannt;

Der Schauspieldirektor (The Impresario) (opera) K. 486 **No. 1**

L — Da schlägt die Ab-schieds- stun-de, um grau-sam uns zu trennen

M — Ein Herz, das so — der Ab- schied krän-ket, dem ist kein Wan-kel-mut —

No. 2

N — Bes-ter Jüng-ling, mit Ent-zü-cken nehm' ich dei-ne Lie-be — an

Le Nozze di Figaro (The Marriage of Figaro) (opera) K. 492 **Act I**

O — Cinque, dieci, venti, trenta, trenta se-i quaranta tre

P — O- ra si, — ch' io — son con- ten- ta

Q — Se a ca-so Ma- da-ma la not-te ti chia-ma

R — Se vuol bal-la - - re, Si-gnor con- ti- no, se vuol bal-ba - - re,

S — La ven-detta Oh! la ven-det-ta è un pia-cer ser-ba-to ai saggi

MOZART
Le Nozze di Figaro (The Marriage of Figaro) (opera) K. 492
Act I

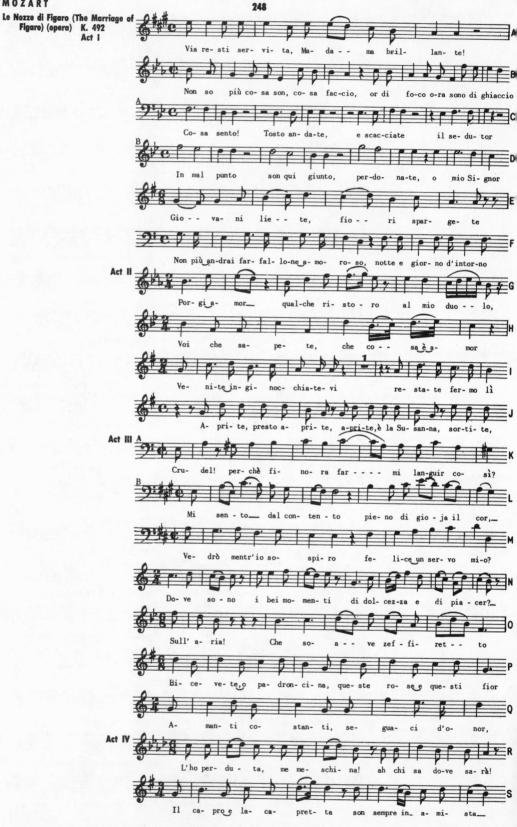

Via re- sti ser- vi- ta, Ma- da- - ma bril- lan- te!

Non so più co- sa son, co- sa fac- cio, or di fo- co o- ra sono di ghiaccio

Co- sa sento! Tosto an- da- te, e scac- cia- te il se- dut- tor

In mal punto son qui giunto, per- do- na- te, o mio Si- gnor

Gio- - va- ni lie- - te, fio- - ri spar- ge- te

Non più_an- drai far- fal- lo- ne_a- mo- ro- so, notte e gior- no d'intor- no

Act II

Por- gi_a- mor_ qual- che ri- sto- ro al mio duo- - lo,

Voi che sa- pe- te, che co- - sa_è_a- mor

Ve- ni- te_in- gi- noc- chia- te- vi re- sta- te fer- mo lì

A- pri- te, presto a- pri- te, a- pri- te,è la Su- san- na, sor- ti- te,

Act III A

Cru- del! per- chè fi- no- ra far- - - - mi lan- guir co- sì?

B

Mi sen- to_ dal con- ten- to pie- no di gio- ja il cor,_

Ve- drò mentr'io so- spi- ro fe- li- ce_un ser- vo mi- o?

Do- ve so- no i bei mo- men- ti di dol- cez- za e di pia- cer?_

Sull' a- ria! Che so- a- - ve zef- fi- ret- - to

Bi- ce- ve- te,o pa- dron- ci- na, que- ste ro- se_e que- sti fior

A- man- ti co- stan- ti, se- gua- ci d'o- nor,

Act IV

L'ho per- du- ta, me me- schi- na! ah chi sa do- ve sa- rà!

Il ca- pro_e la ca- pret- ta son sempre in_a- mi- sta_

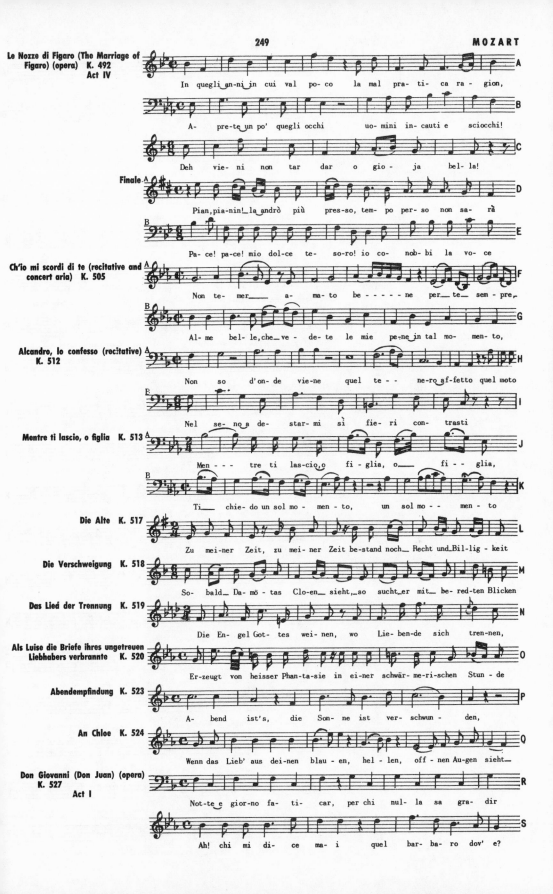

Le Nozze di Figaro (The Marriage of Figaro) (opera) K. 492 Act IV

A — In quegli anni in cui val poco la mal pratica ragion,

B — A- prete un po' quegli occhi uomini incauti e sciocchi!

C — Deh vieni non tardar o gioja bella!

Finale

D — Pian, pia-nin! la andrò più presso, tempo perso non sarà

E — Pace! pace! mio dolce tesoro! io conobbi la voce

Ch'io mi scordi di te (recitative and concert aria) K. 505

F — Non temer amato bene per te sempre,

G — Alme belle, che vedete le mie pene in tal momento,

Alcandro, lo confesso (recitative) K. 512

H — Non so d'onde viene quel tenero affetto quel moto

I — Nel seno a destarmi sì fieri contrasti

Mentre ti lascio, o figlia K. 513

J — Mentre ti lascio, o figlia, o figlia,

K — Ti chiedo un sol momento, un sol momento

Die Alte K. 517

L — Zu meiner Zeit, zu meiner Zeit bestand noch Recht und Billigkeit

Die Verschweigung K. 518

M — So bald Damötas Cloen sieht, so sucht er mit beredten Blicken

Das Lied der Trennung K. 519

N — Die Engel Gottes weinen, wo Liebende sich trennen,

Als Luise die Briefe ihres ungetreuen Liebhabers verbrannte K. 520

O — Erzeugt von heisser Phantasie in einer schwärmerischen Stunde

Abendempfindung K. 523

P — A- bend ist's, die Sonne ist verschwunden,

An Chloe K. 524

Q — Wenn das Lieb' aus deinen blauen, hellen, offnen Augen sieht

Don Giovanni (Don Juan) (opera) K. 527 Act I

R — Notte e giorno faticar, per chi nulla sa gradir

S — Ah! chi mi dice mai quel barbaro dov' e?

MOZART
Don Giovanni (Don Juan) (opera)
K. 527
Act I Catalogue Song

A — Ma- da- mi- na! Il ca- to- lo- go è que- sto,

B — Nel- la bion- da e- gli ha l'u- san- za

C — Gio- vi- net- te, che fa- te all'a- mo- re, che fa- te all'a- mo- re,

D — Ho ca- pi- to, Si- gnor, si! Si- gnor, si!

A — Là ci da- rem la ma- no, là mi di- rai di sì

B — An- diam, an- diam, mio be- ne, a ri- sto- rar le pe- ne

Ah! fug- - - gi il tra- di- tor! Non lo las- ciar più dir;

Or sai, che l'o- no- re ra- pi- re a me vol- se

Dal- la sua pa- ce la mia di- - pen- - - - - de,

Finch'han dal vi- no cal- da la tes- ta u- na gran fes- ta

A — Bat- ti, bat- ti o bel Ma- set- to, la tua po- ve- ra Zer- li- na:

B — Pa- ce, pa- ce o vi- ta mi- a! pa- ce, pa- ce o vi- ta mi- a!

Act II

Serenade — Eh via, buf- fo- ne, eh via, buf- fo- ne, non mi sec- car!

Deh vie- ni al- la fi- ne- stra o mio te- so- ro,

Ve- drai, ca- ri- no, se sei buo- ni- no,

Ah, pie- tà! Si- gno- ri miei! Ah pie- tà, pie- tà, pie- tà, pie- tà

Il mio te- so- ro in- tan- - to an- da- te,

Per que- - ste tu- e ma- ni- ne, Can- di- de e te- ne- rel- le,

Mi tra- di quell' al- ma in- gra- ta, quell' al- ma in- gra- ta

Don Giovanni (Don Juan) (opera) K. 527
Act II

A — O sta- tua gen- ti- lis- si- ma del gran Commen- da- to- re

B — Non mi____ dir,____ bell' i- - dol mi- - o,

C — For- se,____ for- se un gior- no il cie- lo an- co- ra

Finale

D — Gia la men- sa e pre- - pa- - ra- ta.

E — L'ul- ti- ma pro- va dell' a- mor mi- o an- cor vogl' i- o

F — Don Gio- van- ni a ce- nar te- co m'in- vi- ta- sti

G — Ah! dov' è il per- - fi- do? dov' è l'in- degno?

H — Or che tut- ti, O_ mio te- so- ro! ven- di ca- ti- siam dal cie- lo,

I — Que- sto è il fin di chi fa mal di chi fa mal

Bella mia fiamma, addio (Recitative and concert aria) K. 528

J — Re- sta, oh ca- ra, oh ca- - - - - - - ra!

K — Que- sta vi- ta co- sì a- ma- ra più sof- fri- bile non è

Das Traumbild K. 530

L — Wo bist_ du, Bild, das vor mir_ stand als ich im Gar- ten träum- - te

Die kleine Spinnerin K. 531

M — "Was spinnst Du?" frag- te Nach- bars Fritz als er uns jüngst be- such- te;

Un Bacio di Mano K. 541

N — Un ba- cio di ma- no vi fa ma- ra- vi- glio

O — Voi sie- te un po' ton- do, mio ca- - ro Pom- pe- o,

Ave Maria (4-part canon) K. 554

P — A- - - - - ve Ma- ri- a, A- - - - - - ve_ Ma- ri- a

Un moto di gioja K. 579 (alternate aria for "Deh Vieni" in Marriage of Figaro)

Q — Un mo- to di gio- ja mi sen- to in pet- to,

Rivolgete a lui lo sguardo K. 584 (meant for Cosi fan tutte)

R — Ri- vol- ge- te a lui lo sguardo e ve- dre- te co- me sta;

Cosi fan tutte (opera) K. 588 Act I No. 1

S — La mia Do- ra- bel- la ca- pa- ce non è, ca- pa- ce non è;

Das Kinderspiel K. 598

Wir Kin- der, wir schmecken_ der_ Freu-den_ recht_ viel,

Per questa bella mano K. 612

Per que- sta bel- la ma - no, per que- sti va- ghi ra- i

Vol-gi lie- ti o fie- ri sguar- di, dim-mi pur che m'odi_o m'ami

Ave verum corpus K. 618

A- ve,_ a - -ve, ve- rum_ cor- pus, na-tum de Ma-ri-a vir- gi- ne,

Die Zauberflöte (The Magic Flute)
(opera) K. 620
Act I No. 2

Der_ Vo- gel-fän- ger_ bin ich ja, stets_ lus- tig, hei-sa, hop-sa- sa!

No. 3

Dies Bild-niss ist be- zau- bernd schön, wie noch kein Au-ge je ge-seh'n!

No. 4

Zum Lei- den bin ich auser-ko- ren, denn mei-ne Toch- ter feh-let mir,

Du, du du wirst_ sie_ zu be-frei- en ge- - - - - -hen,

No. 5 Quintet

Hm, Hm, Hm, Hm,_ Hm, Hm, Hm, Hm,_ Hm, Hm, Hm, Hm,Hm, Hm,_Hm, Hm!

No. 7

Bei Män-nern, wel-che Lie- be fühlen, fehlt auch_ein gu-tes Her-ze nicht

Finale

Wie_ stark ist_ nicht_ dein_ Zau- - ber- ton!

Schnelle Fü- sse, ra-scher Mut schützt vor Feindes_List_ und_Wuth;

Das_ klinget so herr-lich das_ klin-get so schön!

Act II No. 10

O I- sis und O- si- ris,_ schenket der Weisheit Geist dem_ neuen Paar

No. 11

Bewah- ret euch vor Wei-ber- tü- cken, dies ist des Bun-des er- ste_ Pflicht!

No. 13

Al- les_ fühlt der_ Lie-be_ Freu-den, schnäbelt, tän-delt, herzt und küsst;

No. 14
Queen of the Night Aria

Der Höl-le Ra-che kocht in mei-nem Her-zen, Tod und Ver- zweiflung!

Cadenza

cadenza

No. 15

In die-sen heil'-gen Hal- len kennt man die Ra- che nicht,_

Laut verkünde uns're Freude (Masonic Cantata)   K. 623

Laut ver- kun- de uns'- re Freu- de fro- her In- strumen- ten- schall

Requiem K. 626

No. 1   Re- qui- em ae- ter- nam, ae- ter- nam do- na e- is

Ky- ri- e e- le- i- son, e- le- i- son

No. 2   Di- es i- rae di- es il- la sol- vet sae- chum in fa- vil- la,

No. 3   Tu- ba mi- rum spargens so- num, tu- ba mi- rum

No. 4   Rex! Rex! Rex! Rex tremen- dae ma- je- sta- tis

No. 5   Re- cor- da- re Je- su pi- e,

No. 6   Con- fu- ta- tis ma- le- di- ctis, flam- mis a- cribus ad- di- ctis,

No. 7   La- cri- mo- sa di- es il- la qua re- sur- get

No. 8   Do- mi- ne Je- su Chri- ste Rex glo- ri- ae, Rex glo- ri- ae!

No. 9   Ho- sti- as et pre- ces ti- bi, Do- mi- ne ti- bi, Do- mi- ne,

quam o- lim A- bra- hae promi- si- sti et se- mi- ni e- jus,

No. 10   San- ctus, San- ctus San- ctus Do- mi- nus De- us Sa- ba- oth!

O- sa- na in ex- cel- sis,

No. 11   Be- ne- di- ctus, qui ve- nit in no- mi- ne Do- mini

No. 12   Ag- nus De- i qui tol- lis pec- ca- ta mun- di,

MUDARRA, Alfonso (16th Cent.)

De la sangre de tus nobles

De la san- gre de tus no- bles

La mañana de Sant Juan

La ma- ña- na de- Sant Juan, Al tie...po_ que albore- a- ba

Triste estaba el Rey David

Tris - - te_es- ta - ba_el rey Da- vid_____

MUSSORGSKY, Modeste (1839-1881)

Boris Godunov (opera)
Prologue Scene I Opening Chorus

Wilt thou_ leave us all un - pro- tect- ed, our_ fa - ther?

Coronation Scene (chorus)

As re- splen-dent the sun_ fills the hea- ven with glo- ry,

My soul is sad! I did not seek this charge_

Act I Scene I Pimen's Monologue

Yet one more tale the last of all these re - cords,

Scene II Varlaam's Song

Here's the tale of what hap-pened at Ka- zan,_____

Drunken Scene

I'll hold my tongue_ I'll hold my tongue_ Reason got plen - -ty

Act II Song of the Gnat

Once a gnat, as all gnats should, Did draw wa- ter, hew the wood

Monologue

I have a- chieved the highest 'Tis now six years that I have reign'd with peace_

The hand of God, the aw- ful judge is on me,

Song of the Parrot

Our cock-a- too was play- ing with the at- tend- ants_

Clock Scene

Ah! give me air! this suf- fo- cates my soul!

Act III Scene II Polonaise

Your pro-fessed de - vo-tion,sir I trust not, All in vain your_ sol-emn_oaths

Oh! Tzar-e- vitch, I be- seech thee, do not curse me

Act IV Scene I Revolutionary Chorus

Sirs,'tis time we got to work,what hinders? Sirs, your o- pin-ion first,

Pimen's Tale A

A peace-ful her-mit of sim- ple mind, un- versed in worldly things

B

There came once at vesper hour a herds-man at my door a grey beard old and hoary

Fare-well my son I am dy-ing From now thou wilt be-gin thy reign

MUSSORGSKY

Boris Godunov (opera)
Act IV Scene I Farewell, my son
(chorus)

Weep and mourn, ye mor-tal men,__ for his life is fled__

The Fair at Sorochinsk (opera)
Act I Revery of the Young Peasant

My heart,__ why weep-est thou? Why art__ thou pin-ing

Sor- row, for-sake thou me!__ De- spair, I bid thee go

Act II Song of Khivria

Who would not love me, such a charm-ing love-bird, Who would not gladly

Since the time when first I met my Bru-de- us, Bru-de- us,

Act III Parasha's Revery and Dance

Grieve nev-er, my be-lov-ed, Griev-ing nev-er ban-ish'd sor- row

Hi__ my young and black eyed lov- er Standing up so__ straight and tall.

Khovantchina (opera)
Act II Divination by Water

Spi-rits of ne-ther worlds, Hid-den be-low the floods! Bound by a ma-gic spell,

In shame and disgrace_I be-hold_thee In exile a- lone in a dis-tant__ land

Act III Martha's Song

And by day and by night I fare O- ver mountain and mead - -ow

Shakiltor's Aria

Ah! mal-heu- reu se Rus-si- e, mon__ pa- ys cher!__

SONGS:
After the Battle

He met his death in for-eign land, in bit- ter fight-ing hand to hand,

By the River Don

By the Don__ a gar-den fair__ All a-bloom__ with ro- ses

A Child's Song

In the vale, oh! in the val-ley Grows a little ber- ry,

The Country Feast

They had opened wide the might-y doors of oak; Some on horse and some in sleds

Cradle Song of the Poor

By-bye, by__ By-bye by- bye Lower than the hum- ble way-side flow'rs

Gathering Mushrooms

Mush- rooms brown and tall,__ mus-ter'd, Mush-rooms white and small__

The Goat

Through a field of flow'rs en - chanting, walked a maid, her beau-ty flaunting

Peasant Cradle Song — By - bye,_ by - - -bye sleep,_my_ pret - ty_ boy Sleep, lit-tle one — A

Seminarist — Pa-nis, piscis, cri-nis, fi-nis; ig-nis, la-pis, pulvis, ci-nis, Oh these La - tin_words! — B

Silently floated a spirit — Si - lent-ly float-ed a spir-it a - cross the high heav- ens — C

Song of the Flea (from Goethe's "Faust") — Reign-ing in roy- al splen-dor A King had raised a flea — D

Songs and Dances of Death: I Death and the Peasant (Trepak) — Snow-fields in si - lence, So cold is the night — E

Hey, poor old man with a head so light!_ Too much you drank — F

II Death's Lullaby — Faint ly the child sighs, The lamp dim-ly flickers, Sheds but a phantom of light — G

III Death's Serenade — Sweet-scent-ed breath of Night, soft and ca- ress-- ing, — H

Lone- ly and fet-ter'd, in__ dark - - ness of bond-age — I

IV Death the Commander (Field Marshall Death) — With crash of bat-tle, ar-mor gleam-ing, The can-nons bel-low forth their fire, — J

Sunless No. 1 Within four Walls (In my attic) — Si - lent the lit- tle room Calm it is, dear to me. — K

No. 2 The Throng (After years) — Thine eyes in the crowd now a- void me, No an-swer-ing glance now is there — L

No. 3 All past the Feast Days (Retrospect) — All past the feast days, joy has gone The calm of night now falls on na-ture: — M

No. 4 Alas! It is my lonely fate (Resignation) — A- las! It is my lone-ly fate_ O when is joy with-out a smart? — N

No. 5 Elegy — In sha-dow black as night The moon's pale sil- ver rays give forth — O

And so 'tis with my heart, for thoughts and sights un- bid- den — P

No. 6 On the River (By the Water) — Pale shines the moon- light, Be- low in the wa- ter calm — Q

Yeremushka's Cradle Song — Schlafe, schlaf'_ein Tie-fer als im Feld ein Blü- me-lein, — R

MYLIUS, Wolfgang (17th Cent.)

Ein Mägdlein stund

Ein Mägd-lein stund, Wo stund es denn? Ein Mägd-lein stund

NÄGELI, Hans Georg (1773-1836)

Freut euch des Lebens

Freut euch_des Le - - bens, weil noch_das Lämp - chen glüht

NAGINSKI, Charles (1909-1940)

The Pasture
Copyright 1940, G. Schirmer, Inc.

I'm go- ing out to clean the pas- ture spring

Richard Cory
Copyright 1940, G. Schirmer, Inc.

When- ev- er Rich- ard Co- ry went down town

NANINI, Giovanni Maria (c.1545-1607)

Diffusa est gratia

Dif - - fu-sa est gra - - - - - - - - - - ti-a in la- bi-is,in la - - bi-is

NAPRAVNIK, Eduard (1839-1916)

Cradle Song, from Harold (opera)
Act V
Copyright 1906, G. Schirmer, Inc.

Hush thee, dear one, slumber well! Pain be gone,and grief's e- mo- tion,

NELSON, Sidney (1800-1862)

Mary of Argyle

I have heard the may is sing- ing, His love-song to the morn

NESSLER, Victor E. (1841-1900)

Behüt' dich Gott, from Der Trompeter
von Sakkingen (opera)

Das ist im Le- ben häss- lich ein ge- rich- tet,

Be- hüt' dich Gott!es wär'zu schön ge- we- sen, be- hüt dich Gott,

NEUMARK, Georg (1621-1681)

Gottestrost

Wer nur den lie- ben Gott lässt wal-ten und hof- fet

NEVIN, Ethelbert (1862-1901)

A Life Lesson
There, lit-tle girl, don't cry! They have bro-ken your doll, I know,

Little Boy Blue, Op. 12, No. 4
The lit-tle toy dog is cover'd with dust, But stur-dy and staunch he stands;

Might lak' a rose
Copyright by John Church Co.
Used by permission.
Sweetest li'-l' fel-ler, Ev'-ry bod-y knows; Dun-no what to call him,

Oh! that we two were maying, Op. 2, No. 8
Oh! that we two were may - - ing Down the stream of the soft spring breeze

One Spring Morning
One spring morn-ing, bright and fair, Tra- la- la- la- la- la la

The Rosary
The hours I spent with thee, dear heart, are as a string of pearls to me

NICKERSON, Camille

Michieu Banjo (arr.)
Copyright by Boston Music Co.
Gar- dez pi- ti Mi- latte la, Mi-chieu Ban- jo,

NICOLAI, Karl (1810-1849)

The Merry Wives of Windsor (Die lustigen Weiber von Windsor) (opera)
Act I No. 3
Ver- füh - - - - - - - - - - rer! Wa- rum stellt.... ihr so

Froh- sinn und Lau- ne wür - - - zen das Le - - - ben

Act II No. 5
Als Büb-lein klein an der Mut-ter Brust, hopp hei-ssa bei Re-gen und Wind,

Act II No. 7b
Horch, die Ler-che singt im Hain, lau-sche, lausche Liebchen still,

Act III No. 11
So schweb' ich Dir Gelieb - - ter zu, so kennst Du mich, so na - hest Du,

O se- li- ge Träu- me, o sü - - - - - sses Glück

NIEDERMEYER, Abraham Louis (1802-1861)

Le Lac
Ain- si tou-jours pous- sés vers de nou- veaux ri- va- ges

Un soir t'en sou-vient-il? nous vo- guions en si- len- ce

NIELSEN, Carl (1865-1931)

Irmelin Rose
Copyright by Hansen, Copenhagen

Se, der var en Gang en Kon - - ge man-gen Skat han kald-te____ sin

NIN, Joaquin (1879-   )

Classiques espagnols du chant (arr.)
Alma, sintamos (Pablo Esteve, 1730?-1792?)
By permission Associated Music Publishers, Inc.

Al - ma, sin - ta - mos! O - jos, llo - rar!____

Aria de Acis y Galatea (Antonio Literes, 1680?-1755)

Si de ra-ma_en ra - ma si de flor en flor

Corazón que en prisión (José Marin, 1619-1699)

Co - ra - zon que_en pri - sión de res - pe - tos cau - ti____

Cloris Hermosa (Sebastian Duron, 1645?-1716?)

Gra - cio - sa mo - da e - sa que_han da - do

Desengañémonos ya (José Marin, 1619-1699)

De - sen-ga - ñe - mo - nos ya; mal pa-ga - do pen - sa - mien - to

El jilguerito con pico de oro (Blas de Laterna, 1751-1816)

El jil-que - ti - to con pi - co de_o - ro

Minué cantado (José Bassa, 1670?-1730?)

Si de_A - ma - ri - lis los____ o - jos dis - pa - - - ran

Four Popular Spanish Songs
I Castellana (also No. 3 of Vingt chants populaires espagnols)
By permission Associated Music Publishers, Inc.

Yo me i - ba ma - dre a la ro - me - ri - a

So ell'en-ci-na_en-ci - na So ell'en-ci - na Yo me_i-ba_mi ma-dre,

II Catalana (also No. 16 of Vingt chants populaires espagnols)

Ei-xa nit es nit de vet-lla__n'ha pa-rit u - na__don-ze-lla

A - ni-rem al camp, po - mes a cu - llir, po-me-tes cu - lli-rem

III Gallega (also No. 12 of Vingt chants populaires espagnols)

Meu a - mor meu a - mo - ri - ño Ond'es - tás que no te ve-jo

IV Asturiana (also No. 14 of Vingt chants populaires espagnols)

Fuis - ti_a la sie-ga_y Col-vies - ti____ Fuis - ti_a la sie-ga_y Col-vies-ti

Vingt chants populaires espagnols
I Tonada de Valdovinos
By permission Associated Music Publishers, Inc.

Sos - pi - ras - te, val - do - vi - nos La co - sa que más que - rí - a

II Cantar

Quien a - mo - res ten a - fin-que los ben____ que non he vien-to

IV Montañesa

Se - ga - ba yo_a-que - lla____ tar - de

Vingt chants populaires espagnols
V Tonada del Conde Sol — A
Grandes Guerras se pu- bli- can en-tre Es-pa-ña y Por- tu- ga- le:

VI Malagueña — B
Cuan-do sa- lí de Mar-be-lla___ a Quan-do sa- lí de Mar-be-lla___

VII Granadina (Andaluza) — C
Las fa- ti - - - gues del que- rer___

VIII Saeta — D
A- llá a- rri- bi- ta a-rri- bi- ta___ Há-cia el mon - - - te

IX Jota Tortorina — E
A- dios Tor-to-sa___ fa - - mo- sa Ro-de-a-da de bal - - co- nes

X Jota Valenciana — F
Los ar- bo-les de A-ran- juez___ Los ar- bo-les de A-ran-juez___

XI Canción Gallega I — G
En co- a___mi-ña mon-tei- ra e c'o meu sa-io de lan

XIII Canción Gallega III — H
Can-ta ó ga- la ven Ó di- a Er- gue-te meu ben ê vai-te

XV Pano Murciano A — I
Di-ga us-ted se-ñor pla-te-ro quan-ta pla-ta es me-nes- ter

B — J
Se - - ñor pla-te-ro he pen-sa- do__ que us-ted sa-be en-gar- zar

XVII El canto de los pajaros — K
Al veu-rer des-pun- tar___ Lo ma-jor blu-mi- rar

XVIII El irto — L
U- na vie- ja va-le un re- al y u-na mu-cha- cha dos quar- tos

XIX Canto Andaluz A — M
Ay a - ay

B — N
Por dar-le gus-to a tu gen - - -te y a mi co- ra-zon pe- sar

XX Polo — O
Cuer-po bue-no, al- ma di- vi- na___ que de fa- ti- gas

OBRECHT, Jacob (1430-1505)

Kyrie, from Missa sine Nomine (Credo and Agnus Dei use same theme) — Q
Ky - - - - - - - - - - - ri- e e le- i- son

Missa super Maria Zart
Credo — R
Pa - - trem om - - - ni- po- tem - - - - - - - - - - - - - tem,

Qui propter — S
Qui pro - - - - - - pter, qui pro - - - - - - pter nos___

Missa super Maria Zart Et incarnatus est (A)

Et in-car-na____ tus est de___ Spiri-tu

Tsaat een meskin (No words in score) (B)

OFFENBACH, Jacques (1819-1880)

La Belle Helene (opera) Act I No. 2 (D)

A-mours di- vins ar-den- tes flam- mes! Ve-nus! A- do- nis!

No. 6 Le Jugement de Paris (E)

Au__ mont I-da trois dé- es-ses se que-rel-laient dans un bois__

Act II No. 11 Invocation à Vénus (F)

On me nomme Hé-lè-ne la blon-de, La blon-de fil-le de Lé-da

No. 15 Dream Duet (G)

Oui! c'est un rê-ve, Oui, c'est un rê-ve, Oui! c'est un doux rê-ve d'a-mour__

Couplets des fariniers, from La boulangère a des écus (opera) Act II No. 9 (H)

Les fa-ri-niers, Les char-bon-niers Ont le mêm' sac

Duettino des époux, from Les Braconniers (opera) Act I (I)

Que j'aime tes yeux e-veil-lés! Que j'aime ta no-ble tour- nu-re

Chanson de Fortunio, from La chanson de Fortunio (opera) No. 7 (J)

Si vous cro-yez que je vais di- re Qui j'ose ai- mer

Les Contes d'Hoffmann (The Tales of Hoffmann) (opéra-comique) Act I (K)

Il é-tait u- ne fois à la cour d'Ei-se-nach! À la cour d'Ei-se-nach!

Act II (L)

Ah! vi-vre doux n'avoir qu' une même es-pé-ran-ce Un mê-me sou-ve- nir!

(M)

J'ai des yeux, de vrais yeux, des yeux vi-vants, des yeux de flam - - - - me

(N)

Les oi- seaux dans la char-mil - - - - - - - - - - - - - - le

Act III Barcarolle (O)

Bel- le nuit, ô nuit d'a-mour, Sou-ris__ à nos i-vres-ses!

(P)

Scin- til-le di-a-mant__ Mi-roir où se prend l'a-lou-et-te

(Q)

O Dieu de quelle i- vresse em-bras-ses tu mon â- me

Act IV (R)

Elle a fui, la tour-te-rel-le, Elle a fui loin de toi

(S)

Jour et nuit je me mets en quatre, Au moin-dre si-gne je me tais,

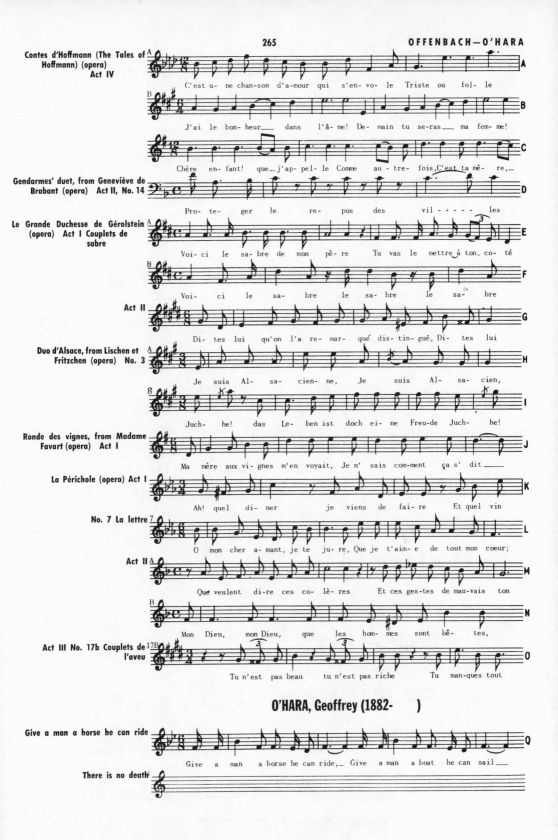

Contes d'Hoffmann (The Tales of Hoffmann) (opera) Act IV

C'est u- ne chan-son d'a-mour qui s'en-vo- le Triste ou fol- le

J'ai le bon-heur___ dans l'â-me! De- main tu se-ras___ ma fem-me!

Chè-re en- fant! que j'ap-pel- le Comme au-tre-fois, C'est ta mè- re,__

Gendarmes' duet, from Geneviève de Brabant (opera) Act II, No. 14

Pro- te- ger le re- pos des vil - - - - les

Le Grande Duchesse de Gérolstein (opera) Act I Couplets de sabre

Voi- ci le sa- bre de mon pè- re Tu vas le mettre à ton co- té

Voi- ci le sa- bre le sa- bre le sa- bre

Act II

Di- tes lui qu'on l'a re- mar- qué dis- tin- gué, Di- tes lui

Duo d'Alsace, from Lischen et Fritzchen (opera) No. 3

Je suis Al- sa- cien- ne, Je suis Al- sa- cien,

Juch- he! das Le- ben ist doch ei- ne Freu-de Juch- he!

Ronde des vignes, from Madame Favart (opera) Act I

Ma mère aux vi- gnes m'en voyait, Je n' sais com-ment ça s' dit___

La Périchole (opera) Act I

Ah! quel di- ner je viens de fai- re Et quel vin

No. 7 La lettre

O mon cher a- mant, je te ju- re, Que je t'aim- e de tout mon coeur;

Act II

Que veulent di-re ces co- lè- res Et ces ges-tes de mau-vais ton

Mon Dieu, mon Dieu, que les hom- mes sont bê- tes,

Act III No. 17b Couplets de l'aveu

Tu n'est pas beau tu n'est pas riche Tu man-ques tout

O'HARA, Geoffrey (1882-)

Give a man a horse he can ride

Give a man a horse he can ride,__ Give a man a boat he can sail

There is no death

OKEGHEM, Jean de (c. 1430-1493)

Ma Maitresse
Ma mai- tres- se____ et ma plus___ grant____ a my - - - - - - - -

OTHMAYR, Casper (1515-1553)

Brauns-Maidelein
Mir ist ein feins brauns Mai- de-lein ge- fal- len in mein Sinn

PADILLA, José (Contemporary)

Princesita
Copyright by E. B. Marks Music Corp., N. Y.
Prin- ce- si- ta ____ Prin- ce- si- ta la de o-jos a- zu- les

Who'll Buy My Violets
(La Violetera)
Copyright 1923, Harms, Inc.
Co-mo a ves pre-cur so- ras de Pri-ma-ve - - - ra

PAISIELLO, Giovanni (1740-1816)

Déserts écartés, from Prosperine
(opera)
De- serts é- car- tés som- bres lieux, Ca- chez mes sou- pirs,

Nel cor più non mi sento, from La
Molinara (opera)
Nel cor più non mi sen- to bril-lar la____ gio- ven- tù

PALADILHE, Emile (1884-1926)

Patrie (opera)
No. 4 Air du sonneur
Copyright by Choudens fils, Paris
Ja- dis el- les chan-taient gaie- ment____

No. 21 Cantabile de Rysor
Pau- vre mar-tyr obs- cur,____ Hum-ble hé- ros d'une heu- re

No. 22 Air de Rysor
Fuir à ja- mais____ fuir en- sem- ble

SONGS: Psyché
Copyright 1911, G. Schirmer, Inc.
Je suis ja- loux, Psy- ché de tou- te la na- tu- re

Le Roitelet
Copyright 1911, G. Schirmer, Inc.
Ra- pi- de comme un rê- ve, Vif comme un feu fol- let

Les Trois Prières
A l'heu- re où notre es-prit moins fier____ S'in- cli- ne comme un Roi

PALESTRINA, Giovanni Pierluigi da (1524-1594)

Hymns: I O crux ave 1
O crux____ a - - - ve, spes____ u- ni- ca,____

Tota pulchra es amica mea (motet) — To- ta pulchra es a- mi-ca me — a ___ A

Tribulationes civitatum (motet) 1 — Tri- bu- la- ti- o — nes ci — vi-ta — tum au- di- vi- mus B

Peccavimus (motet) 2 — Pec- ca- vi- mus pec — ca — vi- mus ___ C

Vox dilecti mei (motet) — Vox vox di- le-cti me — i Vox ___ di- le-cti D

Vulnerasti cor meum (motet) — Vul- ne- ra-sti cor me — um vul- ne- ra-sti cor me- um, E

Offertories:
Bonum est — Bo — num est con- fi- te- ri ___ F

Exaltabo te, Domine — Ex- al- ta- bo- te ___ Do — mi- ne G

Improperium expectavit — Im — pro-pe- ri- um ex-pe-cta-vit ___ cor me — um, H

Laudate Dominum — Lau- da- te Do — mi- num, lau- da- te Do- mi- num ___ I

Super flumina Babylonis — Su — per flu- mi- na Ba- by- lon — nis, ___ J

Alma redemptoris mater (cantus firmus) — Al — ma Re- demp- to-ris ma — ter K

Ecce, quomodo moritur justus (response) — Ec- ce quo- mo- do mo — ri- tur ju- stus, L

Exultate Deo — Ex- ul- ta — te De- o, ad — ju- to- ri nos — tro ___ M

Gloria Patri — Glo- ri- a Pa- tri Et Fi- li- o, Glo- ri- a Pa- tri N

Incipit oratorio Jeremiae Prophetae (lamentation) — In- ci- pit O- ra- ti- o In- ci- pit O- ra- ti- o O

Jubilate Deo (Psalm 99) — Ju — bi- la — te De — o P

Pueri Hebraeorum (Antiphon) — Pu — e- ri He- brae- o — rum, He — brae-o — rum Q

PALMGREN, Selim (1878-)

Finnish Lullaby
Copyright by H. W. Gray Co. — Lit- tle songs I'll sing thee, dear-est, Lit-tle tales I bring thee, dear-est S

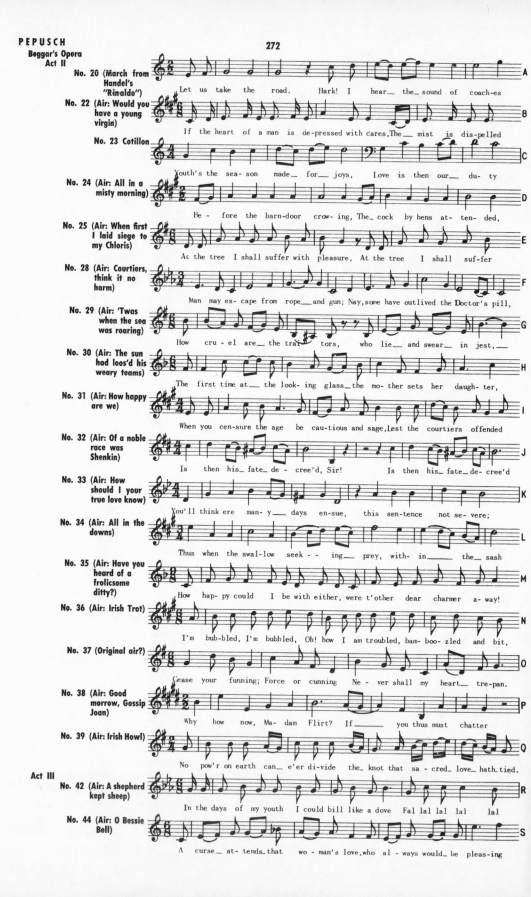

Beggar's Opera
Act III

No. 45 (Air: Come, sweet lass)
Come, sweet lass, Let's ban-ish sor-row till to-mor-row, Come, sweet lass, — A

No. 46 (Air: The last time I went o'er the moon)
Hi-ther, dear hus-band, turn your eyes, Be-stow one glance to cheer me. — B

No. 47 (Air: Tom Tinker's my true love)
Which way shall I turn me how can I de-cide — C

No. 48 (Air: Bonny Dundee)
The charge is pre-pared; the lawyers are met, the judges all ranged — D

No. 50 (Air: Happy Groves) A
O cru-el, cru-el, cru-el case! Must I suf-fer this dis-grace? — E

(Air: Of all the girls) B
Of all the friends in time of grief, when threat'ning death looks grimmer — F

(Air: Did you ever hear of a gallant sailor) C
But can I leave my pret-ty hussies, without one tear, or ten-der sigh? — G

(Air: Why are mine eyes still flowing) D
Their eyes, their lips, their bus - - - - - - ses — H

No. 51 (Air: All you that must take a leap)
Would I might be hang'd! And I would so too! To be hang'd with you — I

No. 52 (Air: Lumps of pudding)
Thus I stand like the Turk, with his do-xies a - - round — J

PEREZ FREIRE, Osman

Ay, ay, ay
Copyright by E. G. Marks Music Corp., N. Y.
A só-ma te a la ven-ta-na Ay, Ay Ay pa-lo-ma del al-ma mi - a — L

PERGOLESI, Giovanni (1710-1736)

Ogni pena più spietata
O-gni pe-na più spie-ta-ta, più spie-ta-ta — N

Se tu m'ami
Se tu m'a-mi, se tu so-spi-ri sol per me, — O

La Serva Padrona (opera) 1.
A-spet-ta - - re e non ve-ni-re, sta-re a let-to e non dor-mi-re — P

2.
Sem-pre in con-tra-sti con te si sta con te si sta, — Q

3.
Stiz-zo-so mio stiz-zo-so voi fa-te il bo-ri-o-so — R

4.
Lo co-no-sco, lo co-no-sco a que-gli och-chietti a que-gli oc-chietti — S

PERGOLESI

La Serva Padrona (opera)

Stabat Mater

PERI, Jacopo (1561-1633)

Euridice (opera)

Gio- i-te al can-to mio   sel- ve fron-do- se; gio-i-te a-ma-ti col-li

Nel pu-ro ar-dor del___ la più bel-la stel-la Au- rea fa- cel- la

PESSARD, Emile (1843-1917)

L'Adieu du Matin
Copyright 1901, G. Schirmer, Inc.

Le ma-tin, dès que je te quit-te, Son-geant aux longs en-nuis

Requiem du Coeur
Copyright by A. Leduc Music Publishers, Paris

Mon coeur est mort! De-dans la biè- re ce___ ma-tin

PESTALOZZA, Alberto (1851-1934)

Ciribiribin

I am wait-ing here for you,_ love,_ as the eve-ning bree-zes blow

Ci- ri- bi- ri- bin, more love than mine for thee

PFITZNER, Hans (1869-   )

Ist der Himmel darum im Lenz so blau? Op. 2, No. 2
By permission Boosey & Hawkes, Inc., copyright owners

Ist der Him- mel da- rum im Lenz so blau, weil er ü- ber die blu-mi-ge

Der Einsame, Op. 9, No. 2
By permission Boosey & Hawkes, Inc., copyright owners

Wär's dun-kel, ich läg im Wal- - de   Im Wal-de rauscht's

Gretel, Op. 11, No. 5
By permission Boosey & Hawkes, Inc., copyright owners

Vor der Tür im Son- nen-schei-ne wo das Kätz-chen sonst_ liegt_

Nachts, Op. 26, No. 2
By permission Boosey & Hawkes, Inc., copyright owners

Ich ste- he in Wal- des-schatten wie_ an des Le- bens Hand,

PIERNÉ, Gabriel (1863-1937)

L'Adieu Suprême

Lais- se- moi ché-rir ton fan- tô- me,_ Mais ne re-viens pas

Complainte des Arches de Noé
By permission J. Hamelle Music Publishers, Paris

Dans la fo- rêt les me-nui-siers, taillez les ar-ches

En Barque

Pestons en- cor, Mi-gnon- ne! Ma barque est douce et bon- ne;

Ils étaient trois petits chats blancs

Ils é- taient trois pe-tits chats blancs Tou-jours pom-pon-nés

Les Marionettes
By permission Heugel & Cie, Paris, copyright owners

Les ma- ri- on- net- tes de bois ont des ro- bes de pa- pier — A

Le Moulin
Copyright by Boston Music Co.

Tour- ne, tour- ne, tour- ne, mon mou- lin _____ — B

Le Petit Rentier
By permission J. Hamelle Music Publishers, Paris

Il s'en est al- lé ____ par la rou- ce le pauvre homme — C

Serenade

Au sein des nuits tout dort ____ L'é- toi- le brille en- cor — D

PIETRI, Giuseppi (1886-   )

Maristella (opera)

Act I

Io co- no- sco un giar- di- no ____ a tut- ti sco- no- sciu- to — F

Act II

U- no stra- no sen- so ar- ca- no pren- de il cuor! ____ — G

Qui di- nan- zi all'al- ta- re giu- ro che quest' ac- cu- sa è u- na men- zogna! — H

PILKINGTON, Francis (d. 1638)

Care for thy Soul

Care for ___ thy soul, care ___ for thy soul ___ care for ___ thy soul — J

Diaphenia

Di- a- phe- ni- a like the daff- down- dil- ly, white as the sun, — K

Down a down

Down a down, down a down, ___ thus Phyllis sung, By fan- cy ones op- press- ed; — L

Rest, sweet nymphs

Rest, sweet nymphs, let gol- den sleep Charm your star- bright- er eyes — M

Underneath a cypress shade

Un- der- neath a cy- press shade the Queen of love sat mourn- ing — N

PINSUTI, Ciro (1829-1888)

The Arrow and the Song

I shot an ar- row in- to the air, ___ It fell to earth — P

Bedouin Love Song

From the des- ert I come to thee ___ on my A- - rab ___ shod with fire — Q

Till the sun grows cold ___ and the stars grow old ___ — R

I fear no foe

I fear no foe in shin- ing ar- mour, Tho' his lance be swift — S

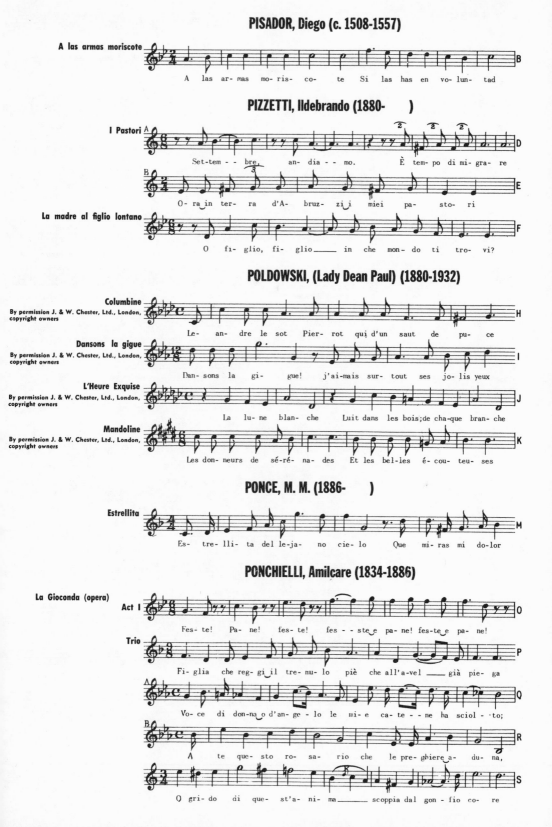

PISADOR, Diego (c. 1508-1557)

A las armas moriscote

A las ar- mas mo- ris- co- te Si las has en vo- lun- tad

PIZZETTI, Ildebrando (1880-   )

I Pastori

Set-tem — bre, an- dia — mo.   È tem- po di mi- gra- re

O- ra in ter- ra d'A- bruz- zi i miei pa- sto- ri

La madre al figlio lontano

O fi- glio, fi- glio____ in che mon- do ti tro- vi?

POLDOWSKI, (Lady Dean Paul) (1880-1932)

Columbine
By permission J. & W. Chester, Ltd., London, copyright owners

Le- an- dre le sot Pier- rot qui d'un saut de pu- ce

Dansons la gigue
By permission J. & W. Chester, Ltd., London, copyright owners

Dan- sons la gi- gue! j'ai- mais sur- tout ses jo- lis yeux

L'Heure Exquise
By permission J. & W. Chester, Ltd., London, copyright owners

La lu- ne blan- che Luit dans les bois; de cha- que bran- che

Mandoline
By permission J. & W. Chester, Ltd., London, copyright owners

Les don- neurs de sé- ré- na- des Et les bel- les é- cou- teu- ses

PONCE, M. M. (1886-   )

Estrellita

Es- tre- lli- ta del le- ja- no cie- lo Que mi- ras mi do- lor

PONCHIELLI, Amilcare (1834-1886)

La Gioconda (opera)

Act I

Fes- te! Pa- ne! fes- te! fes — ste e pa- ne! fes-te e pa- ne!

Trio

Fi- glia che reg- gi il tre- mu- lo piè che all'a-vel ___ già pie- ga

Vo- ce di don-na o d'an- ge- lo le mi- e ca- te — ne ha sciol- to;

A te que- sto ro- sa- rio che le pre- ghiere a- du- na,

O gri- do di que- st'a- ni- ma____ scoppia dal gon- fio co- re

La Gioconda (opera)

Act I — O mo- nu- men - - - to! re- gia e bol- gia do- ga- le!

O cuor! do-no fu- ne - - sto!_ re- tag-gio di_ do- lo - - re.

Act II — Ho! he! ho! he! Fis-sa il ti-mo- ne! Ho! he! ho! he! Fis sa

Siam nel fon- do più_ pro-fon- do del- la na- ve del- la ca- la,

Pes- ca- tor,_ af- fon- da l'es-ca, a te l'on-da sia fe-del,

Cie- lo e mar! l'e- te- res_ ve- lo splen-de co-me un santo altar!

Duet — Deh! non tur- ba- re_ con ree pa- u- ra_ di que-sti i-stan- ti

Lag- giù_ nel-le neb-bie re- mo - - te, lag- giù

Stel- la del ma- ri- nar! Ver- gi- ne San-ta, tu mi di- fen-di

L'a- mo co - - me il ful-gor del cre- a-to, co- me l'au- - ra che av- vi- va

Act III — Là tur- bi-ni e far- ne- ti- chi, la ga- ja ba- ra- on- da

Là del_ pa- tri - - - zio_ ve - - - ne-to

Già ti veg- go im-mo- ta e smor - - - ta

Duet — Bel- la co- sì ma- don- na, io non v'ho mai ve- du- ta

È trop- po, è trop-po or- ri- bi- le! a- ver di- nan- zi,

La ga- ia can- zo - - ne, fa l'e - - co lan- guir_

Act IV — Sui- ci- dio! In que-sti fie- ri mo- men- ti_

La Gioconda (opera)   Act IV

Eb- brez- za! de- li- rio! So- gna- ta mia gio- ia!   A

Raccogli e calma, from Il Figliol Prodigo (opera) Act III

Rac-cog- lie cal-ma sot- to al- la pi- a a la dol- cis- si- ma   B

POULENC, Francis (1899-   )

Airs Chantés

No. 1 Air Romantique
Copyright by Salabert, Paris, N. Y.

J'al- lais dans la cam- pagne a- vec le vent d'o- ra- ge   D

No. 2 Air Champêtre

Bel- le sour-ce bel- le sour-ce, je veux me rap-pe-ler sans ces-se   E

No. 3 Air Grave

Ah! fuy-ez à pré- sent, ma-lheu-reu-ses pen- sées! O co-lère, o! re-mords!   F

No. 4 Air Vif

Le tré- sor du ver- ger, et le jar-din en fête,   G

A sa guitarre
By permission Durand & Cie, Paris; Elkan-Vogel Co., Inc., Phila., copyright owners

Ma gui-ta- re, je te chante, Par qui seu- le je dé- çois   H

Banalités

No. 1 Chanson d'Orkenise
By permission Associated Music Publishers, Inc.

Par les por-tes d'Or-ke-ni- se veut en-trer un char-re-tier   I

No. 2 Hotel

Ma chambre a la for- me d'u- ne ca- ge   J

No. 3 Fagnes de Wallonie

Tant de tris-tes-- ses plé- ni- è- res   K

No. 4 Voyage à Paris

Ah! la char-man-te cho- se Quit-ter un pa- ys   L

No. 5 Sanglots

Notre a-mour est rè- glé par les cal-mes é- toi- les   M

Le Bestiaire
No. 1 Le Dromadaire
Copyright by Ed. de la Sirene, Paris

A- vec ses qua-tre dro-ma-daires Don Pe- dro d'Al-fa-rou- bei- ra   N

No. 2 Le Chèvre du Thibet

Les poils de cet- te chè- vre et mê- me Ceux d'or   O

No. 3 La Sauterelle

Voi- ci la fi- ne sau-te-rel- le La nour-ri- ture de Saint Jean   P

No. 4 Le Dauphin

Dau- phins, vous jouez dans le mer Mais le flot est tou-jours a- mer   Q

No. 5 L'Écrevisse

In-cer-ti- tude, O! mes de- - lices Vous et moi nous nous en al-lons   R

No. 6 Le Carpe

Dans vos vi-viers dans vos e- tangs Car- pes que vous vi-vez long-temps!   S

Bleuet

Jeune homme de vingt ans___ qui as vu des choses si af-freu-ses___   A

C

J'ai tra-ver-sé les ponts de C C'est là que tout a com-men-cé   B

Chansons Gaillardes

La belle jeunesse

Il faut s'ai-mer tou-jours, et ne s'é-pou-ser guè-re   C

Invocation aux parques

Il jure tant que je vi-vrai de vous ai-mer, Syl-vi-e   D

Chanson à boire

Les Rois d'E-gyp-te et de Sy-ri-e, vou-laient qu'on em-bau-mât   E

Chansons Villageoises
I Chansons du clair tamis

Où le be-deau a pas-se Dans les pa-pa-ve-ra-cé-es   F

II Les gars qui vont à la fête

Les gars qui vont à la fête Ont mis la fleur au cha-peau___   G

III C'est le joli printemps

C'est le jo-li prin-temps qui fait sor-tir les fil-les   H

IV Le mendiant

Jean Mar-tin prit sa be-sa-ce Vi-ve le pas-sant   I

V Chanson de la fille frivole

Oh dit la fil-le fri-vo-le Que le vent y vire,   J

VI Le retour du sergent

Le ser-gent s'en re-vient de guer-re Les pieds gon-flés   K

Les Chemins de l'Amour

Che-mins de mon a-mour___ Je vous cherche tou-jours___   L

Dans le jardin d'Anna

Cer-tes, si nous a-vions vé-cu en l'an dix-sept cent soi-xan-te   M

Fêtes Galantes

On voit des mar-quis sur des bi-cy-clet-tes On voit des mar-lous   N

Fiançailles pour rire
No. 1. La dame d'André

An-dré ne con-nait pas la da-me Qu'il prend au-jour-d'hui par la main___   O

No. 2. Dans l'herbe

Je ne peux plus rien di-re Ni rien fai-re pour lui___   P

No. 3. Il vole

En al-lant se cou-cher le soleil Se re-flète au vernis de ma ta-ble   Q

No. 4. Mon cadavre est doux comme un gant

Mon ca-davre est doux comme un gant___ Doux comme un gant de peau gla-cé-e   R

No. 5. Le Violon

Couple a-mou-reux___ aux ac-cents mé-con-nus___   S

Fiançailles pour rire
No. 6. Fleurs
Fleur pro-mi-ses, fleurs te-nues dans tes bras,_ Fleurs sor- ti-es_

Hier
Hi-er,_ c'est ce cha-peau fa-né_ Que j'ai long-temps trai-né.

Hyde Park
Les Fai- seurs de re- li-gions Pré-chaient dans le brouillard

Hymne
Som- bre nuit, a-veu-gles té- né- bres, Fu- yez;

Métamorphoses
I Reine des mouettes
Rei-ne des mouet-tes, mon orphé-li-ne Je t'ai vue ro-se, je m'en souviens

II C'est ainsi que tu es
Ta chair, d'â- me mê-lé- e Che-ve-lure em-mê-lé- e

III Paganini
Vio- lon,_ hip-po-campe et si-rè- ne Ber-ceau des coeurs

Montparnasse
O por- te de l'ho-tel a-vec deux plan-tes ver- tes

Nous voulons une petite soeur A
Ma-dame Eus- tache a dix- sept fil- les ce n'est pas trop

B
Ce n'est pas ça que nous vou- lons_ Nous vou-lons u- ne pe-ti- te soeur

Petites voix (children's choruses)
I La Petite Fille Sage
Le pe-ti-te fil-le sa-ge est ren- trée_ de l'é-co-le a-vec son panier

II Le chien perdu
Qui est-tu, in-con-nu? qui es- tu, chien per-du? Tu rêves, tu som-meil-les;

III En rentrant de l'école
En ren- trant de l'é-co-le par un che-min per-du

IV Le petit garçon malade
Le pe-tit gar-con ma- la-de_ Ne veut plus re-gar-der les i- ma-ges_

V Le hérisson
Quand pa-pa trouve un hé- risson il l'ap-porte à la mai-son.

Poèmes de Ronsard
I Attributs
Les é- pis_ sont à Cé- rès, aux Dieux bou-quins les fo-rêts,

II Le Tombeau
Quand le ciel et mon heu-re ju-ge-ront que je meu- re

III Ballet
Le soir qu'A- mour vous fit en la sal- le des- cen-dre

IV Je n'ai plus que les os
Je n'ai plus que les os, un squelet- te je sem- ble,_

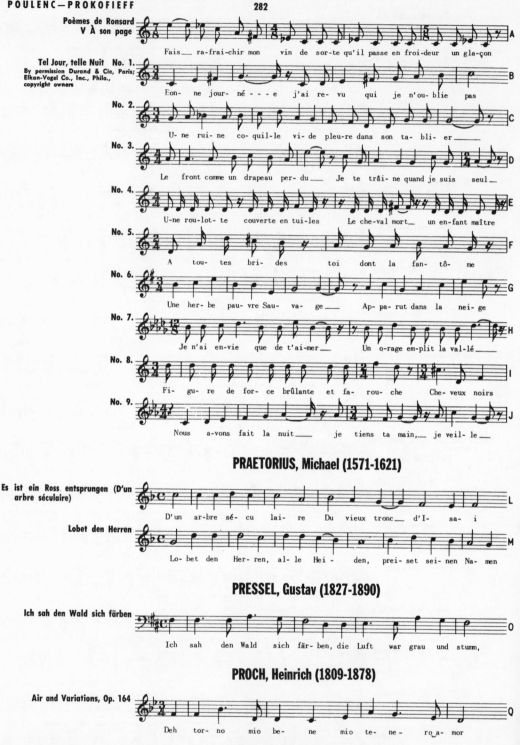

Alexander Nevsky, Op. 78
Part II Song about Alexander Nevsky

Ah! how we did fight,___ how we rout-ed them

Part IV Arise, ye Russian people

A-rise to arms, ye___ Rus-sian folk, in bat-tle just, in_ fight to death

In our Rus-sia great, in our na-tive Rus-sia no foe shall live___

Part VI Field of the Dead

I shall go___ a-cross the snowclad field. I shall fly a-bove the field_of_ death

Snowdrops

Snow-drops grow on___ yon-der hill,___ Snow_ drops blos-som

Snowflakes

O-ver field and plain___ come_ steal - - - - ing

PUCCINI, Giacomo (1858-1924)

La Bohême (opera)
Act I
Copyright by G. Ricordi & Co., Inc.

Nei cie-li bi-gi guar-do fu-mar dai mil-le co-mi-gno-li Pa-ri-gi

Che ge-li-aa ma-ni-na, se la la-sci ri-scal-dar. Cer-cai

Ta- lor dal mio for-zie-re___ ru-ban tut-ti_i gio-iel-li

Si Mi chia-ma-no Mi- mi, ma il mio no-me_è Lu-ci-a___

Mi piaccion quel-le co-se che_han si dol-ce ma-lì-a

Duet

O so-a-ve fan-ciul-la,___ O dol-ce vi-so

Act II Quartet

Questa è Mi-mi, ga-ia fio-ra-ia. Il suo ve-nir com-ple-ta

U-na cuf-fietta_a piz-zi, tut-ta ro-sa, ri-ca-ma-ta

Musetta's Waltz

Quan- do me'n vo'_ quan-do me'n vo so-let-ta per la via

Act III Mimi's Farewell

Don-de- lie-ta u-scì al tuo gri-do d'a-mo-re

A-scol-ta, a-scol-ta. Le po-che ro-be_a-du-na che la-sciai spar-se

Quartet

Ad-di-o dol-ce sve-glia-re Al-la_ mat-ti-na___

La Bohême (opera)
Act IV

O Mi- mi tu più non tor- ni o gior- ni bel- li,

Colline's Song

Vec-chia zi-mar-ra, sen-ti, io re-sto al pian, tu a- scen-de-re il

So- no an-da-ti? fin-ge- vo di dor-mi-re__ per-chè vol-li con te so-la

La Fanciulla del West (The Girl of the Golden West) (opera) Act I
Copyright by G. Ricordi & Co., Inc.

Min- nie, dal-la mia ca- sa son par-ti- to che è là dai mon- ti

Lag- giù__ nel So- le-dad, e- ro pi- ci- na

Io non son che u- na po- ve- ra fan- ci- ulla__

Act II

Oh, se sa- pe- ste co- me il vi- ve-re è al-le- gro!

Or son sei me- si__ che mio pa-dre mo- rì E tutto ap-pre-si

Act III

Ch'el-la mi cre- da li- be-ro e lon-ta- na, so-vra u-na nuo- va via

Gianni Schicchi (opera)
Copyright by G. Ricordi & Co., Inc.

Fi- ren-ze è come un al- be-ro fio- ri- to__ che in piaz-za dei Si-gnori

Oh, mio bab-bi- no ca- ro, mi pia-ce, è bel- lo, bel- lo;

Mes- ser no- ta- io, pre- sto, Via da Buo-so Do- na- ti!

In__ te- sta la cap-pel- li- na! Al vi- so la pez-zo-li-na!

Madama Butterfly (opera) Act I
Copyright by G. Ricordi & Co., Inc.

Do- vun- que al mondo lo Yan-kee va-ga-bon- do si go-de e traf-fi-ca

A- mo- re o gril- lo,__ dir non sa- pre- i. Cer- to co- ste- i

Spi- ra sul ma-re e sul- la ter-ra un pri-ma-ve-ril sof-fio gio- con-do__

Io se- guo il mio de- sti - - - no e pie- na d'u-mil- tà

Bim- ba da- gli occhi pie- ni di ma- lì-a__ o-ra sei tut-ta mi-a

Dam- mi ch'io ba- ci le tue ma- ni ca- re__

Madama Butterfly (opera) Act I
A
Oh__ quan-ti oc-chi fi-si, at-ten-ti d'o-gni par-te a ri-guar-dar!__

Act II Scene 1
B
Un__ bel dì, ve-dre-mo le-var--si un fil di fu-mo

Flower duet
C
Scuo-ti quel-la fron-da di ci-lie-gio e m'in-non-da di fior__

D
Tut-ti i fior? Tut-ti i fior__ Tut-ti-tut-ti. Pe-sco, vio-la

Humming Chorus
E
Hum throughout ___
Act II Scene 2
F
Ad-di-o, fio-ri-to a-sil di le-ti-zia e d'a-mor

G
Tu? Tu? pic-co-lo Id-di-o! A-mo-re, amo-re mi-o,

H
Lo so che al sue pe-ne non ci so-no con for-ti

I
Che tua ma-dre do-vrà pren-der-ti in brac-cio

Manon Lescaut (opera)
Act I
J
Tra voi, bel-le, bru-ne e bion-de si na-scon-de gio-vi-net-ta

K
Don-na non vi-di ma-i si-mi-le a que-sta!

Act II
L
In quel-le tri-ne mor-bi-de nell'al-co-va do-ra-ta

M
L'o-ra, o Tir-si, e va-ga e bel-la, Ri-de il gior-no, ri-de in-tor-no

N
Tu, tu a-mo-re? Tu? Ah__ mio im-men-so a-mo-re?

O
O ten-ta-tri-ce!__ O ten-ta-tri-ce!

P
Ah! Ma-non__ mi tra-di-sce il tuo fol-le pen-sier__

Act III
Q
Guar-da-te, paz-zo son, guar-da-te, co-m'io pian-go e im-plo-ro

Act IV
R
Ve-di, ve-di, son io che pian-go io che im-plo-ro

S
So-la, per-du-ta, ab-ban-do-na-ta,__ per-du-ta,

PUCCINI

La Rondine (opera) Act I
Copyright by Sonzogno, Milan

Chi bel so- gno di Do- ret- ta po- tè in- do- vi- nar

O- re dol- ci e di- vi- ne di lie- ta ba- ra- on- da___

Fan- ciul___ la e sboc- cia- to l'a- mo- re!___ Di- fen- di, di- fen- di

Senza mamma, from Suor Angelica
(opera)
Copyright by G. Ricordi & Co., Inc.

Sen- za mam- ma, o bim- bo, tu sei mor- to Le tue lab- bra

Il Tabarro (opera)
Copyright by G. Ricordi & Co., Inc.

Se tu sa- pes- si gli og- get- ti___ stra- ni

Hai ben ra- gio- ne; me- glio non pen- sa- re pie- ga- re il ca- po

Tosca (opera)
Act I
Copyright by G. Ricordi & Co., Inc.

Re- con- di- ta ar- mo- ni- a di bel- lez- ze di- ver- se!

Non la so- spi- ri la no- stra ca- set- ta

Duet

Qual l'oc- chio al mon___ do può star___ di pa- ro

Duet

Mia ge- lo- sa! Si, lo sen- to___ ti tor- men- to sen- za po- sa

Te De- um Glo- ri- a Vi- va il Re! Si fe- steg- gi la___ vit- to- ria!

Act II

Già!___ Mi di- con ve- nal___ mi di- con ve- nal,

Vis- si d'ar- te, vis- si d'a- mo- re, non fe- ci mai ma- le

Cantata

Sem- pre___ con fe sin- ce- ra la mia pre- ghie- ra

Sa- le a- scen- de___ l'u- man___ can___ ti- co

A te___ que- st'in- no di glo- ria vol- li a te

Act III

E lucevan le stelle
(Not beginning of aria,
but most salient
phrase.)

Oh! dol- ci ba- ci o lan- gui- di ca- rez- ze, mentr' io fre- men- te

O dol- ci ma- ni man- su- e- te e pu- re, o ma- ni e- le- te

A- ma- ro sol per te m'e- ra il mo- re- re, Da te la vi- ta

Turandot (opera)
Copyright by G. Ricordi & Co., Inc.
Act I — Si-gno-re a-scol-ta! Ah si-gno-re a-scol-ta! Liù non reg-ge più!

Non pian-ge-re, Liù___ Se in un lonta-no gior-no io t'ho sor-ri-so

Trio (Ping, Pang and Pong) — Fer--mo! che fai T'arre-sta! Chi sei, che fai,

Non v'è in Chi-na per no-stra for-tu-na'

Act II Turandot's Air — In que-sta Reg-gio, or son mill'an-ni e mil-le

O prin-ci-pi, che a lun-ghe ca-ro-va-ne d'o-gni par-te del mon-do

Trio (Ping, Pang and Pong) — Ad-dio, a-mo-re' ad-dio, raz-za! Ad-dio___

Act III — Nes-sun dor-ma! nes-sun dor-ma! Tu pu-re, o Prin-ci-pes-sa

Tan-to a-mo--re se-gre-to e in-con-fes-sa-to,

Death of Liu — Tu che di gel sei cin-to___ da tan-to fiam-ma vin-ta

Le Villi (opera)
Copyright by G. Ricordi & Co., Inc.
Act I — If I were but like you,___ my frail for-get-me nots fair of a-zure hue___

Act II — O pure and sim-ple soul of her that was my daugh-ter,___

Back to the vanished years,___ My sor-row-ful thoughts re-turn___

PURCELL, Henry (c. 1659-1695)

Ah! how sweet it is to love, from Tyrannic Love Act IV — Ah!___ how sweet, Ah!___ how sweet, how sweet it is to love,

Celia has a thousand charms, from The Rival Sisters Act II — Ce-lia has a thousand, thousand, thou - - - - - - - - - -sand charms,

From Rosy Bowers, from Don Quixote (opera) Part III Act V — From ro-sy bowers, where sleeps___ the God___ of Love

Or if more in-flu-en-cing, Is___ to be brisk___ and ai--ry,

Hence with your trifling deity, from Timon of Athens (masque) No. 5 — Hence! Hence! Hence with your trif-ling dei-ty A great - - - - er,

PURCELL

Music for a while, from Oedipus

Mu- sic, mu - - - sic for a __ while shall all your__ cares be- guile,__ A

Nymphs and Shepherds, from The Libertine (opera)

Nymphs and shep- herds, come__ a- way, come a- way, B

Retir'd from any mortal's sight, from King Richard II Act IV

Re- tir'd__ from a- ny mor-tal's sight The pen-sive Da - - - - mon lay C

Dido and Aeneas (opera)

Act I

Shake_____ the cloud from__ off your brow, D

Ban- ish sor- row, ban- ish care, Grief should ne'er ap-proach__ the__ fair, E

Fear no dan- ger__ to en- sue, The he- ro loves as well as you F

Cu- pid on- ly throws the__ dart__ that's dread-ful, dread-ful, dread-ful G

To the hills and the vales, to the rocks and the moun- tains H

Harm's our de- light and mis - - - chief__ all__ our__ skill, I

But ere we this__ per- form, We'll con- jure__ for a storm_____ J

(echo)

In our deep vault-ed cell -ed cell the__ charm we'll pre - pare K

Ah! Ah!__ Ah! Be- lin- da, I__ am prest__ with__ tor - ment L

Act II

Thanks to these lone- some,__ lone-some vales, These de- sert, de - - sert M

Oft she vis- its this__ lone__ moun- tain, Oft she bathes her N

Haste, haste to town, haste, haste, haste, haste haste_____ to town O

Act III

Come a- way, fel-low sai- lors, come a- way, Your an- chors P

Our next mo- tion must be to storm_____ Q

De- struc-tion's our__ de- light, De- light our great-est sor- row R

Great minds a- gainst them- selves con- spire, great minds S

Dido and Aeneas (opera) Act III — When I am laid,____ am laid _____ in earth. (A)

With droop - - - - - ing wings, ye Cu - pids,_ come (B)

Dioclesian (opera) — What shall I do to show how____ much__ I__ love her? (C)

Let us dance, ____ let us sing, let us sing _____ (D)

The Fairy Queen (opera) Act III — When I have of - ten heard young maids com - plain - ing __ (E)

Act IV — Next, win - ter comes slow - ly, pale, mea - ger and old, _____ (F)

Act V — Hark! Hark! the ech' - ing air a tri - - - - - - - - - - - umph sings (G)

The Indian Queen (opera) — I at - tempt from Love's sick - ness to fly - - - - - - - - - in_ vain__ (H)

Act III A — Ye twice ten hun - dred de - i - ties, to whom, to whom (I)

B — By the croak - ing of the toad, In their caves that make a - bode (J)

We the spir - its of__ the__ air That of hu - man things_ take_ care, (K)

King Arthur (opera) Act II — How blest are shep - herds, how hap - py__ their__ lass - es,__ (L)

Shep - herd, shep - herd, leave_ de - cry - ing: Pipes are sweet on sum - mer's_ day (M)

Act V — Fair - est Isle all Isles__ ex - cell - ing, Seat_ of plea - sures and_ of loves. (N)

The Tempest (opera) Act II — A - rise, a - rise, ye sub - - - - - - - - - - - - - - - - ter - ranean (O)

Act III — Come un - to_ these yel - - - - - - - - - - - low_ sands_ and_ there take hands__ (P)

Full fa - thom five thy fa - ther_ lies; Of his bones are co - - - - - rals_ made__ (Q)

Dry those_ eyes which_ are _____ o'er - - flow - - - - - ing (R)

Kind _____ fortune smiles and she has_ yet _____ in store for thee (S)

The Tempest (opera) Act V — See, see the hea - - - vens smile with clouds no more o'er - cast

Songs:

Ah! how pleasant 'tis to love — Ah! how pleasant 'tis to love, Ev' - ry mo - ment does im - prove:

Ah what pains — Ah what pains Ah what pains

Anacreon's defeat — This po - et sings the Tro - jan wars

Ask me to love no more — Ask me to love no more, no more, no more, no more, no more, no more,

Bess of Bedlam (Mad Bess) — From si - lent shades, and the E - lys - ian groves,

Bright Cyn - thia kept her re - - vels late, while Mab, the Fai - ry Queen

The Blessed Virgin's Expostulation (realization by Benj. Britten) — Tell me, tell me, some, some Pi - - - ty - ing An - gel, tell, quick - ly

Me Ju - dah's daughters once car - ess'd

How, how how shall my soul its Mo - - - - - - - - - - - - - tions guide?

Cease, O my sad soul — Cease O my sad soul, cease to mourn I see my love and faith are paid

Evening Hymn — Now, now that the sun hath veil'd his light,

Fly swift, ye hours — Fly swift, ye hours, make haste, make haste, fly

How delightful's the life — How de - light - - - ful's the life of an in - no - cent swain,

I envy not a monarch's fate — I en - - vy not a mon - - - - - arch's fate,

I fain would be free — I fain would be free and to sev - er all kind, But the dev - il,

If music be the food of love (2nd setting) — If mu - sic be the food of love, Sing on, sing on, sing on, sing on,

I gave her cakes (round) — I gave her cakes and I gave her ale, and I gave her sack and sher - ry

I'll sail upon the Dog-star — I'll sail up - on the Dog - star, and then pur - sue the morn - ing

The Yorkshire Feast Song No. 6

The pale and the pur--ple Rose that af - - ter_cost so ma - - ny_ blows,

PURCELL-COCKRANE, E. (Edward C. Purcell) (Contemporary)

Passing By
Copyright 1932, G. Schirmer, Inc.

There is a la--dy sweet and kind, Was nev-er face so pleas'd_ my mind

QUILTER, Roger (1877-   )

Love's Philosophy, Op. 3, No. 1
By permission Boosey & Hawkes, Inc.,
copyright owners

The fountains min - gle with the riv-er And the riv - - ers with the o-cean;

Come away, death, Op. 6, No. 1
By permission Boosey & Hawkes, Inc.,
copyright owners

Come a - way, come a - way death, And in sad cy - press

O mistress mine, No. 2

O mis-tress mine, where are you roam-ing? O ___ stay and hear

Blow, blow, thou winter wind, No. 3

Blow, blow, thou win-ter wind, Thou art not so un-kind

To Daisies, Op. 8, No. 3
By permission Boosey & Hawkes, Inc.,
copyright owners

Shut not so soon: The dull-eyed night has not as yet be-gun

Weep you no more, Op. 12, No. 1
By permission Boosey & Hawkes, Inc.,
copyright owners

Weep you no more, sad foun-tains; What need you flow so fast?

Fair House of Joy, No. 7

Fain would I change that note to which fond Love hath charm'd me.

Autumn Evening, Op. 14, No. 1
By permission Boosey & Hawkes, Inc.,
copyright owners

The yel-low pop-lar leaves have strown Thy qui-et mound

Song of the Blackbird, No. 4

The Night-in-gale __ has a lyre of gold, The Lark's is a cla-rion call

I will go with my father a-ploughing,
Op. 22, No. 1
By permission of Galaxy Music Corporation,
N. Y., copyright by Elkin & Co., Ltd.

I will go with my fa-ther a-plough-ing,_ To the green field

Fear no more the heat o' the sun,
Op. 23, No. 1
By permission Boosey & Hawkes, Inc.,
copyright owners

Fear no more the heat o' the sun, Nor the fur-ious win-ter's

It was a lover and his lass, No. 3

It was a lov-er and his lass, with a hey and a ho,

Take, O take those lips away, No. 4

Take, O take those lips a-way, That so sweet-ly were for-sworn;

Hey, ho, the Wind and the Rain, No. 5

When that I was and a lit-tle ti-ny boy, With hey, ho,

Go, Lovely Rose, Op. 24, No. 3

The Fuchsia Tree, Op. 25, No. 2
By permission Boosey & Hawkes, Inc., copyright owners

O what if the fowl-er my black-bird has tak-en?

Who is Silvia? Op. 30, No. 1
By permission Boosey & Hawkes, Inc., copyright owners

Who is Sil-via? What is she, that all our swains com-mend her?

Now sleeps the crimson petal
By permission Boosey & Hawkes, Inc., copyright owners

Now sleeps the crimson petal, Now the white;__ Nor waves the cypress

Over the Mountains
Copyright by Boston Music Co.

Ov-er the__ moun-tains and__ ov-er the waves

RABAUD, Henri (1873-   )

Mârouf (opera)
Act I
Copyright by Choudens fils, Paris

Il est des Mu-sul-mans

Act II La Caravane

A tra-vers le dé-sert, mil-le cha-meaux char-gés__ d'é-tof-fes

Act III

Ô__ mar-chand si ri-che ou si pau-vre

Act IV

Dans le jar—din fleu-ri de fleurs,moi, je suis le jet d'eau

Act IV

Viens, ô mon é-pou-se fleu-ri-e

RABEY, René (Contemporary)

Tes Yeux!
By permission Durand & Cie, Paris; Elkan-Vogel Co., Inc., Phila., copyright owners

Tes yeux,__ tes jo-lis yeux__ aux longs regards si doux__

RACHMANINOFF, Sergei (1873-1943)

Romance of the Young Gypsy, from Aleko (opera)

See__ how beneath the dis-tant sky_ dome__ There wanders air-i-ly

Oh stay, my love, Op. 4, No. 1
By permission Boosey & Hawkes, Inc., copyright owners

Oh stay, my love, forsake me not__ The great-est grief

In the silent night, No. 3
Copyright 1943, G. Schirmer, Inc.

Oh, in the si-lent night I see your vi-sion near-ing,

The Songs of Grusia (O, cease thy singing, maiden fair) No. 4
Copyright 1923, G. Schirmer, Inc.

O cease thy sing-ing maid-en fair, The old Gru-se-nian songs

O thou billowy harvest field, No. 5
Copyright 1911, G. Schirmer, Inc.

O thou bil-low-y har-vest field of__ grain!

The Soldier's Bride, Op. 8, No. 4
By permission Boosey & Hawkes, Inc., copyright owners

To my sor-row I fell__ in love with him__ with a poor or-phan,

The Island, Op. 14, No. 2
Copyright 1936, G. Schirmer, Inc.
Far out at sea an is-land lies with gentle slopes and flow'ring masses,

Floods of Spring, No. 11
By permission Boosey & Hawkes, Inc.,
copyright owners
While yet the fields are wrapp'd in snow The waters hear the call of spring

Fate, Op. 21, No. 1
With pil-grim's staff with wear- y gait, With gloom- y brows

The Answer, No. 4
They won-der'd a while: Shall our ves- sel so light

Lilacs, No. 5
Copyright 1910, G. Schirmer, Inc.
Morn-ing skies are a-glow where the li- lac trees blow,

How sweet the place, No. 7
How sweet the place! Far dis - - tant gleams the riv-er in the sun;

Sorrow in Spring, No. 12
How my heart aches! yet fain would I live now that spring

Christ is risen, Op. 26, No. 6
By permission Galaxy Music
Corporation, N. Y.
The Christ is ris'n The choirs are singing My soul is sad,

To the Children, No. 7
By permission Boosey & Hawkes, Inc.,
copyright owners
How oft-en at midnight in days long since fled, Dear children

Before my window, No. 10
By permission Boosey & Hawkes, Inc.,
copyright owners
Be-fore my win-dow stands a flow'ring cher-ry tree,

When yesterday we met, No. 13
By permission Boosey & Hawkes, Inc.,
copyright owners
When yes-ter- day we met, her words and glances fal-ter'd;

All things depart, No. 15
By permission Boosey & Hawkes, Inc.,
copyright owners
All things de-part, no single thing return- eth. Life hur-ries on,

Vocalise, Op. 34, No. 14 (wordless song)
By permission Boosey & Hawkes, Inc.,
copyright owners

Daisies, Op. 38, No. 3
By permission Boosey & Hawkes, Inc.,
copyright owners
Behold, my friend, the dai - - sies sweet and ten-der Wher-e'er I go,

Dreams, No. 5
Say, oh whi- ther art bound, rare en- chant-ment of dreams,

RADECKE, Robert (1829-1893)

Aus der Jugendzeit
Aus der Ju- gend- zeit, aus der Ju- gend- zeit klingt ein Lied

RAFF, Joseph Joachim (1822-1882)

Sei still
Ach, was ist Le- ben doch so schwer, wenn was du lieb hast

RAMEAU, Jean Philippe (1683-1764)

Air Tendre, from Diane et Acteon
(cantata)

Quand le si- lence et le mys-tè- re Dans vos feux

L'Impatience (cantata)

I Air gai

Ce n'est plus le poids de ma chaî- - - - - - - - - - ne

II Air tendre

Pour- quoi leur en- vi- er leur jus- te ré- com- pen- se?

III Air léger

Tu te plais, en- fant de Cy- -the- re, A faire a- che- ter

Musette, from La Musette (cantata)

L'ai-ma-ble Li- set-te for-me ces con- certs, Et sur la mu- set-te

Les Indes Galantes (opera ballet)

Ra- ni- mez vos flam- beaux, rem-plis- sez vos car- quois

Il faut_ que_ l'a- mour_ s'en-vo- - - - - - - - - le

Per-met- tez,_ as- tre du jour, Qu'en chantant_ vos feux

A- mour,_ A- mour, quand du des- tin j'é-prou- ve la ri- gueur

Pa-pil- lon in-cons- tant, vo- le dans ce bo- ca- ge,

Laboravi (motet)

La- bo- ra- - - - - - - - - vi cla- - - - - - - - - - - mans

Beati qui habitant, from Quam dilecta
(motet)

Be- a- ti, be- a- ti qui ha- - bi- tant_ in do- mo tu- a,

Chassons de nos plaisirs, from
Acanthe et Céphise (opera)

Chas- sons De nos plaisirs tran-quil- les Les plaintes i- nu-ti- - les_

Tristes apprêts, from Castor et Pollux
(opera) Act I

Tris- tes ap- prêts pâ- les flam- beaux, Jour plus af- freux

Rossignols amoureux

Ros- si- gnols a- mou- reux, ré- pon- dez à nos voix

RASBACH, Oscar (1888-)

Trees

I think that I shall never see a po- em love-ly as a tree.

RASI, Francesco (c. 1580-c. 1650)

Dove, misero, mai

Do- ve mi- se- ro ma- i   Spe- rar deg- gio con- for- to

Filli mia

Fil- li mi- a,   Fil- li,   Fil- li___ mia dol- ce,

Filli, tu vuoi partire

Fil- li   tu vuoi par- ti- re   E non vuoi___ ch'io so- spi- ri

Occhi sempre sereni

Oc- chi sem- pre se- re- ni   Per cui vi- vo con- ten- to,

RAVEL, Maurice (1875-1937)

Cinq melodies populaires grecques
! Chanson de la mariée
By permission Durand & Cie, Paris; Elkan-Vogel Co., Inc., Phila., copyright owners

Ré- veil- le- toi, Ré- veil- le- toi, per- drix mi- gnon- ne, Ah!

II

Là- bas, vers l'é- gli- se   Vers l'é- glise Ay- io Si- dé- ro

III

Quel ga- - - - - lant, ga- lant m'est com- pa- ra- - - ble,

IV Chanson des cueilleuses de lentisques

O___ joie de mon â- - - - - - - - - me,

V

Tout_ gai! gai, Ha, tout_ gai, tout_ gai, Ha, tout gai!

Deux Épigrammes de Clement Marot
1. D'Anne jouant de l'espinette
By permission Associated Music Publishers, Inc.

Lor- sque je voy en_ or- dre la bru- net- te Jeu- - ne en bon point,

2. D'Anne qui me jecta de la neige

An- ne par jeu me jec- ta de la nei- ge

Deux Mélodies Hebraïques
I Kaddisch
By permission Durand & Cie, Paris; Elkan-Vogel Co., Inc., Phila., copyright owners

Yith- gad- al___ weyith___ kad- dash

B

Yith- ba- - - ra'kh.___ Wey- isch- ta- - ba'h___

II l'Énigme éternelle

Frägt die Velt die al- te Casche Tra la tra la la la la___

Les grands vents venus d'outremer
By permission Durand & Cie, Paris; Elkan-Vogel Co., Inc., Phila., copyright owners

Les grands vents venus d'ou- tre- mer Pas- sent par la ville, l'hi- ver

Histoires Naturelles I Le Paon
By permission Durand & Cie, Paris; Elkan-Vogel Co., Inc., Phila., copyright owners

Il va sûre- - ment se ma- ri- er au- jour- d'hui.

Sainte
A la fe- nê- tre re- cé- lant Le san- tal vieux qui se dé- do- re

Sur l'Herbe
L'abbé di- vague Et toi, marquis, Tu mets de travers ta peruque

Chansons Madécasses
I
Na- han- do- - ve, o bel- le Na- han- do- - ve! l'oiseau noc- turne

II A
Aoua! Aoua! Me- fi- ez- vous des blancs,

B
Du temps de nos pè- res, des blancs descen- dirent dans cette î- le,

III Repos
Il est doux de se cou- cher du- rant la chaleur sous un ar- bre touf- fu,

Don Quichotte à Dulcinée
I Chanson Romantique
Si vous me di- siez que la ter- re A tant tour- ner

II Chanson Épique
Bon Saint Mi- chel qui me don- nez loi- sir de voir ma Da- - me

III Chanson à boire
Foin du bâ- tard, il- lus- tre Da- me, qui pour me perdre

L'Enfant et les Sortilèges (opera-ballet)
Song of the clock
Ding, ding, ding, ding; et encor ding, ding, ding et en- cor ding

Song of the cup
Keng- ça- fou, Mah jong, Keng- ça- fou, Puis' kong, kong, panpa, Ça- oh- rã,

Song of the fire
Je ré- chauf- fe les bons, Je ré- chauf- fe les bons,

Lullaby
Toi, le coeur de la ro- se Toi, le par- fum du lys blanc

Song of the little old man
Deux ro- bi- nets cou- lent dans un ré- ser- voir!

L'Heure Espagnole (comédie-musicale)
Scene IX Inigo's Air
Tant pis, ma foi, si je dé- roge! Je con- çois à l'ins- tant

Scene XV Gonzalve's Air
En dé- pit de cette in- hu- maine Je ne veux pas quit- ter

Scene XVII Concepción's Air
Oh! la pi- toy- able a- ven- tu- re!

Trois Chansons I Nicolette
Ni- co- lette, à la ves- prée, S'al- lait pro- me- ner au pré,

II Trois beaux oiseaux du Paradis
Trois beaux oi- seaux du Pa- ra- dis, (Mon a- mi z-il est à la guer- re

REGER, Max (1873-1916)

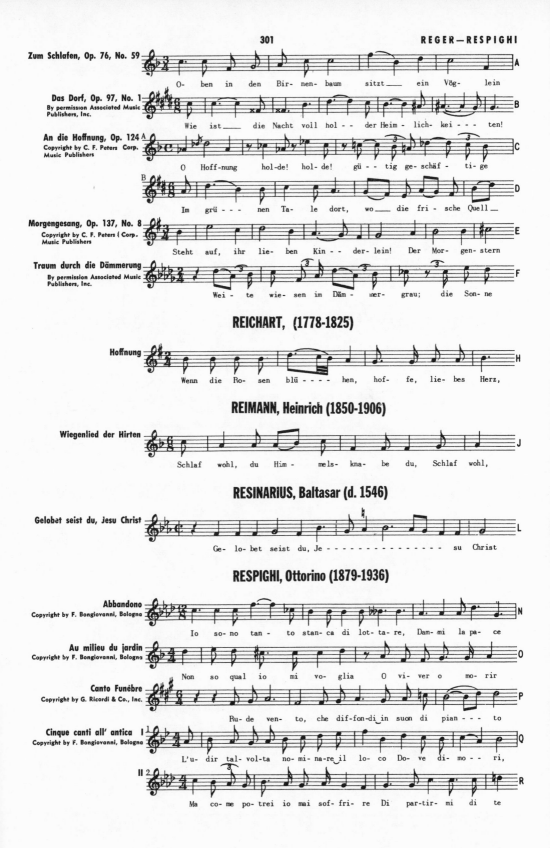

Zum Schlafen, Op. 76, No. 59

O- ben in den Bir- nen- baum sitzt___ ein Vög- lein

Das Dorf, Op. 97, No. 1
By permission Associated Music Publishers, Inc.

Wie ist___ die Nacht voll hol - - der Heim - lich- kei - - - ten!

An die Hoffnung, Op. 124 A
Copyright by C. F. Peters Corp.
Music Publishers

O Hoff- nung hol- de! hol- de! gü- tig ge- schäf - ti- ge

Im grü - - - nen Ta- le dort, wo___ die fri- sche Quell___

Morgengesang, Op. 137, No. 8
Copyright by C. F. Peters (Corp.
Music Publishers

Steht auf, ihr lie- ben Kin - - der- lein! Der Mor- gen- stern

Traum durch die Dämmerung
By permission Associated Music Publishers, Inc.

Wei - te wie- sen im Däm- mer- grau; die Son- ne

REICHART, (1778-1825)

Hoffnung

Wenn die Ro- sen blü - - - - hen, hof- fe, lie- bes Herz,

REIMANN, Heinrich (1850-1906)

Wiegenlied der Hirten

Schlaf wohl, du Him- mels- kna- be du, Schlaf wohl,

RESINARIUS, Baltasar (d. 1546)

Gelobet seist du, Jesu Christ

Ge- lo- bet seist du, Je - - - - - - - - - - - - su Christ

RESPIGHI, Ottorino (1879-1936)

Abbandono
Copyright by F. Bongiovanni, Bologna

Io so- no tan - to stan- ca di lot- ta- re, Dam- mi la pa- ce

Au milieu du jardin
Copyright by F. Bongiovanni, Bologna

Non so qual io mi vo- glia O vi- ver o mo- rir

Canto Funèbre
Copyright by G. Ricordi & Co., Inc.

Ru- de ven- to, che dif- fon- di in suon di pian - - to

Cinque canti all' antica
Copyright by F. Bongiovanni, Bologna

I

L'u- dir tal- vol- ta no- mi- na- re il lo- co Do- ve di- mo - ri,

II 2

Ma co- me po- trei io mai sof- fri- re Di par- tir- mi di te

Cinque canti all' antica III Ballata

Non so qual io mi vo- glia, o vi- ver o mo- rir,

IV

Bel- la por- ta di ru- bi- ni Ch'a- pri- il var- co a' dol- ci ac- cen- ti

V Canzone
di re Enzo

A- mor mi fa so- ven- te Lo me- o co- re pe- na- re

E se un giorno tornasse
Copyright by G. Ricordi & Co., Inc.

E se un gior- no tor- nas- se che do- vrei dir- gli

Invito alla danza
Copyright by F. Bongiovanni, Bologna

Ma- don- na, d'un brac- cio so- a- ve ch'i- o cin- ga

In alto mare
Copyright by F. Bongiovanni, Bologna

E sdru- sci- to il na- vil l'i- ra del flot- te tre- gua non da.

Mattinata
Copyright by F. Bongiovanni, Bologna

Span- do- no le cam- pa- ne a la pri- m'al- ba l'a- ve

Nebbie

Sof- fro, lon- tan lon- ta- no Le neb- bie son- no- len- te Sal- go- no

Nevicata
Copyright by F. Bongiovanni, Bologna

Sui cam- pi e su le stra- de Si- len- zi- o- sa e lie- ve

Notte
Copyright by F. Bongiovanni, Bologna

Sul giar- di- no fan- ta- sti- co Pro- fu- ma- to di ro- sa

Pioggia
Copyright by F. Bongiovanni, Bologna

Pio- ve- a per le fi- ne- stra spa- lan- ca- te

Scherzo
Copyright by F. Bongiovanni, Bologna

U- na not- te al da- van- za- le, e- ro so- la, o pur non e- ro?

Stornellatrice
Copyright by F. Bongiovanni, Bologna

Che mi gio- va can- tar: "Fior di be- tul- la:

Il Tramonto A
Copyright by G. Ricordi & Co., Inc.

Oh! quan- ta te- ne- ra gio- ia, che gli fè il re- spi- ro

B

Ne- ri gli oc- chi ma non ful- gi- de più

REYER, Ernest (1823-1909)

Air des colombes, from Salammbo
(opera)
Copyright by Choudens fils, Paris

Oh! qui me don- ne- ra comme à la co- lombe des ailes, pour fuir

Sigurd (opera) Act II
By permission Heugel & Cie, Paris,
copyright owners

Et toi, Fré- ïa, dé- es- se de l'A- mour Belle é- pou- se

Sigurd (opera) Act II

J'ai gar-dé mon âme in-gé-nue___ A la fi-an-cée in-con-nue___

Es-prits,___ gar-diens de ces lieux vé-né-rés, sa-chez quel nom,

Sa-lut!___ splen-deur___ du jour! Sa-lut! astre au front pur,

Act IV

O pa-lais ra-di-eux___ de la voûte é - - toi-lé- e!

RHEINBERGER, Josef (1839-1901)

In Heaven the Stars now are shining

In Heav'n the stars now are shin-ing, The o-cean waves flash___

RHENÉ-BATON (1879-1940)

Berceuse
By permission Durand & Cie, Paris;
Elkan-Vogel Co., Inc., Phila.,
copyright owners

Quand l'en-fant s'en-dort dans son ber-ceau blanc, son an-ge gar-dien

Il pleut des petales de fleurs, Op. 14, No. 6
By permission Durand & Cie, Paris;
Elkan-Vogel Co., Inc., Phila.,
copyright owners

Il pleut___ des pe-ta-les de fleurs La flam-me

Tendresse, Op. 16, No. 5
By permission Durand & Cie, Paris;
Elkan-Vogel Co., Inc., Phila.,
copyright owners

Mets ta main sur mes yeux Je ne veux plus rien voir

RICHARD, Coeur de Lion (1157-1199)

Ja nun hons pris

Ja nun hons pris ne di-ra sa rai-son

RICHARDSON, T. (Contemporary)

Mary

Kind, kind and gen-tle is she, Kind is my Ma-ry

RIEGO, Teresa del

Homing

O Dry Those Tears!

O dry those tears, and calm those fears, Life is not made___ for sor-row;

RIISAGER, Knudage (1897-)

Mor Danmark
Copyright by Hansen, Copenhagen

Der er et Land, som daar-lig kan bli' me-get min-dre

RIMSKY-KORSAKOFF, Nicolai (1844-1908)

The Czar's Bride (opera)
Lykow's Aria
So an- ders sind__ die Leu- te und das Land.__ B

Ssobakin's Aria
Wer hätt das ah - - - - - - - - nen kön - - - nen__ C

Grjasnoy's Aria
Du Ü - - - ber- muth__ wo- hin bist du ent- schwun- den D

Martha's Aria
Deut- lich liegt vor mir der__ grü - ne Gar- ten E

Die Ver-wand - - ten__ all__ wenn sie sa - - - hen__ uns F

Hymn to the sun, from Le Coq d'Or
(opera) Act II
Sa- lut à toi, so- leil de flam- me! Nous re-viens-tu de l'O - ri - ent G

May Night (opera)
Act I Levko's Song
L'om- bre__ dis - crè- te La nuit mu- et- te, Viens, je t'at- tends__ H

Song to the Village
Mayor
Hé gar-cons, le sa- vez vous? No- tre mai- re perd les jam- bes,__ Hey! I

Act II Slumber Song
Dors, ma dou- ce cré- a- tu- re, dors en paix J

Sadko (opera)
Scene I
Mes__ na- vi- res ra- pi- des aux flancs ver-meils K

Scene II Forest Song
Qu- vre-toi,__ fo- rêt im- pé- ne- trable! Lais-se- moi__ fray-er L

Scene IV Song of the Viking
Guest
Les va- gues en hur- lant as- sie- gent nos ri- va- ges M

Song of India
Les di- a- mants chez nous sont in- nom- bra- bles, N

Dans__ un__ de__ nos__ si - - - - - - tes__ O

Song of the Venetian
Guest
Planche et tout__ en__ mar- bre an- cien__ jo- yaux P

Vil- le su- per- be, bel- le Ve-ni- se, Rei- ne du mon-de Q

Scene VII Berceuse
Sur la ri- ve er- rait le__ Rêve, sur le pré__ le Som- meil. R

Snégourotchka (The Snow Maiden)
(opera)
Act I Air of Snégourotchka
Al - - ler au bois, cueil- ler__ la fram- boise S

ROBINSON, Earl (1911-   )

Ballad for Americans
Copyright by Robbins Music Corp., N. Y.

In sev-en-ty six the sky was red Thun-der rum-bling o-ver-head

No-bod-y___ who was a-ny-bod-y___ be-lieved it

The House I Live In

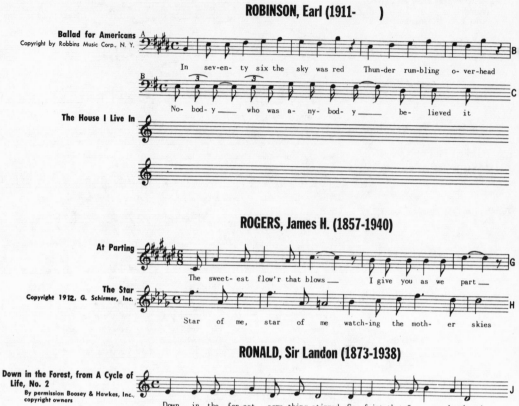

ROGERS, James H. (1857-1940)

At Parting

The sweet-est flow'r that blows___ I give you as we part___

The Star
Copyright 1912, G. Schirmer, Inc.

Star of me, star of me watch-ing the moth-er skies

RONALD, Sir Landon (1873-1938)

Down in the Forest, from A Cycle of Life, No. 2
By permission Boosey & Hawkes, Inc., copyright owners

Down in the for-est some-thing stirred So faint that I scarce-ly heard:

ROOT, George F. (1820-1895)

Just before the Battle, Mother

Just be-fore the bat-tle, mo-ther I am think-ing most of you

The Vacant Chair

We shall meet but we shall miss him, There will be one va-cant chair

ROPARTZ, J. Guy (1864-   )

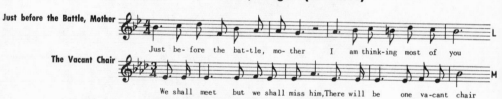

Berceuse
Copyright by Salabert, Paris, N. Y.

O pe-tits en-fants; Voi-ci l'heure où tout bruit cesse

La Mer
Copyright by Salabert, Paris, N. Y.

Le flot, mi-roir mou-vant des cieux, S'é-veille au so-leil

ROSA, Salvator (1615-1673)

Star vicino al bell' Idol

Star vi-ci-no al bell' I-dol che s'a- ma,

Vado ben spesso

Va- do ben spes-so can-gian-do___ lo - - - co

ROSSETER, Philip (c. 1575-1623)

If she forsake me

If she for-sake me, I must die; Shall I tell her so?

ROSSI, Francesco (17th Cent.)

Ah! rendimi quel core, from Mitrane
(opera)

Ah ren-di-mi quel co - - - re, Ren-di-mi quel'a-mo - - -re!

Il tuo fu il mi-o pen-sie - - re Tuo sempre il mi-o vo-le - - - re

ROSSINI, Gioacchino (1792-1868)

La Danza (Tarantella Napoletana)

Già la luna è in mez - -zo al ma - - re, mam - ma mia

La la ra la ra _____ la ra la la ra la

The Barber of Seville (opera)
Act I

Pia - no, pia-ni-si-mo sen - za par-lar! Tut-ti con me veni-te quà,

Ec-co ri-den-te il cie - - - - - lo spun-ta la bel-la au-ro - - - ra

Serenata

Se il mio no - me sa - per voi bra-ma - - - - - - te,

Lar - - - go al fac-to - - tum della cit-tà; lar - go!

All' i - dea di quel me-tal-lo por-ten-to-so on-ni-pos-sente

U - na vo - ce po-co fa qui nel cor mi ri - suo-no,

Io so - - - no do-ci-le, son ri-spet-to - - - -sa,

La ca-lum-nia è un ven-ti-cel-lo, un' au-ret-ta

duet

Dun-que io son? tu non m'in-gan-ni? dun-que io son la for-tu-na-ta?

Ah! tu so - - - - - lo, a-mor, _____ tu se - - - - - - - - l,

A un Dot-tor della mia sor-te que-ste scu-se, Si-gno-ri-na

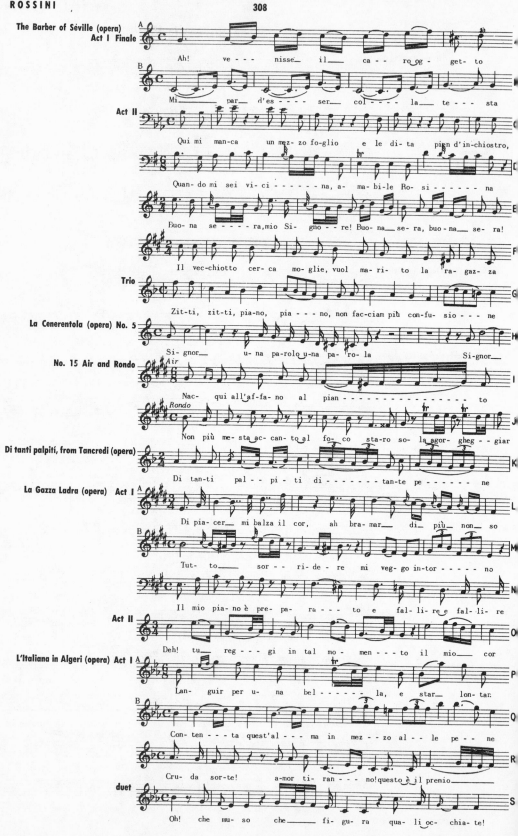

The Barber of Séville (opera)
Act I Finale
A
Ah! ve - - - nisse_ il_ ca - ro og - get - to

B
Mi_ par d'es - - - ser_ col - la_ te - - sta

Act II
Qui mi man - ca un mez - zo fo - glio e le di - ta pien d'in - chiostro,

Quan - do mi sei vi - ci - - - - - - na, a - ma - bi - le Ro - si - - - - na

Buo - na se - - - ra, mio Si - gno - - re! Buo - na_ se - ra, buo - na_ se - ra!

Il vec - chiot - to cer - ca mo - glie, vuol ma - ri - to la ra - gaz - za

Trio
Zit - ti, zit - ti, pia - no, pia - - no, non fac - ciam più con - fu - sio - - ne

La Cenerentola (opera) No. 5
Si - gnor_ u - na pa - ro - lo u - na pa - ro - la Si - gnor_

No. 15 Air and Rondo
Air
Nac - qui all'af - fa - no al pian - - - - - - - - - to

Rondo
Non più me - sta ac - can - to al fo - co sta - rò so - la a gor - gheg - - giar

Di tanti palpití, from Tancredi (opera)
Di tan - ti pal - pi - ti di - - - - - tan - te pe - - - ne

La Gazza Ladra (opera) Act I
A
Di pia - cer_ mi bal - za il cor, ah bra - mar_ di_ più non_ so

B
Tut - to_ sor - ri - de - re mi veg - go in - tor - - - no

Il mio pia - no è pre - pa - ra - - - to e fal - li - re fal - li - re

Act II
Deh! tu reg - - gi in tal mo - men - - to il mio_ cor

L'Italiana in Algeri (opera) Act I
A
Lan - guir per u - na bel - - - la, e star_ lon - tan

B
Con - ten - - - ta quest'al - - - ma in mez - - zo al - le pe - - ne

duet
Cru - da sor - te! a - mor ti - ran - - - no! questo è il premio

Oh! che mu - so che_ - - - fi - gu - ra qua - li oc - chia - te!

ROSSINI

Stabat Mater No. 4

Pro_____ pec - ca - tis su - - - - - ae - gen - tis

No. 6

San - cta ma-ter, is-tud a - gas, cru-ci-fix-i fi-ge pla-gas,

No. 7

Fac ut por-tem Christi mor-tem pas-si-o - - nis e - jus sor - - tem,

No. 8

In - flam-ma - - - tus, in-flam-ma - tus et ac - cen - - - sus

ROUSSEAU, Jean Jacques (1712-1778)

Je vais revoir ma charmante maîtresse, from Le Devin du Village (opera)

Je vais re - voir ma char - man - te Mai - tres - se,

ROUSSEL, Albert (1869-1937)

Le Jardin Mouillé, Op. 3, No. 3
Copyright by Salabert, Paris, N. Y.

La croi-sée est ou - verte; il pleut Com - me mi - nu-ti-eu - se-ment

Nuit d'Automne, Op. 8, No. 2
Copyright by Salabert, Paris, N. Y.

Le cou-chant est si beau par-mi les ar - bres d'or

Invocation, No. 3
Copyright by Salabert, Paris, N. Y.

Pour que la nuit soit douce___ il fau-dra que les ro - ses

A un jeune gentilhomme, Op. 12, No. 1
Copyright by Salabert, Paris, N. Y.

N'en-trez pas, Mon-sieur, s'il vous plaît,_ Ne bri-sez pas mes fou-gè - res,

Amoureux séparés, No. 2
Copyright by Salabert, Paris, N. Y.

Dans le roy-au - me de Yen___ un jeune ga - lant ré - si - de

Light, Op. 19, No. 1
By permission Durand & Cie, Paris; Elkan-Vogel Co., Inc., Phila., copyright owners

Des lar - mes ont cou - lé___ D'un coeur se-cret et ten-dre

Sarabande, Op. 20, No. 2
By permission Durand & Cie, Paris; Elkan-Vogel Co., Inc., Phila., copyright owners

Les jets d'eau dan - sent des sa - ra - ban - des

Réponse d'une épouse sage, Op. 35, No. 2
By permission Durand & Cie, Paris; Elkan-Vogel Co., Inc., Phila., copyright owners

Con - nais-sant, sei - gneur,_ mon é - tat d'é - pou - se.

Jazz dans la nuit, Op. 38
By permission Durand & Cie, Paris; Elkan-Vogel Co., Inc., Phila., copyright owners

Le bal, sur le parc in - cen-dié___ jet - te ses feux

Coeur en Peril, Op. 50, No. 2
By permission Durand & Cie, Paris; Elkan-Vogel Co., Inc., Phila., copyright owners

Que m'im - por - te que l'in-fan - te de Por - tu - gal___

RUBINSTEIN, Anton (1829-1894)

Der Traum, Op. 8, No. 1

Am Wie - sen-hü - gel schlum - mert ich dem brei - ten Weg

Sehnsucht, Op. 8, No. 5

Gönnt mir gold- ne Ta- ges- hel- le, öff- net mir des Ker- kers Schloss

Du bist wie eine Blume, Op. 32, No. 5

Du bist wie ei- ne Blu- me so hold, und schön und rein

Frühlingslied, Op. 32, No. 2

Die blau- en Früh- lings- au- gen schau'n aus dem Gras her- vor

Lied (The Page), Op. 32, No. 4

Es war ein al- ter Kö- nig, sein Herz war schwer, sein Haupt war grau

Persian Songs, Op. 34, No. 1

Nicht mit En- - geln im blau- en Himmels- zelt,

No. 2

Mein Herz schmückt sich mit dir wie sich der Him- mel mit der Son- ne

No. 3

Seh' ich dei- ne Zar- ten Füss- chen an, so be- greif' ich nicht,

No. 4 Die Rose

Es hat die Ro- - - - se sich be- klagt, dass gar zu schnell

No. 9

Gelb rollt mir zu Füs- sen der brau- sen- de Kur

Der Engel, Op. 48

Es schweb- te ein En- gel den Him- mel ent- lang

Nun die Schatten dunkeln, Op. 57, No. 2

Nun die Schat- ten dun- keln, Stern an Stern er- wacht

Clärchen's Lied, No. 4

Freud- voll und leid voll, ge- dan- - - - - - - - - ken- voll sein

Es blinkt der Thau, Op. 72, No. 1

Es blinkt der Thau in den Grä- sern der Nacht, der Mond zieht vor- ü- ber

The Prisoner, Op. 78, No. 6

Im Ker- ker ge- fan- gen ver- schmacht' ich da- hier

Der Asra

Täg- lich ging die wun- der- schö- ne Sul- tans- toch- ter auf und nie- der

Die Lerche (The Lark)

Ler- che stei- get im Ge- sang, zieht hin- auf zu blau- en Räu- men,

Sang das Vögelein

Sang wohl, sang das Vö- ge- lein, und ver- stumm- te

Wanderers Nachtlied

Al- ler Ber- ge Gi- pfel ruh'n in dunk- ler Nacht,

RUSSELL, Henry (1871-1937)

Woodman, spare that tree

Wood-man, spare that tree!__ Touch not a sin-gle__ bough!

SADERO, Geni (1891-)

Amuri, Amuri

A-mu-ri, a-mu--ri__ che m'ai fat-tu

Fa la nana, bambin

Fà la na-na bam-bin, Fà la na-na bel bam-bin

In mezo al Mar

In me-zo al mar ghe xe un ca-min che fu-ma__

SAINT-SAËNS, Camille (1835-1921)

O beaux rêves évanouis, from Étienne
Marcel (opera) Act II
By permission Durand & Cie, Paris; Elkan-
Vogel Co., Inc., Phila., copyright owners

O beaux rê-ves é-va-nouis__ Es-pé-ran-ces tant ca-res-sé-es!

Qui donc commande, from Henry VIII
(opera) Act I
By permission Durand & Cie, Paris; Elkan-
Vogel Co., Inc., Phila., copyright owners

Qui donc com-man-de quand il ai-me Et quel em- pi-re

Samson et Dalila, Op. 47 (opera)
Act I
By permission Durand & Cie, Paris; Elkan-
Vogel Co., Inc., Phila., copyright owners

Ar-rê-tez ô mes frè-res! Et bé-nis-sez le nom de Dieu saint

Ce Dieu que vo-tre voix im-plo-re Est de-meu-ré sourd

Mau-di-te à ja-mais soit la ra-ce des en-fants d'Is-ra-ël!

Voi-ci le prin-temps nous por-tant des fleurs

Je viens cé-lé-brer la vic-toi-re De ce-lui qui regne en mon coeur

Prin-temps qui com-men-ce Por-tant l'és-pe-ran-ce

Act II

A-mour! viens ai-der ma fai-bles-se Ver-se le poi-son

Mon coeur s'ouvre à ta voix, com-me s'ou-vrent les fleurs

Ah!__ ré-ponds à ma ten-dres-se

Act III

Vois ma mi-sère, hé-las vois ma dé-tres-se! Pi-tié! Sei-gneur!

SAINT-SAENS

Samson et Dalila, Op. 47 (opera)
Act III
Gloire à Da-gon vain-queur! Gloire à Da-gon vain-queur! Il ai-dait

Oratorio de Noël (Christmas Oratorio) Op. 12 No. 2
By permission Durand & Cie, Paris; Elkan-Vogel Co., Inc., Phila., copyright owners
Glo-ri- a in al-ti-si-mis De- o

No. 4
Do-mi- ne e- go cre-di-di e- go cre-di-di

No. 5
Be-ne-dic-tus, be-ne-dic-tus, be-ne-dic - - - tus

No. 7
Te - - cum prin-ci-pi-um te-cum prin-ci-pi-um in di-e vir-tu-tis

No. 8
A- le- lu-ia, Al- le- lu-ia, Al- le- lu-ia

No. 10
Tol-li-te hos-ti-as, et a-do-ra-te Do-mi-num in a tri-o

Aimons-nous
By permission Durand & Cie, Paris; Elkan-Vogel Co., Inc., Phila., copyright owners
Ai-mons nous et dor-mons Sans son-ger au res-te du mon-de

L'Attente
By permission Durand & Cie, Paris; Elkan-Vogel Co., Inc., Phila., copyright owners
Monte, é-cu-reuil. monte au grand chê-ne, sur la bran-che des cieux

Ave Verum
By permission Durand & Cie, Paris; Elkan-Vogel Co., Inc., Phila., copyright owners
A- ve A- ve ve - - rum Cor-pus natum de Ma-ri- a Vir-gi- ne

Le bonheur est chose légère
By permission Durand & Cie, Paris; Elkan-Vogel Co., Inc., Phila., copyright owners
Le bon-heur est cho-se lé-gè- re, Pas-sa-gè - - - - - - - re

La Cloche
By permission Durand & Cie, Paris; Elkan-Vogel Co., Inc., Phila., copyright owners
Seule en ta som-bre tour aux fai-tes den-te- lés

Danse Macabre
By permission Durand & Cie, Paris; Elkan-Vogel Co., Inc., Phila., copyright owners
Zig et zig et zig, La mort en ca-den-ce Frap-pant u- ne tombe

Le vent d'hi-ver souffle, et la nuit est som- bre

Guitares et Mandolines
By permission Durand & Cie, Paris; Elkan-Vogel Co., Inc., Phila., copyright owners
Gui-ta-res et man-do-li-nes Ont des sons qui font ai-mer

Mai
By permission Durand & Cie, Paris; Elkan-Vogel Co., Inc., Phila., copyright owners
Mai! les ar-bres du ver-ger Sont pou-drés de nei-ge ro-se

Mélodies Persanes, Op. 26: Au cimetière
By permission Durand & Cie, Paris; Elkan-Vogel Co., Inc., Phila., copyright owners
As-sis sur cet-te blanche tom-be Ouvrons no- tre cœur

La Solitaire
Ô fier jeune homme, ô tu - - eur de ga-zel - les

The Nightingale and the Rose (wordless song), from incidental music to Parysatis
By permission Durand & Cie, Paris; Elkan-Vogel Co., Inc., Phila., copyright owners

Le Pas d'armes du Roi Jean

Par saint Gil - les, Viens nous en, Mon a - gi - le A - le - zan

Los aux da - mes! au roi los! Vois les flammes Des champs clos

Tournoiement

Sans que nul-le part je sé - jour-ne Sur la poin-te du gros or - teil

SALTER, Mary Turner (1856-1938)

The Cry of Rachel

I stand in the dark, I beat on the door: Death, let me in

The Pine-Tree

O pine-tree lone-ly stand-ing, Out-lined a-gainst the blue

SANDERSON, James

Hail to the Chief

Hail to the Chief, who in tri - - umph ad - van - ces,

Heav'n send it hap-py dew, Earth lend it sap a-new

SANDERSON, Wilfrid

Until

No rose in all the world___ un - til you came,___

SARTI, Guiseppe (1729-1802)

Lungi dal caro bene

Lun-gi___ dal ca-ro be-ne, Vi-ve-re non pos-s'i-o

SARTORIUS, Thomas (1577-1637)

Wohlauf, ihr lieben Gäste

Wohl- auf ___ wohl- auf, ihr lie-ben Gä - - - - - - - ste

SATIE, Erik (1866-1925)

Le Chapelier

Le cha-pe-lier s'é-ton - - ne de con-sta-ter que sa mon - tre

Daphénéo

Dis- moi,___ Da-phé-né-o, quel est donc cet ar-bre

Je te veux

J'ai com-pris ta dé tres-se, cher a-mou-reux___

Je n'ai pas___ de re-grets___ et je n'ai qu'u-ne en-vi- e

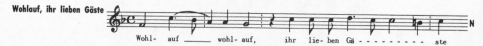

La Statue de Bronze
Copyright by Salabert, Paris, N. Y.
La gre-nou-ille du jeu de tonneau S'en-nu-ie le soir

SCANDELLI, Antonio (1517-1580)

Ein Hennlein weiss
Ein Henn-lein-weiss ein Henn-lein weiss mit gan-zen Fleiss

SCARLATTI, Alessandro (1659-1725)

Chi vuole innamorarsi
Chi vuo-le in-na-mo-rar-si,   Chi vuo-le in-na-ma-rar-si,

Già il sole dal Gange
Già il so-le_ dal Gan-ge,già il so-le dal Gan-ge più chia-ro,

O cessate di piagarmi
O ces-sa-te di_ pia-gar-mi, o las-cia-te-mi mo-rir

Ombre opache, from Correa nel peno
amato (cantata)
Om-bre o-pa- che che il chia-ro-re del-la lu-ce

Povera pellegrina (cantata)
Po - - - ve-ra pel-le-gri-na_ Son io cor mio per te_

Rugiadose, odorose
Ru-gia-do-se, o-do-ro-se, Vi-o-let-te gra-zi-o-se,

Se Florindo è fedele
Se Flo-rin-do è fe-de-le io m'in-na-mo-re - - -rò,

Sento nel core
Sen-to nel co-re cer-to do-lo-re, cer-to do-lo-re,

Se tu della mia morte
Se tu_ del-la mia mor-te a que-sta de-stra for - -te

Son tutta duolo
Son tut-ta duo-lo, non ho che affan-ni e mi_ da mor-te

Su, venite a consiglio
Su, su su, ve-ni-te a con-si-glio,ve-ni-te a con-siglio

SCARLATTI, Domenico (1685-1757)

Consolati e spera
Con-so-la-ti!_ e spe-ra!_ po-trai d'altro ogget - -to

Qual farfalietta amante
Qual far-fal-let-ta a-man - -te in vo-lo a quel-la fiam-ma

SCHEIN, Johann Hermann (1586-1630)

Wenn Filli ihre Liebesstrahl

Wenn Fil-le ih-re Lie-bes-strahl   wirft in mein Herz

SCHILLINGS, Max von (1868-1933)

Wie wundersam, Op. 2, No. 3
By permission Associated Music
Publishers, Inc.

Wie wun - - - der-sam   ist dies Verlo-ren-geh'n in Lie-bes-tie-fen

SCHÖNBERG, Arnold (1874-   )

Erhebung, Op. 2, No. 3

Gieb mir dei-ne Hand, nur den Fin-ger,   dann_ seh ich

Warnung, Op. 3, No. 3

Mein Hund, du,_ hat dich bloss be-knurrt   und_ ich hab ihn

Hochzeitslied, No. 4

So voll und reich wand noch das Le-ben nim-mer euch sei-nen Kranz,

Geübtes Herz, No. 5

Wei-se nicht von dir mein schlichtes Herz, weil es schon so viel ge-lieb-et!

Mädchenlied, Op. 6, No. 3

Ach, wenn es nun die Mut-ter wüsst, wie du so wild mich hast ge-küsst,

Verlassen, No. 4

Im Mor-gen-grau-en schritt ich fort   Ne-bel lag in den Gas-sen

Ghasel, No. 5

Ich hal-te dich in mei-nem Arm,   du_ hältst die Ro-se zart_

Das Buch der hängenden Gärten, Op. 15,
No. 5
By permission Associated Music
Publishers, Inc.

Sa - - get mir, auf wel-chem Pfa-de heu-te sie vor-ü-ber schrei-te,

No. 12

Wenn sich bei heil-ger Ruh   in tie-fen Mat-ten

Gurrelieder, Op. 35
Waldemar's Song
By permission Associated Music
Publishers, Inc.

So tan-zen die En-gel vor Got-tes Thron nicht,   wie die Welt_

Tove's Song

Nun sag ich dir zum er-sten Mal: "Kö-nig Vol-mer, ich lie-be dich!"

Waldemar's Song

Du wun-der-li-che To-ve!   So reich durch dich nun bin ich

Waldtaube's Song   I

Tau-ben von Gur-re   Sor-ge qualt_ mich, vom Weg_

II

Weit_ flog ich,   Kla-ge sucht' ich   fand gar viel!

SCHUBERT, Franz (1797-1828)

Agnus Dei, from Mass in G (No. 2) — Ag- nus De- i, qui tol- lis pec- ca- ta mun- di,

Sanctus, from Mass in F — Sanc- tus, Sanc- tus Sanc- tus Do- mi- nus De- us Sa- ba- oth

Die schöne Müllerin, Op. 25 (song cycle) No. 1 "Das Wandern" — Das Wan- dern ist des Mül- lers Lust, das Wan- - dern!

No. 2 Wohin? — Ich_ hört' ein Bäch- lein rau- - schen wohl_ aus dem Fel- sen- quell,

No. 3 Halt! — Ei- ne Müh- le seh ich blin- ken aus den Er- len her aus

No. 4 Danksagung an den Bach — War es al- so ge- meint, mein rau- - schen- der Freund? dein Sin- gen,

No. 5 Am Feierabend — Hätt' ich tau- send Ar- me zu rüh- ren! Könnt ich brau- send

No. 6 Der Neugierige — Ich fra- ge kei- ne Blu- me, ich fra- ge kei- nen Stern;—

O Bäch- lein mei- ner Lie- be, wie bist du heut_ so stumm!

No. 7 Ungeduld — Ich schnitt' es gern in al- le Rin- den ein, ich grüb es gern

No. 8 Morgengruss — Gu- ten Mor- gen, schö- ne Mül- le- - rin! Wo steckst du gleich_

No. 9 Des Müllers Blumen — Am Bach_ viel klei- ne Blu- men stehn, aus hel- len, blau- en Au- gen_ sehn;

No. 10 Tränenregen — Wir sa- ssen so trau- lich bei- sam- men im küh- len Er- len- dach

No. 11 Mein! — Bäch- lein,_ lass dein Rau- schen_ sein! Rä- der, stellt euer Brau- en_ ein!

No. 12 Pause — Mei- ne Lau- te hab ich ge- hängt an die Wand,

No. 13 Mit dem grünen Lautenbande — Schad' um das schö- ne grü- ne Band, dass es ver- bleicht hier_ an der Wand,

No. 14 Der Jäger — Was sucht denn der Jä- ger am Mühl- bach hier? Bleib trot- zi- ger Jä- ger

No. 15 Eifersucht und Stolz — Wo- hin so schnell, so kraus und wild, mein lie- ber Bach?

Die schöne Müllerin, Op. 25 (song cycle) No. 16 Die liebe Farbe
A
In Grün will ich mich klei- den, in grü- ne Trä- nen- wei- den:

No. 17 Die böse Farbe
B
Ich möch- te ziehn in die Welt hin- aus, hin- aus in die wei- te Welt;

No. 18 Trockne Blumen
C
Ihr Blüm- lein al- le, die sie mir gab, euch soll man le- gen

No. 19 Der Müller und der Bach
D
Wo ein treu- es Her- ze in Lie- be ver- geht,

No. 20 Des Baches Wiegenlied
E
Gu- te Ruh, gu- te Ruh! tu die Au- gen zu!

Schwanengesang (14 Lieder) No. 1 Liebesbotschaft
F
Rau- schen- des Bäch- lein, so sil- bern und hell, eilst zur Geliebten

No. 2 Kriegers Ahnung
G
In tie- fer Ruh liegt um mich her der Waf- fen- bru- der Kreis;

No. 3 Frühlingssehnsucht
H
Säu- seln- de Lüf- te we- hend so mild, blu- mi- ger Düf- te

No. 4 Ständchen (Serenade)
I
Lei- se flie- hen mei- ne Lie- der durch die Nacht zu Dir

No. 5 Aufenthalt
J
Rau- schen- der Strom, Brau- sen- der Wald, Star- ren- der Fels

No. 6 In der Ferne
K
We- he dem Flie- hen- den Welt hin- aus zie- hen- den!

No. 7 Abschied
L
A- de! du mun- tre, du fröh- li- che Stadt, A- de!

No. 8 Der Atlas
M
Ich un- glück- sel- ger At- las, ich un- glück- sel- ger At- las!

No. 9 Ihr Bild
N
Ich stand in dun- keln Träu- men und starrt' ihr Bild- nis an

No. 10 Das Fischermädchen
O
Du schö- nes Fi- scher- mäd- chen, trei- be den Kahn ans Land;

No. 11 Die Stadt
P
Am fer- nen Ho- ri- zon- te er- scheint wie ein Ne- bel- bild,

No. 12 Am Meer
Q
Das Meer er- glänz- te weit hin- aus im letz- ten A- bend- schei- ne

No. 13 Der Doppelgänger
R
Still ist die Nacht, es ru- hen die Gas- sen, in die- sem Hau- se

No. 14 Die Taubenpost
S
Ich hab ei- ne Brief- taub in mei- nem Sold, die ist gar er- ge- ben

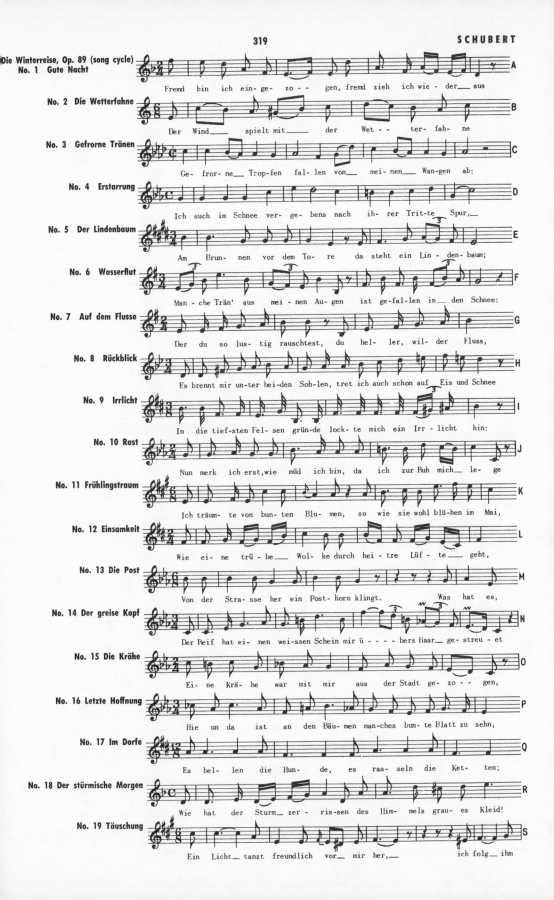

Die Winterreise, Op. 89 (song cycle)
No. 1 Gute Nacht
Fremd bin ich ein-ge-zo — gen, fremd zieh ich wie-der aus   A

No. 2 Die Wetterfahne
Der Wind spielt mit der Wet-ter-fah-ne   B

No. 3 Gefrorne Tränen
Ge-fror-ne Trop-fen fal-len von mei-nen Wan-gen ab: C

No. 4 Erstarrung
Ich such im Schnee ver-ge-bens nach ih-rer Trit-te Spur,   D

No. 5 Der Lindenbaum
Am Brun-nen vor dem To-re da steht ein Lin-den-baum;   E

No. 6 Wasserflut
Man-che Trän' aus mei-nen Au-gen ist ge-fal-len in den Schnee: F

No. 7 Auf dem Flusse
Der du so lus-tig rauschtest, du hel-ler, wil-der Fluss,   G

No. 8 Rückblick
Es brennt mir un-ter bei-den Soh-len, tret ich auch schon auf Eis und Schnee   H

No. 9 Irrlicht
In die tief-sten Fel-sen grün-de lock-te mich ein Irr-licht hin: I

No. 10 Rast
Nun merk ich erst, wie müd ich bin, da ich zur Ruh mich le-ge   J

No. 11 Frühlingstraum
Ich träum-te von bun-ten Blu-men, so wie sie wohl blü-hen im Mai,   K

No. 12 Einsamkeit
Wie ei-ne trü-be Wol-ke durch hei-tre Lüf-te geht,   L

No. 13 Die Post
Von der Stra-sse her ein Post-horn klingt. Was hat es,   M

No. 14 Der greise Kopf
Der Reif hat ei-nen weis-sen Schein mir ü — bers Haar ge-streu-et   N

No. 15 Die Krähe
Ei-ne Krä-he war mit mir aus der Stadt ge-zo — gen,   O

No. 16 Letzte Hoffnung
Hie un da ist an den Bäu-men man-ches bun-te Blatt zu sehn,   P

No. 17 Im Dorfe
Es bel-len die Hun-de, es ras-seln die Ket-ten;   Q

No. 18 Der stürmische Morgen
Wie hat der Sturm zer-ris-sen des Him-mels grau-es Kleid!   R

No. 19 Täuschung
Ein Licht tanzt freundlich vor mir her, ich folg ihm   S

Die Winterreise, Op. 89 (song cycle)
No. 20 Der Wegweiser — A

Was ver-meid ich denn die We- ge, wo die An-dern Wan-drer gehn,

No. 21 Das Wirtshaus — B

Auf ei- nen To- ten- ak- ker hat mich mein Weg ge- bracht

No. 22 Mut! — C

Fliegt der Schnee mir ins Ge- sicht, schüttl ich ihn her- un- ter

No. 23 Die Nebensonnen — D

Drei Son- nen sah ich am Him- mel stehn, hab lang und fest sie an- ge-sehn;

No. 24 Der Leiermann — E

Drü- ben hin-term Dor- fe steht ein Lei- er- mann,

Gretchen am Spinnrade, Op. 2 — F

Mei- ne Ruh ist hin, mein Herz ist schwer; ich fin- de,

Meeres Stille, Op. 3, No. 2 — G

Tie- fe Stil- le herrscht im Was- ser, oh- ne Re- gung ruht das Meer,

Heidenröslein, No. 3 — H

Sah ein Knab ein Rös- lein stehn, Rös- lein auf der Hei- den,

Jägers Abendlied, No. 4 — I

Im Fel- de schleich' ich still und wild ge- - spannt

Der Wanderer, Op. 4, No. 1 — J

Ich kom- me vom Ge- bir- ge her Es dampft das Tal

— K

Wo bist Du, wo bist Du, mein ge- lieb- tes Land?

Wanderers Nachtlied, No. 3 — L

Der du von dem Him- mel bist, al- les Leid und Schmerzen stillst,

Rastlose Liebe, Op. 5, No. 1 — M

Dem Schnee, dem Re- gen, dem Wind ent- ge- gen, in Dampf der Klüf- te,

Nähe des Geliebten, No. 2 — N

Ich den- - ke dein, wenn mir der Son- - - ne Schimmer vom Mee- - re strahlt

Das König in Thule, No. 5 — O

Es war ein König in Thu- le, gar treu bis an das Grab,

Memnon, Op. 6, No. 1 — P

Den Tag hin-durch nur ein- mal mag ich spre- chen,

Am Grabe Anselmos, No. 3 — Q

Dass ich dich ver- lo- - ren ha- - be, Dass du nicht mehr bist,

Der Tod und das Mädchen, Op. 7, No. 3 — R

Vor- ü- ber, ach, vor- ü- ber! geh, wil- der Kno- chen- mann

Erlafsee, Op. 8, No. 3 — S

Mir ist so wohl, so weh' am stil- len Er- laf- see;

Am Strome, Op. 8, No. 4 — A

Ist mir's doch, als sei mein Le-ben an den schö-nen Strom ge-bun-den;

Die Nachtigall, Op. 11, No. 2 (men's chorus) — B

Be-schei-den ver-bor-gen im bu-schich-ten Gang

C

So Freun-de, ver-hall-te manch' himm-li-sches Lied

Gesänge des Harfners, Op. 12, No. 1 — D

Wer sich der Ein-sam-keit er-gibt, ach! der ist bald al-lein,

No. 2 — E

Wer nie sein Brot mit Trä-nen ass, wer nie die kum-mer-vol-len Näch-te

No. 3 — F

An die Tü-ren will ich schlei-chen, still und sitt-sam

Lob der Tränen, Op. 13, No. 2 — G

Lau-e Lüf-te, Blu-men-düf-te, al-le Lenz und Ju-gend-lust;

Der Alpenjäger, No. 3 — H

Auf ho-hem Ber-ges-rü-cken, wo fri-scher al-les grünt,

Suleika I, Op. 14, No. 1 — I

Was be-deu-tet die Be-we-gung? Bringt der Ost mir fro-he Kun-de?

J

Ach, die wah-re Her-zens-kun-de, Lie-bes-hauch

Geheimes, No. 2 — K

Ü-ber mei-nes Lieb-chens Äu-geln stehn ver-wun-dert al-le Leu-te;

Die Nacht, Op. 17, No. 4 (men's voices) — L

Wie schön bist Du, freundliche Stil-le, himm-li-sche Ruh'!

An Schwager Kronos, Op. 19, No. 1 — M

Spu-te dich, Kro-nos! fort den rasseln-den Trott!

Ganymed, No. 3 — N

Wie im Mor-gen-glan-ze du rings mich an-glüh'st

Sei mir gegrüsst! Op. 20, No. 1 — O

O du Ent-riss-ne mir und mei-nem Küs-se, sei mir ge-grüsst,

Frühlingsglaube, No. 2 — P

Die lin-den Lüf-te sind er-wacht, sie säu-seln und we-hen

Der Schiffer, Op. 21, No. 2 — Q

Im Win-de, im Stur-me be-fahr ich den Fluss,

Der Zwerg, Op. 22, No. 1 — R

Im trü-ben Licht ver-schwin-den schon die Ber-ge, es schwebt das Schiff

Wehmuth, No. 2 — S

Wenn ich durch Wald und Flu-ren geh', es wird mir dann so wohl und weh,

Die Liebe hat gelogen, Op. 23, No. 1 — A

Die Lie-be hat ge-lo-gen, die Sor-ge las-tet schwer,

Schwanengesang, No. 3 — B

Wie klag ich's aus, das Ster-be-ge-fühl, das auf-lö-send

Gruppe aus dem Tartarus, Op. 24, No. 1 — C

Horch, wie Mur-meln des em-pör-ten Mee-res wie durch hohler Felsen

Schlaflied, No. 2 — D

Es mahnt der Wald, es ruft der Strom: "du lie--bes Büb-chen,

Romanze, Op. 26, No. 1 (from Rosamunde) — E

Der Voll-mond strahlt auf Ber-ges-höh'n, wie hab' ich dich ver-misst

Der Gondelfahrer, Op. 28 — F

Es tan-zen Mond und Ster---ne den flücht'gen Gei-ster-reih'n

Suleika II, Op. 31 — G

Ach, um dei-ne feuch-ten Schwingen, West, wie sehr ich dich be-nei-de;

Die Forelle, Op. 32 — H

In ei-nem Bäch-lein hel-le, da schoss in fro-her Eil

Nachtstück, Op. 36, No. 2 — I

Wenn ü-ber Ber-ge sich der Ne-bel brei-tet,

Der Pilgrim, Op. 37, No. 1 (words by Schiller) — J

Noch in mei-nes Le-bens Len-ze war ich, und ich wan-dert aus

Der Einsame, Op. 41 — K

Wenn mei-ne Gril-len schwir-ren, bei Nacht, am spät er-wärm-ten Herd,

Die junge Nonne, Op. 43, No. 1 — L

Wie braust durch die Wip---fel der heu-len-de Sturm!

Nacht und Träume, No. 2 — M

Heil'-ge Nacht, du sinkest nie-der nie-der wal-len auch die Träu-me,

Ellen's erster Gesang, Op. 52, No. 1 (from Scott's Lady of the Lake) — N

Ra--ste, Krie-ger! Krieg ist aus, schlaf' den Schlaf,

Ellen's Zweiter Gesang, No. 2 (from Scott's Lady of the Lake) — O

Jä-ger, ru-he von der Jagd! Jä-ger, ru-he von der Jagd!

An die Leier, No. 3 — A — P

Ich will von A-treus' Söh-nen von Kad-mus will ich sin-gen!

B — Q

Doch mei-ne Sai-ten tö-nen nur Lie-be im Er-klin-gen,

Coronach, No. 4 — R

Er ist uns ge-schie-den vom Berg und vom Wal-de

Ave Maria, No. 6 — S

A-ve Ma-ri-----a! Jung-----frau mild,

SCHUBERT

Die Allmacht, Op. 79, No. 2

Gross ist Je - ho - va, der Herr, _____ denn Him - mel und Er - de

Der Wanderer an den Mond, Op. 80, No. 1

Ich auf der Erd, am Him - mel du, wir wan - dern bei - de rüs - tig _ zu:

Alinde, Op. 81, No. 1

Die Son - ne sinkt _____ in's tie - - fe Meer

An die Laute, No. 2

Lei - ser, lei - - ser, klei - ne Lau - te, flü - stre, was _ ich dir - ver - trau - te,

An die Musik, Op. 88, No. 4

Du hol - de Kunst, in wie viel grau - en - Stun - den,

Der Musensohn, Op. 92, No. 1

Durch Feld und Wald zu schwer - fen, mein Lied - chen weg zu pfei - fen,

Im Walde, Op. 93, No. 1

Ich wand' - re ü - - ber _ Berg und Thal und ü - ber _ grü - ne Hai - den

Auf der Bruck, No. 2

Frisch tra - be son - der Ruh' und Rast, mein gu - tes Ross,

Die Sterne, Op. 96, No. 1

Wie bli - tzen die Ster - ne so hell _ durch die Nacht _____

Wanderers Nachtlied, No. 3

Ü - ber al - len Gip - feln ist Ruh, in al - len Wip - feln spü - rest Du

Fischerweise, No. 4

Den _ Fi - scher - fech - ten _ Sor - gen und _ Gram und _ Leid nicht an;

An die Nachtigall, Op. 98, No. 1

Er liegt und schläft an mei - nem Her - zen

Wiegenlied, No. 2

Schla - fe, schla - - fe, hol - der, sü - - sser _ Kna - be,

Mondenschein, Op. 102 (men's chorus)

Des Mon - - des Zau - - ber - blu - - me lacht,

Wiegenlied, Op. 105, No. 2

Wie sich der Äug - lein kind - li - cher Him - mel, schlum - mer - be - las - tet,

Am Fenster, No. 3 (John Gabriel Seidl)

Ihr lie - ben Mau - ern hold und traut, die ihr mich kühl um - schliesst,

Vor meiner Wiege, Op. 106, No. 3

A

Das al - so, das ist der en - ge Schrein, da lag ich ein - stens

B

Dann lach - - - te ich sau - gend zu ihr _ em - - - por

An Silvia, No. 4 (Who is Sylvia?)

Was ist Sil - via, sa - get an _ dass sie die wei - te Flur preist?

A B C D E F G H I J K L M N O P Q R S

Über Wildemann, Op. 108, No. 1

A

Die Win- de sau- sen am Tan- nen-hang, die Quel- len brau- sen

Todesmusik, No. 2

B

In des To- des Fei- er- stun- de wenn ich einst von hin- nen_ schei- de,

Das Lied im Grünen, Op. 115, No. 1

C

Ins Grü- ne, ins Grü- ne, da lockt uns der Früh- ling,

Sprache der Liebe, No. 3

D

Lass dich mit_ ge- lin_ den_ Schlägen rüh-ren_ mei-ne_ zar- te Lau-te!

An die Sonne, Op. 118, No. 5

E

Sin- ke, liebe Son-ne, sin- ke, en- de dei- nen trü - - - ben Lauf_

Die Spinnerin, No. 6

F

Als_ ich_ still und_ ru- hig spann, oh- ne_ nur_ zu_ sto- cken

Der Hirt auf dem Felsen, Op. 129
(for soprano, clarinet and piano)

A

G

Wenn_ auf dem_ hoch - - - - - sten Fels ich_ steh',

B

H

Der Früh- ling_ will_ kom- men, der Früh- ling mei- ne_ Freud',

Das Echo, Op. 130

I

Herz- lie- be, gu- te Mut- ter, O grol- le nicht mit mir,

Psalm, Op. 132, No. 23

J

Gott ist mein Hirt,_ mir wird nichts man - - - - geln Gott ist mein Hirt,

Nachthelle, Op. 134 (men's chorus)

K

Die Nacht ist hei-ter und ist rein, Die Nacht ist hei-ter und ist rein

Ständchen, Op. 135

L

Zo- gernd lei- se, Zo- gernd lei- se in des Dun- kels

Miriams Siegesgesang, Op. 136

A

M

Rührt_ die_ Cym- bel, schlagt_ die_ Sai- ten, lasst_ den_ Hall

B

N

Aus_ E- gyp - - - ten vor_ dem_ Vol- ke

Nachtgesang im Walde, Op. 139b
(men's chorus)

A

O

Sei uns stets ge-grüsst, O Nacht! a- ber dop- pelt hier im Wald,

E

P

Es regt in den Lau- ben des Wal- des sich schon,

Das Bild, Op. 165, No. 3

Q

Ein Mäd- chen ist's, das früh und spät mir vor der See- le schwe- bet,

An die Nachtigall, Op. 172, No. 3

R

Geuss_ nicht so laut_ der lieb-ent- flamm-ten Lie-der ton- reichen Schall

Abendbilder

S

Still be- ginnt's im Hain zu thau-en, ru- hig webt der Dämm'-rung Grau-en

Abendstern — Was weilst du ein- sam an dem Him- mel, o schö- ner Stern? — A

Abschied (Lebewohl) — Le - - be wohl, — le - be wohl, — du___ lie- ber Freund — B

Als ich sie erröthen sah — All'___ mein Wir - - - ken, all'___ mein Le- ben — C

Am Bach im Frühling — Du brachst sie nun, die kal- te Rin- de und rie-selst froh — D

Am Flusse — Ver- flie- sset, viel ge- lieb- te Lie - - der, zum Mee - - - re — E

Am See — In des See- es Wo- gen-spie-le fal- len durch den Son- nen- schein — F

An den Mond — Fül- lest wie- der Busch und Tal___ still mit Ne- bel-glanz, — G

An den Tod — Tod, du Schre-cken der Na- tur, im- mer rie-selt dei- ne Uhr; — H

An die Entfernte — So hab' ich wirk-lich dich ver-lo- ren? Bist du, o Schö-ne mir ent-floh'n, — I

An die Freunde — Im Wald, im Wald da grabt___ mich ein, ganz stil-le oh- ne Kreuz — J

An die Sonne — Kö- nig- li- che Mor - - gen- son- ne, sei___ ge - - grüsst — K

An mein Clavier — Sanf- tes Cla- vier, sanf- tes Cla- vier! wel- che Ent- zü___ ckung- en — L

Arietta, from Claudine von Villabella No. 3 (operetta) — Hin und wie - - - - der flie-gen die Pfei-le, A- mors leich - - - te — M

Auflösung — Ver- birg dich, Son- ne, denn die___ Glu- ten der Won- ne___ ver- ven - - gen — N

Aus "Heliopolis" II — Fels auf Fel- sen hin-ge-wäl- zet, fe- ster Grund und treu- er Halt; — O

Blumenlied — Es ist ein hal- bes Him- mel- reich, wenn, Pa- ra- dies-es- blu- men___ gleich, — P

Der Entfernten — Wohl denk' ich all - ent- hal - - - ben, O du Ent- fern- te, dein___ — Q

Erlkönig A — Wer rei- tet so spät durch Nacht und Wind? Es ist der Va- ter — R

B — Du lie- bes Kind, komm, geh mit mir! Gar schö- ne Spie- le — S

SCHUBERT

Erster Verlust — Ach, wer bringt die schö - - - nen Ta - ge, je - ne Ta-ge — A

Fahrt zum Hades — Der Na - chen dröhnt, Cy - pres - sen flü - - stern, horch, Gei - ster re - den — B

Des Fischers Liebesglück — Dort blin - ket durch Wei - den und win - ket ein Schim - mer — C

Fragment aus dem Aeschylus — So wird der Mann, der son - der Zwang ge - recht ist, nicht un - glück - lich sein — D

Freiwilliges Versinken — A — Wo - hin? O He - li - os! wo - hin? — E

B — Ich neh - me nicht, ich pfle - ge nur zu ge - ben — F

Frühlingslied — Die Luft ist blau, das Thal ist grün, die klei - nen Mai - en - glo - cken blühn, — G

Gebet während der Schlacht — A — Va - ter, ich ru - fe dich! Brül - lend um - wölkt mich der Dampf — H

B — Va - ter, du füh - re mich! Führ' mich zum Sie - ge, führ mich zum To - de — I

Gondelfahrer — Es tan - - zen Mond und Ster - ne den flücht' - gen Gei - - ster - reih'n — J

Gott im Frühlinge — In sei - nem schim - mern - den Ge - wand hast du den Früh - ling — K

Grenzen der Menschheit — Wenn der ur - al - te hei - li - ge Va - ter mit ge - las - se - ner Hand — L

Gretchen (from Goethe's "Faust") — Ach, nei - ge, du Schmer - zen - rei - - - - che, dein Ant - litz — M

Ihr Grab — Dort ist ihr Grab, die einst im Schmelz der Ju - gend glüh - - te — N

Im Abendrot — O, wie schön ist dei - ne Welt, Va - ter, wenn sie gol - den strah - let! — O

Im Frühling — Still sitz' ich an des Hü - gels Hang, der Him - mel ist so klar, — P

Der Jüngling am Bache — An der Quel - le sass der Kna - be, Blu - men wand er sich zum Kranz, — Q

Der Jüngling an der Quelle — Lei - - se, rie - seln - der Quell! ihr wal - len - den, flispern - den Pop - peln! — R

Der Jüngling auf dem Hügel — Ein Jüng - ling auf dem Hü - gel mit sei - nem Kum - mer sass — S

Der Jüngling und der Tod

Die Son-ne sinkt___ o könnt ich, o könnt ich mit ihr schei-den,

Der Knabe

Wenn ich nur ein Vög-lein___ wä-re, ach, wie wollt' ich lu-stig_flie-gen

Der Kreuzzug

Ein Mü-nich steht in sei-ner Zell' am Fen-ster-git-ter___ grau

Die Liebe

Freud-voll und leid-voll, ge-dan---ken-voll sein

Die Liebe

Wo weht der Lie-be ho-her Geist?___ Er weht in Blum' und___ Baum

Liebhaber in allen Gestalten

Ich wollt' ich wär' ein Fisch, so hur-tig und frisch;

Der liebliche Stern

Ihr Stern-lein, still in der Hö-he, ihr Stern-lein, spie-lend im Meer,___

Liebe schwärmt auf allen Wegen, from Claudine von Villabella (operetta) Act I No. 6

Lie-be schwärmt auf al-len We-gen: Treu-e wohnt_für sich_al-lein

Liebeslauschen

Hier un-ten steht ein Rit-ter in hel-len Mon-den-strahl,

Lied der Mignon (Nur wer die Sehnsucht kennt) (two different settings)

Nur wer die Sehn-sucht kennt weiss___ was___ ich___ lei-de!

Nur wer die Sehn-sucht kennt weiss was___ ich___ lei-de!

Litanei auf das Fest "Aller Seelen"

Ruh'n in Frie-den al-----le See------len,

Das Mädchen

Wie_ so in-nig, möcht'_ich sa-gen,sich_ der Mei-ne mir_er-giebt

Die Männer sind méchant

Du sag-test mir es, Mut-ter: Er ist ein Spring ins feld

Minnelied

Hol-der klingt_ der Vo-gel-sang, wenn die En-gel-rei-ne,

Die Nacht

Du___ ver-störst uns nicht, o Nacht! Sieh, wir trin-ken

Nachtgesang

O___ gieb vom wei-chen Pfüh-le träu-mend, ein halb___ Ge-hör

Nachtviolen

Nacht-vi-o-len, Nacht-vi-o-len! dun-kle Au-gen, see-len-vol-le,

Wiederschein — Tom lehnt har-rend auf der Brü-cke, die Ge-liebte___ säumt, — A

Der Winterabend — Es ist so still, so heim-lich um mich, die Sonn' ist___ un-ter, — B

Der zürnende Barde — Wer wagt's, wer wagt's, wer wagt's, wer will mir die Lei-er zer-bre- chen, — C

SCHULTZ, Johann Abraham Peter (1747-1800)

Am Sylvester-Abend — Des Jah-res letz-te Stun- de- er-tönt mit ern-stem Schlag — E

SCHUMANN, Clara (1819-1896)

Liebst du um Schönheit, Op. 37, No. 4 — Liebst du um Schön-heit O nicht mich lie- be! — G

SCHUMANN, Robert (1810-1856)

Der Contrabandiste (Spanish Songs) — Ich bin___ der Con-tra-ban-di-ste, Weiss wohl___ Respect mir zu schaffen, — I

Morgens steh ich auf und frage, Op. 24, No. 1 — Mor-gens steh' ich auf und fra- ge: Kommt fein's Lieb-chen heut'? — J

Es treibt mich hin, No. 2 — Es treibt mich hin, es treibt mich her! Noch we-ni-ge Stun-den, — K

Ich wandelte unter den Bäumen, No. 3 — Ich wan-del-te un-ter den Bäu-men mit mei-nem Gram___ al-lein — L

Lieb' Liebchen, No. 4 — Lieb' Lieb-chen, leg's Händ-chen auf's Her- ze mein; — M

Schöne Wiege meiner Leiden, No. 5 — Schö- ne Wie- - ge mei- ner Lei- den, schö-nes Grab-mal — N

Mit Myrthen und Rosen, No. 9 — Mit Myr-then___ und Ro- sen, lieb-lich und hold, — O

Myrthen, Op. 25, No. 1 Widmung A — Du mei-ne See- le, du mein Herz, du mei-ne Wonn' o du mein Schmerz, — P

B — Du bist die Ruh', du bist___ der Frie-den, du bist vom Him-mel — Q

No. 2 Freisinn — Lasst mich nur___ auf mei-nem Sat-tel gel - - - ten! — R

No. 3 Der Nussbaum — Es grü- net ein Nuss-baum vor dem Haus, duf- tig, luf- tig brei-tet — S

SCHUMANN

Myrthen, Op. 25,

No. 4 Jemand
Mein Herz ist be- trübt, ich sag' es nicht, mein__ Herz ist be- trübt__

No. 7 Die Lotosblume
Die Lo- tos- blu- me äng- stigt sich vor der Son- ne Pracht,

No. 8 Talismane
Got- tes ist der O- ri- ent! Got- tes ist der Oc- ci- dent!

No. 9 Lied der Suleika
Wie, mit in- nig- stem Be- ha- gen, Lied, em- pfind' ich dei- nen Sinn!

No. 11 Lieder der Braut
Mut- ter,__ Mut- ter! Glau- be nicht, weil ich ihn lieb' al_____ so sehr,

No. 12
Lass mich ihm am Bu- sen han- gen, Mut- ter, Mut- ter!

No. 14 Hoch- ländisches Wiegenlied
Schla- fe, sü- - - - sser klei- ner Do- - - - - - nald;

No. 15 Aus den hebräischen Gesängen
Mein Herz ist schwer Auf! von der Wand die Lau- te,

No. 17 Zwei Venetianische Lieder
Leis' ru- dern hier, mein Gon- - - - do- lier, leis', leis'!

No. 18
Wenn durch die Pi- a- zet- - ta die A- bend- luft weht,

No. 21 Was will die einsame Thräne?
Was will die ein- sa- me Thrä- ne? sie trübt mir ja__ den Blick.

No. 23 Im Westen
Ich schau ü- ber Forth, hin- ü- ber nach Nord: was hel- fen mir Nord

No. 24 Du bist wie eine Blume
Du bist__ wie ei- ne Blu- me, so hold und schön__ und rein;

No. 25 Aus den östlichen Rosen
Ich sen- de ei- - - nen Gruss wie Duft der Ro- sen,

No. 26 Zum Schluss
Hier in die- sen erd be- klomm- nen Lüf- ten, wo__ die Weh- mut taut,

Was soll ich sagen! Op. 27, No. 3
Mein Aug' ist trüb', mein Mund ist stumm, du heissest mich re- den,

Jasminenstrauch, No. 4
Grün ist der Jas- mi- nen- strauch A- bends ein- - ge- schla- fen.

Der Page, Op. 30, No. 2
Da ich nun ent- sa- gen müs- sen Al- lem, was mein Herz

Der Hidalgo, No. 3
Es ist so süss zu scher- zen mit Lie- dern und mit Her- zen

Der Hidalgo, Op. 30, No. 3
Die Schö- nen von Se- vil- la, mit Fä- cher-und Man- til- la,

Die Kartenlegerin, Op. 31, No. 2
Schlief die Mut-ter end-lich ein ü- ber ih- rer Haus- po-stil- le?

Liebesgarten, Op. 34, No. 1
Die Lie- be ist ein Ro - - sen-strauch, wo blüht er, wo blüht er?

Unter'm Fenster, No. 3
Wer ist vor mei- ner Kam- mer-thür? Ich bin es, ich bin es!

Familien-Gemälde, No. 4
Gross- va- ter und Gross- mut- ter, die sas- sen im Gar- ten- hag,

Lust der Sturmnacht, Op. 35, No. 1
Wenn durch Berg' und Tha - - le drau- ssen Re- gen schau- ert,

Stirb, Lieb' und Freud, No. 2
Zu Augs- burg steht ein ho - - - - - hes Haus

Wanderlied, No. 3
Wohl- auf! noch ge-trun- ken den fun- kelnden Wein! A- de nun, ihr Lie- ben,

Erstes Grün, No. 4
Du jun- ges Grün, du fri-sches Gras, wie man-ches Herz durch dich ge- nas,

Auf das Trinkglas eines verstorbenen Freundes, No. 6
Du herr- lich Glas, nun stehst du leer, Glas, das er oft

Wanderung, No. 7
Wohl- auf und frisch ge- wan- dert in's un- be- kann- te Land!

Stille Liebe, No. 8
Könnt' ich dich in Lie- dern prei- sen, säng ich dir das läng- ste Lied,

Frage, No. 9
Wärst du nicht, heil' ger A- bend-schein! wärst du nicht,

Stille Thränen, No. 10
Du bist vom Schlaf er- stan- den und wan- delst durch die Au'

Wer machte dich so krank? No. 11
Dass du so krank ge- wor- den, wer hat es denn ge- macht?

Alte Laute, No. 12
Hörst du den Vo- gel sin- gen? Siehst du den Blü-then-baum?

Sonntags am Rhein, Op. 36, No. 1
Des Sonn- tags in der Mor- gen-stund' wie wan-dert's sich so schön

Ständchen, No. 2
Lieb- chen, was zö- gerst Du? Lieb- chen, was zö- gerst Du?

An den Sonnenschein, No. 4
O Son- nen-schein, o Son- nen-schein! wie scheinst du mir in's Herz hinein,

Dichters Genesung, Op. 36, No. 5

Und wie- der hatt' ich der Schön- sten ge- dacht, die nur in Träu- men

A

Liebesbotshaft, No. 6

Wol- ken die ihr nach O- sten eilt, wo die Ei- ne, die Mei- ne,

B

Der Himmel hat eine Thräne geweint, Op. 37, No. 1 (Robt. & Clara)

Der Him- mel hat ei- ne Thrä- ne ge- weint, die hat sich in's Meer

C

Er ist gekommen, No. 2 (Robert & Clara Schumann)

Er ist ge-kom- men in Sturm und Re- gen, ihm schlug be-klommen

D

O ihr Herren, o ihr werthen, No. 3 (Robt. & Clara S.)

O ihr Her- ren, o ihr wer- then gros- sen rei - - - chen Her-ren all!

E

Flügel! Flügel! um zu fliegen, No. 8 (Robt. & Clara S.)

Flü- gel! Flü- gel! um zu flie- gen ü- ber Berg und Thal

F

So wahr die Sonne scheinet, No. 12 (Robt. & Clara S.)

So wahr die Son- ne schei- net, so wahr die Wol- ke wei- net,

G

Liederkreis, Op. 39, No. 1 In der Fremde

Aus der Hei- math hin- ter den Blit- zen rot da kom- men die Wol- ken her

H

No. 2 Intermezzo

Dein Bild- niss wun- der- se- lig hab' ich im Her- zens- grund,

I

No. 3 Waldesgespräch

Es ist schon spät es ist schon kalt, was reit'st du ein-sam

J

No. 4 Die Stille

Es weiss und räth es doch kei- ner, wie mir so wohl ist, so wohl!

K

No. 5 Mondnacht

Es war, als hätt' der Him- mel die Er- de still ge-küsst,

L

No. 6 Schöne Fremde

Es rau-schen die Wi-pfel und schau-ern, als mach- ten zu die-ser Stund'

M

No. 7 Auf einer Burg

Ein-ge-schla- fen auf der Lau- er o- ben ist der al- te Rit- ter,

N

No. 8 In der Fremde

Ich hor die Bäch-lein rauschen im Wal- de her und hin,

O

No. 9 Wehmuth

Ich kann wohl manch-mal sin- gen als ob ich fröh- lich sei;

P

No. 10 Zwielicht

Dämm'- rung will die Flü- gel spreiten, schau-rig rüh- ren sich die Bäu- me

Q

No. 11 Im Walde

Es zog ei-ne Hoch-zeit den Berg ent-lang, ich hör-te die Vö- gel

R

No. 12 Frühlingsnacht

Ü- ber'm Gar-ten durch die Lüf-te hört' ich Wan-der-vö- gel zieh'n,

S

Märzveilchen, Op. 40, No. 1
Der Him- mel wölbt sich rein und blau, der Reif stellt Blu - men

Muttertraum, No. 2
Die Mut- ter be- tet her- zig, und schaut ent- zückt

Der Soldat, No. 3
Es geht bei ge-däm- pfter Trom-meln Klang. Wie weit noch die Stät- te,

Frauenliebe und Leben (cycle), Op. 42, No. 1
Seit ich ihn ge- se- hen, glaub ich blind zu sein,

No. 2
Er, der herr-lich-ste von al- len, wie so mil- de, wie_ so gut

No. 3
Ich kann's nicht fassen, nicht glau-ben, es hat ein Traum mich be-rückt,_

No. 4
Du Ring an mei-nem Fin- - ger, mein_ gol-de-nes Rin- ge- lein,

No. 5
Helft mir, ihr Schwes-tern freundlich mich schmücken, dient_ der Glück- li- chen

No. 6
Sü - - - sser Freund, du bli-ckest mich ver-wun- dert an

No. 7
An mei-nem Her- zen, an mei- ner Brust, du mei- ne Won- ne,

No. 8
Nun hast du mir den er-sten Schmerz ge- tan, der a- ber traf

Der Schatzgräber, Op. 45, No. 1
Wenn al- le Wäl- der schlie-fen, er an zu gra-ben hub,

Frühlingsfahrt, No. 2
Es zo-gen zwei rüst-'ge Ge-sel-len zum_ er-sten mal_ von Haus,

Dichterliebe (cycle), Op. 48, No. 1
Im wun-der schö-nen Mo-nat Mai, als al- le Knos- - pen spran-gen

No. 2
Aus mei nen Thrä-nen sprie-ssen viel blü-hen-de Blu-men her- vor,

No. 3
Die Ro- se, die Li- lie, die Tau- be, die Son- ne,

No. 4
Wenn ich in dei- ne Au-gen seh' so schwin-det all' mein Leid

No. 5
Ich will mei- ne See - - le tau-chen in den Kelch der Li-lie hin- ein;

No. 6
Im Rhein, im hei- li- gen Stro- me, de spie-gelt sich in den Well'n,

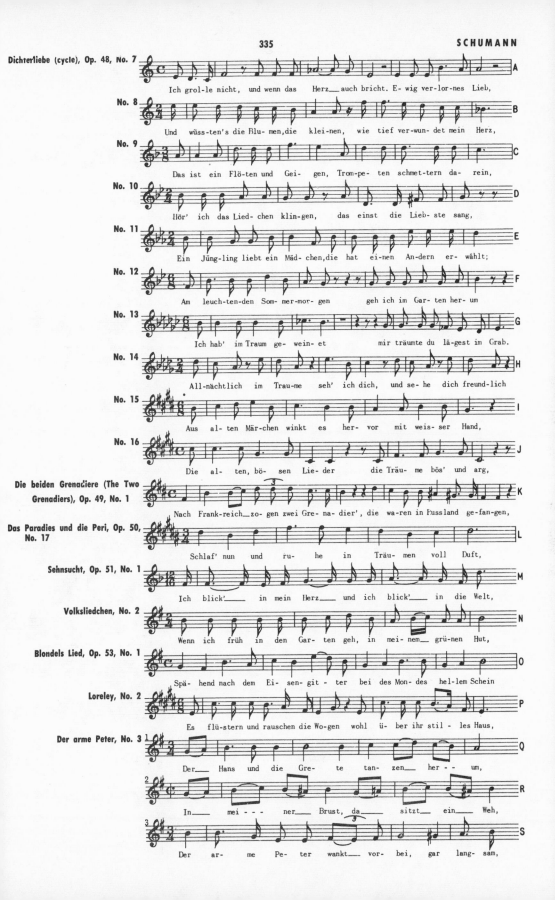

Dichterliebe (cycle), Op. 48, No. 7 — A
Ich grol-le nicht, und wenn das Herz___ auch bricht. E- wig ver-lor-nes Lieb,

No. 8 — B
Und wüss-ten's die Blu-men,die klei-nen, wie tief ver-wun-det mein Herz,

No. 9 — C
Das ist ein Flö-ten und Gei-gen, Trom-pe-ten schmet-tern da- rein,

No. 10 — D
Hör' ich das Lied-chen klin-gen, das einst die Lieb-ste sang,

No. 11 — E
Ein Jüng-ling liebt ein Mäd-chen,die hat ei-nen An-dern er- wählt;

No. 12 — F
Am leuch-ten-den Som-mer-mor-gen geh ich im Gar-ten her- um

No. 13 — G
Ich hab' im Traum ge-wein- et mir träumte du lä-gest im Grab.

No. 14 — H
All-nächt-lich im Trau-me seh' ich dich, und se- he dich freund-lich

No. 15 — I
Aus al-ten Mär-chen winkt es her- vor mit weis-ser Hand,

No. 16 — J
Die al-ten, bö-sen Lie-der die Träu- me bös' und arg,

Die beiden Grenadiere (The Two Grenadiers), Op. 49, No. 1 — K
Nach Frank-reich___ zo-gen zwei Gre-na-dier', die wa-ren in Russland ge-fan-gen,

Das Paradies und die Peri, Op. 50, No. 17 — L
Schlaf' nun und ru- he in Träu-men voll Duft,

Sehnsucht, Op. 51, No. 1 — M
Ich blick'___ in mein Herz___ und ich blick'___ in die Welt,

Volksliedchen, No. 2 — N
Wenn ich früh in den Gar-ten geh, in mei-nem___ grü-nen Hut,

Blondels Lied, Op. 53, No. 1 — O
Spä- hend nach dem Ei-sen-git-ter bei des Mon-des hel-lem Schein

Loreley, No. 2 — P
Es flü-stern und rauschen die Wo-gen wohl ü- ber ihr stil- les Haus,

Der arme Peter, No. 3 1 — Q
Der___ Hans und die Gre-te tan-zen___ her- - um,

2 — R
In mei- - - ner Brust, da sitzt ein___ Weh,

3 — S
Der ar- me Pe- ter wankt___ vor-bei, gar lang-sam,

Belsatzar, Op. 57

Die Mit-ter-nacht zog nä-her schon; in stum-mer Ruh' lag Ba-by-lon

A

Die Soldatenbraut, Op. 64, No. 1

Ach, wenn's nur der Kö-nig auch wüsst', wie wa-cker mein Schätze-lein ist!

B

Das verlassne Mägdelein, No. 2

Früh wann die Häh-ne krah'n eh' die Stern-lein schwin-den,

C

Tragödie, No. 3

1.

Ent-flieh' mit mir und sei mein Weib und ruh' an mei-nem Her-zen aus!

D

2.

Es__ fiel ein Reif in der Früh-lingsnacht,er fiel auf die zar - - - ten Blau

E

Die Rose stand im Thau, Op. 65, No.1
(male chorus)

Die Ro-se stand im Thau,___ es wa-ren Per-len grau.

F

Melancholie, Op. 74, No. 6

Wann, wann er-scheint der Mor-gen, wann denn, wann denn!

H

Geständniss, No. 7

Al- so lieb' ich euch, Ge- lieb- te, dass mein Herz es nicht mag wa- gen,

H

Im Walde, Op. 75, No. 2 (chorus)

Es zog ei- ne Hoch-zeit den Berg ent- lang, den Berg ent- lang

I

Geisternähe, Op. 77, No. 3

Was weht um mei- ne Schlä- fe wie lau- e Früh-ling- luft,

J

Stiller Vorwurf, No. 4

In ein-sa- men Stun- den drängt Weh- muth sich auf,

K

Aufträge, No. 5

Nicht so schnel-le,nicht so schnelle! wart' ein wenig, kleine Wel-le!

L

Er und Sie, Op. 78, No. 2

Seh' ich in das stil- le Thal, wo im Son- nen-schei- ne

M

Ich denke dein, No. 3

3

Ich den- ke dein,wenn mir der Son- ne Schim-mer vom Mee- re strahlt;

N

Wiegenlied, No. 4

Schlaf', Kind-lein, schlaf, wie du schläfst,so bist du brav!

O

Liederalbum für die Jugend, Op. 79,
No. 1 Der Abendstern

Du lieb- li- cher Stern, du leuch- test so fern,

P

No. 4 Frühlingsgruss

So sei ge-grüsst viel tau-send-mal, hol- der, hol- der Früh- ling!

Q

No. 7a Zigeunerliedchen

Un- ter__ die Sol- da - - ten__ ist ein Zi- geu- ner-bub' ge- gan-gen,

R

No. 7b Jeden Morgen

Je- den Mor- gen, in der Frü- he, wenn mich weckt das Ta- ges- licht,

S

SCHUMANN

Drei Gesänge (Hebrew Melodies) Op. 95, No. 1 Die Tochter Jephtas
Da die Hei-math, o Va-ter, da Gott von der Toch-ter — A

No. 2 An den Mond
Schlaf-lo-ser Son-ne, me-lan-chol-scher Stern! Dein thrän-en-voller Strahl — B

No. 3 Dem Helden
Dein Tag ist aus, dein Ruhm fing an, es preist des Volks Ge-sang — C

Nachtlied, Op. 96, No. 1
Ü-ber al-len Gi-pfeln ist Ruh', in al-len Wipfeln spü-rest du — D

Schneeglöckchen, No. 2
Die Son-ne sah die Er-de an, es ging ein mil-der Wind — E

Ihre Stimme, No. 3
Lass' tief in dir mich le-sen, ver-hehl auch dies mir nicht, — F

Himmel und Erde, No. 5
Wie der Bäu-me küh-ne Wip-fel zu des Lich-tes Hö-hen — G

Nur wer die Sehnsucht kennt, Op. 98a, No. 3
Nur wer die Sehn-sucht kennt, weiss was ich lei-de, — H

Wer nie sein Brot mit Thränen ass, No. 4
Wer nie sein Brot mit Thränen ass, wer nie die kum-mer-vol-len Näch-te — I

Heiss' mich nicht reden, No. 5
Heiss' mich nicht re-den, heiss' mich schweigen denn mein Ge-heim-nis — J

Wer sich der Einsamkeit ergiebt, No. 6
Wer sich der Ein-sam-keit er-giebt ach! der ist bald al-lein; — K

So lasst mich scheinen, No. 9
So lasst mich scheinen bis ich wer-de, zieht mir das weisse Kleid nicht aus! — L

An die Türen will ich schleichen, No. 8
An die Tü-ren will ich schlei-chen, still und sittsam will ich stehn, — M

Liebster, deine Worte stehlen, Op. 101, No. 2
Lieb-ster, dei-ne Wor-te steh-len aus dem Bu-sen mir das Herz — N

Mein schöner Stern, ich bitte dich, No. 4
Mein schö-ner Stern! ich bit-te dich, o las-se du dein heitres Licht — O

O Freund, mein Schirm, mein Schutz, No. 6
O Freund, mein Schirm, mein Schutz! o Freund mein Schmuck, mein Putz! — P

An den Abendstern, Op. 103, No. 4
Schweb' em-por am Him-mel, schö-ner A-bend-stern — Q

Viel Glück zur Reise, Schwalben, Op. 104, No. 2
Viel Glück zur Rei-se, Schwalben! ihr eilt, ein lan-ger Zug, — R

Der Zeisig, No. 4
Wir sind ja, Kind, im Mai-e, wirf Buch und Heft von dir — S

SCHUMANN

Die Spinnerin, Op. 107, No. 4

Auf dem Dorf' in den Spinn stu-ben sind lus--tig die Mäd-chen. A

Nänie, Op. 114 (women's chorus)

Un- ter den ro-ten Blu- men schlum-me-re, schlum- me-re, B

Senkt die Nacht den sanf-ten Fit- tig nie-der tönt der Zi- ther C

O bli-cke,wenn den Sinn dir will die Welt ver-wir-ren D

Der Husar, tra-ra! Op. 117, No. 1

Der Hu-sar, Tra- ra! was ist die Ge- fahr? Sein herz-lieb-ster Schatz E

Da liegt der Feinde gestreckte Schaar, No. 4

Da liegt_ der Feinde ge-stre-ckte Schaar, sie liegt in ihrem blutroten Blut F

Frühlingslust, Op. 125, No. 2

Nun ste-hen die Ro-sen in Blü- the, da wirft die Lie- be ein Netz-lein aus, G

Die Meerfee, No. 3

Hel- - le Sil-ber-glöck- lein klin- gen aus der Luft vom Meer; H

Jung Volkers Lied, No. 4

Und die mich trug im Mut-ter-arm, und die mich schwang_ in Kis-sen, I

Dein Angesicht, Op. 127, No. 2

Dein An- ge-sicht,so lieb und schön, das hab' ich jungst im Traum ge-seh'n, J

Es leuchtet meine Liebe, No. 3

Es leuch-tet mei-ne Lie--be in ih--rer dun-keln Pracht, K

Tief im Herzen trag' ich Pein, Op. 138, No. 2

Tief____ im Her- zen trag' ich Pein, muss nach aus-sen stille sein, L

O wie lieblich ist das Mädchen, No. 3

O wie lieb-lich ist das Mäd-chen wie so schön und voll An-muth___ M

Romanze, No. 5

Flu- - ten rei-cher Eb- ro, blü- - - hen-der U- fer, N

Weh, wie zornig ist das Mädchen, No. 7

Weh, wie zor- nig ist das Mädchen, weh,wie zornig, weh,weh! O

Hoch, hoch sind die Berge, No. 8

Hoch, hoch sind die Ber- ge und steil ist der Pfad, P

Provenzalisches Lied, Op. 139, No. 4

In dem Ta- len der Pro- ven- ce ist___ der_ Min-ne-sang entsprossen, Q

SCHÜTZ, Heinrich (1858-1672)

Bringt her dem Herren

Bringt her dem Her- ren,bringt her dem Her- ren,bringt her dem Her- - ren S

SCOTT, Lady John (Alicia Ann Scott) (1810-1900)

SCOTT, Cyril (1879-   )

Blackbird's Song, Op. 52, No. 3
By permission of Galaxy Music Corporation,
N. Y., copyright by Elkin & Co., Ltd.

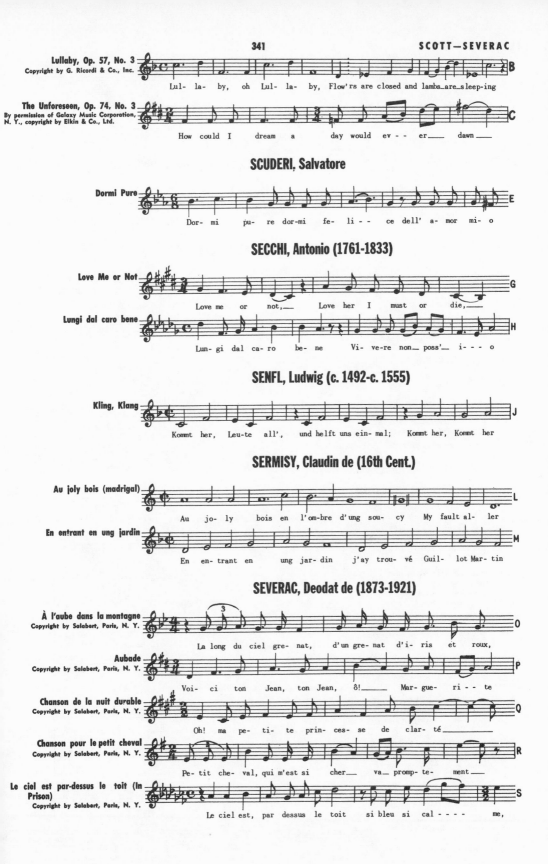

Lullaby, Op. 57, No. 3
Copyright by G. Ricordi & Co., Inc.
Lul- la- by, oh Lul- la- by, Flow'rs are closed and lambs are sleep-ing

The Unforeseen, Op. 74, No. 3
By permission of Galaxy Music Corporation, N. Y., copyright by Elkin & Co., Ltd.
How could I dream a day would ev - - er dawn

SCUDERI, Salvatore

Dormi Pure
Dor- mi pu- re dor-mi fe- li - - ce dell' a- mor mi- o

SECCHI, Antonio (1761-1833)

Love Me or Not
Love me or not, Love her I must or die,

Lungi dal caro bene
Lun- gi dal ca- ro be- ne Vi- ve-re non poss' i - - o

SENFL, Ludwig (c. 1492-c. 1555)

Kling, Klang
Kommt her, Leu-te all', und helft uns ein- mal; Kommt her, Kommt her

SERMISY, Claudin de (16th Cent.)

Au joly bois (madrigal)
Au jo- ly bois en l'om-bre d'ung sou- cy My fault al- ler

En entrant en ung jardin
En en- trant en ung jar- din j'ay trou- vé Guil- lot Mar- tin

SEVERAC, Deodat de (1873-1921)

À l'aube dans la montagne
Copyright by Salabert, Paris, N. Y.
La long du ciel gre- nat, d'un gre- nat d'i- ris et roux,

Aubade
Copyright by Salabert, Paris, N. Y.
Voi- ci ton Jean, ton Jean, ô! Mar- gue- ri - te

Chanson de la nuit durable
Copyright by Salabert, Paris, N. Y.
Oh! ma pe- ti- te prin- ces- se de clar- té

Chanson pour le petit cheval
Copyright by Salabert, Paris, N. Y.
Pe- tit che- val, qui m'est si cher va promp-te- ment

Le ciel est par-dessus le toit (In Prison)
Copyright by Salabert, Paris, N. Y.
Le ciel est, par dessus le toit si bleu si cal - - - - me,

Les Hiboux

Ma poupée chérie
Copyright by Salabert, Paris, N. Y.

SHOSTAKOVICH, Dmitri (1906-)

United Nations
Copyright 1946
Leeds Music Corp., N. Y.
Used by permission.

SIBELIUS, Jean (1865-)

Våren Flyktar Hastigt (Spring is Fleeting), Op. 13, No. 4
Copyright by Oliver Ditson Co.
Used by permission

Vilse (Astray) (Verirrt), Op. 17, No. 4
By permission Associated Music Publishers, Inc.

Lastu lainehilla (Driftwood), No. 7
By permission Associated Music Publishers, Inc.

Svarta rosor (Black Roses), Op. 36, No. 1
By permission Associated Music Publishers, Inc.

Säf, säf, susa (Schilfrohr, säus'le!), No. 4
By permission Associated Music Publishers, Inc.

Den första Kyssen (The First Kiss), Op. 37, No. 1
By permission Associated Music Publishers, Inc.

Var det en dröm? (Was it a dream?), No. 4
By permission Associated Music Publishers, Inc.

Tuol Laulaa Neitonen (A Maiden Yonder Sings), Op. 50, No. 3
Copyright by Oliver Ditson Co.
Used by permission

O wert thou here (Aus banger Brust), No. 4
By permission Associated Music Publishers, Inc.

The Silent Town (Die stille Stadt), No. 5
By permission Associated Music Publishers, Inc.

Kom nu hit, död (Come away, Death), Op. 60, No. 1 (Shakespeare)
By permission Associated Music Publishers, Inc.

Vår förnimmelser (Coming of Spring), Op. 86, No. 1
Copyright by Hansen, Copenhagen

Blåseppan (The Anemone), Op. 88, No. 1
Copyright by Hansen, Copenhagen

Norden (From the North), Op. 90, No. 1
Copyright by Hansen, Copenhagen

SIBELLA, Gabriele

La Girometta (arr.)
Copyright 1919, G. Schirmer, Inc.

Chi t'ha fat- to quel- le scar- pet- te che ti stan si ben

Me l'ha fat- te lo mio A- mo- re,____ me l'ha fat- te lo mio A- mo- re

SIECZYNSKI, Dr. Rudolf

Wien, du Stadt meiner Träume

Mein Herz und mein Sinn schwärmt stets nur für Wien

Wien, Wien, nur du al- lein sollst stets die Stadt meiner Träu- me

SILCHER, Friedrich

Aennchen von Tharau

Aenn- chen von Tha- rau ist, die mir ge- fällt, sie ist mein Le- ben,

Die Lorelei

Ich weiss nicht was soll es be- deu- ten dass ich so trau- rig bin____

SINDING, Christian (1856-1941)

Moderen Synger (The mother sings)

Gret- chen lies in her gloom- y bed in the wet, wet mold

Der Skreg un Fugl (There cried a bird)

There cried____ a bird in its lone- - - - - some flight

Sylvelin, Op. 55, No. 1
Copyright 1912, G. Schirmer, Inc.

O Syl- ve- lin, God's own blessing be on you the whole day through!

SJÖBERG, C.

Tonerna

Tan- ke, hvars stri- der blott nat- ten ser____ To- ner,____

SJÖGREN, Emil (1853-1918)

Lehn' deine Wang', Op. 16, No. 5

Lehn' die- ne Wang' an mei- ne Wang' dann fliessen die Thrä- nen

SMETANA, Bedrich (1824-1884)

OPERAS

The Bartered Bride Act I
Opening Chorus

Seht am Strauch die Knos- - pen___ sprin- gen! Hört die mun- tern Vö- gel____

The Bartered Bride Act I — Duet A

Gern ja will ich dir ver- trau- en, gläu- big bli- cken auf zu dir,

Mit der Mut- ter sank zu Gra- - be mein gan- zes jun- ges Glück

O Du gu- ter, ar- mer Kna- be, wie klang_ ich_ um Dein Ge- schick

Nun in Lust_ und_ Lei- - de, nun in Schmerz und Freu- de sind vereint

Al- les ist so gut wie rich- tig, das Fi- ne ist nur wich- tig

Ge- kom- men_ wär' er mit mir wie_ ger- ne doch zar- te Rück- sicht,

Polka (Finale) A

Durch die Reih- en hin zu flie- gen! Sich zu Zwei- en an- zu schmie- gen!

B

Ging es, wie es uns ge- fällt tanz- - - te mit die gan- ze Welt

Act II Drinking Chorus

Wie schäumst du in den Glä- sern, ed- ler Ger- sten- saft,

Sextet

Noch ein Weil- chen, Ma- rie, be- denk' es Dir

Stuttering Song

Theu- - - - theu- - - - - - - theu- theu- ren Sohn, spra- - spra- - - - sprach Müt- ter- lein,

Ich weiss Euch ei- nen lie- ben Schatz den man- cher schon be- gehrt,

Duet A

Komm, mein Söhn- chen, auf ein Wort! Will dir was ver- trau- - en

B

Wer in Lieb' entbrannt, hält aus Un- ver- stand Wei- ber für En- gel.

Weiss ich doch Ei- ne, die hat Du- ka- ten, hat Du- ka- ten

Es muss ge- lin- gen! Al- les soll nach Wunsch und Wil- len ge- hen

Act III Duet

Al- les geht am Schnür- chen, da man Dich nicht quält

Wie fremd und todt ist Al- les um- her,

Mein lie- ber Schatz, nun_ auf- ge- passt! Ich geb' Dir was zu hö- ren,

SMETANA

The Bartered Bride Act III
Ge- seg- net, ge- seg- net, wer liebt und auch ver- traut!

Finale
Kom- men wir ger- ne, so kom- men wir gleich, gleich, gleich,

So ist's recht, es freut uns Al- le, so ist's recht,

Dalibor Act II Love duet
Ta du- še ta tou- ha, to srd- ce, ten čar tot' lás- ky mé

Duet
Ó nev- ý- slov- né š tě- sti lá - - - - - - sky

The Devil's Wall (Certova Sténa) Act I
Stast- ná vím on přijde dnes přec mě vsr- déč- ku cos trá- nu

Ciž poz- by- la jsi ve mne ví- ry? A kdy- by můj byl kraj ten sí- rý

Tak věč- ně k to- bě ĩnout rtem na rtu spo- či nout

Jen je- di- na- mě zě- ny krá- sna tvář tak do- ja- la

Act II
Kam prch- nout, kam prch- nout před je- jím tak sladkym o- brazem?

Ach, žie se to- mu při- vy- ka Mně se to zvot- lo s nejkrásně jším

Act III
Ti- se krad- me pře- po- zor- ně špe- hům chy- trým pro- ne- snáz,

O Bo- že lá- sky Vté - - to hrů- zné chvi- li mi ro- stou kří- dla

The Kiss Act I Duet
Für e- wig ver- eint treu in Lie- be ist un- ser heisses flehen.

Cradle Song
Schla- fe mein Kind- lein, schlaf' ein, schla- fe ein,

Wie hell am Him- mel die Ster- ne auch steh'n, wie sanft im Mond- licht

Act II Smugglers' Chorus
Lei- se, auf- ge- passt oh- ne Ruh noch Rast; lauscht im Mor- gen- wind

If I knew how to wipe out my fault
Zu süh- nen mei- ne gro- sse Schuld, will ich die Ge- lieb - - - te

Duet
Ach, ar- mer Freund, früh starb dein Gluck, schwer kehrt, was man ver- lor, zu- rück!

The Kiss Act II Duet

Wir su-chen sie wir fin-den sie, du rufst die ganze Nach-bar-schaft

Trio

Ach! Ste-fan schel-tet mei-ne Thor-heit nur! Längst nagt am Her-zen mir

Lark Song

Lass dein Lied er-schal--len dass der Mor-gen neu er-wacht!

Libusa Act I

Bo-ho-vé věč-ní ta-mo nad o-bla-ky vmi-lo-sti shlí-žejte

Act II Scene I

A toz, když vbla-hé tou-ze lá-sky on plal

Za-po-li to-va-ni tě___ pro-sim, za je-di-ný,

Scene III

Již pla-ne slun-ce bla-hý mí-ru sen se vzná-si

A-no, mar-ně vzdo-ru-ji tvé mo-ci lá--sko svo-tá

Ó vy lí-py, o-vy lí-py! pra-ot-cův ru-ká vsa-di-la vás

Act III Scene V

Hoj! tvr-dý Vy-šchrad bud stokrát ví----tan!

Bo------ho-vé moc-ní!___ Za ten-to šta-stný den dik bu-diž vám!

Love Duet from The Brandenburgers
in Bohemia Act II

Ó jak bla-há krás-ná ta-to chir--le ó jak stast-né to

The Secret (Tajemství) Act I

O slyš to pře-da-le-ký svě-te, jak v ob-ci ka-li-na nám kve-te!

Act II

Nač o tom dá-le bá-dat? též ra-dost' a bla-ho chci znát!

Ven, ven, ven! ven z po-dze-mi ven! ó zla-tá ré-vo, chme-li!

Duet

Vše-cko je tvo-je, Vše-cko je tvo-je ze sr-dce tvé-ho

Kdy sly-ším jen tvé-ho ro-hu pě-ni, tvé pu-ský jen rá-nu,

Ó, kdy-by on mé tak byl me-lo-val, tak kdy-by on byl

Jsem vo-ják, jsem vo-ják stál jsem vbi-tvách pro-ti Pru-su

First Songs 4. Vyzvání (Invitation)

Pojď mil- ko, Pojď mil- ko! Hle sklá-ni se les ktobě néž

5. Jaro lásky

Die - ses Sai-ten-spiel der Brust, das__ du hast so reich be- sai- tet

SMITH, John Christopher (1712-1795)

No more dams I'll make for fish

No more dams__ I'll make__ for fish; Nor fetch fir - ing

SPEAKS, Oley (1876-   )

Morning
Copyright 1910, G. Schirmer, Inc.

Nev- er star was in the sky, Win- ter winds went wail-ing by,

Morn- ing on the ho- ly hills, Mead-ows that en- fold the rills

On the Road to Mandalay
Copyright 1907, G. Schirmer, Inc.

By the old Moul-mein Pa- go- da, look- in' east- ward__ to the sea

Come you back to Man-da- lay, Where the old Flo-til- la lay

Sylvia
Copyright 1914, G. Schirmer, Inc.

Syl- via's hair is like the night, Touched with glancing star- ry beams

To You

Some- where, I know, from the blue of the sky

SPILMAN, James E.

Flow gently, sweet Afton

Flow gen- tly, sweet__ Af- ton, a- mang thy green braes

SPOHR, Ludwig (1784-1859)

As pants the Hart

As pants the Hart for cool- ing streams When heat- ed in the chase,

The Last Judgment Part I No. 12

Lord God of Heav'n and Earth, we a- dore_____ thee

Part II No. 19

Blest are the de- part- ed Who in the Lord are sleep- - ing

Rose, softly blooming

Rose soft- ly bloom- ing formed__ to__ al - - lure

SPONTINI, Gaspard (1774-1851)

La Vestale (opera)   Act I

Dans   le   sein   d'un   a-mi   fi-dè---le

L'a-mour   est   un   mon-stre,est   un   mons-tre   bar-ba-re

O   ma   fil-le, ma   fil---le,   ton   coeur   s'é-ga-re

Act II

Toi   que   j'im-plo-re   a-vec   ef-froi   re-dou-ta-ble   dé-es--se

O   Nu--me   tu-te-lar   degl'   in-fe-li-ci,

Act III

Toi   que   je   lais-se   sur   la   ter----re,   mor-tel

STANFORD, C. Villers (1852-1924)

A Carol of Bells   A

Ring,   Christ-mas   bells   of   Lon-don,   Swing   wild-ly   with   a   will

B

"Greet-ings   to   all!"   Boom   the   Bells   of   St.   Paul;

Cavalier Songs   No. 1

Kent-ish   Sir   Byng   stood   for   his   King,   bid-ding   the   crop-head-ed

No. 2

King   Charles!   and   who'll   do   him   right   now!   King   Charles!

No. 3

Boot,   sad-dle,   to   horse   and   a-way!   Res-cue   my   Cas-tle

Coelos ascendit hodie, Op. 38
By permission Boosey & Hawkes, Inc.,
copyright owners

Coe-los   as-cen-dit   ho-di-e   Je-sus   Christus   Rex   glo-ri-ae

Father O'Flynn

Of   priests   we   can   of-fer   a   charm-in'   va-ri-e-ty

**Oh! Breathe not his Name (Air, the
Brown Maid)**

Oh   breathe   not   his   name,   let   it   sleep   in   the   shade,

A Soft Day, Op. 140, No. 3
Copyright by Stainer & Bell, Ltd., London;
Galaxy Music Corporation, N. Y.,

A   soft   day,   thank   God!   A   wind   from   the   south   with   a   hon-ey'd   mouth

Songs of the Fleet, No. 5.   Fare Well
Copyright by Stainer & Bell, Ltd., London;
Galaxy Music Corporation, N. Y.,
U. S. agents

Mo-ther,   with   un-bowed   head   Hear   thou   a-cross   the   sea

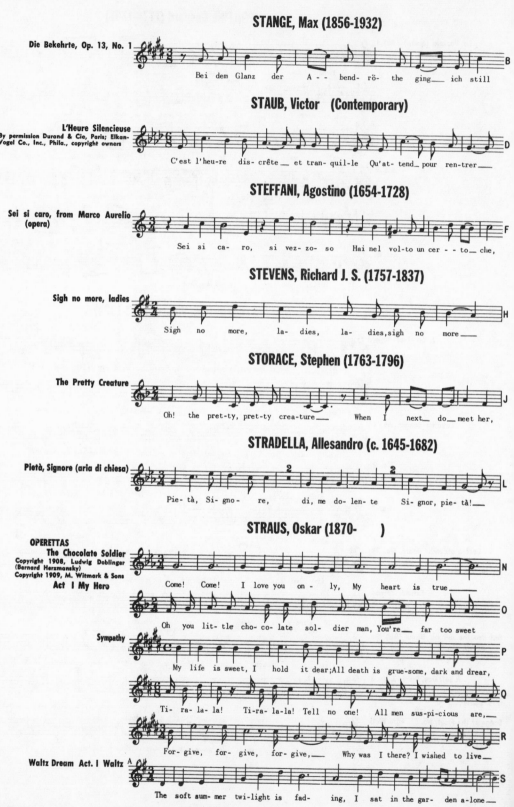

STANGE, Max (1856-1932)

Die Bekehrte, Op. 13, No. 1

Bei dem Glanz der A--bend-rö-the ging___ ich still

STAUB, Victor (Contemporary)

L'Heure Silencieuse
By permission Durand & Cie, Paris; Elkan-Vogel Co., Inc., Phila., copyright owners

C'est l'heu-re dis-crête___ et tran-quil-le Qu'at-tend___ pour ren-trer___

STEFFANI, Agostino (1654-1728)

Sei si caro, from Marco Aurelio (opera)

Sei si ca-ro, si vez-zo-so Hai nel vol-to un cer--to-che,

STEVENS, Richard J. S. (1757-1837)

Sigh no more, ladies

Sigh no more, la-dies, la-dies,sigh no more___

STORACE, Stephen (1763-1796)

The Pretty Creature

Oh! the pret-ty, pret-ty crea-ture___ When I next do___meet her,

STRADELLA, Allesandro (c. 1645-1682)

Pietà, Signore (aria di chiesa)

Pie-tà, Si-gno-re, di, me do-len-te Si-gnor, pie-tà!

STRAUS, Oskar (1870-   )

OPERETTAS
The Chocolate Soldier
Copyright 1908, Ludwig Doblinger (Bernard Herzmansky)
Copyright 1909, M. Witmark & Sons
Act I My Hero

Come! Come! I love you on--ly, My heart is true___

Oh you lit-tle cho-co-late sol-dier man, You're___ far too sweet

Sympathy

My life is sweet, I hold it dear;All death is grue-some, dark and drear,

Ti-ra-la-la! Ti-ra-la-la! Tell no one! All men sus-pi-cious are,___

For-give, for-give, for-give,___ Why was I there? I wished to live___

Waltz Dream Act. I Waltz

The soft sum-mer twi-light is fad--ing, I sat in the gar-den a-lone___

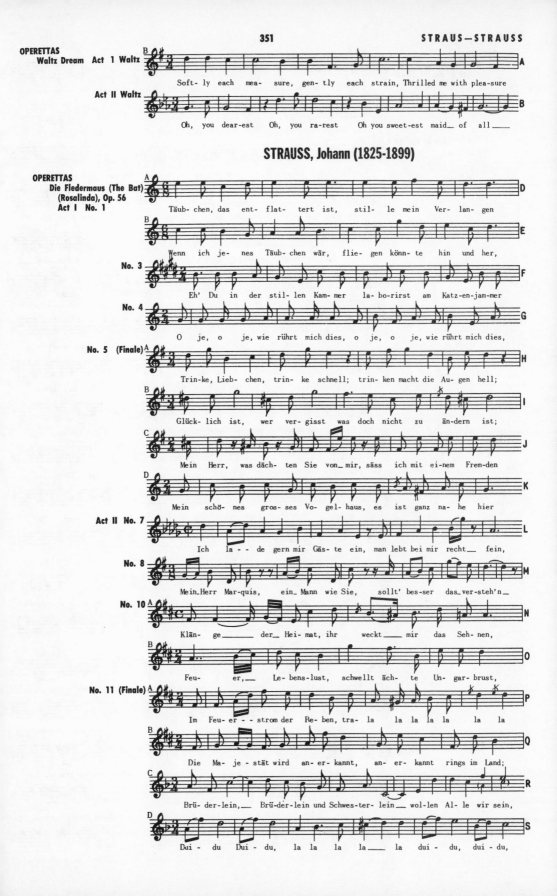

OPERETTAS
Waltz Dream Act I Waltz

B / A
Soft- ly each mea- sure, gen- tly each strain, Thrilled me with plea-sure

Act II Waltz
B
Oh, you dear-est Oh, you ra-rest Oh you sweet-est maid_ of all___

STRAUSS, Johann (1825-1899)

OPERETTAS
Die Fledermaus (The Bat)
(Rosalinda), Op. 56
Act I No. 1

A / D
Täub- chen, das ent- flat- tert ist, stil- le mein Ver- lan- gen

B / E
Wenn ich je- nes Täub- chen wär, flie- gen könn- te hin und her,

No. 3 / F
Eh' Du in der stil- len Kam- mer la- bo-rirst am Katz-en-jam-mer

No. 4 / G
O je, o je, wie rührt mich dies, o je, o je, wie rührt mich dies,

No. 5 (Finale) A / H
Trin- ke, Lieb- chen, trin- ke schnell; trin- ken macht die Au- gen hell;

B / I
Glück- lich ist, wer ver- gisst was doch nicht zu än-dern ist;

C / J
Mein Herr, was däch- ten Sie von_ mir, säss ich mit ei-nem Frem-den

D / K
Mein schö- nes gros- ses Vo- gel- haus, es ist ganz na- he hier

Act II No. 7 / L
Ich la- - de gern mir Gäs- te ein, man lebt bei mir recht_ fein,

No. 8 / M
Mein_Herr Mar-quis, ein_ Mann wie Sie, sollt' bes-ser das_ver-steh'n_

No. 10 A / N
Klän- ge_____ der_ Hei- mat, ihr weckt_ mir das Seh- nen,

B / O
Feu- er,_ Le- bens-lust, schwellt äch- te Un- gar-brust,

No. 11 (Finale) A / P
Im Feu- er - -strom der Re- ben, tra- la la la la la la la

B / Q
Die Ma- je - stät wird an- er- kannt, an- er- kannt rings im Land;

C / R
Brü- der-lein,_ Brü-der-lein und Schwes-ter- lein_ wol-len Al- le wir sein,

D / S
Dui- du Dui- du, la la la la_ la dui- du, dui- du,

OPERETTAS
Die Fledermaus Op. 56
Act II No. 11 Finale

Mar- ian- ka, komm und tanz' me' hier! Heut ist's schon schetzko jedno mir!

Ha, welch ein Fest, wel-che Nacht voll Freud! Lie- be und wein

Act III No. 14

Spiel' ich die Un-schuld vom Lan-de, na- tür-lich im kur-zen Ge- wan- de

Wenn Sie das ge-sehn, müs-sen Sie ge-steh'n, es wär der Scha-den

Al- les___ mach'n voll Ehr-furcht mir Spa-lier; lauscht den Tö- nen___

Spiel' ich 'ne Da- me von Pa- ris, ach,___ ach,___

No. 15

Ein selt-sam A- ben-teu- er ist ge-stern mir pas- siert

Ja, ich bins, den Ihr be- tro-gen, ja, ich bins den Ihr be- tro-gen

No. 16

O Fle- der-maus, o Fle-der-maus, lass end-lich jetzt dein O- pfer aus;

Die ganze Nacht durchschwärmt,
from Waldmeister

Die gan- ze Nacht durch schwärmt ge -trun- ken und ge- lärmt

Eine Nacht in Venedig (A night in
Venice) Act I

Dein___ Lied von Lieb und Treu- e hat ei-nen fal-schen Ton

Pel- le- gri- na ron- di-nel- la, ron- di-nel-la pel- le- gri- na

Al- le mas-kirt, Al- le mas- kirt, cos-pet- to! wie a- mu-sant

Sei mir___ ge-grüsst___ du hol-des Ve- ne - - - tia,

Komm'___ in die Gon - - del, mein Lieb-chen, o stei-ge doch ein,

Act II

Treu sein, das liegt mir nicht,___ weil ich leicht den Kopf ver-lier,

Act III Lagunen
Walzer

Ach, wie so herr-lich zu schau'n___ sind all' die lieb-li-chen Frau'n___

Wie sie schmei- cheln, Lie- be heu- cheln,___ uns durch Thrä - nen___

Nature, from Der Lustige Krieg (The
Merry War)

Na - - ture loved she___ fair to see___ and so free,___ She'd be roam-ing

The Queen's Lace Handkerchief
Act I Truffle Song

Such dish by man not oft is seen As that which once___ I tast-ed

Act II

Where the wild rose sweet-ly doth blow, There must I go;

Bright as a ray from the heav'nly heights gleam-ing,

Der Zigeunerbaron (The Gypsy Baron)
Act I No. 2

Als flot-ter Geist doch früh ver-waist hab ich die gan-ze Welt durch-reist

Ja das al-les auf Ehr____ Das kann ich und noch mehr,____

No. 3

Ja, das Schrei-ben und das Le-sen, ist___ nie mein Fach' ge-we-sen,

No. 5

Ah____ sieh da,____ ein herr-lich Frau-en-bild, das ganz mit Stau-nen

No. 6

So e-lend und so treu ist kei-ner auf Er-den

Flieh' wie du kannst und fürch-te den Zi-geu-ner

No. 7 (Finale)

Hier im die-sem Land Eu-re Wie-ge stand.___ Ach, als Kind___ habt Ihr___

Um frech den Ü-ber-mut zu fröh-nen, ver-let-zet ihr den Stolz

Act II No. 8

Mein Aug' be-wacht___ bei Tag und Nacht, dies hol-de jun-ge Blut___

Dies En-gels-ge-sicht, dies up-pi-ge Haar, dies Aug' voll Licht,

No. 9

Ha seht es winkt,___ es blinkt,___ es klingt. Ach, un-sern Bli-cken,

No. 11

Wer uns ge-traut? Ei sprich: Sag Du's!___ Der Dom-pfaff,

Und mild sang die Nach-ti-gall ihr Lied-chen in___ die Nacht,___

No. 12½

Her die Hand, es muss ja sein, lass' dein Lieb-chen fah-ren,

No. 13 (Finale)

So voll Fröh-lich-keit gibt es weit und breit, kei-ne Stadt

Ein Für-sten-kind ein Wun-der ist ge-scheh'n, ha sie ver-dient,

Zigeunerbaron (The Gypsy Baron) A
Act III No. 16

Von des Tay- o Strand wo mit star- ker Hand wir die Fein- de

B

"Gib Acht, es kracht" schreit mich ein Spa-nier an, schiess du nur zu,

No. 17 A

Hur- rah die Schlacht mit-ge-macht hab'n wir im fer-nen Land

B

Lus- tig oft un- ver hofft geht es auch im Krie-ge zu,

STRAUSS, Richard (1864-1948)

OPERAS: Die Ägyptische Helena
Act I
By permission Boosey & Hawkes, Inc.,
copyright owners

Bei je- ner Nacht, der keu-schen ein- zig ei- nen,

Act II

Zwei - - - - - - - - - te— Brant - - - nacht! Zau- ber-nacht,—

Arabella Act I (Duet) A
By permission Boosey & Hawkes, Inc.,
copyright owners

Ab- er der Rich- ti- ge wenn's ei- nen gibt für mich auf die- ser Welt

B

Ich weiss nicht wie du bist, ich weiss nicht ob du recht hast da zu

A

Mein E- le- mer das hat so ei- nen son-der-ba-ren Klang

B

Nach dem Mat- te- o sehnt sich nichts— in mir

Act II (Duet) A

So wie Sie sind— so hab' ich— kei-nen Men - - schen je ge-sehn!

B

Und du wirst mein Ge- bie- ter sein, und ich dir un- ter- tan—

Act III A

Das war sehr gut Man-dry- ka dass Sie noch nicht fortgegangen sind

B

Und die-sen un- be-rühr- ten Trunk— kre-denz' ich mei- nem Freund

Ariadne auf Naxos Prologue:
Composer's Song
By permission Boosey & Hawkes, Inc.,
copyright owners

Seien wir wie-der gut Ich se- he jetzt al- les mit an - de-ren Au-gen!

Act I

Sie lebt— hier ganz al- lein. Sie at - - met leicht,—

Ein Scho - - - - - - - - - - nes war:— hiess Theseus A-riadne

(Zerbinetta's Aria) A

Gross- mäch-ti- ge Prin- zes- sin wer ver-stun-de nicht,

STRAUSS

Ariadne auf Naxos (Zerbinetta's Aria)

Noch glaub' ich dem ei - nen ganz mich ge - hö - rend,

Als ein Gott kam je - der ge - gan-gen und sein Schritt schon

Capriccio, Op. 85
By permission Boosey & Hawkes, Inc., copyright owners

Kein An - dres, das mir so im Her - - zen loht, nein, Schö - ne,

Ih - re Lie - - be schlägt mir ent-ge - gen, zart_ ge-wo - ben

Du Spie - gel - bild_ der ver - lieb - - ten Made - leine, _

Daphne, Op. 82
By permission Boosey & Hawkes, Inc., copyright owners

O wie ger - ne blieb_ ich bei dir

Göt - - - ter! Bru - der im ho - hen O - lym - pos!

Wind_ spie - le mit mir! Se - li-ge Vö - gel woh-net in mir

Der Rosenkavalier, Op. 59
Act I Italian Serenade
By permission Boosey & Hawkes, Inc., copyright owners

Di - ri - go - ri_ar - ma-to il se - - no con-tro a-mor_mi ri-be - llai

Da geht er hin, der auf - ge-blas - ne, schlech - te Kerl_

Kann mich auch an ein Mä - del er - in-nern, die frisch aus dem Klos-ter

Die Zeit, die ist ein son - der - bar Ding, Wenn man so hin - lebt

Act II Presentation of the Rose

Mir ist die Eh - - re wi - der fah - ren dass ich der hoch

Hat ei - nen star - - ken Ge - ruch_ wie Ro - sen,

Ich kenn ihn schon recht wohl, _ mon Cou - sin!

Mit Ih - ren Au - gen voll Trä - - - nen kommt Sie zu mir

Herr Ca - va - lier Den mor - gi - gen A - bend hätt' i frei.

Act III Trio

Hab'_ mir's ge - lobt, ihn lieb_ zu ha - ben in der rich-ti-gen Weis',_

Duet

Ist ein Traum, kann nicht wirk - lich sein_ dass wir zwei_bei ei - nan-der sein, _

Songs, Op. 10, No. 1 Zueignung
By permission Associated Music Publishers, Inc.

Ja, du weisst es, theu- re See- le, dass ich fern von dir__ mich quä-le,

No. 3 Die Nacht

Aus dem Wal - - - de tritt die Nacht, aus den Bäu-men schleicht sie lei-se

No. 4 Die Georgine

Wa- rum so spät erst, Ge- or- gi- ne? Das Ro- sen-mär-chen ist er-zahlt

No. 5 Geduld

Ge- duld, sagst du und zeigst mit weis-sem Fin- ger

No. 6 Die Ver- schwiegenen

Ich ha- be wohl, es sei hier laut vor al- ler Welt ver- kün-digt,

No. 7 Die Zeitlose

Auf frisch ge- mäh- tem Wei- de-platz steht ein- sam die Zeit- lo- se,

No. 8 Allerseelen

Stell' auf den Tisch die duf- ten- den Re- se- den,

Op. 15, No. 1 Madrigal

In's Joch beug' ich den Nak- ken de- mut- voll, beug' lä- chelnd

No. 2 Winternacht

Mit Re- gen und Sturm- ge-brau- se sei mir will-kom- - men,

No. 5 Heimkehr

Lei- ser schwan- ken die Ä - - - ste, der Kahn fliegt u- fer-wärts,

Op. 17, No. 1 Seitdem dein Aug' in meines schaute

Seit-dem dein Aug' in mei- nes schau- te und Lie- be wie von Him- mel

No. 2 Ständchen (Serenade)

Mach' auf,__ mach' auf, doch lei- se, mein Kind um Kei- nen vom Schlummer

No. 3 Das Geheimnis

Du frag'st mich, Mäd- chen, was__ flüs-ternd der West

No. 6 Barkarole

Um der fal- - len-den Ru-der Spi-tzen zit-tert und leuch- tet

Op. 19, No. 1 Wozu noch, Mädchen
By permission Associated Music Publishers, Inc.

Wo- zu noch, Mäd- chen, soll es from- men, dass du vor mir

No. 2 Breit über mein Haupt

Breit' ü- ber mein Haupt dein schwarzes Haar, heig' zu mir dein An- ge- sicht,__

No. 4 Wie sollten wir geheim sie halten

Wie soll- ten wir ge- heim sie hal- ten, die Se- lig- keit

No. 6 Mein Herz ist stumm

Mein Herz ist stumm, mein Herz ist Kalt, er-starrt__ in des Win-ters Ei-se

Op. 21, No. 1 All mein Gedanken
By permission Associated Music Publishers, Inc.

All mein Ge-dan- ken, mein Herz und mein Sinn da, wo die Lieb- ste ist,

STRAUSS

Songs, Op. 21, No. 2 Du meines Herzens Krönelein

Du mei-nes Her - - zens Krö- ne-lein, du bist von lau-trem Gol-de A

No. 3 Ach Lieb, ich muss nun scheiden

Ach, Lieb, ich muss nun schei- den, geh'n ü-ber Berg und Thal, B

Op. 26, No. 1 Frühlingsge- dränge
By permission Boosey & Hawkes, Inc., copright owners

Früh- lings- kin- der im bun-ten Ge- drän- ge; flatternde Blü- ten, C

Op. 27, No. 1 Ruhe, meine Seele
By permission Associated Music Publishers, Inc.

Nicht ein Lüft-chen regt sich lei- se, sanft ent-schlummert ruht der Hain; D

Ru- he, ru- he,mei-ne See- le dei- ne Stür- me gin-gen wild E

No. 2 Cäcilie

Wenn du es wüss-test was träu-men heisst von bren-nen-den Küs-sen F

No. 3 Heimliche Aufforderung

Auf, he- be die fun- keln-de Schaa-le em- por zum Mund, G

No. 4 Morgen

Und mor-gen wird die Son- ne wie- - der schei- nen H

Op. 29, No. 1 Traum durch die Dämmerung
By permission Associated Music Publishers, Inc.

Wei- te Wie- sen im Däm- mer-grau; die Son- ne ver- glomm, I

No. 2 Schlagende Herzen

Ü- ber Wie- sen und Fel- der ein Kna-be ging; kling,klang J

No. 3 Nachtgang

Wir gin- gen durch die stil- le mil- de Nacht, dein Arm in mei- nem, K

Op. 31, No. 1 Blauer Sommer
By permission Boosey & Hawkes, Inc. copyright owners

Ein blau- er Som- mer glanz und glu- ten-schwer geht- ü-ber Wie-sen, L

No. 3 Weisser Jasmin

Blei- che Blü- te, Blü- te der Lie-be, leuch- te ü- ber dem Lau- ben-dach M

Op. 32, No. 1 Ich trage meine Minne vor Wonne stumm
By permission Associated Music Publishers, Inc.

Ich tra- ge mei-ne Min- ne vor Won- ne stumm im Her- zen N

No. 2 Sehnsucht

Ich ging den Weg ent-lang, der ein- sam lag den stets allein O

No. 3 Liebeshymnus

Heil je- nem Tag, der dich ge-bo- ren, Heil ihm, P

No. 4 O süsser Mai

O sü- sser Mai, o ha-be du Er- bar- men, o sü- sser Mai, Q

Op. 33, No. 4 Pilgers Morgen- lied
By permission Associated Music Publishers, Inc.

Mor- gen- ne- - bel Li- la, hül- len dei- nen Thurm ein. R

Op. 36, No. 2 Für fünfzehn Pfennige
By permission Boosey & Hawkes, Inc., copyright owners

Das Mägd- lein will ein' Frei- er habn, und sollt sie'n aus der Er- de grabn, S

STRAUSS   358

Songs, Op. 36, No. 3 Hat gesagt, bleibt's nicht dabei

Mein Va-ter hat ge-sagt ich soll das Kindlein wie-gen, wie----gen,

Op. 37, No. 1 Glückes genug
By permission Boosey & Hawkes, Inc., copyright owners

Wenn sanft du mir im Ar--me schliefst,

No. 2 Ich liebe dich

Vier ad-li-ge Ros-se vo-ran un-serm Wa-gen,

No. 3 Meinem Kinde

Du schläfst und sach-te neig' ich mich ü-ber dein Bett-chen

No. 4 Mein Auge

Du bist mein Au-ge!   Du durch-dringst mich ganz

Op. 39, No. 4 Befreit
By permission Boosey & Hawkes, Inc., copyright owners

Du wirst nicht wei-nen Lei-se, lei--se wirst du lä-cheln

No. 5 Lied an meinem Sohn

Der Sturm be-horcht mein Va-ter-haus, mein Herz

Op. 41a, No. 1 Wiegenlied
By permission Associated Music Publishers, Inc.

Träu-----me, träu--me du, mein sü-sses Le-ben

No. 3 Am Ufer

Die Welt ver-stumt, dein Blut er-klingt in seinem hel-len Ab-grund

No. 5 Leise Lieder

Lei-se Lie-der sing' ich dir bei Nacht, Lie--der, die kein sterb-blich Ohr

Op. 43, No. 2 Muttertändelei
By permission Boosey & Hawkes, Inc., copyright owners

Seht mir doch mein schö--nes Kind, mit den gold'--nen Zot--tel

Op. 46, No. 4 Morgenrot
By permission Boosey & Hawkes, Inc., copyright owners

Dort wo der Mor-gen-stern her-geht und wo der Mor-gen-wind herweht,

Op. 47, No. 2 Des Dichters Abendgang

Er-gehst du dich im A-bend-licht (das ist die Zeit)

Op. 48, No. 1 Freundliche Vision
By permission Boosey & Hawkes, Inc., copyright owners

Nicht im Schla-fe hab ich das ge-träumt hell am Ta-ge sah ich's

No. 2 Ich schwebe

Ich schwe-be wie auf En-gels-schwin-gen, die Er-de kaum be-rührt

No. 3 Kling

Kling! Mei-ne See-le gibt rei--nen Ton. Und ich wähn-te die Ar-me

No. 4 Winterweihe

In die-sen Win-ter-ta-gen, nun sich das Licht ver-hüllt,

No. 5 Winterliebe

Der Son-ne ent-ge-gen in Lie-bes-glu-ten wand'r ich

No. 7 Wer lieben will, muss leiden

Wer lie-ben will, muss lei--den oh'n Lei-den, oh'n Lei-den liebt man nicht,

Songs, Op. 49, No. 1 Waldseligkeit
By permission Boosey & Hawkes, Inc.,
copyright owners
Der Wald be-ginnt zu rau - - schen, den Bäu - men naht die Nacht:

No. 3 Wiegenliedchen
Bien- chen, Bien- chen, wiegt sich im Son-nen-schein

Op. 51, No. 2 Der Einsame
By permission Boosey & Hawkes, Inc.,
copyright owners
Wo ich bin, mich rings um- dun- kelt Fin- ster- nis

Op. 56, No. 1 Gefunden
By permission Associated Music
Publishers, Inc.
Ich ging im Wal- de so für mich hin, und nichts zu su- chen,

No. 2 Blindenklage
Wenn ich dich fra- ge, dem das Le - - - ben blüht:

No. 3 Im Spätboot
Aus der Schiffs-bank mach' ich mei-nen Pfühl, end - - - lich wird

No. 4 Mit deinen blauen Augen
Mit dei- nen blau - - - en Au- gen siehst du mich lieb- lich an,

No. 5 Frühlingsfeier
Das ist des Früh-lings trau- ri- ge Lust! Die blü - - hen-den Mäd- chen

No. 6 Die heiligen drei Könige aus Morgenland
Die heil'-gen drei Kön'-ge aus Mor- gen- land, sie fru- gen

Op. 68, No. 4 Als mir dein Lied erklang
Dein Lied er- klang! ich ha - - be es ge- hört,

No. 5 Amor
An dem Feu - - - - - - - - - - - er sass das Kind A- mor

Op. 69, No. 3 Einerlei
By permission Boosey & Hawkes, Inc.,
copyright owners
Ihr Mund ist stets der- sel - - - - - - - - - - - be,

No. 5 Schlechtes Wetter
Das ist ein schlech-tes Wet-ter, es reg - - - - - - - - net und stürmt

Olympische Hymne
Völ - - - ker! Seid des Vol- kes Gä - ste, kommt durch's off-ne Tor her-ein

STRAVINSKY, Igor (1882-   )

Symphonie de Psaumes No. 1
By permission Boosey & Hawkes, Inc.,
copyright owners
E - - xau- di o - - ra-ti-o-nem me-am, Do - - mi - - ne,

Quo- ni- am ad- ve - - na e- go sum a - - - - - pud te

No. 2
Ex- pec - - - tans ex- pec- ta - - - - - vi Do- mi- num

Et im- mi- sit in os me- um can- ti- cum nov- um

STRAVINSKY

360

Symphonie de Psaumes No. 3

Lau- da- te, Lau- da- te, Lau- da- te Do- mi- num

Lau- da- te E- um in tim- pa- no et cho- ro

Lau- da- te E- um in cym- ba- lis be- ne so- nan- ti- bus

Les Noces

Tableau I Chez la mariée

By permission J. & W. Chester, Ltd., London, copyright owners

Tres- se, tres- se, ma- ma tres- se à moi,

On tresse on tres- sera la tresse à Nas- ta- sie

Con- so- le toi con- so- le toi pe- tit oi- seau

Dai- gne, dai- gne très ai- ma- ble mè- re

Tableau II Chez le marié

Dai- gne ai- ma- ble mère, daigne en- trer dans la chau- mière,

A- vec quoi qu'on pei- gne- ra les bou- cles de Fé- é- é- tis?

Hier soir Hier soir en- co- re Fe- tis é- tait

Et vous père et mè- re be- nis- sez votre en- fant

Tableau IV Le Repas de Noces

Ya deux fleurs sur la branche u- ne rouge une blan- che

J'é- tais loin sur la mer, j'é- tais loin sur la mer im- mense

Sou- laud, vieux sa- laud Père de Nas- ta- sie

Le beau lit bien fait, le beau lit car- ré!

Pulcinella, (ballet) (music after Pergolesi) I

By permission J. & W. Chester, Ltd., London, copyright owners

Men- tre l'er- bet- ta pas- ce l'a- guel- la

II

Con- ten- to for- se vi- ve- re nel mi- o mar- tir po- trei

III

Con que- ste pa- ro- li- ne, pa- ro- li- ne

IV

Sen- to di- re no' nce pa- ce sen- to di- re

Pulcinella IV

Chi di - - - se ca__ la fem - me - na

V

U - na te fa - lanz em - pre - ce ed è ed è

VI

Pu - pil - let - te fiam - met - te__ d'a - - mo - - re

Four Russian Peasant Songs
I On Saints' Days at Chigisakh
By permission J. & W. Chester, Ltd., London,
copyright owners

On,__ on Saints' Days__ on Saints' Days__ in Chi-gi - sakh

II Ovsen

Ov-sen, ov-sen, ov - sen__ I'm a hunt - ing the grouse,__

III The Pike

Once a pike swam out of Nov-go - rod Glo - ry!

IV Master Portly

Mas - ter Port - ly__ tramp'-d__ thro' the big tur - nip_field

Pastorale (without words)
By permission Associated Music
Publishers, Inc.

A__ a - ou A - ou__ A__ A - ou

Trois Histoires pour Enfants
I Tilimbom
By permission J. & W. Chester, Ltd., London,
copyright owners

Ti - lim - bom, ti - lim - bom, c'est la cloche du feu qui sonne

II Les canards, les cynges, les oies

Les ca-nards, les cy - gnes, les oies__ qui sont ve - nus_ de Sa - voie__

III Chanson de l'ours

Grin-ce, grin-ce, grin - ce patte en bou - leau__ De-dans, de-hors

STRICKLAND, Lily (1887-   )

Mah Lindy Lou
Copyright 1920, G. Schirmer, Inc.

Hon-ey__ did you heah dat mock - in - bird sing las' night__

My Lover is a Fisherman

Oh, my lov - er is a fish - er - man, and he sails on the big

STROZZI, Barbara (c. 1644-1664)

Amor dormiglione

A - mor, a - mor, mon dor-mir più! Su. su, su, su, Sveg - lia-te,

STULTS, R. M. (1861-1923)

The Sweetest Story Ever Told
Copyright by Oliver Ditson Co.
Used by permission

Oh, an - swer me a ques - tion, love, I pray,__

Tell me, do you love me? Tell me soft - ly, sweet-ly, as of old,__

SULLIVAN, Sir Arthur (1842-1900)

OPERAS
The Gondoliers Act I, No. 1

List and learn, list and learn, List and learn ye dain-ty ro-ses,

We're called___ gon-do- lier- i, but that's a va- ga- ry,___

Thank you, gal-lant gon-do- lier-i: In a set and for-mal mea-sure

Gay and gal-lant gon-do-lier-i Take___us both and hold___us tight-ly

No. 3   In___ en-ter-prise of mar-tial kind, when there was an-y___ fight-ing

No. 6   I stole the Prince and brought him here,and left him gai- ly pratt-ling

No. 8   Try we life long, we can nev-er, Straighten out___life's tan-gled skein,

No. 9   When a mer-ry mai-den mar-ries, Sor-row goes and plea-sure tai-ries,

No. 10   Kind sir, you can-not have the heart our lives to part
Finale

Oh,___ 'tis a glo-rious thing,I ween to be a regu-lar Roy-al Queen

Then a-way___ they go to an is-land fair___ That lies in a Southern sea:

Act II, No. 1   Of hap-pi-ness the ve-ry pith___In Ba-ra-ta- ria you may see:

No. 3   Take a pair of spark-ling eyes,___ Hid-den ev-er and a- non,___

No. 5   Dance a___ ca- - chu-cha, fan-dan-go, bo- le- ro,

No. 6   Old Xe- res we'll drink Man-za- nil- la, Mon-te-ro,

No. 7   There lived a King, as I've been told,In the won-der-work-ing days of old

No. 9   In a con-tem-pla-tive fa-shion, And a tran-quil frame of mind

On the day when I was wed-ded to your ad-mi-ra-ble sire,

OPERAS
The Gondoliers Act II, No. 10

Small ti-tles and or-ders for Mayors and Re-cor-ders — A

No. 11

I__ am a cour-tier grave and se-rious Who__ is a-bout to kiss your hand, — B

No. 12
Finale

Here is a fix un- pre- ce-den- ted! Here are a King and Queen ill-starr'd! — C

H. M. S. Pinafore Act I, No. 1

We__ sail the o- cean blue, and our sau-cy ship's a beau-ty; — D

No. 2

I'm called lit-tle But-ter-cup, dear lit-tle But-ter-cup, though I could never tell why — E

No. 3

A maid-en fair to see, the pearl of min-strel-sy, A bud of blush-ing beau-ty, — F

No. 4 A

I am the cap-tain of the Pin- a- fore,—and a right__ good__ cap-tain too — G

B

Then give three cheers, and one cheer more, For the har- dy cap-tain — H

No. 5 A

Sor-ry her lot__ who loves__ too well, Hea-vy the heart__ that hopes — I

B

Hea- vy the sor-row that bows__ the head, When love is a- live__ — J

No. 8

I am the mon-arch of the sea, The ru-ler of the Queen's Na- vee, — K

No. 9

When I was a lad I serv'd a term as of-fice boy__ — L

No. 11 A

Re- frain, au- da- cious tar, Your suit__ from__ press- ing — M

B

I'd laugh my rank to scorn, in u- - nion__ ho- ly, — N

No. 13

Fair moon to thee__ I__ sing! Bright re-gent of the hea- vens — O

No. 14 A

Things are sel- dom what they seem, Skim milk mas-que- rades as cream, — P

B

Stern con- vic-tion's o'er__ him__ steal-ing, That the mys-tic la- dy's__ deal-ing — Q

No. 15

A sim- ple sail- or, low- ly born, un- let-ter'd and un- known, — R

No. 16

Nev-er mind the why and where- fore, Love can lev- el ranks — S

OPERAS
H. M. S. Pinafore Act II, No. 17

Kind Cap-tain, I've im- por-tant in- for- ma- tion Sing hey,

No. 18

Care- ful- ly on tip-toe steal- ing, breathing gently as we may

No. 18A

For___ he him- self has said___ it, and it's great-ly to his cred- it,

No. 19

Fare- well, my own, Light of my life, fare-well! For crime un-known I go

No. 20

A ma-ny years a- go, when I was young and charm- ing,

No. 21

Oh joy, oh rap-ture un- for-seen, The cloud-ed sky is now se- rene

Iolanthe Act I, No. 1

Trip- ping hi- ther, trip- ping thi- ther, No- dy knows why or whi-ther

We are dain- ty lit- tle fai- ries E- ver sing-ing e- ver danc-ing

No. 3

Good mor- row, good mo-ther___ Good mo- ther, good mor-row___

No. 5

None shall part us from each o- ther, One in life and death are we:

No. 6

Bow, bow, ye low- er mid- dle class- es, Bow, bow, ye trades-men,

We are___ peers of___ high- est sta- tion,

No. 7

The Law is the true em- bo- di-ment of ev'- ry-thing that's ex - cel-lent

No. 8

Of all the young la-dies I know,___ This pret-ty young la-dy's the fair-est,

No. 10

Spurn not the no- bly born With love___ af - fect- ed!

No. 12

When I went to the bar as a ve- ry young man,

No. 13 Finale

When dark- ly looms the day, and all is dull and grey,

Go a- way, ma- dam; I should say, ma- dam, You dis- play, ma- dam,

Act il, No. 2

Stre-phon's a Mem-ber of Par- lia-ment! car-ries ev-'ry Bill_ he choos- es

OPERAS
Iolanthe Act II, No. 3
When Bri- tain real- ly rul'd the waves (In good Queen Bess- 's____ time)

No. 5
Oh, fool-ish fay, Think you, be-cause His brave ar-ray my bo- som thaws,

No. 7
When you're lying a- wake with a dis-mal head-ache, And re- pose is ta-boo'd

No. 8
He____ who shies at such a prize is____ not worth a ma- ra- ve- di,

No. 9
If we're weak e- nough to tar- ry Ere we mar- ry, You____ and I,

The Mikado Act I, No. 1
If you want to know who we are____ We are gen-tle-men of Ja- pan____

No. 2
A wan- d'ring min- strel I a thing of shreds____ and patch-es

No. 3
Our great Mi- ka- do, vir-tuous man, When he to rule our land be-gan

No. 4
Young man de-spair, Like- wise go to Yum- Yum the fair you must not woo.

No. 5
And the brass will crash, and the trum- pets bray; and they'll cut a dash

No. 5
Be-hold the Lord High ex- e- cu-tion-er! A per-son-age of no- ble rank

Ta- ken from the coun- ty jail By a set of cu-rious chan-ces

No. 5a
As some- day it may hap-pen that a vic- tim must be found,

No. 7
Three lit- tle girls from school are we, Pert as a school-girl well can be,

No. 9
Were you not to Ko- ko plight- ed, I would say in ten- der tone,

No. 10
I am so proud, if I al-lowed my fa- mi- ly pride To be my guide,

No. 11 Finale
The threat-en'd cloud has passed a - - way, And brightly shines the dawning day

With joy- ous shout, with joy- ous____ shout and____ring- ing____ cheer

If true her tale, thy knell is rung, Pink cheek, bright eye, rose lip,

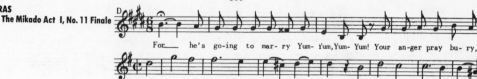

For he's go-ing to mar-ry Yum-Yum, Yum-Yum! Your an-ger pray bu-ry,

We do not heed their dis-mal sound, For joy reigns ev-'ry-where

Act II, No. 1

Braid the ra-ven hair, Weave the sup - - - - - - ple tress,

No. 2 A1

The sun, whose rays are all a-blaze with ev-er liv-ing glo-ry

A2

I mean to rule the earth, as he the sky, we real-ly know our worth,

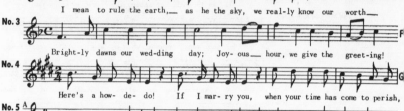

No. 3

Bright-ly dawns our wed-ding day; Joy-ous hour, we give the greet-ing!

No. 4

Here's a how-de-do! If I mar-ry you, when your time has come to perish,

No. 5 A

Mi-ya sa-ma, mi-ya sa-ma, On n'ma-ma no ma-ye ni

B

From ev-'ry kind of man O-be-dience I ex-pect

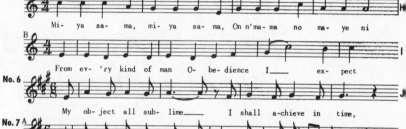

No. 6

My ob-ject all sub-lime I shall a-chieve in time,

No. 7 A

The cri-mi-nal cried, as he dropp'd him down, In a state of wild a-larm

B

Oh, never shall I for-get the cry, or the shriek that shriek-ed he,

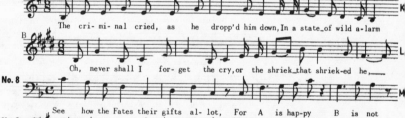

No. 8

See how the Fates their gifts al-lot, For A is hap-py B is not

No. 9

The flow-ers that bloom in the spring, Tra-la Breathe pro-mise

No. 10

Oh liv-ing I come, tell me why, when hope is gone, Dost thou stay on?

No. 11

On a tree by a riv-er a lit-tle tom-tit Sang "Wil-low,

No. 12 A

There is beau-ty in the bel-low of the blast,

B

If that is so, Sing der-ry down der-ry! It's e-vi-dent ve-ry,

Patience Act I, No. 1

Twen-ty love-sick mai-dens we, Love-sick all a-gainst our will.

Patience Act 1, No. 2

I can-not tell what this love may be That com-eth to all

No. 4

In a dole-ful train two and two we walk all day for we love in vain!

Through my book I seem to scan In a rapt ec-sta-tic way

No. 5

When I first put this u-ni-form on, I said, as I looked in the glass

No. 6

If you're anx-ious for to shine— in the high aes-the-tic line—

And ev-ery one will say As you walk your mys-tic way,

No. 8

Pri-thee, pret-ty mai-den pri-thee, tell me true (Hey, but I'm dole-ful,

No. 9 Finale

Let the mer-ry cym-bals sound, Gai-ly pipe Pan-dae-an plea-sure

Now tell us, we pray you, Why thus they ar-ray you, Oh po-et,

List Re-gi-nald, while I con-fess a love that's all un-sel-fish-ness

Act II, No. 2

Sil-vered is the ra - - ven—hair, Spread-ing is the part-ing—straight,

No. 3

Turn, oh turn in this di-rec-tion, Shed, oh shed a gen-tle smile

No. 4

A mag-net hung in a hard-ware shop And all a-round was a lov-ing crop

No. 5

Love is a plain-tive song. Sung by a suf-fering maid

Love that no wrong can cure, Love that is al-ways new,

No. 6

So go to him and say to him, with com-pli-ment i-ron-i-cal

Sing "Hey to you good-day to you" Sing "Bah to you ha! ha! to you"

No. 7

You hold your-self like this, You hold your-self like that, By hook and crook

No. 8

If Sa-phir I choose to mar-ry, I shall be fixed up for life;

OPERAS
Patience Act II, No. 8

In that case un-pre-ce-dent-ed, Sin-gle he will live and die,

No. 9

When I go out of door of da-mo-zels a score All sighing and burning,

The Pirates of Penzance
Act I, No. 1

Pour, O King, the pi-rate sher-ry, Fill, O King, the pi-rate glass!

No. 2

When Fred'ric was a lit-tle lad He proved so brave and da-ring,

No. 3

Oh bet-ter far to live and die Un-der the brave black flag I fly

For I am a Pi-rate King! And it is, it is, a glo-rious thing

No. 5

Climb-ing o-ver rock-y moun-tain, Skip-ping ri-vu-let and fountain,

Let us gai-ly tread the mea-sure, Make the most of fleet-ing pleas-ure

No. 7

Oh, is there not one mai-den breast which does not feel the mo-ral beau-ty

No. 8

Poor wan-d'ring one Tho' thou hast surely strayed, Take heart of grace,

Take heart, no dan-ger lowers, Take a-ny heart but ours

No. 10

How beau-ti-ful-ly blue the sky, The grass is ris-ing ve-ry high

Did e-ver mai-den wake from dream of home-ly du-ty

No. 11

Now here's a first rate op-por-tu-ni-ty To get mar-ried

No. 13

I am the ve-ry pat-tern of a mo-dern Ma-jor Ge-ne-ral

Finale

These chil-dren whom you see are all that I can call my own.

I'm tell-ing a ter-ri-ble sto-ry, but it does-n't di-min-ish

Act II, No. 1

Oh, dry the glis-t'ning tear that dews that mar-tial cheek!

No. 3

When the foe-man bares his steel, Ta-ran'-ta-ra, ta-ran-ta-ra

OPERAS
The Pirates of Penzance
Act II, No. 3

Go_____ ye he-roes, go_____ to glo-ry Though_____ ye die in com-bat go--ry

No. 5

When you had left our pi-rate fold, we tried to raise our spi-rits faint.

A pa-ra-dox, a pa-ra-dox, a most in-ge-nious pa-ra-dox

No. 6

A-way, a-way_____ my heart's on fire!_____ I burn this base de-cep-tion

No. 8

Ah, leave me not to pine a-lone and de-so-late

Oh, here is love, and here is truth, and here is food for joy-ous_____ laugh-ter

No. 10

When a fe-lon's not en-gaged in his em-ploy-ment, his em-ploy-ment,

No. 12

With cat like tread up-on our prey we steal; In si-lence dread

Come, friends, who plough the sea, truce to na-vi-ga-tion,

No. 14 Finale

Soft-ly sigh-ing to the ri--ver, Comes the lone-ly breeze_____

We tri-umph now for well_____ we trow Your_____ mor-tal ca-reer's cut_____ short

Princess Ida Act I, No. 1

Search through-out the pa-no-ra-ma, For a sign of roy-al Ga-ma

No. 2

Now heark-en to my strict com-mand On ev'-ry hand, on ev'-ry hand

No. 3

I-da was a twelve-month old twen-ty years a-go

No. 5

We are war-riors three,_____ Songs of Ga-ma Rex,_____ Like most sons are we_____

Bold_____ and fierce and strong, ha, ha! For_____ a war we burn

No. 6

If you give me your at-ten-tion, I will tell you what I am:

No. 7 Finale

P'raps if you 'ad-dress the la-dy most po-lite-ly, most po-lite-ly

Ex-press-ive glan-ces shall be our lan-ces and pops of Sil-le-ry

OPERAS

Princess Ida Act I, No. 7 Finale

For a month to dwell in a dun-geon cell, grow-ing thin and wi-zen

Act II, No. 8

To- wards the em- py- re- an heights___ of ev'- ry kind of love,

No. 9

Migh- ty mai-den with a mis- sion, Pa- ra-gon of com-mon sense

No. 10

Oh, god-dess wise that lov--est___ light En- dow with___ sight

No. 11

Come might- y Must! In- e- vi- ta-ble Shall! In Thee I trust.

No. 13

I am a mai- den cold___ and state- ly Heart-less I,

No. 14

The world is but a bro-ken toy, Its plea-sures hol-low false its joy,

No. 15

A La- dy fair, of___ lin-eage high, When loved by an Ape

No. 16

The wo- man of the wis- est wit may some-times be mis- ta- ken, O!

No. 19

Would___ you know the kind___ of maid Sets___ my heart a- flame- a?

No. 22 A

When- e'er I spoke sar- cas- tic joke Re- plete with mal- ice spite-ful,

B

Oh, don't the days seem lank and long When all goes right

No. 23

I built up- on a rock, But ere De-struc-tion's hand

No. 24

When an- ger spreads his wing, and all___ seems___ dark as___ night for it,

No. 25

This hel- met, I sup-pose was meant to ward off blows, It's ve- ry hot

Ruddigore Act I, No. 1

Fair___ is Rose as bright May day, Soft___ is Rose as warm west wind,

No. 2 A

Sir Ru- pert Mur- ga-troyd His lei- sure and___ his rich- es

B

This sport___ he much en- joy'd,___ Did Ru- pert Mur- ga- troyd___

No. 3

If some- bo- dy there chanced to be Who loved me in a man- ner true

OPERAS
Ruddigore Act I, No. 3

No. 3 — Had I the love of such as he, Some qui-et spot he'd take me to,

No. 4 — I know a youth who loves a lit-tle maid (Hey, but his face is a sight

No. 5 — From the bri-ny sea comes young Rich-ard, all vic-to-rious!

No. 7 — If you wish in the world to ad-vance, Your me-rits You're bound to en-hance

No. 8 — The bat-tle's roar is o-ver, O my love! Em-brace thy ten-der lov-er,

No. 10 — In sail-ing o'er life's o-cean wide Your heart should be your on-ly guide;

No. 11 — To a gar-den full of po-sies Com-eth one to ga-ther flowers,

No. 12 — Wel-come, gen-try, For your en-try sets our ten-der hearts a-beat-ing,

No. 12 — When thor-ough-ly tir-ed of be-ing ad-mir-ed By la-dies

No. 13 — Oh why am I mood-y and sad? Can't guess! And why am I guil-ti-ly mad?

No. 14 — You un-der-stand? Like-wise the Bride The mai-dens are ve-ry E-lat-ed

No. 15 Finale — Hail the Bride of seven-teen sum-mers: In fair phra-ses Hymn her prai-ses

No. 15 — Leaves in au-tumn fade and fall Win-ter is the end of all, Fa la la la

No. 15 — When i'm a bad Bart. I will tell ta-ra-did-dles! He'll tell ta-ra-did-dles

No. 15 — Oh, hap-py the li-ly when kiss'd by the bee; And sip-ping tran-quil-ly,

Act II, No. 2 — Hap-pi-ly cou-pled are we, you see I am a jol-ly Jack Tar, my star,

No. 4 — Paint-ed em-blems of a race All ac-curst in days of yore

No. 5 — When the night wind howls in the chim-ney cowls, and the bat in the moon-light flies

No. 7 — I once was a ve-ry a-ban-doned per-son mak-ing the most of e-vil chances

My eyes are ful-ly o-pen to my aw-ful sit- u- a- tion,

No. 10 A

There grew a lit- tle flow- er 'Neath a great oak tree

Sing___ hey, lack- a- day, let the tears fall free

The Sorcerer Act I, No. 1 A

Ring forth, ye bells, with cla- rion sound, For- get your knells,

For to- day young A- lex- is, Young A- lex- is Point- dex- tre

No. 2 A

When he is here I sigh with plea-sure,When he is gone I sigh with grief

No. 3 A

Time was, when love and I were well ac- quain- ted,

No. 5

With heart and with voice Let us wel- come this ma-ting to the youth

No. 6 A

Oh, hap- py young heart___ Comes thy young lord a- woo- ing

No. 8

With heart and with voice let us wel- come this mat- ing

No. 9

Wel- come joy! a-dieu to sad - ness! As Au- ro- ra gilds___the day

No. 10

All is pre-pared for seal-ing and for sign-ing, The contract has been drafted

No. 11

Love feeds on ma- ny kinds of food, I know; Some love for rank,

No. 12

My name is John Wel-ling-ton Wells___ I'm a deal- er in ma-gic and spells

No. 13
(Incantation)

Sprites of earth and air! Fiends of flame and fire! Demon souls,come

No. 14 Finale A

Eat, drink and be gay, Ba- nish all wor- ry and sor- row

B

Oh love, true love! un- world- ly, a- bid- ing, Source of all pleasure

Act II; No. 15

Hap- py are we in our lov- ing fri- vol- i- ty Hap-py and jol- ly

No. 16 A

Dear friends,take pi- ty on my lot, My cup is not of nec- tar

OPERAS
The Yeomen of the Guard
Act I, No. 9

A

I've wis- dom from the East and from the West,

No. 10

B

Though tear and long drawn sigh ill fit a bride___ no sad-der wife than I

No. 11

C

Were I thy bride, then all the world be- side were not too wide

Act II, No. 1

D

Night___ has spread her pall once more, and_the pris - 'ner still is free

No. 2

E

Oh! a pri- vate buf- foon is a light heart- ed loon,

No. 3

F

Here-up- on we're both a- greed, all that we two Do a- gree to

No. 4

G

Far from his fet-ters grim Free to de- part;___ Free both in life and limb

No. 5

H

Strange ad- ven -ture!Mai-den wed- ded To a___ groom she'd nev-er___ seen!

No. 7

I

If he's made the best use of his time,___ His twig he'll so care-fully lime___

No. 8

J

Oh, the hap- py days of do- ing! Oh, the sigh-ing and the su- ing

No. 9

K

Rap- ture, rap- ture, when love's vo- ta- ry;Flushed with cap-ture,

God shall wipe away all tears, from
The Light of the World (oratorio)

L

God shall wipe a- way all tears from their eyes,There shall be no more death

The Golden Legend Evening Hymn

M

O glad- some Light of the Fa- ther im- mor - - - - - tal,

The Night is calm

N

The night is calm and cloud-less, And still as still___ can be

How many hired servants, from The
Prodigal Son

O

How ma- ny hi- red ser-vants of my fa-ther's have bread e-nough

Songs: Birds in the Night

P

Birds___ in the night___ that soft - - ly___ call

Ho, Jolly Jenkin, from Ivanhoe
(grand opera)

Q

Then ho, jol- ly Jen- kin I spy a knave in drink- in

The Long Day Closes

R

No star is o'er the lake, Its pale watch keep- ing,

The Lost Chord

S

Seat- ed one day at the or- gan, I was wea- ry and ill at ease

Songs: Onward Christian Soldiers (hymn) — On- ward, Chris-tian sol - - - diers Mar- ching as to war,

Orpheus with his Lute — Or - - - - - pheus with his lute, with his lute made trees

SUPPÉ, Franz von (1819-1895)

Boccaccio (operetta) No. 3 — Hol-de Schö-ne, hör' die-se Tö-ne, hör' mein zärt-li-ches Lie-ber- ge- stöh- ne!

No. 6 — Hab' ich nur dei-ne Lie-be, die Treu- e brauch'_ich nicht,

No. 18 — Flo- renz hat schö- ne Frau- en,_ die Schön - - ste bist du

SWEELINCK, Jan Pieterzoon (1562-1621)

Hodie Christus natus est — Ho- di- e, ho-di- e Chri- stus na - - - - - - - tus est,

Or sus, serviteurs du Seignour — Or sus,_ ser- vi- teurs du Sei-gneur, or sus,

Psalm 138 — Il faut que de tous mes e- sprits_

Tu as tout seul — Tu as tout seul, Jan, Jan, Jan, Jan, vi- gnes et prez,

SZULC, Joseph (1874-1935)

Clair de Lune, Op. 83, No. 1
Copyright 1920, G. Schirmer, Inc. — Votre âme est un pa- y- sa- ge choi- si Que vont char- mant

La Lune Blanche No. 8
Copyright by Salabert, Paris, N. Y. — La lu- ne blan - che luit dans le bois, de cha-que bran - che

En Sourdine No. 9 — Cal- mes dans le de- mi jour, Que les bran-ches hau- tes font,

Mandoline No. 10 — Les don-neurs de sé-ré- na-des et les bel-les e-cou- teu - - - - - ses

TAUBERT, Wilhelm (1811-1891)

Birdling, why sing in the forest wide — Bird- ling why sing in the for - - est wide? Say, why?

TAVERNER, John (c. 1495-1545)

Audivi

Au- di - - - - - - - - - - - - - - - - - - - vi:

TAYLOR, Deems (1885-   )

Captain Stratton's Fancy
Copyright 1923, J. Fischer & Bro., N. Y.
Used by permission

Oh, some are fond of red wine and some are fond of white

The King's Henchman (opera) Act I
Copyright 1926, J. Fischer & Bro., N. Y.
Used by permission

Oh, Cae- sar, great wert thou! and Jul- ius was thy name!

Act III

Nay, Mac- cus, lay him down What man hath met the thrust of

May-Day Carol, Op. 15, No. 9 (transcribed)
Copyright 1920, J. Fischer & Bro., N. Y.
Used by permission

The moon shines bright, The stars give a light, A lit-tle be-fore 'tis day

TCHAIKOVSKY, Peter Ilyich (1840-1893)

Moscow (cantata) Arioso No. 2

Ist ein Him- mels-licht, das so strahlt und blinkt durch die fin- stre Nacht.

Arioso No. 5

Wird mir, Herr mein Gott, nicht zu schwer das Kreuz, das mir auf-er- legt

OPERAS
Adieu, forêts, from Jeanne d'Arc

A- dieu, fo- rêts, a- dieu, près fleur- is champs d'or

Eugene Onegin, Op. 24 Act I, No. 1

Did'st thou not hear? how like the night- in- gale One sang by night

No. 6 Lenski's Aria

Yes, I love you, yes, I love you, Ol- ga fierce and hot,

No. 9 Letter scene

Tho' I should die for it I've sworn now I first shall live

No, ne- ver a- ny oth- er, For an- y oth- er I had loathed!

No. 11

Come, ye maid-ens all, and dance, Run while yet ye have a chance

No. 12 Onegin's Aria

If in this world a kind-ly for-tune for house-hold cares had destined me

Act II, No. 13 Waltz

Re- gale you all! Hail, hail to all beau- ty

(Instrumental acc. to waltz)

Instrumental accompaniment to Waltz

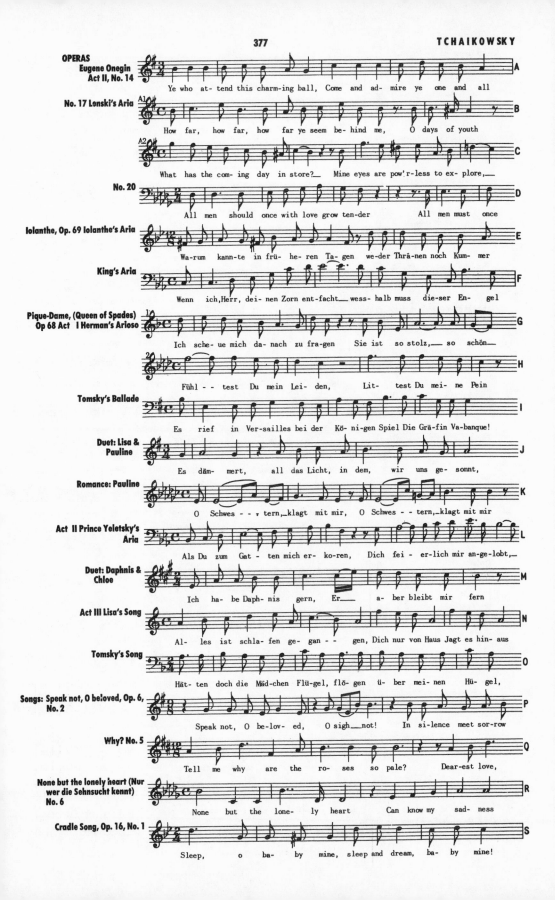

Songs: Linger yet, Op. 16, No. 2
Lin-ger yet! Thought of part-ing O ban-ish! Like an ar - - - row

Wherefore? Op. 28, No. 3
Why did you come in dreams to me, My ab-sent love, I ne-ver for-get

Er liebt mich so sehr! No. 4
Nein, nim-mer lieb-te ich! Und doch sah ich ihn kom-men,

Kein Wort von dir, No. 5
Kein Wort von dir, der Freu-de o-der Kla-ge,

One small word, No. 6
Small head droop-ing, here you stand be-fore me

Don Juan's Serenade, Op. 38, No. 1
All Gra-na-da li - - -eth qui-et In thy bal-co-ny__ap-pear

It was in days of early spring, No. 2
It was in days of ear-ly spring, when ten-der grass was grow-ing

At the Ball, No. 3
I know not how love-ly your face is, For that,when I met you

Oh, but to hear thy voice (I wish) No. 4
Oh would but Heav'n in pi-ty grant a boon to me!

Pimpinella (Florentine Song) No. 6
Non con-tras-tar__cogl' uo - - mi - ni, fal-lo per ca-ri-ta!

Whether Day Dawns, Op. 47, No. 3
Whe-ther day dawns__or night sha-dows are fall-ing Whe-ther I dream

Pilgrim's Song (Benediction) No. 5
My bless-ing rest on ye, o woods, o val-leys moun-tains

Toujours à toi, No. 6 (confused with Toi seul, Op. 57, No. 6)
Que le jour bril-le ou que l'om-bre nous cou-vre

Was I not a blade of grass in meadow green, No. 7
Was I not a blade of grass in mead-ow green

Ah. my__heart, how hard is life to bear! Ah! my__heart,

Songs for Young People, Op. 54, No. 5 Legend
Child Je-sus in his gar-den fair Some sweet red ro-ses once had grown

No. 8 The Cuckoo
From out the ci-ty thou hast flown: Now prith-ee, what word

No. 14 Autumn
De broui-llards mo-ro-ses Les cieux sont cou-verts;

The Nightingale, Op. 57, No. 1
O Sprich wo-von die Nach-ti-gall wenn rings die Welt ver-sank

OPERAS
Hamlet, Act I, Scene I

A — Dou-te de la lu-miè-re Dou-te du so-leil et du jour,

B — Pour mon pa-ys,__ en ser-vi-teur fi-dè-le

Scene II

C — Spectre in-fer-nal! I-ma---ge vé-né-ré-e!

Act II

D — A-dieu, dit il, a-yez foi!__ Mon coeur vous aime, ai-mez moi!

E — Les ser-ments_ont des ai-les! Dans le coeur des in-fi-dè--les__

F — Dans son re-gard plus som--bre,__ J'ai vu passer__ comme un é-clair!

G — Ô vin dis-si-pe la tris-tes----se Qui pè-se sur mon coeur__

Act III

H — Ê--tre ou ne pas ê-tre! ô mys-tè-re! Mou-rir! dor-mir! dor-mir!

I — Je__ t'im-plo-re Ô__ mon frè-re!__ Si tu m'en-tends,__

Act IV

J — Pâle et blon-de dort sous l'eau pro-fon-de Les wil-lis au re-gard de feu!

Act V

K — Comme u-ne pâ-le fleur É-close au souf-fle de la tom-be

Mignon Act I

L — Bons bour-geois et no-ta-bles, as-sis au-tour des ta-bles,

M — Fu-gi-tif et trem-blant,__ je vais de porte en por-te,

N — Oui, je veux, par__ le mon--de pro-me-ner li-bre-ment__

O — Si l'a-mour__ sur ma rou-te Ce soir m'é-tend la main,

A1 — Con-nais-tu le__ pays où fleu-rit l'o-ran-ger__

A2 — C'est là que je vou-drais vi--vre, Ai-mer, ai-mer et mou-rir,

R — Lé-gè----res hi-ron-del-les, Oi-seaux bé-nis de Dieu,__

Act II Madrigal

S — Belle, a-yez pi-tié de__ nous, Belle a-yez pi-tié de__ nous

OPERAS
Mignon Act II Styrienne

Je con-nais un pauvre en-fant,___ Un pauvre en-fant de Bo-hê-me___

Ah! la la___ la la ta___ ta la___ ral la

Me voi- ci dans son bou-doir, et je sens mon coeur

A- dieu, Mi- gnon!___ cou- ra- ge Ne pleu- re pas!

Elle est ai-mé- e Il l'aime! eh! bien! je le savais!

As- tu souffert? as- tu pleu- ré? As- tu lan-gui sans es- pé- ran- ce?

Je___ suis Ti- ta- ni- a la blon- - - - -de,

Act III Berceuse
De son coeur j'ai cal-mé la fiè-vre! Un sou- ri- re doux et joy- eux

Romance
El- le ne croy- ait pas, dans sa can- deur na- ï- ve,

Ô___ prin- temps don- - ne- lui ta gout- te de___ ro- sé- e!

Le Soir (song)
La terre em- bra- sé- e At- tend___ la ro- sé- e

THOMAS, Christopher J. (1894-   )

O men from the fields!
Copyright 1938, Galaxy Music Corp., N. Y.

O, men from the fields! come gen- tly with- in, Tread soft- ly,

THOMÉ, Francis (1850-1909)

Sonnet d'amour
Copyright 1901, G. Schirmer, Inc.

Sous le so- leil___ qui les___ ir- ri- - se,

THOMPSON, Randall (1899-   )

Alleluia
Copyright 1940, E. C. Schirmer, Boston

Al- le- lu- ia, al- le- lu- ia, al- le- lu- ia, al- le- lu- ia,

Velvet Shoes
Copyright 1935, Harcourt, Brace

Let us walk in the white snow, In a sound- - less space

THOMSON, Virgil (1896-)

Four Saints in Three Acts
Prologue
Copyright by Arrow Music Press, N. Y.

To know to know to love her so. Four saints pre-pare for saints

Act I

There are a great man-y per-sons and pla-ces near to-geth-er

She can have no one no one can have an-y-one

A scene and with-ers Scene three and scene two. How can a sis-ter

Could they grow and tell it so if it was left to be to go

There can be no peace on earth with calm with calm

They nev-er knew a-bout it green and they nev-er knew a-bout it

Act II

Can an-y-one feel an-y one mov-ing and in mov-ing can

How man-y saints are there in it There are ver-y man-y man-y saints

There are as man-y saints as there are in it.

Act III

Pi-geons on the grass a-las. Pi-geons on the grass a-las.

He asked for a dis-tant mag-pie as if they make a dif-fer-ence

There are ver-y sweet-ly ver-y sweet-ly Hen-ry

Once in a while and where and where a-round a-round

Let-ting pin in let-ting let in let in in in in in let

Variant

With wed led said with led dead said with dead led said

Act IV

Be-gin to trace be-gin to race be-gin to place be-gin and in

The Mother of Us All
Act I Scene I
Copyright by Arrow Music Press, N. Y.

Yes I was, said Su-san. You mean you are, said Anne

They be- gan to trav- el, not to trav- el you know but to go

Men are so__ con- ser- va- tive, so sel- fish so bore- some,

Do come Su- san B. An- tho- ny, do come no- bod- y no- bod- y

Scene II   Pit- y the poor__ per - - se- cu- tor   If mon- ey is mon- ey,

He digged a pit, he digged it deep, he digged it for his bro- ther.

Dan- iel was his fa- ther's name,   fa- ther's name,   fa- ther's name

Not an- y more   I am not a mar- tyr an- y- more__

Hush, I hush, you hush, they hush, we hush, Hush, we hush,

Scene III   I be- lieve in pub- lic school ed- u- ca- tion

Dear Miss Con- stance Fle- tcher, it is a great plea- sure

Scene IV   If I be- lieve__ that I am right and I am__ right if they be- lieve__

We are the cho- rus of the V. I. P.   Ve- ry im- por- tant per- sons

Scene V   Will they re- mem- ber that it is true that neither they, that neither you,

So beau- ti- ful. It is so beau- ti- ful   to meet you here,

Act II, Scene II   I have just con- vert- ed Lil- li- an Rus- sell to the cause

Dear friends, it is so beau- ti- ful__ to meet__ you all__

That so long that the gor- geous en- sign of the re- pub- lic

Scene III   The vote,   wo- men have the vote.   They have it each and ev'ry one

THRANE, Waldemar (1790-1828)

Kom Kjyra (Norwegian Echo Song)

Kom Kjy- ra! Kom Kjy - ra mi! kom kjy - - - ra!

TIERSOT, Julien (1857-1936)

Noel Provençal I (arr.)
By permission Heugel & Cie, Paris, copyright owners

Un flam- beau,_ Jean-nette, I- sa- bel- le! Un flam- beau_

Noel Provençal II (arr.)

Guil- laume, An- toi- ne, Pier- re, Clau- de, Jac- ques, Ni- co- las_

Noel Provençal III (arr.)

Ah! quand re- vien- dra- t-il le temps, ber- gè- re? Ah!

Le Pauvre Laboreur (arr.)
By permission Heugel & Cie, Paris, copyright owners

Le pau- vre la- - - bou- reur, Il_ a bien du mal- heur

Le Retour du Marin (chanson Poitevine)
By permission Heugel & Cie, Paris, copyright owners

Quand le ma- rin re- vint de guer- re,_ Tout doux

TOMKINS, Thomas

(madrigals)
Oyez! Has any found a lad

O- yez has a- ny found a lad, has a- ny found

See, see, the shepherds Queen

See, see, see, the shep- herds' Queen, fair Phyl- lis all_ in green

When David heard

When, When Da- - - - vid heard that Ab- sa- lom was slain

TORELLI, Giuseppe (1650-1708)

Tu lo sai

Tu lo_ sa- i Quan-to t'a- ma- i, Tu lo_ sa- i,

TOSELLI, Enrico (1883-1926)

Serenade (Rimpianto)
By permission Heugel & Cie, Paris, copyright owners

Co- me un so- gno d'or scol- pi- to,è nel co- re

Ma fu mol- to bre- ve,in me la dol-cez- za di quel ben

TOSTI, F. Paolo (1846-1916)

L'Alba sepàra dalla luce l'ombra
By permission Heugel & Cie, Paris, copyright owners

L'al- ba se- pà- ra dal- la lu- ce l'om- bra_

TOSTI

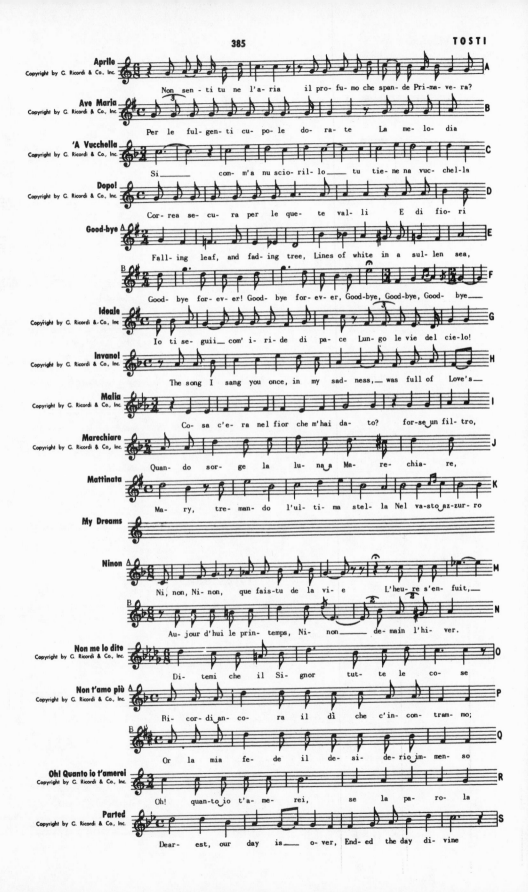

Penso!
Copyright by G. Ricordi & Co., Inc.

A

Pen- so al- la pri- ma vol- ta in cui vol- ge- sti

Ridonami la calma
Copyright by G. Ricordi & Co., Inc.

B

A- ve Ma- ri- a, per l'a- ria va il suon d'u- na cam- pa- na

La Serenata

C

Vo- la, o se- re- na- ta: La mia di- let- ta è so- la,

Sogno
Copyright by G. Ricordi & Co., Inc.

D

Ho so- gna- to che sta- vi a gi- noc- chi Co- me un san- to

L'Ultimo Canzone (The Last Song) A
Copyright by G. Ricordi & Co., Inc.

E

M'han det- to che do- ma- ni, Ni- na, vi fa- te spo- sa

B

F

Fo- glia di ro- sa,___ O fio- re d'a- ma- ran- to___

Vorrei (Could I) A
Copyright by G. Ricordi & Co., Inc.

G

Vor- rei__ al- lor che tu pal- li- do e mu- to pie- ghi la fron- te

B

H

Vor- rei___ per in- can- te- si- mi d'a- mo- re pia- na- men- te

Vorrei morir A
Copyright by G. Ricordi & Co., Inc.

I

Vor- rei mo- rir ne la sta- gion del l'an- no,

B

J

Vor- rei mo- rir, vor- rei mo- rir quan- do tra- mon- ta il so- le

TOURS, Frank E. (1877-   )

Mother o' Mine!

TOYE, Francis (1883-   )

The Inn
Copyright 1925, F. Toye

N

Do you re- mem- ber an inn, Mi- ran- da?

TRADITIONAL

Barbara Allen

P

In Scar- let town, where I was born, There was a fair maid dwel- lin'

Early one morning

Q

Ear- ly one morn- - - ing just as the sun was ris- ing

The Holly and the Ivy

R

The hol- ly and the i- vy Now both are full well grown,

The Lincolnshire Poacher

S

When I was bound__ ap- pren- tice, in fam- ous Lin- coln- shire,___

O Can Ye Sew Cushions

O can ye sew cush- ions and can ye sew sheets,

TROTERÉ, Henry (1855-1912)

In Old Madrid

Long years a- go in old Mad- rid where soft- ly sighs

TURINA, Joaquin (1882-1950)

Cantares
Copyright by Unión Musical Española

Ay!

Mas 'cer-ca de mi te sien- to___ cuan-do mas hu-yo de tí___

Las locas por amor
Copyright by Unión Musical Española

Te a-ma- re ___ dio-sa Ve - - - - - - - - - - - nus

Rima
By permission Associated Music
Publishers, Inc.

Yo soy ar- den- te yo soy mo- re- na

Saeta en forma de Salve a la Virgen de la Esperanza

Dios te sal- ve, Ma-ca- re - - - - na ma-dre de los se-vi- lla- - nos

Triptico I. Farruca
Copyright by Unión Musical Española

Es- tá tui- ma-gen que ad- mi-ro, tan pe- ga-da a mi de- se- - o

II. Cantilena

Por un a- le-gre pra-do de flo-res es-mal-ta- - - - - - - to

III. Madrigal

Tus o- jos, o-jos no son, ni- ña si- no dos na- va-jos

VALDERRABANO, Enriquez de (16th Cent.)

A monte sale (Soneto)

A mon-te sa-le el a- mor___ · de la Is- la muy nom- bra-da

Señora, si te olvidaré

Se- ño- ra, si te ol-vi-da- ré La___ mi dies-tra ol vi-de à mi

VALVERDE, Joaquin (1846-1910)

Clavelitos (Carnations)
Copyright by E. B. Marks Music Corp., N. Y.

Cla- ve- li- tos___ a quien le doy cla- ve - - - les!___

VANDERPOOL, Frederick W. (1877-1947)

Values (Another Hour with Thee)
Copyright 1918, M. Witmark & Sons

Ah, love, could I but take the hours That once I spent with thee

VARNEY, Louis (1844-1908)

Valse du Colibri, from L'Amour Mouillé (comic-opera)
Copyright by Choudens fifi, Paris

P'tit fi! P'tit mi- gnon! gen-til com-pag-non

VAUGHAN WILLIAMS, Ralph (1872-   )

Bushes and Briars
Copyright by Novelli & Co., Ltd., London

Through bush- es and through bri- ars I late- ly took my   way

A farmer's son so sweet
Copyright by Stainer & Bell, Ltd., London;
Galaxy Music Corporation, N. Y.,
U. S. Agents

A far- mer's son so sweet was keep- ing of his sheep

The House of Life 1. Love-Sight
Copyright by Edwin Ashdown, London

When   do I see   thee most, be- lov- ed one

2. Silent Noon

Your hands lie o- pen in the long fresh grass

3. Love's Minstrels

One flame- winged brought a white winged harp play- er

4. Heart's Haven

Some- times she is a child with- in my arms

5. Death in Life

There came an im- age   in Life's   ret- in- ue

6. Love's Last Gift

Love to his sin- ger held a glis- ten- ing leaf,

How can the tree but wither
By permission Oxford Univ. Press, London,
copyright owners

How can   the tree but waste   and wi- ther a- way

Linden Lea
By permission Boosey & Hawkes, Inc.,
copyright owners

With- in the wood-lands, flow'-ry glad- ed, by the oak-trees moss- y moot,

Mass in G Minor I. Kyrie
Copyright 1922, J. Curwen

ky - - - - - - ri e - - e lei - - - - - - - - - - son

II. Gloria in excelsis

Et in ter- ra pax ho- mi- ni- bus bo-nae vo- lun- ta- tis

III. Credo

Pa- trem o- mni- pot- en- tem, fac- to- rem cae- li

IV. A. Sanctus

San - ctus

VAUGHAN WILLIAMS

Mass in G Minor IV. B. Osanna

O- san- na, O- san- na in ex- cel- sis   O- san- na

C. Benedictus

Be- - - - - - - - - ne- di- ctus qui ve-nit in no- mi- ne Do- mi- ni

V. Agnus Dei

A- - - gnus De- i qui tol- lis pec- ca- ta mun- di

On Wenlock Edge 1. On Wenlock Edge
By permission Boosey & Hawkes, Inc.,
copyright owners

On Wen- lock Edge_ the wood's in trou-ble,_ His for- est fleece

2. From far, from
eve and morning

From far,_ from eve_ and morn-ing And yon twelve-wind-ed sky,

3. Is my team
ploughing

Is my team plough- ing, that I was used_ to_ drive

4. Oh, when I was in
love with you

Oh, when I was in love with you, Then I was clean and brave

5. Bredon Hill

In sum- mer-time on Bre- don The bells they sound so_ clear

6. Clun

In val-leys of springs_ of ri- vers, By On- y and Teme and Clun

Orpheus with his Lute

Or - - pheus with his lute_ made trees, And the moun-tain tops that freeze

A Piper
By permission Oxford Univ. Press, London,
copyright owners

A pi- per in the streets to-day Set up, and tuned and start-ed to play,

Serenade to Music
By permission Oxford Univ. Press, London,
copyright owners

How sweet the moon- light sleeps up - - on this bank!

I am nev- er mer - - - ry when I hear_ sweet_ mus - - - - - - ic

Songs of Travel 1. The Vagabond
By permission Boosey & Hawkes, Inc.,
copyright owners

Give to me the life I love, Let the lave go by me

2. Bright is the ring of
words

Bright is the ring of words_ when the right man rings them,

3. The Roadside Fire

I_ will make you broo- ches and toys for your de- light

Three Poems by Walt Whitman
1. Nocturne
By permission Oxford Univ. Press, London,
copyright owners

Whis- pers of heaven- ly death_ mur-mur'd I hear,

2. A Clear Midnight

This is thy hour, O Soul, thy free flight in-to the word- less

3. Joy, Shipmate, Joy

Joy, ship-mate, joy! Pleased to my soul_ at death I cry

The Twilight People
By permission Oxford Univ. Press, London, copyright owners

It is a whis-per a-mong the ha- - -zel bush- -es;   A

The Water Mill
By permission Oxford Univ. Press, London, copyright owners

There is a mill, an an-cient one, Brown with rain and dry with sun,   B

The Winter is gone
Copyright by Novello & Co., Ltd., London

The win- ter is gone and the sum-mer is come   C

Arrangements: Ca' the yowes
Copyright 1922, J. Curwen

Ca' the yowes, tae the knowes, Ca' them whar the hea-ther grows   D

The Dark Eyed Sailor
Copyright by Stainer & Bell, Ltd., London; Galaxy Music Corporation, N. Y., U. S. agents

It was a come-ly young la- -dy fair, Was walk-ing out   E

Down in yon forest
Copyright by Stainer & Bell, Ltd., London; Galaxy Music Corporation, N. Y., U. S. agents

Down in yon for-est there stands a hall, The bells of Par-a-dise   F

Just as the tide was flowing
Copyright by Stainer & Bell, Ltd., London; Galaxy Music Corporation, N. Y., U. S. agents

One morn-ing in the month of May, Down by some roll-ing ri-ver   G

Loch Lomond
Copyright by Stainer & Bell, Ltd., London; Galaxy Music Corporation, N. Y., U. S. agents

By yon bon-ny banks and yon bon-ny braes,where the sun shines   H

The Springtime of the year
Copyright by Stainer & Bell, Ltd., London; Galaxy Music Corporation, N. Y., U. S. agents

As I walked out one morn-ing, in the spring-time of the year   I

The Turtle Dove
Copyright 1919, J. Curwen

Fare you well my dear, I must be gone, and leave you   J

Wassail Song
Copyright by Stainer & Bell, Ltd., London; Galaxy Music Corporation, N. Y., U. S. agents

Was- sail, Was- sail all o-ver the town   K

Wassail Song
Copyright by Stainer & Bell, Ltd., London; Galaxy Music Corporation, N. Y., U. S. agents

We've been a-while a- wan-der-ing A- mongst the leaves   L

VECCHI, Orazio (1550-1603)

Il bianco e dolce cigno

Il bian- - -co e dol-ce cig- no can-tan- - -do mo- re   N

Can- tan- - - - - - - - - - - - - do, can-tan- - - - - - do   O

VEHANEN, (1887-   )

Tuku, tuku, lampaitani (arr.) (Finnish folk tune)
By permission Galaxy Music Corporation, N. Y.

Tu- ku, tu-ku, lam-pai-ta-ni, ki- li, ki-li, ki-li-a-ni   Q

VERACINI, Francesco (1690-1750)

Pastoral, from Rosalinda (opera)

Me- co ver-rai su quel-la, A- me-na col-li- net-ta   S

VERDI, Giuseppe (1813-1901)

OPERAS
Aida Act III (Nile Song)

O cieli az- zur- ri o dol-ci au- re na- ti - - - - - ve,

Ri- ve- drai le fo- re- ste im- bal- sa- ma- te, le fre- sche val- li

Su, dun - - - - - que! sor- get- te e- gi- zie co- or- ti!

Duet

Pur ti ri- veg - - - - - go mia dol- ce A- i - - - - da

Là tra_ fo- re- ste ver- gi- ni, di fio - ri pro- fu- ma- te

Si: fug- giam da que- ste mu- ra al_ de- ser- to in- siem

Act IV Scene I Duet

Già i sa- cer- do- ti a- du- nan- si ar - - bi- tri del tuo fa- to;

Ah!_ tu dei vi- ve- re!_ Sì, al- l'a- mour mio vi- vra- i;

Scene II Finale

Mo- rir!_ si pu- ra e bel- la Mo- rir!_ per me d'a- mo- re

Ve- di? di mor- te l'an- ge- lo radian- te a noi s'ap- pres- sa

O ter- ra ad- di- o; ad- di- o val- le di pian- ti

Attila Act II

Dagl' im- mor- ta- li ver - - ti- ci bel- li di glo- ria,

Act III Trio

Te sol,_ te sol quest' a- ni- ma a- ma im- men- so a- mo- re

Un Ballo in Maschera (The Masked Ball)
Act I Scene I

La re- ve- drà nel l'e- sta- si rag- gian- te_ di pal- lo- re

Al- la vi- ta che t'ar- ri- de di spe- ran- ze e gau- dio pie- na,

Vol - - ta la ter- re a_ fron- te al- le stel- le

Scene II

Re - - dell' a- bis- so af- fret- ta- ti, pre- ci - - pi- ta per l'e- tra,

È lui è lui ne' pal- pi- ti co - - me ri- sen- to a- des- so

Di' tu - - se fe- de - - le flut- to m'a- spet - - - - ta,

OPERAS
Un Ballo in Maschera (The Masked Ball)
Act I Scene II

A — È scher-zo o d'è fol-li - - a si f-fatta pro-fe-zi - a

Act II
B — Ma dal-l'a-ri-do stelo di-vul - sa co-me a-vrò di mia ma-no

Love duet
C — Non sai tu che se l'a-ni-ma mi-a - - - il ri-mor-so

D — Oh qual so-a-ve bri-vi-do l'ac-ce-so pet-to ir-ro-ra!

E — Ve' se di not-te qui col-la spo-sa l'in-na-mo-ra - to

Act III
F — Mor-rò, ma pri-ma in gra - - zia deh! mi con-sen-ti al-me-no

G — E-ri tu che mac-chia-ve quel-l'a - - -ni-ma, la de-li-zia

H — Ma se m'è for-za per-der ti per sem-pre o lu-ce mi-a

(Air of the page)
I — Sa-per vor-res-te di che si ves-te, quan-do l'è co-sa

Don Carlos Act I
J — Io la vi-di e al su - - - o sor-ri-so scin-til - lar,

Act II
K — Dio, che nell' al-ma in-fon - - - de-re a-mor

L — Nel giar-din del bel-lo sa-ra-cin o-stel-lo,

M — Non pian-ger, mia com-pa - - gna, non pian-ger no,

Act IV
N — Dor-mi-rò sol nel man-to mio re-gal, quan-do la mia gior-na-ta

O — O don fa-ta-le, o don cru-del che in suo fu-ror

P — O mia Re-gi-na, io t'im-mo-la-i

Q — Per me giun-to è il dì su-pre-mo, no, mai più ci ri-ve-drem;

R — Io mor-rò, ma lie-to in co-re, chè po-tei co-sì ser-bar

Act V
S — Tu che le va-ni-tà co-no-sce-sti del mon-do

VERDI

OPERAS

Don Carlos Act V

S'an-cor si pian-ge in cie - - - lo pian-gi sul mio do- lo - - - re,

I Due Foscari Act I

Dal più re- mo- to e- si- glio, sull'a- li del_ de- si - o

Tu al ciu squardo onni- pos- sen - - - - - te tut- to esul- ta o

O vec-chio cor che bat - - - - - - ti come a'prim' an- ni in se - - - - - no

Act II

Non ma- le- dir-mi o pro - - - de se son del Do- ge fi - - glio;

Act III

Al- l'in- fe- li- ce ve-glio con- for - - ta tu il do- lo - - - re,

Que- sta dun- que è l'i- ni- qua mer- ce- de, che ser- ba- ste

Ernani Act I

Co- me ru-gia- da a al co- spi- te d'un ap- pas-si- to fio - - - - - re

Ev- vi - - va! be- viam! be- viam! Nel vi-no cer- chiam

Er- na-ni! Er-na - - - ni in-vo-la- mi all' ab-bor-ri- to am-ples- so

Tut- to_ sprez- zo_ che d'Er- na - ni non_ fa - vel- la

Da quel dì_ che t'ho ve- du- ta bel- la co- me un pri mo a-

In- fe- li- ce! e tu cre- de- vi si bel ci- glio

Act II

Lo ve- dre - - mo o ve- gli au-da - - ce se re- si- ster- mi

Vie- ni me- co, sol di ro - - - se in- trec-ciar ti vo' la vi - - ta,

Act III

Oh de' verd'an - - - - ni_ mie - - - - i so gui e bugiar de_ lar - - - ve

Si ri- des- ti il Le- on di_ Ca- sti - - - glia, e d'I- be - - - ria

O som- mo Car- lo, più del tuo no- me le tue vir- tu - - di_

Act IV

So- lin- go, er- ran- te e mi- se- ro, Fin da prim' an- ni mie- i

OPERAS
La Forza del Destino
Act II Scene II

Deh! non m'ab-ban-do-nar, pie-tà, pie-tà di me, Si-gno-re.

Il san-to no-me di Di-o Si-gno-re sia be-ne-det-to.

Ma-le-di-zio-ne, ma-le-di-zio-ne, ma-le-di-zion!

La Ver-gi-ne de-gli an-ge-li mi co-pra del suo man-to,

Act III Tarantella

Nel-la guer-ra e la fol-li-a

So-len-ne in que-st'o-ra giu-rar-mi do-ve-te

Or muo-io tran-quil-lo, Vi strin-go al cor mi-o

Oh, tu che in se-no a-gli an-ge-li e-ter-na-men-te pu-ra,

Toh, toh! Pof-fa-re il mon-do! oh che tem-po-ne

Ur-na fa-ta-le del mio de-sti-no, va,t'al-lon-ta-na,

E-gli è sal - - vo! oh gioja im-men-sa che m'in-non - - - di

(chorus)

Com-pa-gni, so-stia-mo, il cam-po e-splo-ria-mo;

Sle-a-le! Il se-gre-to fu dun-que vio-la-to?

No,d'un i-me-ne il vin-co-lo strin-ga fra noi la spe - - - me;

(chorus)

Lor - - chè pif - - fe - - ri il tam - - bu-ri

(soprano & chorus)

Ra-ta-plan, ra-ta-plan, del-la glo-ria pel sol-da-to

Act IV

Le me-nac-cie,fie-ri ac-cen-ti por-tin se-co in pre-da i ven-ti,

Pa-ce, pa-ce, pa-ce, mio Di-o, pa-ce mio Di-o!

(Trio)

Non im-pre-ca-re,u-mi-lia-ti a Lui che è giu-sto

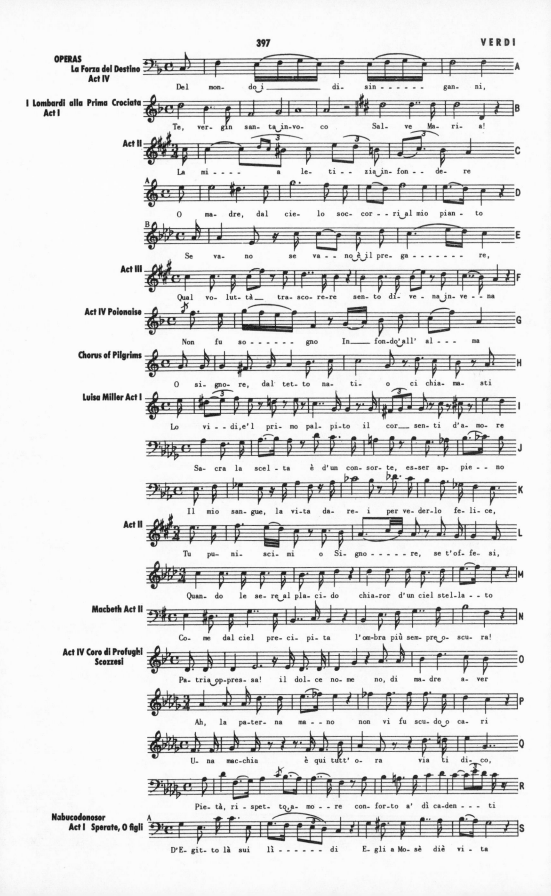

OPERAS
Rigoletto Act I (Duet)

A — Fi-glia! Mio pa-dre! A te d'ap-pres-so

B — Deh non par-la-re al mi-se-ro del suo per-du-to be---ne

C — Ve-glia o don-na, que-sto fio-re che a te pu-ro con-fi-da---i;

D — È il sol del-l'a-ni-ma, la vi-ta è a-mo---re

E — Ad-di-o, ad-di-o, spe-ran-za ed a-ni-ma

F — Ca-ro no-me che il mio cor fe-sti pri-mo pal-pi-tar

(Final chorus)
G — Zit-ti, zit-ti mo-via-mo a ven-det-ta, ne sia col--to

Act II
H — Par-mi ve-der le la-gri-me scor-ren-ti da_ quel ci-glio,

(chorus)
I — Scor-ren-do u-ni----ti re-mo-ta vi---a

J — Pos-sen-te a-mor mi chia----ma, vo-lar io deg--gio a le-i;

K — La rà, la rà, la la, la rà, la rà la rà, la rà,

A
L — Cor-ti-gia-ni, vil raz-za dan-na-ta,

B
M — Miei si-gno-ri per-do-no, pie-ta------te

N — Tut-te le fe-ste al tem-pio men-tre pre-ga-va Id-di--o,

A
O — So-lo per me l'in-fa---mia a te chie-de-va o Di-o

B
P — Pian-gi, pian-gi, fan-ciul----la, fan-ciul-la, pian-gi.

Q — Sì, ven---det-ta, tre-men-da ven-det--ta

Act III
R — La don-na è mo-bi-le qual piu-ma al ven--to,

(Quartet) A
S — Un dì, se ben ram-men-to-mi o bel-la, t'in-con-tra-i

OPERAS
Rigoletto Act III (Quartet)

Bel- la fi-glia del- l'a- mo- re, schia- vo son de'vez- zi tuo- - i;

Ah! ah! ri- do ben di co- re chè tai ba- ie co- stan po- co

In- fe- li- ce co- re, cor tra- di- to, per an- go- scia non

V'ho in-gan- na- to col- pe- vo- le fu- i l'a- mai trop- po

Las- su in cie- - lo, vi- ci- na al la ma- dre

Simon Boccanegra Prologue

Il la- ce- ra- to spi- ri- to del me- sto ge- ni- to- re

Act I

Co- - me in que-st'o- ra bru- - na sor- ri- - - -don gli a- stri

Fig- lia a tal no- me io pal- pi- to qual se m'a-pris- se i cie- - li

Ple- be! Pa-tri- zi! Po- po- lo dal- la fe-ro- ce sto- ria

Pian- go su voi sul pla- - ci- do- rag- gio del vo- stro cli- vo

Act II

Sen- to av-vam- par nel l'a- ni- ma fu- ren- te- ge- lo- si- - - a

Cie- lo pie-to- so, ren- di- la ren- di- la a que-do co- re

La Traviata Act I Brindisi

Li- bia- - - - mo, li- bia- mo ne' lie- - ti ca- - li- ci,

Un dì fe-li- ce, e- te- re- a, mi ba- le- na-ste in-nan- - - - - te

Ah, for- s'e lui che l'a- ni- ma so-lin- ga ne' tu- mul- - ti,

A quel- l'a- mor, quel l'a- mor- - ch'e pal- pi- to,

(Part 2 of Ah fors'e lui)

Sem- pre li- be- ra- deg- g'i- o fol- leg- gia- re

Act II Scene I

De- miei bol- len- ti spi- ri- ti il gio- va- ni-le ar- do- - re

O- - mio ri- - mor- so! oh in- fa- mia! io- - vis- si

OPERAS

OPERAS
Il Trovatore Act II

Stri- de la vam- - - - -pa, la____ fol-la in-do - - - -mi-ta

Chi del gi- ta- - no i gior- ni ab- bel- la?

Con-dot- ta el- l'era in cep- pi al su- o de-stin tre- men- do

Mal reg- - gen- do all' a- - - - -spro as- sal- to,

Pe- ri gliar-ti an-cor lan-guen- - te per cam- min sel- vag- gio

Il ba- len del suo sor- ri- so d'u- - na____ stel- la

Per me o- ra fa- ta- - le, i tuoi mo- men- ti af- fret- ta

Finale

E deg- gio e pos- so cre- der- lo? Ti veg- go a me d'ac-can-to!

Act III Soldiers'
Chorus

Or co da- di, ma fra po- co gio-che- rem ben_ al- tro gio-co!

Squil- li e cheg- gi la trom- - ba guer-rie- ra, chia- mi all' ar- mi

Ah si, ben mio coll' es- se- re io tuo, tu mia con- sor- te,

Di quel- la pi- - - - -ra l'or- ren- do fo- - - - - co

All' ar- mi! All' ar- mi all' ar- mi all' ar- - - mi!

Gior- ni po- ve- ri vi- ve- - a, pur con- ten- ta

Act IV Scene I

D'a- mor sull' a- - li ro- se- - e van-ne, sos-pir_ do- len- - -te;

Miserere

Quel son, quel- le pre- - - - ci so- len- ni, fu- ne- ste

Ah ____ che la morte o- gno- - ra è____ tar- da nel ve- nir

Tu ve-drai che a-more in ter- ra mai del mio non fa più for- te

Mi- ra, di a-cer- be la-gri- me spar- go al tuo piedi un ri- o!

OPERAS

Il Trovatore Act IV Scene II

Si, la stan- chez- za m'op- prime, o fi - - glio

Ai nos-tri mon - - ti ri- tor- ne- re - - mo, l'an- ti- ca pa- ce

Vi - vra! Con-ten- de il giu- bi- lo i det- ti a me, Sig- no- re

I Vespri Siciliani Act II

O tu, Pa- ler- mo, ter- ra a- do- ra- ta, a - - me si ca - - ro

Act III

In bra- ccio alle do- vi - - zie, nel se- no de- gli o- nor,

Quan-do al mio sen per te par- la- va pie- tà sin- ce- ra

Act IV

Gior- no di pian - - to, di fier do- lo - - re! Men- tre l'a- mo- re

Act V Siciliana

Mer - - cè, di- let- te a- mi - - che di quoi leg- gia-dri fior;

La brez- za a-leg- gia in-tor- no a car- ez- zar- mi il vi- so e

Sacred Music:
Ave Maria (scala enigmatica)

A- ve Ma- ri - - a, gra- ti- a ple- na,

Requiem I Requiem and Kyrie A

Re- qui- em Re- qui- em Re- qui-em ae-ternam do- na, do- na e- is,

B

Te de- cet hym- mus, De - - - - - - us, in Si- on,

M

Ky- ri- e e- le - - - - - - - - - - - i- son

II Dies Irae A

Di- es i- rae, Di-es i - - - - - - - - - - - - - - - - - rae,

B

Tu- ba mi - - - - rum spar - - gens - - so- num

C

Quid sum, mi - - - - ser! tunc - - dic- tur- us

D

Rex tre- men- dae maj- es- ta - - - tis

E

Re - - - - cor- da - re, Je - - - su- pi- e Quod - - sum cau- sa

F

In- ge- mi - - sco tam- quam re- us, Cul- pa ru- bet vul-tus me- us:

Requiem II Dies Irae — Qui ___ Ma-ri-am ab-sol vis _____ ti,

O- ___ ro sup-plex et ac-cli-nis, Cor con-tri-tum qua-si ci-nis,

La- cry- mo-sa di- es _ il-la! Qua re-surg-et ex fa-vil-la

III Domine Jesu — Do - - ne Do - - mi-ne Je- su Chris-te,

li- _ be- ra a ____ ni ____ mas

Quam o- lim A- bra-hae, quam o- lim Ab- ra- hae,

Ho - - - - sti- as et pre - - - ces _ ti- bi, Do- mi- ne

IV Sanctus (fugue for two choirs) — San-ctus, san-ctus, san-ctus, Do- mi-nus De- us _ Sa- ba-oth,

San- ctus, san-ctus, san-ctus Do - - mi-nus De-us _ Sa- ba-oth

V Agnus Dei — Ag-nus De- i, A- - - gnus De- i, qui _ tol- lis pec-ca-ta mun-di,

VI Lux aeternam — Lux ae- ter- na lu- ce- at e- is Do- mi- ne

Re- qui-em ae-ter - - nam do na _ e - - - - - - - - is,

et ___ lux _ per- pe- tu- a lu - - ce- at _ e- is

VII Libera me — Li- be- ra me, Do- mi- ne, de mor- te ae- ter- na, ___

VIDAL, Paul (1863-1931)

Ariette — Si j'é- tais ray- on, j'i- rais, jeu- ne fil- le

Le Fidèle Coeur
Je se- rai ta dou-ceur pro-fon-de Ta der-niè-re joie

VIDE, Jacques (15th Cent.)

Las! j'ay perdu mon espincel — Las! j'ay per- du mon es- pin - - - cel

Vit encore ce faux Dangier

Vit en-co-re ce faux Dan-gier

VILLA-LOBOS, Heitor (1884-   )

Bachianas Brasileiras No. 5
By permission Associated Music
Publishers, Inc.

Ah

Tar-de u-ma nu-vem ro-sea len-ta e tran-spa-ren-te

Canção de Saudade

Ah

Mi-nha mae que-ri-da Tu es meu pen-sa-men-to

Estrella é lua nova (Brazilian folk
song) (arr.)
By permission Associated Music
Publishers, Inc.

Es-trel-la do céo é lu-a no-va cra-ve-ja-da

Nozani - ná (Brazilian folk song) (arr.)
By permission Associated Music
Publishers, Inc.

No-za-ri ná ô-re ku-á ku-á,___ Ka-za ê-tê

Serestas No. 1 Pobre Céga

Po-bre cé-ga, por-que cho-ram as-sim tan-to esses teus o-lhos

No. 2 O anjo da guarda

Quan-do min-ha ir-mã mor-reu (De-via ter si-do as-sim

No. 3 Canção de folha morta

Fol-ha ca-his-te ao meu la-do La-gri-ma ver-de dos ra-mos!

No. 4 Saudades da minha vida

Sau-da-de-do tem-po, Do tem-po pas-sa-do,

No. 6 No paz do outono

Na paz do ou-to-no, Gra-ve, pro-fun-da

No. 7 Cantiguo do viuvo

A noi-te ca-in na minha al-ma, Fi-quei tris-te sem que-rer

No. 8 Canção do carreiro

Na, na! na na na na na na na na na na na na na na

No. 9 Abril

De-pois da chu-va-ra-da su-bi-ta que i-num-dou

No. 10 Desejo

Pe-la ja-nel-la a-ber-ta eu ve-ja a lu-a a-pen-du-ra-da

No. 11 Redondilha

A vi-da Fin-gi da Me cha-ma Me bei-ja Me fo-go

No. 12 Realejo

Be-a-le-jo é co-mo os ou-tros são, que vao e vem___

Sino da Aldeia, Op. 87

Si- no, co- ra- ção d'al- de- - - - ia, Co- ra- ção

Viola quebrada (Brazilian folk song) (arr.)
By permission Associated Music Publishers, Inc.

Quan- do da bri- sa no a- çoite a frô da noi- te se cur- vó

Xangô
By permission Associated Music Publishers, Inc.

Xan- gô Ô le gon- di- le O lá lá gon gon gon

VITTORIA, Tomas Luis de (c. 1535-1611)

Animan meam

A- - - ni- mam me- am di- le- - - - - - ctam

Ave Maria

A- ve Ma- ri- - - - - - a Gra- ti- a ple- na

Caligaverunt oculi mei

Ca- li- ga- ve- runt O- cu- li me- i a fle- tu me- - - o

Domine, non sum dignus

Do- mi- ne non sum dig- nus, non sum dig- - - - - nus

Gaudent in coelis

Gau- dent in coe- lis a- ni- moe Sanc- to- - - - - - rum,

O Domine Jesu

O- - - - Do- mi- ne Je- su Chri- ste O Do- mi- ne Je- su Chri- ste,

O magnum mysterium

O ma- gnum mys- te- ri- um et ad- mi- ra- bi- le sa- cra

O quam gloriosum

O- - - - quam glo- ri- o- - - - - sum est re- - - - - - - gnum

O vos omnes

O vos- - - om- - - nes qui tran- si- tis per vi- - - am,

(both themes sung simultaneously)

O- - - vos- - - om- - - nes qui tran- si- tis per vi- am

Popule meus

Po- pu- le me- us, quid fe- ci ti- bi aut in quo con- tri- sta- vi- te

Tantum ergo

Tan- tum er- go Sa- - - cra- men- - - - - - tum

Tenebrae factae sunt

Te- - - ne- brae fac- - - - - tae sunt dum cru- ci- fi- xes- sent Je- sum

VIVALDI, Antonio (c. 1680-1743)

Stabat Mater I Largo

Sta- bat ma- ter do- lo- ro- - sa jux- sta cru- cem

Stabat Mater II Rocitative
Cu- jus a- ni- ma ge- men- tem con- tri- stan- tem

III Andante
Pro- pec- ca - - - tis su - - e gen- ti

IV Largo
E - ja, Ma - - ter fons a- mo - - - - - - - ris,

V Lento
Fac ut ar - de at cor me - - um in a- man- do

VUILLERMOZ, Emile (1878-)

Jardin d'amour
Copyright by Salabert, Paris, N. Y.
Quand je vais au __ jar- din, jar- din d'a- mour

WAGNER, Richard (1813-1883)

OPERAS

Der fliegende Holländer (The Flying Dutchman)
Act I Sailor's song
Mit Ge- wit- ter und Sturm aus fer- nem Meer, mein Mä- del, bin dir nah'!

Wie oft in Mee - res tief- sten Schlund stürzt' ich voll Sehn- sucht mich hin- ab,

Dich fra- ge ich, ge- pries'ner En- gel Got - - - tes

Durch Sturm und bö- sen Wind ver- schla- gen, irr' auf den Was- sern ich

Act II Spinning Chorus
Summ' __ und __ brumm', du __ gu- tes Räd - - - - - - - - chen

Senta's Ballad
Jo- ho- hoe! Jo- ho- ho- hoe! Ho- ho- hoe! Jo - - - - hoe

Traft ihr das Schiff im Mee- re an; blut- rot die Se- gel,

Doch kann dem blei- chen Man- ne Er- lö- sung ein- stens noch wer - - den

Mein Herz voll Treu- e __ bis __ zum Ster- ben,

Erik's dream
Auf ho- hem Fel- sen lag' ich träu- mend, sah un- ter mir des Mee- res Flut;

Daland's Aria
Mögst du, mein Kind, den frem- den Mann will- kom- men hei- ssen;

Wie aus der Fer- ne längst ver- gang' ner Zei- ten

OPERAS
Der fliegende Holländer (The Flying Dutchman)
Act II

Wohl hub auch ich voll Sehn-sucht mei- ne Bli- cke

Love Duet

Wirst du des Va- ters Wahl nicht schel- ten? was er ver-sprach,

Ach! könn- test das__ Ge-schick du ah- nen, dem dann__ mit mir

Ver-sank ich jetzt in wun-der-ba- res Träu- men?

Act III Sailor Chorus

Steu- er-mann! Lass__ die Wacht! Steu- er-mann! Her__ zu uns

Willst je- nes Tag's__ du__ nicht dich mehr ent-sin- nen

Lohengrin Act I Elsa's Dream

Ein- sam in trü- ben Ta- gen hab' ich zu Gott ge- fleht,

Ge- grüsst__ du gott-ge-san-dter Held! Sei ge- grüsst, sei ge- grüsst,__

Nun sei be-dankt, mein lie-ber Schwann! Zieh' durch die wei-te Flut__ zurück

Wenn ich im Kam-pfe für dich sie-ge willst du dass ich dein Gat- te sei?

Mein Herr und Gott, nun ruf' ich dich, dass du dem Kampf

Du kun-dest nun dein wahr__ Ge- richt; mein Gott und Herr,

Des rei- nen Arm gieb Hel- den-kraft; des Fal-schen Stär- ke

O fänd__ ich Ju- bel-wei- sen dei- nem Ruh- me__ gleich,

Dank, Kö- nig dir, dass du zu rich- ten kamst

Act II

Durch dich__ musst' ich ver- lie- ren mein Ehr', all' mein-en Ruhm

Euch Lüf- ten, die mein Kla- gen so trau- rig oft er- füllt,__

Ent- weih - - - - te Got- ter Helft jetzt mei-ner Ra- che

OPERAS
Lohengrin Act II

Ge- seg- net soll sie schreiten die lang' in De- muth litt

Du Ärm- ste kannst wohl nie er- mes- sen wie zwei- fel- los

Act III Bridal Chorus

Treu- lich ge- führt zie- het da- hin wo euch der Se- gen

Das sü- sse Lied ver- hallt; wir sind al- lein, zum er- sten Mal al- lein,

Ath- mest Du nicht mit mir die sü- ssen Düf- te O_ wie so hold

Lohengrin's narration

In fer- nem Land un- nah- bar eu- ren Schrit- ten liegt eine Burg,

Mein lie- ber Schwan! Ach, die- se let- zte traur'_ ge Fahrt

Kommt er dann heim, wenn ich ihm fern im Le- ben, dies Horn, dies Schwert,

Die Meistersinger von Nürnberg
Act I Scene I

Da zu dir_ der Hei - - - land kam wil- lig dei- ne Tau- fe nahm,

Scene II Chorus of Apprentices

Schuh- ma- che- rei und Po- e- te- rei die lern ich da all- ei- ner- lei

Al- ler End' ist doch Da- vid der al - - ler ge- scheit'st

Das Blu- men- kränz- lein aus Sei- den fein, wird das dem Herrn Rit- ter

Scene III

Das schö- ne Fest,_ Jo- han- nis- tag, ihr wisst, be- geh'n wir mor- gen

Am stillen Herd_ in Win- ters zeit_ wann Burg und Hof mir ein- ge- schneit

So rief der Lenz_ in den Wald, dass laut es ihn durch- hallt_

Scene V

Ja, ihr_ seid es; nein! Du_ bist es Al- les_ sag' ich

"Ein Meis- ter - - sin- ger muss es sein; nur_ wen ihr krönt_

Act II Scene I

Jo- han- nis- tag! Jo- han- nis- tag! Blu- men_ und_ Bän - - der

Scene III Sach's Monologue

Was duf- tet doch der Flie - - der so mild, so stark und voll

OPERAS

Die Meistersinger von Nürnberg
Act III Scene V

Ver- ach- tet mir die Meis- ter nicht, und ehrt mir ih- re Kunst!

Ehrt eu- re deut- schen Meis- ter, Dann bannt ihr gu- te Geis - - - - ter

Parsifal Act I Guileless fool motive

„durch Mit- leid wis- send, der rei- ne Tor, har- re sein', den ich er- kor"

Des Hai- nes Tie- re nah- ten dir nicht zahm; grüssten dich freund- lich

Vom Ba- de kehrt der Kö- nig heim; hoch steht die Son- ne

Zum letz- ten Lie- bes- mah - - le ge- rüs- tet Tag für Tag

Weh - - vol- les Er - be, dem ich ver- fal- len, ich_ einz'- ger Sün- der

Der Glau- be lebt; die Tau- be schwebt des Hei - - - lands hol - - der Bo- te:

„Neh- met hin mei- nen Leib, neh- met hin mein_ Blut_

Act II Flower Maidens' Waltz

Komm'! Komm'! Hol- der Kna- be! Komm'! Oh hol- der Kna- be

Im Lenz_ pflückt uns der Mei- ster! Wir wach - - - - - - sen_ hier_

Ihr kin- di- schen Buh- len, wei- chet von Ihm_ früh- wel- ken- de Blu- men

Ich sah das Kind an sei- ner Mut - - ter Brust

Am- for- tas! Die Wun- de! Die Wun- de!

Act III

Wie dünkt mich doch die Au- e heut' so schön _

Amfortas' Prayer

Mein Va- ter Hoch- ge- seg - - - - ne- ter der_ Hei- den

Nur ei- ne Waf- fe taugt: die Wun- de schliesst der Speer

Höch- sten Hei- les Wun- der!

Rienzi Act I

Die Frei- heit Rom's sei dies Ge- setz, ihn un- ter- than sei je- der Rö- mer,

OPERAS
Rienzi Act II — Ich sah_ die Stä-dte, sah_ das Land, ich zog_ ent - - lang

Act III — In sei- ner Blü-the bleicht_ mein Le-ben, da-hin da - - hin

Act V Rienzi's Prayer — All-mächt' ger Va - - ter, blick her- ab! Hör' mich im Stau- be

Der Ring des Nibelungen
Das Rheingold
Scene I Woglinde's Song — Weia! Waga! Wo- ge, du Wel- le, wal- le zur Wie- ge!

Scene II — Im- mer ist Un- dank Lo- ge's Lohn! Für dich nur be- sorgt_

So weit Le- ben und We- ben   im Was- ser, Erd' und Luft,

Ü- ber Stock und Stein zu Thal stap- fen sie hin

Scene IV Erda's Warning — Wei- che, Wo- tan, wei- che! Fleih' des Rin- ges Fluch!

Entrance of the Gods
into Valhalla — Zur Burg führt die Brü- cke   leicht, doch fest eu-rem Fuss:

Wotan's Song on
entrance to Valhalla — A- bend- lich strahlt der Son- ne Au- ge; in präch- ti- ger Gluth

Song of the
Rhinemaidens — Rhein- gold! Rhein- gold! rei - - - - - - - nes Gold!_

Die Walküre
Act I Scene III — Ein Schwert verhiess mir der Va- ter, ich fänd' es in höch-ster Noth

Der Män- ner Sip- pe sass hier im Saal, von Hun- ding zur Hoch- zeit

Finale: Love Duet — Win- ter- stür- me wi- chen dem Won- ne- mond, ___

Du bist der Lenz nach dem ich ver- lang- te

O süs- ses- te Won- ne! se- lig- stes Weib!

Sieg- mund heiss' ich und Sieg-mund bin ich be- zeug, es diess Schwert

Act II Scene I Call of the
Walküre — Ho- jo- to- ho! __ Ho- jo- to- ho! __ hei- a- ha! hei- a- ha! __

Fricka-Wotan
Duet — Der al- te Sturm, die al- te Müh'! Doch Stand muss ich hier - hal- ten

So ist es denn aus mit den e- wi- gen Göt- tern, — A

O _____ was ___ klag' ich um E- he und Eid, — B

Dei- ner ew- gen Gat- tin hei- li- ge Eh- re be-schir- me heut' — C

Scene IV

Sieg- mund! Sieh' auf mich! Ich bin's der bald du folg'st — D

Act III Scene I

Fort ___ denn ei- le nach O - - - sten ge- wandt! — E

Scene II

Nicht send' ich dich mehr aus ___ Wal- hall; nicht weis' ich dir mehr — F

Scene III Brunnhilde's pleading

War es so schmäh- lich, was ich ver-brach, dass mein Ver- bre- chen — G

Wotan's farewell

Leb' wohl, du Küh- nes, herr- li- ches Kind! Du mei- nes Her- zens — H

Der Au- gen leuch-ten-des Paar das oft ich lä-chelnd ge- kos't, — I

Siegfried Act I Scene I

Zwang- vol- le Pla- ge! Müh' oh- ne Zweck! Das bes- te Schwert, — J

Da hast du die Stü- cken, schänd- li- cher Stüm- per — K

Als zul- len- des Kind zog ich dich auf wärm- te mit Klei-den — L

Es san- gen die Vög- lein so se- lig im Lenz — M

Aus dem Wald fort in die Welt zieh'n!___ nim- mer kehr' ich zu- rück! — N

Scene II

Auf wol- ki- gen Höh'n woh- nen die Göt- ter Wal-hall heisst_ihr Saal — O

Scene III

No- thung! No- thung! Neid- li- ches Schwert! Was muss- test du — P

Zu Spreu nun schuf ich die schar- fe Pracht, im Ti- gel — Q

Schmie- de,mein Ham- mer, ein har-tes Schwert! Ho- ho! Ha- hei! — R

Act II Scene II

Du hol- des Vög- lein, dich hört' ich noch nie: — S

OPERAS
Der Ring des Nibelungen
Siegfried Act II Scene III
Voice of
Forest Bird

Hei! Sieg- fried ge- hört nun der Helm und der Ring!

Lus- tig im Leid   sing ich von — Lie — — — be

Act III Scene I A

Wa- che, Wa- la! Wa- la! Er- wach'! Aus lan- gem Schlaf

B

Er- da! Er- da! E- wi- ges Weib. Aus hei- mi- scher Tie- fe

Stark ruft das Lied   kräf- tig reizt der Zau- ber Ich bin er- wacht

Scene III

Was ruht dort schlum- mernd im schat- ti- gen Tann Ein Ross ist's

A

Heil dir, Son- ne! Heil dir, Licht! Heil dir, Leuchtender Tag!

B

O Heil der Mut- ter, die mich ge- bar!

A

E — — — wig — war ich, e — — — wig — bin ich

B

Sieg — — fried, Herr — — li- cher! Hort — der Welt!

Götterdämmerung
"Twilight of the Gods"
Prologue: Brünnhilde & Siegfried

Zu neu- en Tha- ten   theu- er Hel- de wie liebt' ich dich,

Act I Scene I Hagen's Watch

Hier sitz' ich zur Wacht, wah- re den Hof, weh- re den Hal- le dem Feind.

Scene III Waltraute's
Narrative

Hö- re mit Sinn, was ich dir sa- ge! Seit er von dir ge- schie- den,

Act II Scene III Hagen's Call

Hoi- ho! Hoi- ho— ho- ho! Ihr Gi- bichs- man- nen, wa- chet euch auf

(Chorus)

Gross Glück und Heil lacht nun dem Rhein, da Ha- gen, der Grim- me,

Scene IV

Hel- le Wehr! Hei- li- ge Waf- fe Hilf mei- nem e- wi- gen Ei- de!

Act III Scene I Song of the
Rhinemaidens

Frau Son — — — ne sen- det lich- te Strah- len;

Scene II Siegfried's
Narration

Mi — — me hiess ein mür- ri- scher Zwerg; in des Nei- des Zwang

OPERAS Der Ring des Niebelungen
Götterdämmerung
Act III Scene II Siegfried's
Narration

In Leid_____ zu dem Wi- pfel lausch ich hin - ein_____

Scene III Brünnhilde's
Immolation

Star- ke Schei- te schichtet mir dort am Ran- de des Rhein's zu Hauf'!

Wie Son- ne lau- ter strahlt mir sein Licht!

Oh ihr, der Ei- de e- wi- ge Hü- ter

Tannhäuser
Act I Scene I Baccanale
(Chorus of Sirens)

Naht euch dem Lan - - - de! Wo in den Ar - - - men glü-hender Lie- be_____

Scene II

Dir tö - - ne_____ Lob! Die Wun- der sei'n ge- prie - - sen,

Ge- lieb- ter, komm! Sieh' dort die Grot- te von ros'gen Düf- ten mild

Scene III Shepherd Song

Frau Hol- de kam aus dem Berg_____ her- vor zu zieh'n durch Flu- ren

Scene IV

Als du im küh- nem San- ge uns be- strit- test,

War's Zau- ber, war es rei- ne Macht, durch die solch' Wun- der

Act II Scene I

Dich, teu- re Hal - - - le, grüss' ich wie- der, froh grüss' ich dich,

Ver- zeihe, wenn ich nicht weiss, was ich be- gin- ne!

Der Sän- ger Klu- gen Wei - - - sen lausch ich_____ sonst

Der Un- glück- sel'- ge, den ge- fan- gen ein furcht-bar mächt' ger

Scene II Elizabeth &
Tannhäuser
Duet

Ge- prie - - sen sei_____ die Stun- de, ge- prie- sen sei_____ die Macht!

Scene III

Noch blei- be denn un- aus- ge- spro- chen dein süss Ge- heim- niss

Scene IV Entrance of the
Guests

Freu- dig be- grü - - - ssen wir die ed- le Hal- le

Freu- dig_____ be- grü - - - ssen wir die ed- le_____ Hal- le

Wo_____ lan- ge noch der Ru- fer-schal- le, Wo_____ lan- ge noch der Ru- fer-schalle

OPERAS
Tannhäuser
Act II Scene IV Landgrave's
Welcome

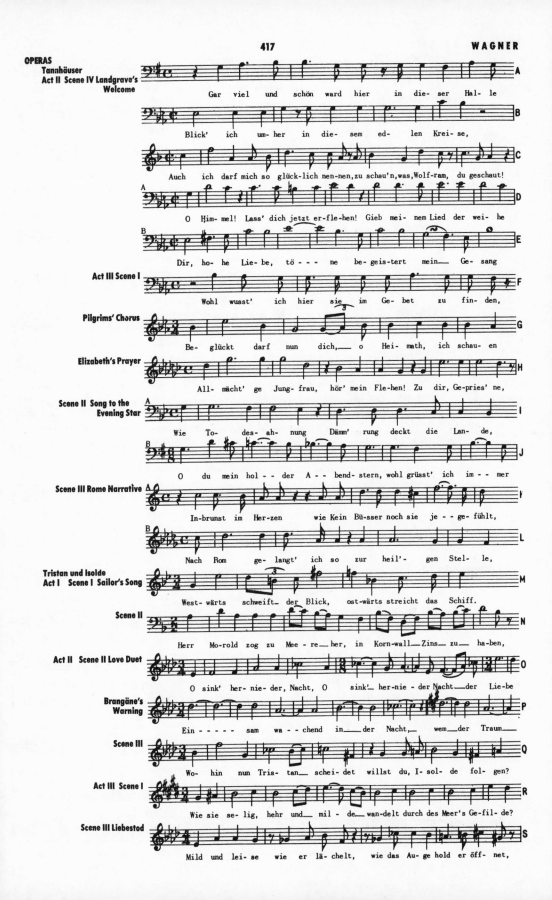

Gar viel und schön ward hier in die- ser Hal- le

Blick' ich um- her in die- sem ed- len Krei- se,

Auch ich darf mich so glück- lich nen- nen, zu schau'n, was, Wolf- ram, du geschaut!

O Him- mel! Lass' dich jetzt er- fle- hen! Gieb mei- nem Lied der wei- he

Dir, ho- he Lie- be, tö- - - ne be- geis- tert mein_ Ge- sang

Act III Scene I

Wohl wusst' ich hier sie im Ge- bet zu fin- den,

Pilgrims' Chorus

Be- glückt darf nun dich,_ o Hei- math, ich schau- en

Elizabeth's Prayer

All- mächt' ge Jung- frau, hör' mein Fle- hen! Zu dir, Ge- pries' ne,

Scene II Song to the
Evening Star

Wie To- des- ah- nung Dämm' rung deckt die Lan- de,

O du mein hol- - der A- - bend- stern, wohl grüss' ich im- - mer

Scene III Rome Narrative

In- brunst im Her- zen wie Kein Bü- sser noch sie je- ge- fühlt,

Nach Rom ge- langt' ich so zur heil'- gen Stel- le,

Tristan und Isolde
Act I Scene I Sailor's Song

West- wärts schweift_ der Blick, ost- wärts streicht das Schiff.

Scene II

Herr Mo- rold zog zu Mee- re- her, in Korn- wall Zins zu ha- ben,

Act II Scene II Love Duet

O sink' her- nie- der, Nacht, O sink' her- nie- der Nacht_ der Lie- be

Brangäne's
Warning

Ein- - - - sam wa- - chend in_ der Nacht,_ wem_ der Traum

Scene III

Wo- hin nun Tris- tan_ schei- det willst du, I- sol- de fol- gen?

Act III Scene I

Wie sie se- lig, hehr und_ mil- de_ wan- delt durch des Meer's Ge- fil- de?

Scene III Liebestod

Mild und lei- se wie er lä- chelt, wie das Au- ge hold er öff- net,

Songs: L'Attente
Monte, é-cu-reuil monte au grand chê- ne, Sur la bran- che des cieux___

Les Deux Grenadiers
Long- temps cap- tifs chez le Rus- se loin- tain

Peut- ê- tre bien qu'en ce choc meur- tri- er,

Five Wesendonck Songs
1. Der Engel
In der Kind-heit frü- hen Ta- gen hört' ich oft von En - geln sa- gen,

2. Stehe still!
Sau- sen-des, brau-sen-des Rad der Zeit, Mes- ser du der E- wig-keit;

3. Im Treibhaus
Hoch- ge-wölb- te Blät- ter-kro- nen, Bal- da-chi- ne von Sma- ragd,

4. Schmerzen
Son- ne, wei-nest je- den A- bend dir die schö-nen Au- gen roth;

5. Träume
Sag',welch' wun-der-ba- re Träu-me hal- ten mei- nen Sinn um- fan-gen

Mignonne
Mi- gnon- ne, al-lons voir si la Ro- se qui ce ma-tin___

Schlaf', holdes Kind
Schlaf ___ hol- des Kind,___ ich wieg'dich in Schlum- mer,

Der Tannenbaum
Der Tan- nen-baum steht schwei-gend ein- sam auf grau- er Höh';

WALLACE, William Vincent (1812-1865)

Maritana (opera) Act I No. 4
An- gels___ that a-round us___ ho- ver, Guard us till the___close of day

Act II No. 13
Yes! let me like a Sol- dier fall up- on some o- pen plain

No. 14
In hap- py mo- ments day by day, The sands of life___ may pass,

No. 19
There is a flow'r that bloom- eth when au- tumn leaves are shed,

Act III No. 22
Scenes that are bright- est, May___ charm___ a - - - while

WALTHER von der Vogelweide (12th-13th Cent.)

Kreuzfahrlied (Crusader's Song)
(also called Palästinalied)
Al- ler erst lebe___ ich mir___ wer- de, sit mie sün- dic___

WALTON, William (1902-   )

By the wa - - - - - - ters of Ba - by - lon   There___ we sat down

Sing us one of the songs of Zi - on

How___ shall we sing___ the Lord's___ song, the Lord's___ song___

If   I for-get thee,___ for- get___ thee

In Ba - - - - - by-lon   Belshazzar the King made a great___ feast

Bring ye the cor - - - - - - - - - - net

Praise___ ye the___ god of sil- ver

Praise___ ye praise___ ye

Then sing___ a- loud to God___ our strength

Then sing, sing a- loud___ to God our strength;Make a joy- ful noise

Then___ sing,___ sing a- loud,___ Sing a- loud___

Al- le- lu- ja   Al- le- lu - - - ja, al- le- lu- ja

WARD, John (16th-17th Cents.)

Hope of my heart

Hope___ of___ my heart, Hope of my___ heart O where- fore

Out from the vale

Out from___ the vale___ of deep de - - - spair, of deep de- spair

Upon a bank of roses

Up- on a bank with Ros- es set a- bout, up- on a bank

WARE, Harriet (Contemporary)

Boat Song

Where will you take___ me lit- tle boat, All on a sum- mer's day___

WARLOCK, Peter (1894-1930) (Philip Heseltine)

As ever I saw
By permission Boosey & Hawkes, Inc., copyright owners
She is gen-tle and al--so wise; of all___ o-thers

Captain Stratton's Fancy
By permission of Augener, Ltd., London
Oh, some are fond of red wine and some are fond of white,

Chop Cherry
By permission J. & W. Chester, Ltd., London, copyright owners
When as the rye reach___ to the chin, and chop-cher-ry,

Corpus Christi (old English carol) (arr.)
Copyright 1921, J. Curwen
Lul-ly, lul-lay, lul-ly, lul-lay, The fau-con hath borne my make___ a-way

Fair and True
By permission Oxford Univ. Press, London, copyright owners
Love-ly kind, and kind-ly lov-ing, Such a mind were worth the mov-ing;

The Fox
By permission Oxford Univ. Press, London, copyright owners
At 'The Fox Inn' the tat-ter'd ears, the fox'-s grin

Good Ale
By permission of Augener, Ltd., London
Bring us in no brown bread___ for___ that is made of bran,

Jillian of Berry
By permission Oxford Univ. Press, London, copyright owners
For Jil-lian of Ber-ry she dwells on a hill, And she hath good beer

Passing by
By permission Oxford Univ. Press, London, copyright owners
There is a la-dy sweet and kind, Was nev-er face so pleased my mind

The Passionate Shepherd
By permission of Galaxy Music Corporation, N. Y., copyright by Elkin & Co., Ltd.
Come live with me, and___ be my love, And we will all

Piggesnie
By permission of Augener, Ltd., London
She is so pro-per and so pure, Full stead-fast, sta-ble and de-mure

Pretty Ring Time
By permission Oxford Univ. Press, London, copyright owners
It was a lov-er and his lass, With a hey and a ho

Rest, sweet Nymphs
By permission Oxford Univ. Press, London, copyright owners
Rest, sweet nymphs, let gold-en sleep Charm your star-bright-er eyes,___

Sigh no more, Ladies
By permission Oxford Univ. Press, London, copyright owners
Sigh no more, la-dies, sigh no more;___ Men were de-cei-vers ev-er.

Sleep
By permission Oxford Univ. Press, London, copyright owners
Come, sleep, and with thy sweet de-ceiv-ing Lock me in de-light a-while;

Take, O take those lips away
By permission Boosey & Hawkes, Inc., copyright owners
Take, O take___ those lips___ a-way that so sweet--ly

Willow, willow (arr.)
By permission Oxford Univ. Press, London, copyright owners
The poor soul sat sigh-ing By a sy-ca-more tree

WEAVER, Powell (1890-   )

The Abbot of Derry
Copyright 1935, G. Schirmer, Inc.

The Ab- bot of Der- ry hates Sat- an and Sin

Moon Marketing
Copyright 1924, G. Schirmer, Inc.

Let's go to the mar- ket in the moon _____

WEBER, Carl Maria von (1786-1826)

OPERAS
Abu Hassan No. 2

Ich ge- be_ Gas- ter- ei- en, Mit Lied- ern_ und mit Tän- zen,

O Fa- ti- me, mei- ne Trau- te, die so zärt- - lich zu_ mir_ spricht,

No. 5

Wird Phi- lo- me- - le trau- ern, dem Kä- fig kaum_ ent- schlüpft,

Euryanthe Act I

Un- ter blüh'nden Man- del- bäu- men, an der Loi- re grü- nem Strand,

O mein Leid ist un- er- mes- sen, du kannst mir_ dein_Herz_ ent- zieh'n

Act II

Schweigt glüh'nden Seh- nens wil- de Trie- be, ihr Au- ge sucht·

We- hen mir Lüf- te Ruh, strö- men mir Düf- te zu,

O Se- lig- keit, dich fass' ich kaum, O Se- lig- keit,dich fass' ich kaum

Act III

Hier dicht am Quell wo Wei- den steh'n, die Ster- ne hell durchschau- en,

Jaegerchor

Die Tha- le damp- fen die Hö- hen glühn!

Der Freischütz Act I

Durch die Wäl- der,durch die Au- en zog ich leich- ten_ Sinns_da- hin!

Jetzt ist wohl ihr Fen- ster of- fen und sie horcht auf mei- nen Tritt,

Hier im ird' schen_ Jam- mer- thal war doch nichts als.Plack und_ Qual

Schweig'! schweig'! da- mit dich Nie- mand warnt, schwei- ge!

Der Höl- le Netz hat dich _____ um- - garnt,

OPERAS
Der Freischütz Act I

A

Tri- umph! _____ die Ra- che ge- lingt!

Act II Brides-
maids'
Chorus

B

Wir win- den_ dir den Jung- fern- kranz mit veil- chen- blau- er_ Sei- de

C

Kommt ein schlan- ker Bursch ge- gan- gen, blond_ von_ Lo- cken_ o- der braun

D

Lei- se, lei- se, from- me_ Wei- se, schwing' dich auf zum Ster- nen- krei- se

E

Al- les pflegt schon längst_ der_ Ruh'! Trau- ter Freund, wo wei- lest_ du?

Act III

F

Und ob die Wol- ke sie_ ver- hül- le, die Son- ne bleibt

Romanze
and Aria

G

Einst träum- te mein- er sel' gen Ba- se, die Kam- mer- thür er- öff- ne sich,

H

Trü- be Au- gen, Lieb- chen_ tau- gen ei- nem_ hol- den Bräut- chen_ nicht,

Hunting
Chorus

I

Was gleicht wohl auf_ Er- den dem Jä- ger- ver- gnü- - gen

Oberon Act I No. 5

J

Von Ju- gend auf in dem Kampf- ge- fild, die Lan- - - - ze_ hoch

K

Jetzt giesst_ sich aus ein sanft'- - rer Glanz

No. 6

L

Ja o Herr! mein Heil,_ mein_ Le- ben Re- zia ist_ für_ e- - wig_ dein!

Act II No. 11 Prayer

M

Va- ter! Hör' mich fleh'n zu dir Va- ter Hör' mich fleh'n zu dir!

No. 12 Ocean, thou
mighty
monster

N

O- ze- an Du Un- ge- heu- er! schlan- gen- gleich hältst du um- schlun- gen

O

Noch seh ich die Wel- len to- ben durch_ die_ Nacht_

P

Wol- ken- los strahlt jetzt die Son- ne auf die Pur- pur- wel- len nie- der

Q

O Won- - - - - - ne! Mein Hü- - on! Zum U- - fer her- bei!

No. 14

R

A- ra- bi- en, mein Hei- mat- land, du Land so teu- er mir

No. 17 Cavatina

S

Trau- - re, mein_ Herz, um ver- schwun- de- nes Glück!

Der kleine Fritz an seine jungen Freunde
Ach, wenn ich nur ein Lieb - - - - chen hät - te, so gross wie ich   A

Leyer und Schwert, Op. 42, No. 2
No. 2 Lützows wilde Jagd
Was glänzt dort vom Wal-de im Son-nen-schein? Hör's nä-her   B

No. 6 Schwertlied
Du Schwert an mei-ner Lin-ken, was soll dein heit-res___ Blin-ken?   C

Schwertlied (variant)
Du Schwert an mei-ner Lin-ken, was soll dein hei-tres Blin-ken?   D

No. 7 Gebet vor der Schlacht
Hör uns, All-mäch-ti-ger! Hör uns, All-gü-ti-ger   E

Wiegenlied, Op. 13, No. 3
Schlaf, Herz-ens-söhn-chen, mein Lieb-ling bist du!   F

WECKERLIN, Jean Baptiste (1821-1910)

Bergerettes (arrangements)
Aminte
Viens dans ce bo-ca-ge, belle A-min-te, Sans con-train-te   H

L'Amour s'envole
L'a-mour est un en-fant ti-mi-de, La sé-vé-ri-té   I

Bergère Légère
Ber-gè-re Lé-gè-re, Je crains tes ap-pas;___   J

Chantons les amours de Jean
Chan-tons, chan-tons les a-mours de Jean-ne, chan-tons, chan-tons   K

Chaque chose a son temps
Cha-que chose a son temps, Fil-let-te, Cha-que chose a son temps   L

Je connais un berger discret
Je con-nais un ber-ger dis-cret, qui se plaint__ et sou-pi-re,   M

Jeunes fillettes A
Jeu-ne fil-le-te, pro-fi-tez du temps, La vi-o-let-te   N

B
Cet-te fleu-ret-te Passe en peu de temps Toute a-mou-ret-te passe   O

Lisette
En me-nant pai-tre mon trou-peau Je vis dans un bo-ca - - - - - ge   P

Maman, dites-moi
Ma-man, di-tes-moi ce qu'on sent quand on ai-me,   Q

Menuet d'Exaudet
Cet é-tang Qui s'e-tend dans la plai-ne, Ré-pète, au sein de ses eaux,   R

Le mère Bontemps
La mè-re Bon-temps s'en al-lait dis-ant aux fil-let-tes: S

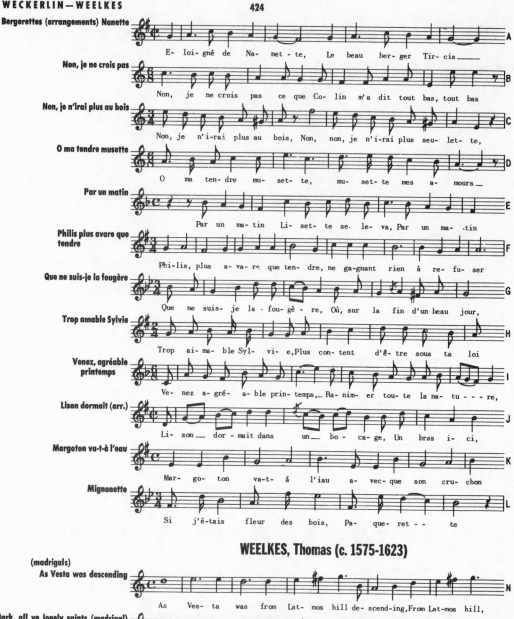

Bergerettes (arrangements) Nanette

E- loi- gné de Na- net- te, Le beau ber- ger Tir- cis____ A

Non, je ne crois pas

Non, je ne crois pas ce que Co- lin m'a dit tout bas, tout bas B

Non, je n'irai plus au bois

Non, je n'i-rai plus au bois, Non, non, je n'i-rai plus seu- let- te, C

O ma tendre musette

O ma ten-dre mu- set- te, mu- set- te mes a- mours____ D

Par un matin

Par un ma-tin Li- set-te se. le- va, Par un ma- .tin E

Philis plus avare que tendre

Phi-lis, plus a- va- re que ten-dre, ne ga-gnant rien à re- fu- ser F

Que ne suis-je la fougère

Que ne suis- je la- fou- gè- re, Où, sur la fin d'un beau jour, H

Trop amable Sylvie

Trop ai- ma- ble Syl- vi- e, Plus con- tent d'ê- tre sous ta loi I

Venez, agréable printemps

Ve- nez a- gré- a- ble prin-temps,_ Ra- nim- er tou- te la na- tu - - re, I

Lison dormait (arr.)

Li- son____ dor- mait dans un__ bo- ca-ge, Un bras i- ci, J

Margoton va-t-à l'eau

Mar- go- ton va-t- á l'iau a- vec- que son cru- chon K

Mignonette

Si j'é-tais fleur des bois, Pa- que-ret - - te L

WEELKES, Thomas (c. 1575-1623)

(madrigals)
As Vesta was descending

As Ves- ta was from Lat- mos hill de- scend-ing, From Lat-mos hill, N

Hark, all ye lonely saints (madrigal)

Hark, all ye love- ly saints a- bove, Di- an- a hath a- greed with love O

Hence, Care, Thou Art Too Cruel

Hence Care; thou art____ too____ cru - - - - el, P

Lady, the birds right fairly

La- dy the birds right_ fair- ly, La-dy the birds right fair - - - - ly Q

O Care, thou wilt despatch me

O Care, thou wilt____ des - - - - patch me,____ if Mu- sic do R

On the Plains

On the plains Fai- ry trains were a tread-ing meas- ures, S

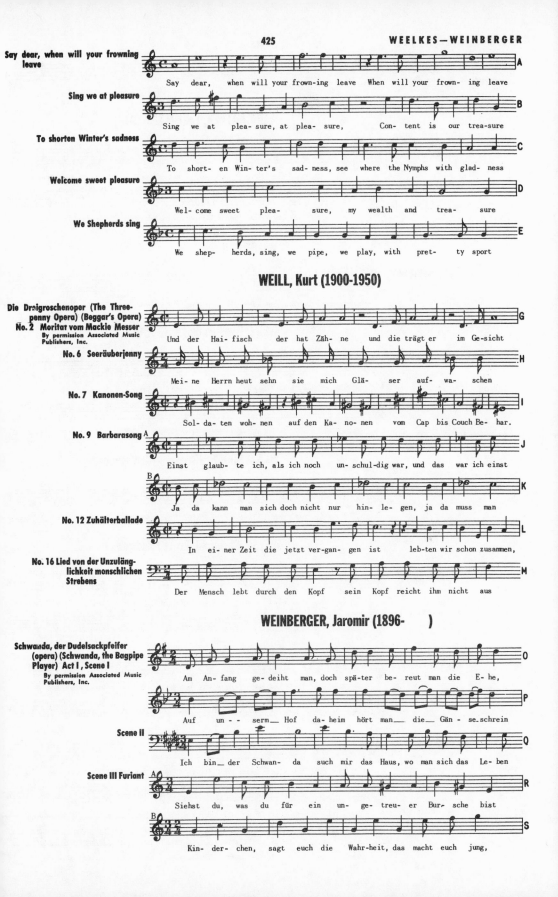

Say dear, when will your frowning leave

Say dear, when will your frown-ing leave When will your frown- ing leave

Sing we at pleasure

Sing we at plea-sure, at plea- sure, Con- tent is our trea-sure

To shorten Winter's sadness

To short- en Win-ter's sad-ness, see where the Nymphs with glad- ness

Welcome sweet pleasure

Wel- come sweet plea- sure, my wealth and trea- sure

We Shepherds sing

We shep- herds, sing, we pipe, we play, with pret- ty sport

WEILL, Kurt (1900-1950)

Die Dreigroschenoper (The Three-penny Opera) (Beggar's Opera) No. 2 Moritat vom Mackie Messer
By permission Associated Music Publishers, Inc.

Und der Hai- fisch der hat Zäh- ne und die trägt er im Ge-sicht

No. 6 Seeräuberjenny

Mei- ne Herrn heut sehn sie mich Glä- ser auf- wa- schen

No. 7 Kanonen-Song

Sol- da- ten woh- nen auf den Ka- no- nen vom Cap bis Couch Be- har.

No. 9 Barbarasong

Einst glaub- te ich, als ich noch un-schul-dig war, und das war ich einst

Ja da kann man sich doch nicht nur hin- le- gen, ja da muss man

No. 12 Zuhälterballade

In ei- ner Zeit die jetzt ver-gan- gen ist leb-ten wir schon zusammen,

No. 16 Lied von der Unzuläng-lichkeit menschlichen Strebens

Der Mensch lebt durch den Kopf sein Kopf reicht ihm nicht aus

WEINBERGER, Jaromir (1896-   )

Schwanda, der Dudelsackpfeifer (opera) (Schwanda, the Bagpipe Player) Act I, Scene I
By permission Associated Music Publishers, Inc.

Am An- fang ge-deiht man, doch spä-ter be- reut man die E- he,

Auf un- serm Hof da-heim hört man die Gän- se schrein

Scene II

Ich bin der Schwan- da such mir das Haus, wo man sich das Le- ben

Scene III Furiant

Siehst du, was du für ein un- ge-treu- er Bur- sche bist

Kin- der- chen, sagt euch die Wahr-heit, das macht euch jung,

Schwanda, der Dudelsackpfeifer (opera) (Schwanda, the Bagpipe Player) Act II, Scene IV

Wie kann ich denn ver-ges-sen, was mein Lieb-stes war,

WEINGARTNER, Felix (1863-1942)

Du bist ein Kind, Op. 28, No. 12
By permission Associated Music Publishers, Inc.

Du bist ein Kind und sollst es e-wig blei-ben;

Liebesfeier, Op. 16, No. 2

An ih-rem bun-ten Lie-derin Klet-tert die Ler-che

WERNER, H.

Haidenröslein

Sah ein Knab' ein Rös-lein stehn, Rös-lein auf der Hai-den

WERT, Giaches de (1536-1596)

Ah dolente partita (madrigal)

Ah do-len-te par-ti - - - ta! Ah fin del-la mia vi-ta

Un jour je m'en allai

Un jour je m'en al-lai, cueil-lant de vi-o-let-tes,

WESTENDORF, Thomas (Contemporary)

I'll take you home again, Kathleen

I'll take you home a-gain, Kath-leen A-cross the o-cean wild and wide

WEYSE, Christoph Ernst Friedrich

De klare Bolger rulled, from Sovedrikken (opera)

De Kla-re Bol-ger rul-led mod dunk-le Af-ten lund

Gud skee Tak og Lov

Gud skee tak og Lov! vi saa dei-lig sov:

Han gik til Ludlams Hule, from Ludlams Hule (opera)

Han gik til Lud-lams Hu-le i mör-ke Mi-die-nat

I Osten stiger Solen op

I O-sten sti-ger So-len op: den spre-der Guld paa Sky

Lysets Engel gaar med Glands

Ly-sets En-gel gaaer med Glands gjen-nem Him-mel-por-te

Nu ringer alle Klokker mod sky

Nu rin-ger al-le klok-ker mod sky, det Ki-mier

Nu vaagne alle Guds Fugle smaa

Nu vaag-ne al-le Guds Fug-le smaa, de fly-ve fra Re-de

Teklas Sang (from Schiller's Wallenstein)
Der Eich-wald brau-set, die Wol- ken ziehn, das Mägd- lein wan- delt

WIDOR, Charles Marie (1845-1937)

L'Aurore, Op. 22, No. 2
By permission J. Hamelle Music Publishers Paris
L'au- ro- re s'al- lu- me, L'ombre é- pais-se fuit

Je ne veux pas autre chose, Op. 43, No. 1
By permission J. Hamelle Music Publishers Paris
Je ne veux pas au-tre cho-se que ton sou- rire et ta voix

Mon bras pressait, Op. 43, No. 3
By permission J. Hamelle Music Publishers Paris
Mon bras pres-sait ta tail-le, frêle et sou-ple com-me le ro- seau,

Non Credo
By permission Durand & Cie, Paris; Elkan-Vogel Co., Inc., Phila., copyright owners
Je ne crois pas que le Sa- veur soit né   Je ne crois pas,

Nuit d'Étoiles, Op. 14, No. 1
By permission J. Hamelle Music Publishers, Paris
Nuit d'é- toi-les, sous tes voi-les, sous ta bri- se et tes par-fums,

Le Plongeur, Op. 43, No. 4
By permission J. Hamelle Music Publishers, Paris
Le plon-geur, sur qui la va-gue dé-fer-le, m'a cri-é du fond

WILBYE, John (1574-1638)

Madrigals: Adieu, sweet Amaryllis (4-voice)
A-dieu, a- dieu, a- dieu, sweet A- ma-ril-lis! A- dieu,

Draw on Sweet Night
Draw on sweet night, draw, draw on sweet night

Flora gave me fairest flowers (5-voice)
Flo- ra gave me fair-est flow-ers, Flo- ra gave me fair-est flow-ers,

Lady, when I behold
La- dy, when I be- hold   the ros- es sprout - ing

Stay, Corydon thou Swain
A1
Stay, Stay Co- ry- don thou swain, talk not so soon of dy - - - ing,

A2
Stay Co- ry- don thou swain, talk not so soon of dy- ing

Sweet honey-sucking bees (5-voice)
Sweet ho- ney- suck-ing bees, Sweet ho- ney- suck-ing bees,

WILLAERT, Adrian (c. 1480-1562)

Con lagrime e sospir
Con la- gri- me e so- spir ne- gan-do por- ge

WILSON, H. Lane

Carmena

Dance and song make glad the night.

Ah! now rings a voice I know from ev'-ry voice a-part

WOLF, Hugo (1860-1903)

Abschied

Un-an-ge-klopft ein Herr tritt a-bends bei mir ein:

Der glei-chen hab' ich nie ge-sehn, all' mein Leb-ta-ge nicht ge-sehn,

Ach, des Knaben Augen

Ach, des Kna-ben Au-gen sind mir so schön und klar er-schie-nen,

Ach, im Maien war's

Ach, im Mai-en war's, im Mai-en

Agnes

Ro-sen-zeit! wie schnell vor-bei, schnell vor-bei, bist du doch ge-gan-gen!

Alle gingen, Herz, zur Ruh

Al-le gin-gen, Herz, zur Ruh, al-le schla-fen, nur nicht du.

Alles endet, was entstehet

Al-les en-det, was ent-ste-het, Al-les, al-les rings ver-geh-et

Als ich auf dem Euphrat schiffte

Als ich auf dem Eu---phrat schiff-te

Anakreons Grab

Wo die Ro-se hier blüht, wo Re-ben um Lor-beer sich schlin-gen,

Andenken

Ich den--ke dein wenn durch den Hain

An den Schlaf

Schlaf! su-sser Schlaf! ob-wohl dem Tod, wie du, nichts gleicht,

An die Geliebte

Wenn ich, von dei-nem An-schaun tief ge-stillt, mich stumm

An eine Aeolsharfe

An-ge-lehnt an die E-pheu-wand die-ser al-ten Ter-ras-se

Auch kleine Dinge

Auch klei-ne Din-ge kön-nen uns ent-zü-cken,

Auf dm grünen Balkon

Auf dem grü-nen Bal-kon mein Mäd-chen schaut, nach mir durchs Git-ter-lein,

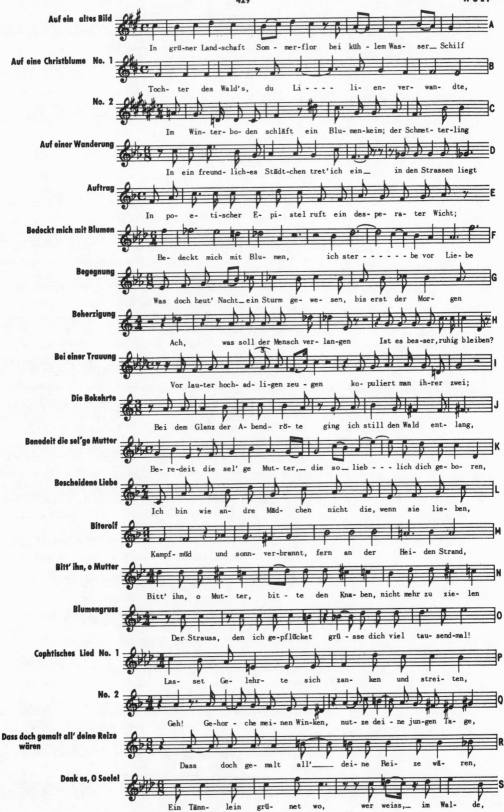

Auf ein altes Bild — In grü-ner Land-schaft Som-mer-flor bei küh-lem Was-ser Schilf   A

Auf eine Christblume No. 1 — Toch-ter des Wald's, du Li - - - li-en-ver-wan-dte,   B

No. 2 — Im Win-ter-bo-den schläft ein Blu-men-keim; der Schmet-ter-ling   C

Auf einer Wanderung — In ein freund-lich-es Städt-chen tret'ich ein_ in den Strassen liegt   D

Auftrag — In po - e-ti-scher E-pi-stel ruft ein des-pe-ra-ter Wicht;   E

Bedeckt mich mit Blumen — Be-deckt mich mit Blu-men, ich ster - - - - be vor Lie-be   F

Begegnung — Was doch heut' Nacht_ein Sturm ge-we-sen, bis erst der Mor-gen   G

Beherzigung — Ach, was soll der Mensch ver-lan-gen Ist es bes-ser, ruhig bleiben?   H

Bei einer Trauung — Vor lau-ter hoch-ad-li-gen zeu-gen ko-puliert man ih-rer zwei;   I

Die Bekehrte — Bei dem Glanz der A-bend-rö-te ging ich still den Wald ent-lang,   J

Benedeit die sel'ge Mutter — Be-re-deit die sel'ge Mut-ter,_ die so_ lieb - - - lich dich ge-bo-ren,   K

Bescheidene Liebe — Ich bin wie an-dre Mäd-chen nicht die, wenn sie lie-ben,   L

Biterolf — Kampf-müd und sonn-ver-brannt, fern an der Hei-den Strand,   M

Bitt' ihn, o Mutter — Bitt' ihn, o Mut-ter, bit-te den Kna-ben, nicht mehr zu zie-len   N

Blumengruss — Der Strauss, den ich ge-pflücket grü-sse dich viel tau-send-mal!   O

Cophtisches Lied No. 1 — Las-set Ge-lehr-te sich zan-ken und strei-ten,   P

No. 2 — Geh! Ge-hor-che mei-nen Win-ken, nut-ze dei-ne jun-gen Ta-ge,   Q

Dass doch gemalt all' deine Reize wären — Dass doch ge-malt all'_ dei-ne Rei-ze wä-ren,   R

Denk es, O Seele! — Ein Tänn-lein grü-net wo, wer weiss,_ im Wal-de,   S

Der Gärtner A
Auf ih - rem Leib-röss- lein, so weiss wie der Schnee,

Gebet B
Herr!_ Schi-cke was du willt, ein Lie- bes o - der Lei- des,

Geh', Geliebter, geh' jetzt C
Geh',_ Ge-lieb- ter, geh' jetzt!_ Sieh, der Mor-gen däm - - mert.

Der Genesene an die Hoffnung D
Töd - - lich grau- te mir der Mor-gen: doch schon lag mein Haupt, wie süss!

Genialisch Treiben E
So wälz_ ich oh - ne Un-ter-lass, wie Sankt Di - o - - - - - - ge- nes,

Gesang Weyla's F
Du bist Orp-lid, mein Land! das fer - - - ne leuch- tet;

Gesegnet sei das Grün G
Ge- seg - - net sei das Grün und wer es trägt! Ein grü-nes Kleid

Gesegnet sei, durch den die Welt entstund H
Ge- seg - net sei, durch den die Welt ent- stund;

Gesellenlied I
"Kein Mei- ster fällt vom Him-mel". und das ist auch ein grosses Glück!

Geselle, woll'n wir uns in Kutten hüllen J
Ge-sel- le, woll'n wir uns in Kut- ten hül - - len

Ghasél K
Im Was- ser wogt die Li - - lie, die blan- ke, hin_ und_ her_

Gleich und Gleich L
Ein Blu- men-glöck - - chen vom Bo- den her- vor

Grenzen der Menscheit M
Wenn _ der ur-al- te hei-li- ge Va- ter mit ge-las-se-ner Hand

Harfenspieler No. 1 N
Wer sich der Ein-sam-keit er- gibt, ach! der ist bald al-lein;

No. 2 O
An die Tü- ren will_ ich schleichen, still und sitt-sam will ich stehn;

No. 3 P
Wer nie sein Brot mit Trä- nen ass, wer nie die kum- mer - vol-len Näch- te

Heb' auf dein blondes Haupt Q
Heb' auf dein blon- des Haupt und schla- fe nicht,_

Heimweh R
An- ders wird die Welt mit je- dem Schritt den ich wei - - - - ter

Heimweh S
Wer in der Frem- de will wan-dern, der muss mit der Lieb- sten gehn,

Herr, was trägt der Boden hier

Herr, was trägt der Bo-den hier, den du tränkst so bit-ter-lich? — A

Herz verzage nicht geschwind

Herz — ver-za-ge nicht ge-schwind, weil die Wei-ber Wei---ber sind. — B

Heut' Nacht erhob ich mich um Mitternacht

Heut' Nacht er-hob ich mich um Mit-ter-nacht, da war — mein Herz — C

Hoffärtig seid Ihr, schönes Kind

Hof-fär-tig seid Ihr, schö-nes Kind, und geht mit Eu-ren Frei-ern um — D

Ich esse nun mein Brot nicht trocken mehr

Ich es-se nun mein Brot nicht tro-cken mehr — E

Ich hab' in Penna einen Liebsten wohnen

Ich hab' in Pen-na ei-nen Lieb-sten woh--nen — F

Ich liess mir sagen

Ich liess mir sa-gen und — mir ward er-zählt — G

Ihr jungen Leute

Ihr jun-gen Leu-te, die ihr zieht ins Feld, — H

Die ihr schwebet

Die ihr schwe-bet um die-se Pal-men in Nacht und Wind, — I

Ihr seid die Allerschönste

Ihr seid die Al-ler schön---ste weit und breit, — J

Im Frühling

Hier lieg' ich auf — dem Früh----lings-hü-gel — K

In dem Schatten meiner Locken

In dem Schat-ten mei-ner Lo-cken schlief mir mein Ge-lieb-ter ein. — L

In der Frühe

Kein Schlaf noch kühlt das Au-ge-mir dort ge-het schon der Tag her-für — M

Der Jäger

Drei Ta-ge Re-gen fort und fort, kein Son-nen-schein zur Stun-de — N

Jägerlied

Zier-lich ist-des Vo-gels Tritt im Schnee, wenn er wan-delt — O

Karwoche

O Wo-che, Zeu-gin hei-li-ger Be-schwer-de! — P

Klinge, klinge, mein Pandero

Klin-ge, klin-ge mein Pan-de-ro, doch an an-dres denkt mein Herz — Q

Der Knabe und das Immlein

Im Wein-berg auf der Hö-he ein Häus-lein steht so win-de-bang — R

Das Köhlerweib ist trunken

Das Köh-ler-weib ist trun----ken und singt im Wald — S

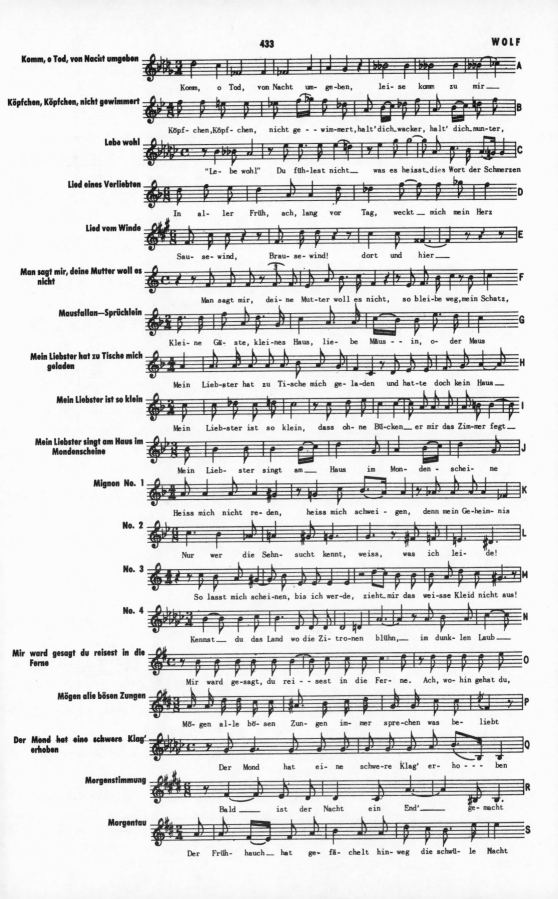

Komm, o Tod, von Nacht umgeben

Komm, o Tod, von Nacht um-ge-ben, lei-se komm zu mir___

Köpfchen, Köpfchen, nicht gewimmert

Köpf-chen, Köpf-chen, nicht ge--wim-mert, halt' dich wacker, halt' dich mun-ter,

Lebe wohl

"Le- be wohl" Du füh-lest nicht___ was es heisst_dies Wort der Schmerzen

Lied eines Verliebten

In al- ler Früh, ach, lang vor Tag, weckt_ mich mein Herz

Lied vom Winde

Sau- se-wind, Brau- se-wind! dort und hier___

Man sagt mir, deine Mutter woll es nicht

Man sagt mir, dei- ne Mut-ter woll es nicht, so blei- be weg, mein Schatz,

Mausfallen—Sprüchlein

Klei- ne Gä- ste, klei-nes Haus, lie- be Mäus--in, o- der Maus

Mein Liebster hat zu Tische mich geladen

Mein Lieb-ster hat zu Ti-sche mich ge- la-den und hat-te doch kein Haus___

Mein Liebster ist so klein

Mein Lieb-ster ist so klein, dass oh- ne Bü-cken er mir das Zim-mer fegt___

Mein Liebster singt am Haus im Mondenscheine

Mein Lieb- ster singt am___ Haus im Mon- den- schei- ne

Mignon No. 1

Heiss mich nicht re- den, heiss mich schwei- gen, denn mein Ge-heim- nis

No. 2

Nur wer die Sehn- sucht kennt, weiss, was ich lei- de!

No. 3

So lasst mich schei-nen, bis ich wer-de, zieht_mir das wei-sse Kleid nicht aus!

No. 4

Kennst_ du das Land wo die Zi- tro-nen blühn, im dunk- len Laub___

Mir ward gesagt du reisest in die Ferne

Mir ward ge-sagt, du rei--sest in die Fer- ne. Ach, wo-hin gehst du,

Mögen alle bösen Zungen

Mö-gen al-le bö-sen Zun-gen im-mer spre-chen was be- liebt

Der Mond hat eine schwere Klag' erhoben

Der Mond hat ei- ne schwe-re Klag' er- ho--- ben

Morgenstimmung

Bald___ ist der Nacht ein End'___ ge- macht

Morgentau

Der Früh- hauch_ hat ge- fä- chelt hin- weg die schwü- le Nacht

A
B
C
D
E
F
G
H
I
J
K
L
M
N
O
P
Q
R
S

Mühvoll komm' ich

Müh - - voll komm' ich und be- la - - - - den, nimm mich an, ___   A

Der Musikant

Wan- dern lieb' ich für mein Le- ben, le- be e- ben, wie ich kann,   B

Nachtzauber

Hörst du nicht die Quel-len ge- hen zwi-schen Stein und Blu-men weit ___   C

Nein, junger Herr

Nein, jun - - ger Herr, so treibt man's nicht, für- wahr;   D

Neue Liebe

Kann auch ein Mensch des an- dern auf ___ der Er- de ganz,   E

Nimmersatte Liebe

So ist die Lieb'! So ist die Lieb'! Mit Küs-sen nicht zu stil- len: F

Nixe Binsefuss

Des Was- ser- manns sein Töch-ter- lein tanzt auf dem Eis ___ im Voll- mond   G

Nun lass uns Frieden schliessen

Nun lass uns Frie- den schlie - - - ssen, lieb-stes Le - - ben   H

Nun wandre Maria

Nun wan- dre, Ma- ri - - a, nun wan- dre nur fort,   I

O wär dein Haus durchsichtig wie ein Glas

O wär dein Haus durch- sich- tig wie ein Glas, mein Hol- der   J

Peregrina I

Der Spie- gel die- ser treu- en brau- nen Au - - gen   K

II

Wa- rum Ge- lieb- te, denk' ich dein auf ein - - mal   L

Phänomen

Wenn zu der Re- gen- wand Phö- bus sich gat- tet,   M

Philine

Sin- get nicht in Trau - - er- tö- nen von der Ein- sam- keit   N

Prometheus

Be- dek- ke dei- nen Him- mel, Zeus, ___ mit Wol- ken- dunst   O

Rat einer Alten

Ein jung ge- we- sen, kann auch mit re- den, und alt ge- wor- den,   P

Der Rattenfänger

Ich bin der wohl- be- kann- te Sän- ger, der viel ge- rei - - ste   Q

Schlafendes Jesuskind

Sohn der Jung- frau, Him- mels- kind! am Bo- den auf dem Holz der Schmerzen   R

Der Scholar

Bei dem an- ge- nehm- - sten ___ Wet- ter sin- gen   S

Treibe nur mit lieben Spott
Trei- be nur mit Lie- ben Spott, Ge- liebte— mein;

Über Nacht
Ü- ber Nacht, ü- ber Nacht kommt still das Leid, und bist du er- wacht,

Um Mitternacht
Ge- las- sen stieg die Nacht— ans Land,— lehnt träu- mend

Und steht Ihr früh am Morgen auf
Und steht ihr früh am Mor- gen auf vom Bet- te,

Und willst du deinen Liebsten sterben sehen
Und willst du deinen Liebsten ster- ben se-hen so tra-ge nicht dein Haar

Unfall
Ich ging bei Nacht einst ü - - - ber— Land, ein Bürsch-lein traf ich

Verborgenheit
Lass, o Welt, O lass mich sein! lo-cket nicht mit Lie- bes- ga- ben

Das Verlassene Mägdlein
Früh wann die Häh- ne krähn, eh' die Stern-lein schwin- den,

Verschling' der Abgrund
Ver- schling' der Ab - - - grund mei - - nes Lieb-sten Hüt- te,

Verschwiegene Liebe
Ü- ber Wip- fel und Saa- ten in den Glanz— hin- ein—

Der verzweifelte Liebhaber
Stu- die- ren will nichts brin-gen, mein Rock hält kei- nen Stich

Wanderers Nachtlied
Der du von dem Him- mel bist, al- les Leid— und Schmer- zen stillest,

Was für ein Lied soll dir gesungen werden
Was— für ein Lied soll dir ge- sun- gen wer- den,

Was soll der Zorn, mein Schatz
Was soll der Zorn, mein Schatz, der dich er- hitzt?

Wenn Du, mein Liebster, steigst zum Himmel auf
Wenn Du, mein Lieb- ster, steigst zum Him- mel auf,

Wenn du mich mit den Augen streifst
Wenn du mich mit den Au- gen streifst und lachst,

Wenn du zu den Blumen gehst
Wenn du zu den Blu - - men gehst, pflü- cke die schön-sten,

Wer rief dich denn?
Wer rief dich denn? Wer hat dich her-be-stellt? Wer hiess dich kom-men

Wer sein holdes Lieb verloren
Wer sein hol- des Lieb ver- lo-ren, weil er Lie- be nicht ver- steht,

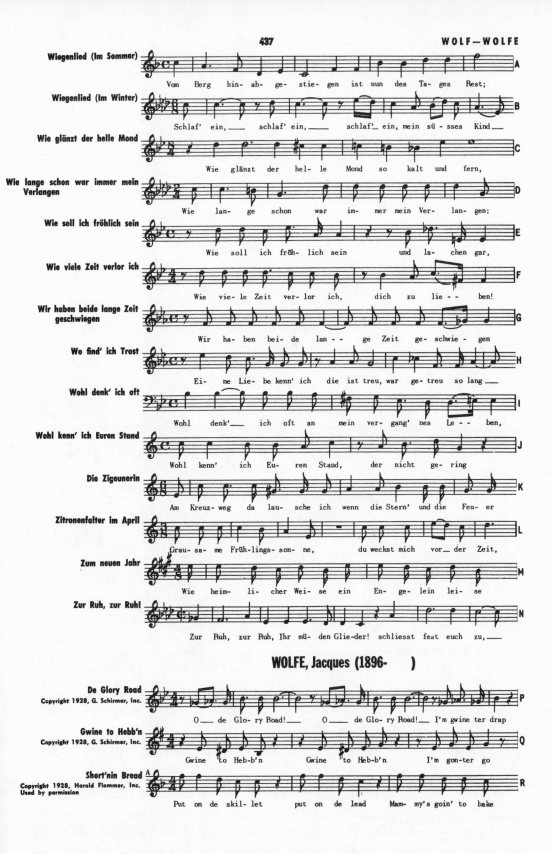

Wiegenlied (Im Sommer)   A

Vom Berg hin-ab-ge-stie-gen ist nun des Ta-ges Rest;

Wiegenlied (Im Winter)   B

Schlaf' ein,__ schlaf' ein,__ schlaf' ein, mein sü-sses Kind__

Wie glänzt der helle Mond   C

Wie glänzt der hel-le Mond so kalt und fern,

Wie lange schon war immer mein Verlangen   D

Wie lan-ge schon war im-mer mein Ver-lan-gen:

Wie soll ich fröhlich sein   E

Wie soll ich fröh-lich sein und la-chen gar,

Wie viele Zeit verlor ich   F

Wie vie-le Zeit ver-lor ich, dich zu lie--ben!

Wir haben beide lange Zeit geschwiegen   G

Wir ha-ben bei-de lan--ge Zeit ge-schwie-gen

Wo find' ich Trost   H

Ei-ne Lie-be kenn' ich die ist treu, war ge-treu so lang__

Wohl denk' ich oft   I

Wohl denk'__ ich oft an mein ver-gang'nes Le--ben,

Wohl kenn' ich Euren Stand   J

Wohl kenn' ich Eu-ren Stand, der nicht ge-ring

Die Zigeunerin   K

Am Kreuz-weg da lau-sche ich wenn die Stern' und die Feu-er

Zitronenfalter im April   L

Grau-sa-me Früh-lings-son-ne, du weckst mich vor-der Zeit,

Zum neuen Jahr   M

Wie heim-li-cher Wei-se ein En-ge-lein lei-se

Zur Ruh, zur Ruh!   N

Zur Ruh, zur Ruh, Ihr mü-den Glie-der! schliesst fest euch zu,__

WOLFE, Jacques (1896-   )

De Glory Road
Copyright 1928, G. Schirmer, Inc.   P

O__ de Glo-ry Road!__ O__ de Glo-ry Road!__ I'm gwine ter drap

Gwine to Hebb'n
Copyright 1928, G. Schirmer, Inc.   Q

Gwine to Heb-b'n Gwine to Heb-b'n I'm gon-ter go

Short'nin Bread
Copyright 1928, Harold Flammer, Inc.
Used by permission   R

Put on de skil-let put on de lead Mam-my's goin' to bake

Short'nin Bread

Mam- my's lit- tle ba- by loves short'- nin', short'- nin'

WOLFF, Erich (1874-1913)

Alle Dinge haben Sprache

Al- le Din- ge ha- ben Spra- che, seit du da bist,

Aus der Ferne in die Nacht, Op. 12, No. 5

Wenn im brau- nen Ha- fen al- le Schif- fe schla- fen,

Entzücket dich ein Wunderhauch?
By permission Associated Music Publishers, Inc.

Ent- zück- et dich ein Wun- - der- hauch, der ein- zig ist

Es werde Licht!
By permission Associated Music Publishers, Inc.

Es wer- de Licht! _____ so tö- ne- te _____ der Ruf Got- tes

Fäden, Op. 13, No. 1

Vie- le Fä- - - den glei- ten zwi- schen mir ___ und dir,

Friede
By permission Associated Music Publishers, Inc.

A- bend- ru- - - - he liegt ü- ber dem Land

Horch, hörst du nicht
By permission Associated Music Publishers, Inc.

Horch hörst du nicht ___ von Him- mel her ___

Ich bin eine Harfe, Op. 13, No. 6

Ich bin ei- ne Har- fe mit gol- de- nen Sai- ten auf einsamen Gip- fel

Im Entschlafen
By permission Associated Music Publishers, Inc.

Blas- se Blü- - ten nei- gen ih- re duf- - ten- de Pracht,

Immer wieder, Op. 8, No. 3

Eh' wir uns tren- nen konn- ten, o wie hielt mich dein ___ Ge- sicht

Knabe und Veilchen, Op. 9, No. 4

Blü- he, blü- he lie- bes Veil- chen, das so lieb- - lich ___ roch, —

Märchen
By permission Associated Music Publishers, Inc.

Glaub' es mir ju- beln- de Kin- der- schar, all die schö- nen Mär- chen

Maria und der Schiffer
By permission Associated Music Publishers, Inc.

Ma- ri- a wollt' zur Kir- - - che gehn, da kam sie

Marienruf
By permission Associated Music Publishers, Inc.

Ma- ri- a, du zar- te! Du bist ein Ro- sen- gar- te,

Meine Lebenszeit verstreicht
By permission Associated Music Publishers, Inc.

Mei- ne Le- bens- zeit ver- streicht, stünd- lich eil' ich hin

Recht wie ein Leichnam
By permission Associated Music Publishers, Inc.

Recht wie ein Leich- nam wand- le ich um- her nachts zu sei- ner Tür

Soll ich denn sterben
By permission Associated Music Publishers, Inc.

Soll ich denn ster- ben, bin noch so jung? Wenn das mein Va- ter wüsst;

Ein Sonntag, Op. 17, No. 5
By permission Associated Music Publishers, Inc.

Von Me-lo-di-en die mich um-flie-hen bin ich im Raum um-ringt,

Spaziergang, Op. 12, No. 1

Ü-ber wei-te Wie-sen schweif ich wo's_ aus tau-send Kei-men bricht,_

Der süsse Schlaf
By permission Associated Music Publishers, Inc.

Der sü-sse Schlaf, der sonst stillt al-les wohl,

Täuscht euch, ihr Augen, nicht
By permission Associated Music Publishers, Inc.

Tauscht_ euch, ihr Au-gen, nicht, die Zeit ver-ge-het,

Der Trauende
By permission Associated Music Publishers, Inc.

Mein Mu-ter mag mi net, und kein Schatz han i net,

Viel bin ich umhergewandert
By permission Associated Music Publishers, Inc.

Viel bin ich um-her-ge-wan-dert, um zum Hei-le zu ge-lan-gen

Wer hat's Lieben erdacht?
By permission Associated Music Publishers, Inc.

Zum Ster-ben bin_ i ver-lie-bet in di,

Wüsst' ich nur
By permission Associated Music Publishers, Inc.

In der See-le ein Wach-sen und Kei-men, so viel

WOLF-FERRARI, Ermano (1876-1948)

OPERAS
Le Donne Curiose Act II
Copyright 1911, G. Schirmer, Inc.

Ah_ tut-ta per te, mio be-ne

Il cor, il cor nel con-ten-to im-prov-vi-so

I Gioielli della Madonna (The Jewels of the Madonna) Act I
Copyright 1911, G. Schirmer, Inc.

Ma-don-na con so-spi-ri, in lun-ghe ve-glie ar-den-di

Be-ne-di-ci-mi tu_ Ma-dre mia buo-na

Act II Serenata

A-pri-la, bel-la, la_ fe-ne-strel-la a-pri la por-ta,

Lucieta e un bel nome, from I Quattro Rusteghi

Lu-cie-ta, Lu-cie-ta, Lu-cie-ta xe un bel no-me

Non sono buffone, from Sly
Copyright by Sonzogno, Milan

Non so-no buf-fo-ne, io so-no un po-ver uo-mo

The Secret of Suzanne
Copyright 1911, G. Schirmer, Inc.

Oh tell me, be-lov-ed, Do you re-mem-ber Those blissful moments

No, I can not let you leave me I've been weep-ing, lone-ly, lone-ly

Oh, joy to be mus-ing with half closed eyes, to fol-low the va-pour

The Secret of Suzanne

All the world is but smoke__ and__ va - - - - - por and a puff__ of wind__   **A**

WOOD, Haydn

A Brown Bird Singing

Roses of Picardy

WOODFORDE-FINDEN, Amy (d. 1919)

Indian Love Lyrics 1. The Temple Bells
By permission Boosey & Hawkes, Inc., copyright owners

The Tem- ple bells are ring - ing, the young green corn is spring - ing,   **F**

2. Less than the Dust

Less than the dust be- neath thy cha- riot wheel__   **G**

3. Kashmiri Song

Pale hands I loved be- side the Sha- li- mar,__ Where are you now?   **H**

4. Till I Wake

When I am dy - - - ing, lean o- ver me,__   **I**

A Lover in Damascus
By permission Boosey & Hawkes, Inc., copyright owners
1. Far across the desert sands

Far, far a- cross the de- sert__ sands I hear the__ ca- mel bells   **J**

2. Where the Abana flows

Through the old ci-ty's si - - - lence__ Where the A- ba- na flows   **K**

3. Beloved in your absence

Be- lov- ed, in your ab- sence, I__ have__ told   **L**

4. How many a lonely caravan

How ma- ny a lone- ly ca- ra- van sets out__   **M**

5. If in the great bazaars

If in the great__ ba- zaars__ They sold the gol- den stars__   **N**

6. Allah be with us

Ah, when the dark on ma- ny a heart de- scends   **O**

WOODMAN, A. Huntington

A Birthday
Copyright 1909, G. Schirmer, Inc.

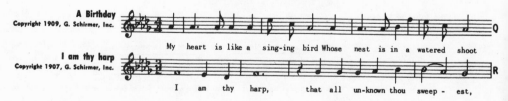

My heart is like a sing- ing bird Whose nest is in a watered shoot   **Q**

I am thy harp
Copyright 1907, G. Schirmer, Inc.

I am thy harp, that all un- known thou sweep- est,   **R**

YOUNG, Anthony

Phillis has such charming graces

Phil - - - lis__ has __ such __ charm - ing - gra - ces

YRADIER, Sebastian (1809-1865)

El Areglito
(Bizet admitted using this for the Habanera in Carmen)

Chi-ni-ta mi a ven por a - qui que tu ya sa-bes que mue-ro por tí

si tu me quie-res di - lo que di - to y_en-se-gni - di - ta

La Calesera

Ya sue-nan las_ cam-pa - ni - les__ Mi ca - le - se - ro ha lle-ga - o

La Paloma

Cuan - do - - - - - sa - li de la Ha-ba - na val-ga - me Dios

ZONDONAI, Riccardo (1883-   )

OPERAS
Giuliano Prologue
Copyright by G. Ricordi & Co., Inc.

Non toc-che-rò mai più ar-co_e sa-et-ta__ più il fo-co - la - re

Act I Love Duet

Re - i - na bel - la! Mi do-na-ste pa - ce il dì che ven - ni

Si Qua - le vuoi,__ sa - rò. Om-bra lon - ta - no

Oc - chi so - a - vi come in sul la se - ra

Act II

Dal - la gai - - ba fug-gi-to_è il lu-si-gno - lo

Giulietta, son io, from Giulietta e Romeo
Copyright by G. Ricordi & Co., Inc.

Giu - liet-ta! Son i - o! I - o, non mi ve-di Io che non pian-go più__

Paolo, datemi pace, from Francesca da Rimini
Copyright by G. Ricordi & Co., Inc.

Pa - o - lo, da-te-mi pa - ce È dol-ce co-sa vi - ve - re

ZELLER, Karl (1842-1898)

OPERETTAS
Der Obersteiger

Wo __ sie war die Müll - ler- in; Zog __ es auch den Fi-scher hin

Sei nicht bös', es kann __ nicht sein,__ Sei nicht bös',

Der Vogelhändler Act I

Schenkt man sich Ro - sen in Ti - rol, Schenkt man das Herz

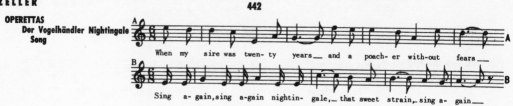

HOW TO USE
THE NOTATION INDEX*

To identify a given theme, play it in the key of C (C major for major themes, C minor for minor themes) and look it up under its note sequence using the following alphabet as a guide:

A Ab A♯ **B** Bb B♯ **C** Cb C♯ **D** Db D♯
E Eb E♯ **F** Fb F♯ **G** Gb G♯

Double flats follow flats; double sharps follow sharps.

The number and letter to the right of the definition indicate the page and listing where the theme may be found in its correct key with the name of the composition and the composer. For example, 32B signifies page 32, theme B.

Trills, turns, grace notes, and embellishments are not taken into consideration here. However, it must be remembered that the appoggiatura is a regular note. In some cases the grace note may be of such nature as to give the aural impression of being a regular note, in which case the theme is indexed both with and without the grace note.

Keys are, in the main, determined by the harmonic structure of the opening bars, not by the cadence. The phrase that begins in C and goes to G is considered to be in C. Themes that may be analyzed in two keys are listed under both keys.

There are themes that defy key definition. However, if the melodic line carries a key implication of its own, if only for the first few notes, that key is used. If the theme carries no such implication, then, for the sake of convenience, the first note is assumed to be C and the rest transposed accordingly.

Each definition is carried to six places except in the case of duplication. Duplicates are continued to a point of difference. When a note is repeated many times, for space conservation an exponent is used; i.e., $GGGGGGG = G^7$.

H. B.

* Publisher's Note: The Notation Index was conceived by Harold Barlow.

NOTATION INDEX

Notes	Code	Notes	Code	Notes	Code
A A A A A D	284D	A C D C D D	239F	A G G B A A	222P
A A A A B C#	333L	A C D E F G	108O	A G G C D B	66O
A A A A F G	277K	A C D G E G	219G	A G G C E F	96K
A A A B B C	412E	A C E C B A	410L	A G G C G G	118G
A A A C C C A A	218R	A C E G G F	177R	A G G E E G	313S
A A A C C C A E	310L	A C G A D C	51S	Ab Ab A A Bb B	404N
A A A G F E	410D	A C G A D C	52A	Ab Ab Ab A A Ab Ab	316R
A A B C G G	35K	A C G G B A	222D	Ab Ab Ab Ab Ab Ab	88F
A A C C G G	216G	A C# F E D F	340C	Ab Ab Ab Ab Ab C	310H
A A C E A D	433G	A D C B A G	80O	Ab Ab Ab Ab Ab G	433F
A A D D D C#	143M	A D C B C D	337N	Ab Ab Ab Ab E G	431C
A A D D F E	89B	A D D E F G E	337F	Ab Ab Ab G F Ab	435Q
A A D E G F	414M	A D D E F G F	55N	Ab Ab Ab G F Eb Eb	243Q
A A D# D# G B	301B	A D D G G D	410R	Ab Ab Ab G F Eb G	43C
A A E E E E	367Q	A D E F A G	51D	Ab Ab Ab G G	23K
A A F D A B	63J	A D E F C B	32G	Ab Ab Ab G G F#	286F
A A F F F F	186A	A D F E D A	184B	Ab Ab Ab G G G Ab	224J
A A G E A A	185S	A D F F G A	316Q	Ab Ab Ab G G G C	220Q
A A G F D G	409N	A E G A E G	222M	Ab Ab Bb Bb Cb Cb	430J
A A G F E D	184K	A E G E F G	173B	Ab Ab F Eb D Eb	428I
A A G F F E A	377H	A F E D G A	379A	Ab Ab G C Eb G	404P
A A G F F E D	410K	A F G E D C	218B	Ab Ab G D D D	66A
A A G F F F	356G	A F# D G G G	333F	Ab Ab G F Eb F	185K
A A G G E E	296R	A G A B C A G	117B	Ab Ab G G F G	177M
A A G G F E	288K	A G A B C A C	440D	Ab Ab G G G Ab	224J
A A G G F F	104I	A G A E D B	179R	Ab B C D Eb F	432D
A Ab G C C D	432L	A G A E E D	298E	Ab B C G Eb D	33B
A Ab G D C B	338N	A G A G A C	413K	Ab Bb Ab C C C	437P
A Ab G F D B	80C	A G A G A G A	114I	Ab Bb Ab G F Eb	337C
A Ab G F# F C	429F	A G A G A G D	402P	Ab Bb Ab G G C	256Q
A B A B C B	146N	A G B C F E	361S	Ab Bb Bb C C D	41G
A B A G F E	377G	A G C A G C	295E	Ab Bb C C G F#	396C
A B B A C C	377R	A G C B B B	211A	Ab Bb C D Eb Eb	435I
A B C B C D	395J	A G C F E C	395F	Ab Bb C Eb Eb D	120G
A B C C C C	272D	A G C G F E	121K	Ab D Eb D Eb F	376D
A B C C E G	133A	A G D C F E	277O	Ab D G G C C	439D
A B C D C D	374F	A G D C# E D	372C	Ab E Ab C Ab E	413R
A B C D D D	395L	A G D D F E	381D	Ab F Ab F D F#	319P
A B C D E F	391K	A G D D F F	129G	Ab F Ab G Eb C	69M
A B C E B D	430I	A G D E A G	80L	Ab F D Ab Ab F	422O
A B C E C B	75Q	A G D G C B	66N	Ab F D Ab Ab G	259N
A B C G A B	339Q	A G E A E G	254D	Ab F G C Ab F	256I
A B C G E F	429D	A G E C C G	399Q	Ab F G C G Eb	171E
A B C G G A	420B	A G E C D E	354I	Ab F# G Eb F# G	234O
A B D C C B	354A	A G E C E G	225G	Ab G A A A A	435A
A B D C G A	339Q	A G E D C G	413D	Ab G Ab F Ab G	219N
A B G A B D	284E	A G E D D C	90R	Ab G Ab F G Ab	55F
A B G#A A B	236E	A G E D F D	400C	Ab G Ab G Bb Ab	59M
A Bb C Bb C D	194N	A G E F D E	357S	Ab G Ab G Bb Ab	61K
A C A B B A	276D	A G E F E D	115J	Ab G Ab G C B	63E
A C A C C F	41S	A G F E D C E	329H	Ab G Bb Ab G Bb	91L
A C A G E F	270R	A G F E D C G	146Q	Ab G C C Ab G	315Q
A C B A G A	196M	A G F E D E C A	308E	Ab G D D F Eb	336K
A C B B G G	386J	A G F E D E C G	180D	Ab G D Eb E F	316G
A C C C C B	286G	A G F F E E	286L	Ab G E C B C	259L
A C C E D C	246H	A G F F E E	410B	Ab G Eb C C Ab	401O
A C C# C# E C#	300D	A G G A G E	371D	Ab G Eb C D C	87H

Notation	Ref.
G G G Ab G F Eb	47I
G G G Ab G G G C	320M
G G G Ab G G G G	248R
G G G B D C	104K
G G G Bb A Bb	404G
G G G Bb A G	241I
G G G Bb Ab G	269O
G G G Bb Bb Bb	189R
G G G Bb G F	316B
G G G Bb G G	272B
G G G C A B	133L
G G G C A C	298D
G G G C Ab Bb	94F
G G G C B A A	216J
G G G C B A G F	44O
G G G C B A G G	35L
G G G C B B	247Q
G G G C B D	39B
G G G C B G A	305M
G G G C B G G	198R
G G G C Bb Ab	261R
G G G C Bb F	57S
G G G C C A	133J
G G G C C B A	187E
G G G C C B B	362K
G G G C C B G	284P
G G G C C Bb	106C
G G G C C C B A E	389L
G G G C C C B A G	35R
G G G C C C B B	385Q
G G G C C C B D	39A
G G G C C C Bb	385P
G G G C C C C A	332O
G G G C C C C A	332P
G G G C C C C B	236G
G G G C C C C C	36G
G G G C C C C D	401A
G G G C C C C E	174F
G G G C C C E C A	355Q
G G G C C C E C G	401A
G G G C C C Eb D Eb	318C
G G G C C C Eb D G	335C
G G G C C C F	436H
G G G C C D D B	334J
G G G C C D D D	169M
G G G C C D E E F	227P
G G G C C D E E G	39F
G G G C C D Eb	397D
G G G C C E A	5E
G G G C C E D	363R
G G G C C E E D	410F
G G G C C E E F	243M
G G G C C Eb D Bb	125M
G G G C C Eb D Eb	322B
G G G C C Eb Eb D	125B
G G G C C Eb Eb Eb	345Q
G G G C D B	142K
G G G C D B	416J
G G G C D D	169N
G G G C D E C	38K
G G G C D E E	297E
G G G C D E F G A B	22L
G G G C D E F G A F	22K
G G G C D E G	257J
G G G C D F	357N
G G G C E D C A	227F
G G G C E D C B	250S
G G G C E D C C B	39L
G G G C E D C C D	181B
G G G C E D C G	97N
G G G C E F	32F
G G G C Eb D C	17O
G G G C Eb D D	221R
G G G C F# G	416G
G G G C G Ab	11N
G G G C G B	355J
G G G C G C B	330G
G G G C G C D	259J
G G G C G D	141K
G G G C G Eb	318G
G G G C G Eb Eb	253Q
G G G C G Eb G	408I
G G G C G F E	300N
G G G C G F G	218S
G G G C G G A A	36F
G G G C G G A G F	313G
G G G C G G A G F#	98S
G G G C G G F	416M
G G G C G G G B	42L
G G G C G G G C C	356R
G G G C G G C G G A	190S
G G G C G G C G G G	369D
G G G C G G G E	270Q
G G G C G G G F	180G
G G G C G G G G	45S
G G G D B G	238O
G G G D C D	179O
G G G D D C	77G
G G G D E F E	194F
G G G D E F G	126Q
G G G D G G	199P
G G G E C Ab	3L
G G G E C C B	111H
G G G E C C C	75B
G G G E C D	352K
G G G E C G A	216B
G G G E C G E	5I
G G G E D C C	95C
G G G E D C G	317L
G G G E E C	329B
G G G E E D C	131J
G G G E E D F	226L
G G G E E E A	23P
G G G E E E D	187C
G G G E E E E C	368A
G G G E E E E E	396B
G G G E E E E G	67O
G G G E E E F	122M
G G G E E G	369Q
G G G E E F	375D
G G G E F F	181L
G G G E F G A E	120C
G G G E F G A G	152G
G G G E G A D	378S
G G G E G A G	115F
G G G E G B	23H
G G G E G C	346E
G G G E G G A	116N
G G G E G G G	231Q
G G G Eb Ab Ab Ab	105F
G G G Eb Ab Ab F	129I
G G G Eb C Ab	43E
G G G Eb C C Ab	74C
G G G Eb C C C	189H
G G G Eb D C C	396H
G G G Eb D C G	210L
G G G Eb D D	240C
G G G Eb D Eb	58F
G G G Eb D G	192F
G G G Eb F F	256A
G G G Eb F G Ab	120O
G G G Eb F G G	293J
G G G Eb G G	257H
G G G F Ab C	58E
G G G F Ab G	240M
G G G F C G	360O
G G G F D G	139D
G G G F E A	115C
G G G F E C A	351F
G G G F E C C	138C
G G F E D C A C D E C	178N
G G F E D C A C D E G	305C
G G G F E D C#	432J
G G G F E D E	193E
G G G F E D F	266Q
G G G F E D G	16D
G G G F E E	252I
G G G F E G	134E
G G G F Eb D D Bb	241L
G G G F Eb D D C	144P
G G G F Eb D D C#	429Q
G G G F Eb D Eb	139F
G G G F Eb Db	119C
G G G F Eb F Eb	149H
G G G F Eb F G	368D
G G G F Eb G	407G
G G G F F Eb Eb D	432G
G G G F F Eb Eb F	80P
G G G F F F E	131K
G G G F F F Eb D	235O
G G G F F F Eb Eb	208L
G G G F G A F	176O
G G G F G A G	175M
G G G F G Ab Bb Ab	91F
G G G F G Ab Bb G	304I
G G G F G D	342K
G G G F G E D C	236I
G G G F G E D D	361G
G G G F G G	381Q
G G G F# A G	356F
G G G F# E F#	108J
G G G F# F Ab	429N

INDEX TO SONGS AND FIRST LINES